Melusine

Jean, Alexander Karley Donald

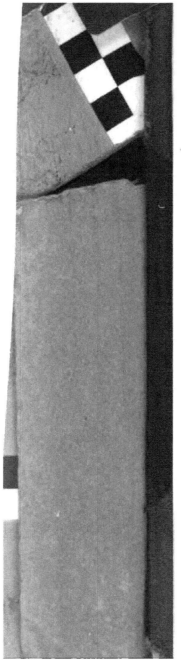

820.6
E 12e

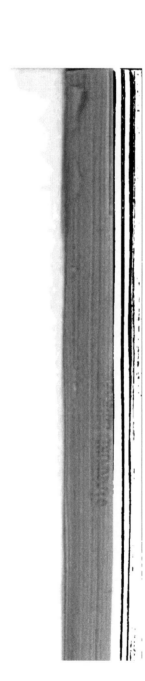

Melusine.

Early English Text Society.

Extra Series, LXVIII.

1895.

Comment guion et ses gens
desconfirent les galees des
sarrazins sur mer Et com

G.K.

Melusine.

COMPILED (1382-1394 A.D.) BY

JEAN D'ARRAS

ENGLISHT ABOUT 1500.

EDITED FROM A UNIQUE MANUSCRIPT

IN

THE LIBRARY OF THE BRITISH MUSEUM

BY

A. K. DONALD.

PART I.

TEXT, NOTES, AND GLOSSARY.

Extra Series, LXVIII.

R. CLAY & SONS, LIMITED, LONDON & BUNGAY.

TABLE OF CONTENTS.

TABLE OF CONTENTS.

TABLE OF CONTENTS.

Melusine.

[A Chronicle of Melusine in olde Englishe.
compyled by Ihon of Arras, and dedicated
to the Duke of Berry and Auuergne, and
4 translated (as yt shoulde seeme) out of
Frenche into Englishe.[1]]

IN the begynnyng of all werkes / men oughten first
of alle to calle the name of the creatour of all   May the Creator
8 Creatures, whiche is very & trew maister of alle
thinges made & to be made, that oughten somwhat to
entende to perfection of wele. Therfore att the begyn-
nynge of this present historye / though that I ne be not
13 worthy for to requyre hym / beseche ryght deuoutly
his right highe & worthy mageste / that this present   help me to bring
this book to a
history he wyl helpe me to bring vnto a good ende / &   good end!
to fuldoo it att hys glorye & praysyng. And to the
16 plaisire of my right high, mighti, and doubtid lord
Iohan, sone to the kyng of Fraunce, Duc of Berry & of
Auuergne. The whiche hystory I haue bygonne after   This History was
compiled (in
the veray & true Cronykles, whiche I haue had of hym   French)
20 and of the Erle of Salesbury in England, & many other
bokes that I haue sought & ouerredde for to accomplysshe hit. And bycause that his noble sustir Marye,
doughtir to the kyng Iohanne of Fraunce, duchesse of   for the Duchess
of Bar,
24 Bar, had requy²red my said lord for to haue the said   ² fol. 1 b.
historye / the whiche in fauour of her hath doon as
moche to his power as he might, to serche the very

[1] This title is added in xvijth cent. handwriting.

at the command
of her brother
John, Duke of
Berry and Au-
vergne,

trouth & true historye / and hath commanded me
for to do drawe alle alonge thystory whiche heraftir
foloweth /.   And I as of herte dyligent / of my pouere
witt & connyng, [do] as nygh as I can the pure trouth 4
of hys gracyous commandement.   Wherfore I humbly
& denoutly beseche & pray to my Creatour, that my
said lord wil take it in gree / and also all them that
schall rede or here it / that they wil pardonne me yf I 8
haue said eny thinges that ben not to theire good gree.

and was com-
menced on St.
Clement's Day,
Nov. 23, 1387.

Whiche this present hystorye I byganne the Wens-
day, saynt Clementis day in Wynter, the yere of our
lord Ml. ccc. lxxx. vij. beseching alle them that shall 12
rede, or here it redde, that they wil pardonne me
my fawte, yf their be eny.   ffor certaynly I haue com-
posed it the moost justly that I coude or haue mowe,
aftir the Cronykles whiche I suppose certaynly to 16
be trew.

*   *   *   *   *   *   *

Cap. I.   How Melusyne & her two sustirs shewid them to Raymondyn at the fontayne of Soyf or thurst /.   20

1 fol. 2.

David said that
the judgments
of God are un-
fathomable.

DAuid [1] the prophete saith, that the Iuggements and
the punysshinges of god ben as abysmes without
bottom & without ryuage.   And he is not wyse that
suche thinges supposeth to comprehende in his wit / & 24
weneth that the meruaylles that ben thrugh the vni-
uersal world, may nat be true, as it is said of the thinges
that men calle ffayrees / and as it is of many other

It is foolish,
therefore, not
to believe that
marvellous
things are true,

thinges wherof we may not haue the knowleche of alle 28
them.   Now thenno the Creature ought nat therfore for

for the Creature
cannot compre-
hend the designs
of God.

to traueille, by outrageous presumyng to knowe & to
comprehende in his wit & vnderstanding the Iugements
of god / but men oughten / thinkynge / to be meruaylled 32
of hym / and meruaylling / to considere / how they may

worthily & deuoutly prayse and glorify hym that Iugith Men should rather think how worthily to praise him.
so, and ordeynith suche thinges after hys plaisure &
wille without eny gaynseying./

4 The creature of god that is raisonable, oughte moche Reasonable creatures
besily to vnderstande aftir the sayeng of Aristote,
that the þynges which he hath made & creatid here
bynethe, by the presence þat they haue in themself, should believe what is seen,
8 certifyen to be suche as they are / As saynct paule
seyth in thepistle that he made to the Rommains /
sayeng in this manere / that the thinges that he hath
doon, shalbe knowen & seen by the Creatures of the
12 world / that is to wete, by the men that can rede &
adiousten seyth to þactoures whiche haue ben byfore and should give credence to travellers
vs / as to wete & knowe the landes, the prouinces & the
straunge Countrees. and to haue ouerseen & vysyted
16 the dyuerse Royaumes / haue founde so many of dyuerse
meruaylles aftir common exstimacion, that thumayn
vnderstanding is constrayned of god / that soo as he is who see many marvels.
without ryuage & without bottom / soo are the thinges
20 meruayllous & wounderfull in many dyuerse landes.
aftir their dyuerse nature / that saaf theire Iuggement.
I suppose that neuer no man / but only Adam. hadd Adam alone had perfect knowledge;
parfytt knowlege of the thinges Inuysible or that may
24 not be seen. Wherfore I me bethink fro day to day but the author daily learns more and more,
to proufytte in science, & to here & see many thinges /
which men suposen not to be true. the whicħ, yf they
be trew / I putte them fourth into this termes byfore and tells what he has seen, that his history may be believed.
28 you / to thende that the grette meruaylles that ben
conteyned in this present hystory may be byleued.
Wherfore I ¹think to treate to the playsure of god / ¹ fol. 2 b.
and after the commandement of my said right mighty
32 and noble lord./

Late vs now leue the Auctoures witħ peas / and Leaving the Authors, let us turn to what has been seen in Poitou.
retourne we to that we haue herde say and telle
of our auncyent and old tyme / and that this day we
36 haue herd sey what in the land of Poitow was seen in

dede / for to couloure[1] *our* hystory to be trew / as we
holde hit soo / and for to shew & publysshe it thrugh
the true Cronykles / as we suppose to doo /.

      We haue thenne herd say and telle of *our* auncyents, 4
that in many partes of the sayd lande of Poytow haue
ben shewed vnto many oon right famylerly many ma-
nyeres of thinges / the whiche som*me* called Gobelyns /
the other ffayrees, and the other 'bonnes dames' or good 8
ladyes / and they goo by nyght tyme and entre wit*h*in
the houses without opnyng or brekyng of ony doore /

and take & bere somtyme with them the children out of
theire cradel*les*. and somtyme they tourne them out of 12
theyre wit / and somtyme they brenne & roste them
before *þe* fyre / and whan they departe fro them, they
leue ham as hoole as they were byfore / and som*me* gyue
grette happe & ffortune in this world. And yet haue 16

I herd say of oon Geruayse, a man worshipfull & of credence, that som*me* other fauntasyes appyeren by nyght
tyme vnto many oon in dyuerse places, in lyknes of
wymen with olde face, of low and lytil stature or body / 20

whiche dide scoure pannes & potts, and dide suche
thing*es* as a mayde or *ser*uau*n*t oughte to doo / lyberaly
& without dooyng of ony harme. And also he saith
for certayn, that in his tyme he hadd a frend that was 24
auncyent & old, whiche recounted for trouth / that in
hys dayes he hadd seen many tymes suche thinges.

and saith yet the said Geruayse, that the sayd fayrees
toke somtyme the fourme & the fygure of fayre & 28
yonge wymen / of whiche many men haue hadd som

doughtirs, and haue take to theire wyues by meanes of
som couena*un*tes or promysses that they made them to
swere vnto them / the som / that they shuld neu*er* see 32
eche other / on the satirday / and that by no man*er*
wyse they shuld nat enquyre where they were bycomme / the other / that *y*f they had eny children /

---

[1] Fr. *coulourer*.

that theire husband*es* shuld neu*er* see them in theyr
child bedd / And as long' as they kept theyre cove-
naunt*es* they had good fortune and were eu*er* in pros-
4 peryte / but assoone as they faylled of theyr promysses
or couena*u*ntes they fell doun fro[1] theyr good happ &
fortune / and aftir these thing*es* so happed to haue
broken theyr couena*u*ntes / the other were conuerted &
8 tourned into serpentes.   And yet more sayth the [2]said
Geruayse, that he byleueth this to be permytted & doon
for som mysded*es* that were doon ayenst the playsure
of god / wherfore he punysshed them so secretly & so
12 wounderly wherof none hath parfytte knowlege / but
alonely he / and they may be therefore called the
secrets of god, abysm*es* without ryuage and wi*th*out
bottom / For none knoweth nothing perfyttly to the
16 regarde of hym / how be it that sometyme of his pro-
uysion ben many thinges knowen / not only of oon /
but of many other.   It is seen often whan a man
hath yssued out of hys co*u*ntree / and hath seen many
20 awounder & meruayllo*us* thynges whiche he neuer wold
haue byleued hit by here sayeng', without he had hadd
the sight of hit / but as for me that haue nat walked
ferre, I haue seen som*me* things that many oon shuld
24 nat byleue without they sawe it.   With this seyth
the said Geruayse, & setteth fourth an ensaumple of a
knyght, named Sir Robert du Chastel Roussel of the
prouince of Asy / the whiche knight by auenture on an
28 euen founde oon of the fayree in a medowe / and wold
haue had her to his wyf / and in dede she assentid to
hit / by suche couena*u*nce that neuer he shuld see her
naked / and were longe togider / and the knight grew
32 & wexed prospero*us* fro day to day.   It happed long
tyme after that / that he wold haue seen the said
Nymphe naked / as he dede / in so moche that the
said nymphe putte her heed in to a watre and was

and so long as
the conditions
were kept, they
were prosperous
and happy;
but when they
were broken,
they became
poor, and their
wives were
turned into ser-
pents.

[2] fol. 3.

Gervaise thinks
this is because of
some misdeeds,
for which God
has punished
them.

Travellers often
see marvellous
things;

but even I, who
have not been
far, have seen
some marvels.

Sir Robert du
Chastel Roussel
found a fairy in
a meadow,

and was married
to her on condi-
tion that he
should never see
her naked.

For a long time
he was prosper-
ous;

but one day
he broke his
promise,

---

[1] MS. has 'for.'

and his wife was changed into a serpent, whilst he himself grew poor.

tourned in to a serpent, whiche was neuer seen after that / And the knyght fro day to day wexed pouere and declyned from his prosperyte. As for prouerbes & exemples I wil none bryng⁴ more vnto you / and 4 that / that I haue doon / it was bycause þat I suppose to treate how the noble ffortresse or Castell of Lusyg-nen was bylded & made of a woman of the fayree, and the manyere how / after the juste & trewe cronykle / 8 without to applye ne adiouste to it nonething / but that it be approued Iuste & trew, and of the propre or owne matere / And ye shall here me spek & say of the noble lynee whiche yssued of the said woman / that shall 12 regne for euer vnto thend of the world / aftir that it appiereth that it hath euer regned vnto this tyme present. But bycause that I byganne first to treate of the fayree / I shall telle you how & of whens cam 16 the said woman whiche bilded the noble ¹ffortress of Lusygnen, beforsayd.

I have to tell how the Castle of Lusignen was built by a fairy,

and how from the same woman a noble race descended, which shall reign for ever.

First I will tell you whence she came.

¹ fol. 3 b.

The children of Melusine and Raymondin were

Herafter folowen the names of the estates of the children whiche yssued of Melusyne, and were 20 bygoten of Raymondyn in wedlok. And first yssued kyng Uryan, whiche regned in Cypre. Aftir hym cam King Guyon, which regned myghtily in Armenye. Item, King Regnald, whiche regned right mightily 24 in Behaygne. Item, Anthony that was due of Lucem-bourgh. Item, Raymond that was Erle of fforest. Item, Geffray with the grette toth, that was lord of Lusygnen. Item, there yssued also theoderyk, which 28 was lord of Partenay. Item, ffroymonde, that was monke into thabbey of Mailleses⁴ the whiche Geffray with the grette toth brent the said Abbey, & thabbot also with an hundred religyous or monkes. 32

Uryan, King of Cyprus; Guyon, King of Armenia; Raynald, King of Bohemia; Anthony, Duke of Luxemburg; Raymond, Earl of Forest,

Geoffroy, of Lu-signen; Theode-ric, of Partenay;

Froment, of Maillares.

Once upon a time, in Albany, lived a brave King

It is true that there was somtyme in Albany³ a kynge that was moche worthy & valyaunt. And as sayth thystory he had of hys wyf many children /

¹ Fr. Maillieres. ² Fr. Albanie.

& that Mathas whiche was fader to fflorymond was
hys first sone / and this kinge had to name Elynas, *named Elynas.*
and was right worthy & mighty knight of his land./

4 And it happed that after the decess of his first wyf / as *After his first wife's death he*
he chaced in a fforest nighe to the see, in the which *was hunting,*
forest was a moche fayre fontayn*ne* / that sodaynly he
had so grett athurst / that as constreyned[1] he tourned *and being thirsty, went towards a*

8 & yede toward the said fontayn*ne*. And whan he ap- *fountain.*
prouched to the said fontayne / he herde a voyce that *When he approached, he heard beautiful*
song' so melodyously & so swetly / that he suposed none *singing, which he thought must*
other / but it had the voyce of an Angel / but soone aftir *be of some angel;*

12 he knewe that hit was the voyce of a woman. Thenne
descendid he & alyghted fro hys hors to thende he
shulde not make gret affray / and walked fayre & softly
toward the fontayn in the most couer*ed* wyse that he

16 coude. And whan he cam*me* nygh to the fontayne / *but, walking towards the*
he sawe there the fayrest lady that eu*er* he the dayes *fountain, he sees a beautiful lady*
of hys lyf had seen to his aduys or semynge. Thenne *(Pressyne).*
he stode styl al abasshed of the grett beaulte that he

20 perceyued in the same ladye, which eu*er* songe so
melodyously and so swetly. And thus he stood styl /
asmoche for the bewte of the lady / as for to here her
swette & playsaunt voyce / and hyd hym in the best *He hides himself to listen to her,*

24 wyse that he coude vnder the leevis of the trees / to
²thende that the said lady shuld not perceyue hym / & *² fol. 4.*
forgate all the chasse and grett thurst that he had afore.
And byganne to think on the songe & on the beaulte *and to look upon her beauty: by*

28 of the lady. In so moche that he was as rauysshed *both he is entranced.*
& knew nat yf it was daylight or nyght, ne yf he slept
or wakked./

Thus as ye shall now here was kynge helynas so *As he stands there,*
32 abused / aswel of the right swete songe / as of
the bewte of the said lady that he ne wyst whether he
slept or waked, For eu*er* styl she songe so melodyously
that it was a swete & melodyo*us* thing to here / Thenne

---

[1] 'honstreyned' in MS.

the kynge Elynas was so rauysshed & abused[1] that he
remembred of nothinge worldly ' but alonely that he
he remembers
nothing;
herd & sawe the said lady, and abode there long tyme.
Thanne camme rannyng toward him two of hys houndis 4
but two hounds
at last disturb
him.
whiche made to hym grett feste,[2] and he lept & mevyd
hym as a man wakynge from slep ,' and thenne he
remembred of the chasse, and had of new so grett
athurst / that without hauyng aduys ne mesure he yede 8
fourth vpon the ryuage of the fountaynne, and toke the
He goes to
the fountain to
drink,
basyn which heng' therby & drank of the watre.   And
thenne he beheld the said lady whiche had lefte her
songe & salued[3] her right humbly / beryng vnto her 12
and humbly
salutes the lady,
the gretest honour & reuerence that he might.   Thanne
she that coude & wyst moche of wele & of honour,
rendred to hym his salutacion right gracyously,
who returns his
salutation.
'Lady,' said Elynas, the kinge ,' ' of your curtoysye be 16
nat you dyspleased yf I requyre of you to knowe of
your estate / of your beyng & what ye are / For the
He asks her who
she is.
cause that moueth me therto is suche ,' as now I shall
reherse to you.   Right dere lady vouche ye saaf to 20
weto & knowe that I can & know[4] so moche of the
beyng of this countree, that there nys within this
He knows all the
lords and ladies
of the neighbour-
hood,
foure or fyue myle neyther Castel ne ffortres, but þat
I knowe / except that same fro whens I departed this 24
day by the mornyng', whiche is two myle hens or theraboute. Nor there nys neyther lord ne lady within
this Countrey but that I knowe them wel, and therfore
gretly I meruaylle & wounderly am abasshed, fro whens 28
and is surprised
that she is with-
out retinue.
may be suche a fayr and so gent a lady as ye be / so
exempt & vnpurveyed of felawship. and for godis loue
pardonne me / For grette outrage is to me to demande
He asks her
pardon for his
rudeness in
questioning her.
of you therof / but the grette desire & good wylle that 32
my herte bereth toward your gracyous personne, hath
caused hardynes within me for to doo it.' ,

[1] Fr. abusé.   [2] Fr. feste.   [3] Fr. salua.
[4] Fr. sçay et congnois.

¹ "Sire Knight,' said the lady / ' there is none outrage /
but it commeth to you of grette curtoysye &
honour.   And knowe you, sire knight, that I shall nat
4 be longe alone whan it shal playse me / but from me
I haue sent my seruaunts, while þat I dysported me.'
Thenne cam fourth to² that word oon of her seruaunts,
wel arayed, whiche rode on a fayre Courcer, and att his
8 right hand ledd a palfroy so richely enharnashed³ that
the kyng Elynas was moche abasshed of⁴ the grette
richesse & noble aray that was about the said palfray.
Thanne said the seruaunt to his lady : 'Madame, it is
12 tyme whan it shall playse you to comme.'   And she
fourthwith said to the kinge : 'Sire knight, god be
with you, and gramercy of your curtoisye.'   thenne she
went toward the palfray / and the kinge hyed hym,
16 & helped to sette her on horsbak moche prately.⁵
And she thanked hym moche of hit, and departid /.
And the kyng yede to his hors, and lept on his bake.
thanne camme hys meney, whiche sought hym, and
20 sayd that they had taken the herte.   And the king
said to them / 'that playseth me.'   Thenne he byganne
to thinke on the beaulte of the said lady, and so moche
he was surprysed of her loue, that he ne wyst what
24 contenaunce or manyere he shuld hold / and said to
his meyne / 'goo you alle before / and I shall folow
you soone.'   They yede at hys commandement theire
way / and wel they perceyued & knew that he hadd
28 found som thinge / And the king hastly tourned his
hors, & toke the way that the said lady had ytaken / &
folowed her.

T hystory recounteth to vs, that so long folowed the
32 kinge Elynas the lady, that he found her in a
fforest, where as were many trees high & strayt / and
[it] was in the season that the tyme⁶ is swete &

² Fr. à.   ³ Fr. enharnacié.   ⁴ Fr. de.
⁵ Fr. doulcement.   ⁶ Fr. temps.

The lady, hear-
ing the noise of
his horse,
waits for him;

but when he
comes up,

King Elynas is
much abashed.

¹ fol. 5.

The lady asks
him why he
follows her,

to which he re-
plies that he is
ashamed to let
her go unaccom-
panied through
his land.

She excuses him,
and begs him
not to delay his
return merely
for that,

upon which he
declares his love
for her,

gracyous, & the place within the forest was moche
delectable.¹ And whan the lady herde the noyse
of the hors of the kynge Elynas, that rode fast, she
said to her seruaunt: 'Stand we styl, and late vs 4
abyde this knight, For I byleue that he cometh vnto
vs for to telle to vs a part of his wille, wherof he was
nat as tofore aduysed, For we sawe hym lepe on his
hors all thoughtfull.' 'Madame,' said the seruaunt / 8
'at your plaisure.' Thanne camme the kinge nigh vnto
the lady / and as he had neuer seen her before, he
salewed her, moche affrayenge, For he was so sur-
prysed² of her loue that he coude nat holde conten- 12
aunce. Thanne the lady, that knew ynoughe as it
was, and that ³she shuld comme to her entrepryse /
said to hym : 'Kynge Elynas, what goost thou sechyng
aftir so hastly / haue I oughte borne away of thyn 16
owne?' / And whan the king herde hym named, he
was moche abasshed, For he knew nat what she was
that spak with hym / and neuertheles he ansuerde to
her : 'My dere lady, nought of myn owne ye withbere / 20
but only that ye passe & goo thrugh my land / and it
is grett shame to me / sith that ye be astraunger,⁴ that
I ne doo you to be conueyed worshipfully thrugh my
land / whiche I wold moche gladly doo yf I were 24
in place, & had tyme & space for to doo it.' Thenne
ansuerde the lady : 'Kynge Elynas, I hold you for
escused, & pray you yf ye wyl of vs none other thinge /
that ye leue ne lette nat your retourne for that cause.' 28
And Elynas ansuerde / 'wel other thing I seke,
lady' / 'And what is it?' said she / 'telle it to me
hardyly.' 'My right dere lady, sith that it is your
wille & plaisir for to knowe it / I shall telle it to you. 32
I desire moche more than eny other thing in the
world forto haue your good loue & your good grace.'
'By my feith,' said she, 'kyng Elynas, to that haue ye

¹ Fr. delectable.   ² Fr. surpris.   ⁴ Fr. estrangière.

and greets her joyfully.

She reproaches him for breaking his promise, saying he has lost her for evermore,

but that she knows Nathas is the cause of all;

whereupon she disappears with her three daughters, and is never seen again.

King Elynas is much afflicted at the loss of his wife Pressyne and his daughters,

and laments for seven years.

His people think him mad, and make Nathas their king,

whom they marry to the Lady of Yerys;

4 fol. 4.

and from the two is born Florymond,

with whom the history is not concerned.

Pressyne goes with her daughters to Avalon, or the Isle Lost,

this manere : 'god blesse the moder & the doughters,' & toke of them grette Ioye. And whan pressyne herde hym, she answerde to hym, 'Fals kinge, thou hast faylled thy couenaunt, wherof grett euyl shal 4 comme vnto the / and hast lost me for euermore. And wel I wot that thy sone Nathas is cause therof, & departe I must fro the lightly.[1] but yet I shalbe auenged me on thy sone by my sustir & felow, my 8 lady of the yle lost.' And these thinges said / [she] toke her thre doughtirs & had them withher / and neuer aftir she was seen in the land /

Thystorye saith to vs, that whan the kinge had lost 12 pressyne his wyf, and his thre doughters, he was so wofull & so abasshed that he wyst not what he shuld doo or say. but he was by the space of seuen yere that he dede none other thinge, but compleyned 16 & sighed, & made grette playntes & piteous lamentacions for loue of Pressyne his wyf, whiche he louyd of lawfull[2] loue. and the peuple in hys land said that he was assoted.[3] and in dede they gaue & betoke the 20 gouernement ouer them & of aile the lande to Nathas his sone. Which gouerned valiauntly, and held hys fader in grette charyte. And thenne the barons of Albanye gaf to hym vnto hys wyf agentyl woman, 24 whiche was lady of Yerys. And of these [4]two yssued florymond, whiche afterward toke moche of peyne & traueyll. Neuertheles, oure hystory is not enterprysed ne begonne for hym and thérfore we shall hold oure 28 peas of hym, and we shall retourne to oure hystorye.

Thistorye saith, that whan Pressyne departed & yede with her thre doughtirs, she went in to Aualon, that was named the yle lost, bycause that all 32 had a man ben there many tymes[5] yet shuld not he conne retourne thither hymself alone but byhapp &

---

[1] Fr. sundainement.   [2] Fr. loué.   [3] Fr. assoté.
[4] Fr. tant y ent este de foys.

grett auenture. And there she nourysshed her thre
doughtirs vnto the tyme that they were xv. yere of
age / and ledd them euery mornyng on a high
4 mountaynne whiche was named, as thystory saith &
recounteth, Elyneos, whiche is asmoche for to say in
englissh as fflorysshed hyll.[1] For from thens she sawe
ynough the land of Albany.[2] and often said to her
8 thre doughtirs, waymentyng & sore wepyng : 'See, my
fayre doughters, yonder is the land wher ye were born /
and ye shuld haue had your wele & honour, ne had be
the dommage of your fader, that bothe you & me hath
12 putte in grett myserye without ende vnto the day of
dome, whan god shal punysshe the euyl folk / and the
good he shall enhaunse in theire vertues.'

Melusyne, tholdest doughtir, demanded of her
16 moder Pressyne : 'What falshed[3] hath doon
oure fader, wherby we must endure so longe this greef
& sorow?' Thanne the lady, theyre moder, byganne
to telle & shew vnto them all the manere of the
20 faytte, so as ye haue herd tofore. And thenne when
Melusyne had herde her moder, and that she vnderstode all the faitte or dede, She tourned the talke of
her moder,[4] & demanded of her the commodytees of
24 the land / the name of the Cites, tounes, & Castels of
Albanye / and rehercyng these thinges they al descendid
doun fro the hyll, & retourned to the yle of Aualon.
And thanne Melusyne had & drew [5]apart her two
28 sustirs, that is to wete Melyor & Palatyne, & said to
them in this manyere : 'My dere sustirs, now loke &
byhold we the myserye wherin oure fader hath putt
both oure moder & vs all, that shuld haue be so wel att
32 ease & in so grette worship in oure lyues. what think
you good of your best aduys for to doo / For as for

where she brings
up her daughters.

She takes them
every morning to
a high mountain,

called Elyneos,

and shows them
the land in which
they were born.

Melusine asks
what was their
father's wrong
doing,

and Pressyne
tells them the
whole story.

[5] fol. 5 b.

Melusine then
conspires with
her sister

---

[1] Fr. *montaigne florie.*   [2] Fr. *Ybernie.*
[3] Fr. *faulceté.*
[4] Fr. *remist sa mere en aultres parolles.*

my parte I think to auenge me therof / and as lytel
myrthe & solas that he hath Impetred[1] to oure moder
by hys falshed / as lytel joye I think to purchasse
vnto hym /.' Thenne her two sustirs ansuerde to her 4
in this manere : ' Ye be our oldest sustir, we shall
folowe & obey you in all that ye wil doo & shall
ordonne theirof.' And Melusyne said to them / 'ye
shew good loue, & to be good & lawfull[2] to oure moder, 8
For by my feyth ye haue said right wel.   and I haue

aduysed yf it semeth you good that we shall close or
shett hym on the high mountayne of Northomberland,
named Brombelyoys / and in myserye he shalbe there 12
all[3] his lyf.' ' My sustir,' said either of bothe sustirs /
'lette now hye vs for to doo this / For we haue
gretto desyre to see that oure moder be auenged of
the vnlawfulnes that our fader dede shew vnto her.' 16

Thanne the thre doughtirs dide so moch, that by
theyre false condycion they toke theyr fader, & closed
or shett hym on the said mountayne.   And after that
they had so doon, they retourned to theire moder, 20

and to her they said in this manere : 'Moder, ye ne
oughte to retche[4] ne care more of the vnlawfulnesse[5] &
falshed of our fader / For therof he hath receyued
hys payment, For[6] neuer he shal yssue ne departe fro 24
the mounteyne of Brombelyoys, wheron he is closed &
shett by vs / and þere he shall waste hys lyf & his

tyme with grett dolour and woo.' / ' Ha / ha / alas !'
said theire moder Pressyne to them / 'how durst you 28
so doo / euyl herted doughters, & without pyte / ye
haue not doon wel, whan he that begat you on my

body ye haue so shamfully punysshed[7] by your
proude courage.   For it was he of whom I toke all 32
the playsaunce that I had in this mortall world,

---

[1] Fr. *impetré.*   [2] Fr. *leal.*   [3] MS. has ' as.'   Fr. *toute.*
[4] Fr. *challoir.*   [5] Fr. *desleaulté.*
[6] MS. has ' ffro.' . Fr. *car.*

whiche ye haue taken fro me.   therfore, knowe ye wel For punishment she condemns Melusine, the eldest and the most in fault,
that I shall punyssh you of the meryte aftir youre
descrte.   thou, Melusyne, that art tholdest, & that
4 oughtest to haue be the moost knowyng / all this is
comme & doon thrughe thy counseyll, For wel I wot
that this pryson hath be gyuen to thy fader by the /
and therfore thou shalt be she that shalbe first
8 punysshed therof.   For notwithstandyng the vnlaw-
fuluess of thy fader / bothe thou & thy sustirs he
shuld haue drawen to hym, and ye shuld shortly haue
ben out of the handes of the Nymphes[1] & of the
12 fairees, without to retourne eny more.   And fro hens
fourthon I gyue to the / the gyfte that thou shalt be to be turned into a serpent every Saturday, until she finds some one who will marry her, and promise never to see her on that day.
euery satirday tourned vnto a serpent fro the nauyll
dounward / but yf thou fynd ony man þat wil take
16 the to hys wyf / and that he wil promytte to the that
neuer on the Satirday he shall see the, ne þat shall
declare ne reherce thy faytt or dede to ne personne /
thou shalt lyue thy cours naturell, and shall dey as a
20 naturel & humayn woman / and out of thy body
shall yssue a fayre lynee, whiche shalbe gret & of
highe proesse.   but yf by hap or som auenture / thou If he break his promise,
shuldest be seen & deceyued[2] of thyn husband /
24 knowe thou for certayn that thou shuldest retourne she must return to her punish-ment until the Day of Judg-ment,
to the tourment & peyne wher as thou were in afore /
and euer thou shalt abyde therinne vnto the tyme that
the right highe Iugge shal hold his jugement.   And
28 thou shalt appiere by thre dayes byfore the fortresse appearing before her castle for three days, when-ever it shall have a new lord, or when one of her descendants is about to die,
or Castel whiche thou shalt make, and thou shalt
name it aftir thy name / at euery tyme whan it shall
haue a new lord, and lykwyse also whan a man of thy
32 lynee shal dey.   And thou, Melyor, to the I gyue a Mellor is con-demned to keep a sparrowhawk in a castle in Armenia, until the judgment day;
Castel in the grette Armenye, whiche is fayre & riche,
wher thou shalt kepe a [3]Sperohak vnto the tyme that
the grett maister shall hold his Iugement.   And al

---

[1] Fr. japhes.   [2] Fr. devellée.   [3] fol. 7 b.

and all knights
who shall watch
there a certain
time without
sleep,

shall have any
gift they desire,

except herself in
marriage.
Those that per-
sist in this last
request shall be
unfortunate to
the ninth genera-
tion.
Palatyne is to
be imprisoned on
Mount Guygo,
with the treasure
of King Elynas,
until one of their
lineage shall de-
liver her,
and obtain the
treasure.

noble and worthy knightes descended & comme of
noble lynee, that wil goo watche there the day byfore
the euen, and theuen also of saint Iohan baptiste,
whiche is on the xx. day of Iung,[1] without eny slep,
shal haue a yeft of the of suche thinges that men may
haue. corporelly / that is to wete, of erthly þinges
without to demande thy body ne thy loue by maryage
nor other wyse.   And al thoo that shal demande the
without cesse, and that wyl not forbere & absteynne
them þerof / shalbe infortunate vnto the ix. lynee, and
shul be putt from theire prosperytees /.   And thou
shalt be closed, palatyne, & shette on the mountayn of
Guygo, with al the tresoure of thy fader, vnto the
tyme that a knight shal comme of our lynee whiche
shal haue al that tresoure to help therwith for to gete
& conquyre the land of promyssion / & shal delyure
the from thens /.'   Thenne were the thre sustirs full
heuy of herte & sorowfull, & departed fro their
moder.   And Melusyne went & toke her way al alone

The sisters then
go their several
ways.

thrughe the forest & thikk busshes.   Melyor also
departed, & yede toward the Sperhaak Castel in the
gretto Armenye.   And Palatyne also went to the
mounteyne of Guygo, wher many a man hath seen
her /.   And I myself herd it say of the kinge of
Arragon and of many other of hys royaume.   And

Be not displeased
that I tell you
these things.

I will now pro-
ceed to the
history itself,

but will first
tell you how
King Elynas
ended his days.

be nat you displessed yf I haue recounted vnto you
this auenture, For it is for to adiouste more of feyth
& for to veryfy thistory, And fro hens fourthon I
wil entre into the matere of the very & true hystory.
but first I shall telle to you how the king Elynas
fynysshed his dayes in this world / and how Pressyne
his wyf buryed hym within the said mountayn in a
moche noble tombe, as ye shal here heraftir. /

After living a
long time upon
the mountain,
he died.
   ² fol. 8.

Longe tyme was the Kyng Elynas on the said moun
tayne in so moch, that deth which bringeth ²euery

¹ Fr. juing.

personne to an ende toke hym. Thanne cam*me* ther
Pressyne his wyf and buryed hym there / and on hym
made to be sette oon so noble & so riche a tombe, þat
4 neu*er* byfore ne syn that tyme was seen none suche ne
so riche. For on the tombe were riches wi*th*out comparacion as of precyo*us* stones and other Jewellis / and
about it were grett & highe Candelstyke*s* of fyn gold,
8 and lampes & torches whiche brennen both day &
nyght continuelly. And on the said tombe stood vp
right a Statue or ymage of Alabaster, kerued & made
aftir the lengthe, lyknes, & fourme of Kinge Elynas /
12 and the said ymage held in her hand*es* a table[1] of gold,
whereon was writon the forsaid auenture. And there
the lady Pressyne stablysshed a stronge geaunt to the
sauegarde of the tresoure byfore said / the whiche
16 Geaunt was wounder fyers & horryble, and al the
Countre therabout he held vnder his subgection. And
also aftir hym many other geaunts kept it vnto the
tyme & com*m*yng of Geffray wi*th* the grett toth / of
20 the whiche ye shall more here herafter. Now haue ye
herde of the King*i* Elynas and of Pressyne his wyf.
And from hens fourthon I wil bigynne & shew the
trouth of thystory of the meruaylles of the noble Castel
24 of Lusignen in Poitow. And why & by what manere
hit was bilded & made./

T̲hystory recounteth to vs that there was somtyme
in the Brut Brytayne[2] a noble man whiche fell at
28 debate with the nevew of the king*i* of Bretons. and in
dede he durst therfore nomore dwelle wi*th*in the land /
but toke wi*th* hym al his fynau*n*ce & goode*s*, and went
out of the land by the high mountaynes. And as
32 telleth thistorye he founde on a day nighe by a fontayne a fayr lady to whom he told al his Fortune &
aduenture / so that fynally they enamourod[3] eche other,

Side notes:
and Pressyne buries him, and erects a rich tomb to his memory,

bearing a statue of the King.

She places a giant to guard the tomb and the treasure,

who was suc-ceeded by many others, until Geoffrey with the Great Tooth came.

Now I will tell you of the mar-vellous Castle of Lusignen.

A noble man of Brut Britain, falling out with the nephew of the King,

leaves the land;

and meeting a beautiful lady near a fountain,

---

[1] Fr. *tablier*.   [2] Fr. *la brute bretaigne*.
                  [3] Fr. *s'amouérent.*

and the lady shewed to hym grett loue, & dide vnto hym mocĥ comfort. and he began witĥin her land, that was wast & deserte for to byldͤ & make fayre tounes & strong Castels. and was the land witĥin 4 ¹short tyme peupled raisonably / And they dede calle the land forestz, bycause that they founde it full of grett wodes & thikk bushes, And yet at this day it is called Forestz. It haped that this knight & this lady 8 fel at debate togidre. I ne wot not goodly how ne wherfore / but that right sodaynly departed the lady fro the knight, wherfore he was woful & heuy. and notwitĥstandinge he grew & encreaced euer in worship 1 and in prosperite. The noble men thanne of this land / seeyng that they were witĥout a lady purveyed hym of oon to hys wyf, a moche gentil & fayre woman, sustir to the Erle of Poiters, whicĥ regned at that tyme, & 1 he begate on her many children males. emonge the whiche was oon / that is to wete the iijde borne, whiche was named Raymondyn, and was fayre, goodly & gracyous, moche subtyl & wyty in all thinges. And 2 that same tyme² the said Raymondin might be xiiij yere of age./

Cap. II. How the Erle of Poytiers prayde the Erle of Forests for to comme to the Feste 2 that he made of³ hys sone./

⁴The Erle of Poyters held a grett feste of a sone that he had, and wold haue made hym to be dowbed a knight. And no more children he had, but 2 only a fayre mayde that was called Blanche / and the sone had to name Bertrand. [Thanne the Erle Emery]⁵ manded & desyred a mocĥ fayre company for loue of the knighthode of his sone / and amonges other he bode 3

Marginal notes: he marries her, and in her land builds many towns and castles; ¹ fol. 8 b. and the country is called Forests. The knight, quarrelling with the lady, she suddenly disappears. He afterwards marries the sister of the Earl of Poitiers, and has many children by her, of whom the third born was named Raymondin. ⁴ fol. 9. The Earl of Poitiers holds a great feast in honour of his son Bertrand,

² Fr. *icelluy temps.*
³ Fr. *pour.*   ⁵ omitted by the translator.

& prayed the Erle of Forests to comme to the feste, *to which the Earl of Forests and his sons are invited.*
& that he shuld bring with him thre of his sones, the
oldest, For he wold see them. Thanne the Erle of
4 Forestz went at his mandement in the moost honourable wyse that he coude, and with hym he led thre of
his sones. The feste was grette, and there were made *At the feast many are knighted.*
and dowbed many a knight for loue of Bertrand, sone
8 to the Erle of Poyters, that was þat day preferred to
thonourable & worshipfull ordere of knighthod. And
also was ther made and dowbed to a knight, theldest
sone of the Erle of Forestz, for he jousted moche wel
12 & fayre. And was the fest contynued and holden the
space of viij dayes. And the Erle of Poyters made &
gaf many & moche fayre & grett yeftes. [1]And at the *When it is over, the Earl of Poitiers asks the Earl of Forests to leave Raymondin in his charge,*
departyng of the feste the Erle of Poyters demanded
16 of the Erle of Forestz, & prayed hym to loue *with* hym
Raymondin his nevew, and that he shuld *neuer* care
for hym For he wold purvey for him wel. And the
erle of Forestz graunted it / and thus dwelled the said *which is done.*
20 Raymondyn with the Erle of Poyters his vncle, that
loued hym wel. And after toke the feste an ende
moche honourably & frendly. And as now cesseth
thistory to spek of the Erle of Forests, whiche re-
24 tourned with his two sones & al his fellowship vnto
his Countre. And begynneth oure hystory to procede fourth / and to spek of the Erle Emery, and of
Raymondyn. /

28 Cap. III. How a forester cam*me* to denounce
to the Erle Emery how there was within the
Forest of Coulombyers the moost meruayllo*us* wildbore that euer was sen byfore. /

32 Thystorye certyffyeth to vs and also the veray *The grandfather of Earl Emery was St. Willam.*
Cronykles that this Erle Emery was grauntfader

[1] In French version Cap. III. begins from this point.

to saynt William that was Erle, and left al worldly
pocessyons for to serue oure Creatour, and toke on
hym the ordre & Religion of the whit mauntelles, an
ordre or Religion so called.   And therof I wil not 4
make grett locucion or talking'; But I will procede
fourth on our matere, and to spek of the Erle Emery.

The Earl was
worthy, and
learned in
astronomy,
Thistory thanne telleth to vs that this Erle was moche
worthy & valyaunt a knight / and that loued euer 8
noblesse, And was the most wyse in the science of
Astronomye that was in hys dayes, ne byfore syn that
Aristotles regned.   That tyme that the Erle Emery
regned / thistory sheweth to vs that [he] coude many a 12
science,[1] & specially he was parfytte in the science of
Astromy, as I haue said tofore.   And knowe ye that

and devoted to
his nephew
Raymondin.
he loued so moche his nevew Raymondin that he might
no more.   and so dide the child his vncle, and peyned 16
hym moche to playse & to serue hym at gree, and to

² fol. 10.
doo hym playsir in all maners.   It is wel trouth [2]that

He had houndes
and hawks,
this Erle had many houndes and many haskes of al
maneres.   and [it] befell as thystory recounteth that 20
oon of the Foresters camme vnto the Erlis Court, & demanded[3] or told that in the Forest of Coulombiers was

and one day
went to hunt a
wild boar in the
Forest of Cou-
lombiers.
the moost meruayllous wildbore that had be seen of
longe tyme byfore, and that at hym shuld be the best 24
& fayrest dysport that eny gentylman shuld euer haue.
'By my feyth,' said the Erle, 'these tydynges plaise
me wel. late the hunters & houndes be redy to morow
by tymes. & we shall goo to the chasse.' 'My lord,' 28
said the Forester, 'at your playsire.'   And al thus he
departed fro the Erle / and made redy al that aparteyned to the chasse for to hunte at thoure that he had
apoynted./   32

---

[1] Fr. *que de moult de sciences estoit plain.*
[3] Fr. *denoncier.*

Cap. IV.   How the Erle went to the chace and Raymondyn with hym.

AND whan the day was comme that Erle Emery with grette foyson of barons and knightes departed out of the Cite of Poyters / and Raymondyn rode euer byside hym on a gret Courser the swerde girded about hym and the shelde [1] hehge ouer hys sholder.   And whan
8 they were comme to the Forest they byganne fourthwith to hunte, And the wildbore was founde that was fel & proude, & deuoured & kyld many houndes and toke his cours thrugh the Forest, For he was strongly
12 chaffed, and they byganne for to folowe hym waloping a good paas, but the wildbore doubted nothinge / but meuyd & wered hym in suche a manere that there ne was so hardy a dogge ne hound that durst abyd hym,
16 ne so hardy a hunter that durst hold the spere styl anenst hym for to hit & broche hym.   And thanne camme bothe knightes and esquyers / but neuer oon was there so hardy that he durst sette foot on the grounde
20 for to withstande & haue launched at hym.   Thenne camme the Erle that cryed with a highe voyce. sayeng. 'shal this swyne[2] abasshe us all.'   And whan Raymondyn herde thus spek hys vncle, he was in hymself
24 vergoynouse[3] and shamed / and alighted from his courser and sette feet on grounde / and holding the swerde naked, yede courageously toward the said bore, and gaf to hym a strok with grette anger / And the
28 bore dressed toward hym and made hym to fall on hys knees, but soone he stood up, And as preu[4] hardy and valyaunt wold haue broched and threst hys swyrde within the booris heest / but the bore fledd, and so
32 fast he ranne that there was neyther man ne hound but that he lost the sight of hym, but alonely Raymondyn that was on horsbak, and so fast he folowed

Earl Emery, his nephew Raymondin, and many knights

[1] fol. 10 b.

go to the forest.

They come upon the boar,

but the dogs and the knights are afraid of him.

Earl Emery cries, 'Shall this swine abasshe us all?'

Raymondin, ashamed, dismounts,

and attacks the boar,

which runs away;

Raymondin follows on horseback,

[2] Fr. filz de truye.   [3] Fr. vergongne.   [4] Fr. preus.

leaving all the
hunters behind.
the bore that he outranne al thoo that were at the
chace, & lefte them behinde and founde hym self alone.

His uncle, afraid,
gallops to him,
and bids him
give up the
chasse,
Wherof the Erle, his vncle, was aferd / les that the
bore shuld distroye hym.   Wherfore the Erle waloped 4
aftir hys nevew Raymondin and with a high voyce
escryed hym. 'Fayre nevew, leve this chasse, and cursed
be he that anounced it to vs, For yf this swyne hurt
you I shall neuer haue joye in my herte.' But Ray- 8

but Raymondin
heeds not;
mondyn, whiche was chaffed,[1] doubted not of hys lyf,
ne toke heede to none euyl Fortune that might befall

[2] fol. 11.
[2]to hym therof / but euer withoute cesse folowed the

and the hunt
continues.
said bore, For he was well horsed. And the erle folowed 12
euer hys nevew.   What shuld auayll yf herof I shuld

The horses fag,
leaving Earl
Emery and his
nephew alone on
the track.
make a longe tale.   Alle theire horses byganne to be
chaffed and wery, & abode fer behinde, saaf only the
Erle and Raymondyn, whiche chaced the bore so longe 16
that the nyght fell on them./   Thanne the Erle & his

They rest under
a tree,
nevew stode styl and rested þem vnder a gretta tree.
And the Erle gan to sey to Raymondin, 'Fayre nevew
here shall we abyde tyl it be mone shyn.' And Ray- 20
mondyn said to hym, 'Sire, aftir your wille shall I
doo.' And soone aftir roos the moone fayre and
bright./ Thenne the Erle that knew moche of the

from which the
Earl studies the
sky,
science of Astronomy dide loke & behelde the skye and 24
sawe the sterres full bright & clere, and the moone that
was moche fayre without tache or spot, ne none obscurte or darknes was seen about it /. he ganne sore to
wepe.   And aftir gretto & deep sighynges said in this 28

and praises God,
manere. 'Ha / ha / right mighty and veray god, how
gretto ben the meruaylles that thou haste lefte here
bynethe / as to knowe parfytly bothe the vertues &
the nature of many wounder and dyuerse condycions 32
of thinges, and of theire significacions or betoknynges.
This might not be perfightly knowen, yf thou shadd
nat vpon the men somwhat of thy full & deuyne grace,

[1] Fr. eschauffé.

And specyally of this meruayllous aduenture, the
whiche I now see by the sterres whiche thou hast created & sitte by ordre on the firmament or skye / and
4 that I knowe by the high science of astronomye / of
the whiche by thy grace þou hast lente to me oon
braunche of knowlege wherof I oughte to preyse /
to thanke and to regracy[1] the hertily in thy highe
8 mageste, wher to none may be compared. O veray &
highe sire, how might this be raisonably as to knowlege humayne without it were by thy terrible jugement,
For no man shuld not mowe haue & receyue wel for
12 to do euer euyl.   And notwithstandyng I see & perceyue wel by [2]the highe science of Astronomy / of   [2] fol. 11 b.
whiche somme vnderstandyng I haue / to me leued[3]
of thy pure grace what hit segnyfyeth or betokneth,
16 wherof moche meruailled I am.'   These wordes said /
the Erle byganne to wepe and to sighe more strongly   and weeps.
than he dide byfore.   Thanne Raymondin whiche hadd   Raymondin
kyndled the fyre with hys fyreyron and that had herde   kindles a fire,
20 the moost part of all that the Erle Emery had sayd /
said to hym in this manere / 'My lord, the fyre is wel
kyndled, comme and warme you. and I byleue that within   and asks the
Earl to warm
a while we shall haue somme tydynges of your meyne,   himself,
24 For as my thought ryght now I herd barking of dogges.'   and says he hears
the dogs barking.
'By my feith,' said the Erle. 'of the chace I gyue
nomore force / but of that I see ' / And thanne he be-
helde vpward vnto the sky and wept ful sore / And   The Earl being
still in tears,
28 Raymondyn þat so moche loued hym, said to hym /
'Ha / ha / my lord, for godis loue lette that thing be.
For it apparteyneth not to so highe a prince as ye be,   Raymondin tries
to divert his
For to putte or sette hys herte therto / ne for to en-   attention,
32 quyre of suche artes, ne of suche thynges. but wel it
behouyth to you, and that shalbe wel doon to regracye,
and to thanke god of that he hath puruéyed you and
promoted vnto so highe and so noble a lordship as

[1] Fr. gracier.   [3] Fr. presté.

youre is. And as me semeth it is grette symplenes to
take ony sorowe or heuynes of suche thinges that may
not helpe / hyndre ne lette' / 'Ha ; ha / fole,' said the
Erle, 'yf thou wyst and knew the grette mernaylles & 4
wounderfull auentures that I see, thou shuldest be al
abasshed.' Thanne Raymondyn, that thought none euyl,
answeryd in this manere. 'My right dere & doubted
lord, I pray you to telle it to me / yf it is thinge that I 8
may knowe.' 'By god,' said the Erle, 'thou shalt
knowe it / and I wold that neyther god ne the world
shuld demande of the nothinge of it / and that thaduenture shuld befall to the, on myn owne self / For I2
from hens fourth I am old and haue frendes ynoughe
for to hold my lordshipes. but yet I loue the so moche
that I would that so grett a worship were haped to
thee / And the auenture is suche / that yf at the same 16
ooure a subget dide 'slee hys lord he shuld becomme the
moost mighty and moost worshiped that euer camme out
of hys lynage or kynrede, And of hym shuld procede
and yssue so subtle a lynee / that of it shuld be 20
mencioun and remembraunce made vnto thende of the
world. And know thou for certayn that this is trouth
which I telle to the.' Thanne ansuerde Raymondyn
that neuer he shuld mowe byleue that it were trouth / 24
and that it were ayenst al right and reason / that a
man shuld haue wele for to doo euyl, and for to doo
suche a mortal treson. 'Now byleue thou it surely,'
said the Erle to Raymondyn, 'For it is as I tell to the.' 28
'By my feith,' said Raymondin 'yet shall I nat byleue it.' And as the Erle Emerye and Raymondin
spak of the said auenture togidre, they herd al alonge
the wod a grette affray ; and Raymondyn toke thanne 32
hys swerd that lay on the erthe. and lyke wyse dede
the erle, And abode longe thus thinkinge for to knowe
what it was, and stode byfore the fyre ; on that syde
as them semyd that the stryf was. And longe in suche 36

but he says he
sees wonderful
adventures in
the sky.

Raymondin asks
what they are.

The Earl says,
that if a subject
¹ fol. 12.
were to slay his
lord, then

that subject
would found
a noble line.

Raymondin
answers, that he
cannot believe it,

because it is
against right
and reason.

While they speak
they hear a great
affray;

they stop and
listen;

a state they abode tyl that they sawe a wounder grette *soon the boar*
& horryble bore moche chaffed commynge toward *approaches*
them. Thanne gan sey Raymondyn, 'My lord, clemme *them.*
4 you vpon som tree lest that this wyld bore hurte you,
and lette me dele with hym.' 'By my feyth,' said the
Erle / 'god forbede that I leue the in suche auenture
al alone.' And whan Raymondyn herde this, he went
8 & stode byfore the bore hauyng hys swerd on his feet,[1] *Raymondin goes*
and wilfull[2] for to dystroye & slee hym / and the wild *to slay him.*
bore tourned hym and went toward the Erle. Thenne
bygganne the dolour of Raymondyn / and the grette
12 hape that therof camme aftirward to hym, As the very
& trew history recounteth to vs.

Cap. V. How Raymondyn slew the Erle of Poyters, his vncle.

16 [3]IN this part recounteth thystory, that whan Ray-   *fol. 12 b.*
mondyn cam ayenst the said bore for to kepe
hym that he shuld not hurte his lord / the bore anoone
hurted to hym, & ranne fast toward the Erle, whiche *The boar comes*
20 seeyng the wyld bore comme / lefte his swerd, and toke *near the Earl,*
a short spere, and strayght held it dounward before
hym. And the Erle, that knew & wyst moche of the
chasse, broched the bore thrughe the brest / but the *who pierces him.*
24 Erle fell doun on his knees. And thanne Raymondyn,
holdyng hys swerde in his hand, camme toward the bore,
and wold haue smytte hym betwene the foure[4] legges,
For he leye vpsodounne the bely vpward. and suche *Raymondin*
28 a stroke gaaf Raymondyn to the bore, that the blade of *strikes also,*
hys swerde brake / so that the poynte of it sprang *but his sword*
ayenst the Erlis stomak, & wounded hym sore / in so *wounds the Earl,*
moche that he deyed therof. And Raymondyn, which *so that he dies.*
32 was sore chaffed / seeyng hys wepen broken, and not

---

[1] Fr. *l'espée au poing*, mistranslation for 'in his fist.'
[2] Fr. *par bonne voulenté de la destruire.*
[4] Fr. *quatre.*

1 fol. 12.

Raymondin kills the boar,

and then sees that his uncle is dead.

He weeps and laments piteously,

and remembers that such an adventure would make a man famous.

2 fol. 12 b.

yet percey[1]uyng' his mortal werk / toke the spere, & so strongly broched it thrughe the bore, that he slew hym.   But whan he dide loke toward his vncle, and that he sawe hym all bloody / he went, and wold haue 4 had hym to stand vpon his feet, but it was for nought. he thenne pulled out of hys brest the piece of the swerd, and knew that it was hys dede /.   Moche meruayllously thanne byganne Raymondin to sighe & 8 to complayne, & wept and lamented piteously, sayeng in this manere : 'Ha / ha / false fortune, how moche art thou peruerse & euyl, that hath doon to be slayn by me hym that loued me so moche, and that had doon to me 12 so moche good ?   Ha / god fader almighty / wher shal now be the land where this harde & false synner shal mowe abyde / For in certayn all they that shall here spek of this grett mysdede shal juge me / & with good 16 right, to dey of a shamfull deth, For a more false ne more euyl treson dide neuer no synner. / Ha / erthe cleue & open the / & deuoure thou me fourthwith, and lete me fall with the moost obscure & derk angel 20 within helle, þat somtyme was the fayrest of all other in heuen, For wel I haue deserued it.'   In this dolour & woo was Raymondyn a longe space of tyme, & was moche þoughtfull & wroth / and bethought hym self, 24 & said in this manere / 'My lord & vncle, that lyeth deed yonder, sayd to me / that yf suche an auenture shuld comme to me, that I shuld be worshiped more than ony man of my lynage.   but I now see wel al the 28 contrary / For truly I shalbe þe moost vnhappy & dyshonoured man that euer was borne of woman / and by my feyth I haue wel deserued it / it is wel raison & right.   But notwithstanding [2]syth that now it may 32 none oþerwyse be / I shal dystourne me out of this land, and shal goo som wher for to purchasse myn aduenture, suche as god wil send to me in to somme good place, where as I may take & do penitence for my 36

synne.' And thanne Raymondyn cam*me* to hys lord / Raymondin sadly kisses his dead lord,
aud sore wepyng, kyssed hym with so heuy & wooful
herte / that thenne he had nat mow say one only word

4 for all the gold in the world /.   And soone aftir that
he had kyssed hym, he layed his foot on the sterop
and lepe vpon his hors / and departed, holding his way leaps on his horse, and rides through the forest
thrugh the myddel of the Forest, moche dyscomforted,

8 & rode apas vnknowing the way, ne whether he
went / but only by hap & att auenture, And made
suche a sorowe that there nys no personne in the world
that coude thinke ne sey the vth part of hys dolour /.

12 When Raymondyn departed fro his lord, and that
he had lefte hym deed beside the fyre, and
the wild bore also / he rode so longe thrugh the
Forest, euer wepyng and complaynyng so sore that

16 it was gret pite for to see & here hym / that about
mydnyght he aprouched nygh to a fontayne of fayerye, till he comes nigh to the fairy Fountain of Soif.
named þe fontayne of soyf / And many one of the
Countre þer about called hit the fontayne of fayerye,

20 bycause that many a meruaylle fell & happed there
many tymes in tyme passed.   And was this fontaynne
in a wounderfull & meruayllous place / and ouer it was
a roch of meruayllous height / and al alonge the said

24 Fontaynne was a fayre medowe, nygh to the high Forest,
And wel trouth it is that the moone dide shynne at that
tyme ryght clere & bright, And the hors ledd Ray-
mondyn whiche way that he wold, For no heede nor He falls asleep on his horse, ¹ fol. 14.

28 ¹aduys he had of nothing, for cause of the gret
dysplaysaunce that he had wi*th*in hym self. And
notwithstanding that he slept, hys hors ledd hym in which journeys on to the fountain,
this state so longe that he was com*me* wel nygh to the

32 fontayne. And at that same tyme were there [thre]
ladyes, that played & dysported them / among*is* the where three ladies disport themselves.
whiche oon was auctorised of the other as maistresse &
lady ou*er* them, Of the whiche lady I wil now spek

36 aftir that thistory telleth.

Cap. VI. How Raymondyn camme to the Fontayne of soyf, wher he founde Melusyne, and two other ladyes with her.

[Unknown to himself Ray mondin is carried by his horse.

[fol. 14 b.

[past the Fairy Fountain.

[the chief lady there originally complained of Raymondin not saluting them.

[he seems to be asleep.

[so says the lady.

THystory saith, that so longe bare the hors Ray- 4
mondyn thus pensefull[1] & heuy of herte of the
myshap that was comme to hym, that he ne wyst where
he was, ne whither he went / ne in no manere he ledd
hys hors / but his hors ledd hym where that he wold, 8
For Raymondin touched [2]not the brydell / and herd
ne saw nought / so sore was hys wit troubled. And
thus he passed byfore the fontaynne where the ladyes
were, without hauyng eny sight of them. but the 12
hors that sawe them, was sodaynly afrayed, and fledd
thens, rennyng moche fast. And thanne she that was
the gretest lady of them thre, sayd in this manere:
' By my feyth, he that rode now & passed byfore vs, 16
semyth to be a moche gentyl man / and, neuertheles,
he maketh of it no semblaunt / but he sheweth the
semblaunt of a vylayne or kerle, that hath passed
so before ladyes without to haue salewed them.' And 20
all this said she feynyngly to thende that the other
shuld not perceyue to what thinge she tended. For she
wist & knew wel how it was with hym, as ye shal
here say in thystory hereafter. And thanne she gan 24
say to the other ' I goo to make hym speke. For he
semeth to be asleep.' She departed fro the other
two ladyes and yede to Raymondin, and toke the
hors by the brydel & make hym to stand styll, and 28
seid in this manere ' By my feyth, sire vassal, his
vassail to you is grete vousur / grete vilanie for
a man of your age asleep & thus spekyng it is more
vilanie but he coude saie nothinge & spake 32
... And anone ... asshe ... shoke hym
... so harde. Sire Raymondin here he ... waked as
... a sleep & the

answerd her not. And she, as angry & wroth, sayd   which enrages
ones ayen to hym : 'And how, sire musarde, are ye so   her ;
dyspytous that ye dayne nat ansuere to me ?' And yet
4 he answered neuer a word. 'By my feith,' sayd she
within her self, 'I byleue nonne other / but that this
yong man slepeth vpon his hors / or ellis he is eyther   she sees he
dombe or def / but as I trow I shal make hym wel to   sleeps,
8 spek, yf he euer spak byfore.' And thenne she toke
and pulled strongly hys hand, sayeng in this manere :   and wakes him
'Sire vassal, ye slep.' Thanne Raymondyn was   suddenly,
astonyed ¹and affrayed, as one is whan another awaketh   ¹ fol. 15.
12 hym fro slepe / and toke hys swerd, wenyng to hym   whereat he is
that it had be hys vnclis meyne, that wold haue take   affrighted,
and slayn hym. And the lady thanne perceyued wel
that he yet had not seen her, and, al lawghing, bygan
16 to say to hym, 'Sire vassal, with whom wyl you   but the lady
bigynne the bataille ? / your enemys ben not here,   soothes him.
And knowe you, fayre sire, that I am of your party or
syde ?' And whan Raymondyn herd her spek, he be-
20 held her, and perceyued the gret beaulte that was in   He admires her
her, and toke of hit grett meruayll, For it semed to   beauty,
hym that neuer byfore he had not seen none so fayre.   for he had seen
And thenne Raymondyn descendid from hys hors, and   none so fair
  before.
24 bowed hys knees, and made reuerence vnto her, and
said : 'My dere lady, pardonne to me myn Ignoraunce   He asks pardon
& vylonny that I haue doo toward you, For certaynly   for his neglig-
I haue mystaken ouermoche anenst your noble per-   ence.
28 sonne. And neuertheles, I ne sawe ne herd neuer
what ye haue said tyl that ye toke me by the hand.
and knowe ye, that I thoughte moche at that tyme on
a thinge that sore lyeth nygh to my herte / and vnto
32 god I pray deuoutly that amendes I may make vnto
you / and that of hys grace I may at myn honour be
out of this peyne, whiche hurteth myn herte sore.'
'By my feyth,' sayd the lady / 'it is wel said, For as
36 for to bygynne eny thinge, the name of god most first

be called to mans help / and I byleue you wel / that
ye herd not what I haue said / but, fayre sire, whither

The lady asks
Raymondin
where he travels
to ;

goo you att this tyme of nyght / telle hit hardyly
to me / yf goodly ye may dyscouere it. And yf you 4
knowe not the way / wel I shaH dresse you to it / For
there nys neyther way ne patH but that I knowe it
wel, and therof ye may trust on me hardyly.' 'By

¹ fol. 15 b.

my feith,' said Raymondyn, ¹'gramercy, lady, of 8
your curtoysye. And ye shal knowe it, my dere lady,

he says he has
lost his way,

sith that youre desyre is for to know it, I haue lost the
high way syn almost yestirday none vnto now / and
I ne wot where I am.' Thanne perceyued she that 12
he² kept hys faytte secret fro her / and said to hym :

but she calls him
by his name,
and tells him
not to deceive
her.

'By god, fayre frend Raymondyn, ye shuld not hyde
nothinge fro me, For I wot wel how it standeth with
you.' And thenne whan Raymondyn herd that she 16
named hym by hys owne name, he was so abasshed

This abashes
Raymondin.

that he wyst not what he shuld answere. And she þat
sawe wel that he was shamfull of that she had named
hym, and that she wyst so moche of hys secret & 20
Counseyll, sayd to hym in this manere : 'Forsouthe,
Raymondyn, I am she after god that may best counseylle the / and that may furthre and enhaunse the in
this mortal lyf. and all thin aduersytees & mysdedes 24
most be tourned in to wele / nought auaylleth to the

The lady
recounts to him
his adventure,

for to hyde them from me. For wel I wot that thou
hast slayn thy lord / as moche by myshap / as wylfully / how be it that at that ooure thou supposest not 28
to haue doon it. and I wot wel all the wordes that he
told vnto þe of the arte of Astronomye, wherin duryng
hys lyf he was right expert.' Whan Raymondyn

which abashes
him yet more.

herde this he was more abasshed than he was tofore / 32
and said to the lady : 'Right dere lady, ye telle to me
the trouth of alle thinges that ye say ; but moche I

He asks how she
knows of it.

meruaylle me how ye may so certaynly knowe it / and

² 'she' in MS.

who told it so soone to you?' And she ansuerd to
hym in this manere: 'Be not thou abasshed therof,
For I knowe the full trouth of thy faytte.   And wene
4 nor suppose thou nat that it be fauntesye or dyuels
werk of me and of my wordes, For I certyfye the,
Raymondyn, [1]that I am of god, and my byleue is / as
a Catholique byleue oughte for to be.   and I lete the
8 to wete that without me and my counseyll / thou
mayst not comme to theude of thy faytte.   but yf thou
wilt byleue stedfastly all that thyn vncle Emerye said
vnto the, hit shalbe profytable to the, with the help of
12 god and of me.   And I say so moche that I shal make
the for to be the gretest lord that euer was of thy
lynage, and the gretest and best lyuelod[2] man of them
all.'   Whan Raymondyn vnderstod the promysse of
16 the lady / he remembred the wordes that hys lord
told vnto hym.   And consyderyng within hym self the
grete parels[3] wherin he was as exilled and banysshed
out of hys Countre & fro his frendes, said [to hym-
20 self][4] that he shuld take thauenture for to byleue the
lady of all that she shuld doo or say to hym, For but
ones as he said he shuld passe the cruell pass of the
deth.   And to the lady he ansuerde full humbly in
24 this manere: 'My right dere lady, I thanke you moche
of the promysse that ye do and proffre to me.   For ye
shall see & knowe that this shal not abyde or tarye by
me for no traueyll that ye can aduyse / but that I
28 shall euer doo your playsire, yf it is possible to be
doo / and that a cristen man may, or ought to doo,
with honour.'   'By my feyth, Raymondin,' said the
lady / 'that is said of free herte, For I shall not say
32 nor counseille you nothing / but that good & wele shal
comme therof.   but first of alle,' said she / 'ye most
promyse to me that ye shall take me to your wyf.
and make you no doubts of me / but that I am of

Marginal notes:
'Not by witch-craft,' she replies,
[1] fol. 15.
and advises him to believe what Earl Emery foretold,
and promises to make him a great lord.
He thanks her,
and undertakes to do her pleasure.
She asks him to marry her;

[2] Fr. *terrien*.   [3] Fr. *pérclz*.   [4] Fr. *s'advisa*.

god.'[1] And thanne Raymondyn yede & ganne say, &
sware in this manere, 'Lady dere / by my feith / sith

that ye ensure me that it is soo / I shal doo aftir[2] my
power all that ye wyl commaunde me for to doo / And 4

indide I lawfully[3] promytte you that so shal I doo.'
'Yet Raymondyn,' sayd she, 'ye most swere another
thinge.' 'What it is, my lady,' said Raymondyn, 'I
am redy / yf it be thinge that goodly I may doo.' 8
'ye,' said she / 'and it may not tourne to you to no
dommage[4] / but to all wele. Ye muste promytte to
me, Raymondyn, vpon all the sacraments & othes that
a man very catholoque & of good feith may doo and 12

swere, that neuer while I shalbe in your company, ye
shal not peyne ne force your self for to see me on the
Satirday / nor by no manere ye shal not enquyre that
day of me, ne the place wher I shalbe.' And whan 16
she had thus said to Raymondyn, he yet ageyn said to
her in this manere : 'On the parel of my sowle I swere

to you / that neuer on þat day I ne shal doo nothing
that may hyndre ne adommage[5] you in no manere of 20
wyse' / 'and I,' said she, 'ne shal doo nor thinke to
none other thing but in what manere I shall mowe
best encresse in worship and honour, both you and
your lynee.' And Raymondyn yede & gan sey to her 24
in this manere, 'Soo shall I doo it to the playsire of
god.'/

'THanne,' said the lady / 'I shal now telle how ye

most doo / doubte you not of nothing. but goo 28
fourthwith vnto Poyters, And when ye shal comme
there / many one ye shal fynd commyng fro the chasse

that shall axe to you tydynges of the Erle, your vncle.
and to them ye shall ansuere in this manere / "how / 32
is he not yet comme ayen ?" And they shal sey "nay."

and thanne ye shal say, "I neuer sawe hym syn that

---

[1] Fr. *de par Dieu.*   [3] Fr. *leaulment.*
[4] Fr. *prejudice.*   [5] Fr. *soit en vostre prejudice.*

the chasse was at the strengest, and whan ye lost
hym" / and semblaunt ye most mak to be abasshed
more than eny other. And soone after shul comme the

4 hunters and other of hys meyne, and [1]shal brynge with
them the corps deed within a litere / & his woundes
shal seme to euery man aduys to be made by the wild-
bores teth. and they shal say alle, that the wildbore

8 hath slayn hym, And yet they shall say that the Er'e
kyled the sayd bore / and many one shal hold it for a
hardy & valiaunt dede. thus the dolour & woo shal
bygynne to be moche grete. The Erle Bertrand, his

12 sone, & hys doughtir Blanche, & alle oper of hys
meyne, bothe lesse & grete togidre, shal make grete
sorowe / and so shall ye doo with them. and ye shall
putte on you the blak gowne as they shall. And aftir

16 this nobly doon, and the terme assigned & take whan
the barons shall comme for to doo theire obeysaunce &
homage vnto the yong Erle, ye shal retourne hither to
me the day byfore the lordes & barons make theire

20 homage / and that tyme att this same place ye shall
fynde me.' Thanne as Raymondyn wold haue departed
from Melusyne to haue take hys leve of her / she said
to hym in this manere: 'Hold, my redoubted frend /

24 for to bygynne & assemble our loue, I gyue you these
two rynges, of whiche the stones ben of grette vertue.
For the one hath suche approprieté, that he to whomme
hit shal be gyuen by paramours[2] or loue, shal not dey

28 by no stroke of no manere of wepen, ne by none
armes / as longe as he shal bere it on hym / And the
other is of suche vertue, that he that bereth it on hym
shal haue victory of all his euyl willers or enemyes / al

32 be it pletyng in Courtes, or fyghtyng in feldes,[3] or ellis
whersoeuer it be : and thus, my frend, ye may goo
surely.' Thanne toke Raymondin leue of the lady,
and embraced & kyssed her swetly & moch frendly

Sidenotes:

and to feign sur-
prise at his ab-
sence.

[1] fol. 17.

When Emery's
body is found
they will think
the boar killed
him,

and will mourn,

which Ray-
mondin must do
too.

After doing hom-
age to the new
earl

he is to return to
the Fountain.

Before Ray-
mondin leaves
Melusine she
gives him two
rings;

one has power to
keep him safe
from hurt,

the other will
insure victory to
the wearer.

Then Raymondin
leaves his lady

---

[2] Fr. par amours.   [3] Fr. en plaidoirie ou meslée.

MELUSINE.

D

fol. 17 b.   [1]as she on whom all hys hoop was leyd. For he was
as thenne[2] so moche esprised[3] of her loue / that al that
she sayd / doubtles he held it for trouth. and raison
it was,[4] as ye shall here herafter in thystorye./   4

Cap. VII. How Raymondin, by the counseyl of the lady, went to Poytiers.

Raymondyn lepte vpon his hors, and the lady
dressed and putte hym in to the high way of 8
Poytiers, and [he] departed fro the lady. And at
departyng Raymondyn was ful sory, For he loued
alredy so moche her felawship, that wel he wold eu*er*

and rides fast to Poitiers.   haue be w*ith* her. Thenne thinkynge, he byganne 1
fast to ryde toward the Cite of Poyters. And the
said lady retourned toward the said Fontayn*ne*, where
the two other ladyes were, & abode her there / of
which ladyes thystory leueth here to speke/.   1

Now saith thystorye, that Raymondyn rode so fast
that soone he was com*me* into Poytiers, where

[5] fol. 18.   he [5]founde many one that were retourned fro the

When he arrives they ask for his lord;   chasse, which demanded of hym, 'where is my lord?' 2
'how,'[6] said thanne Raymondyn / 'is he not com*me*?' /
and they ansuerd 'nay.' And he said to them, 'I

he answers that he has not seen him since the great chase began.   sawe hym neu*er* syn that the grete chasse bygan, and
that the bore scaped fro the hound*es*.' And while that 2
they spak of this matere among* them alle / the hunters

Others arrive,   & other folk arryued there fro the chasse, som now
and thenne, the whiche all said as Raymondyn had
sayd. And som said that neu*er* they had seen suche 2
& so meruayllo*us* a chasse, ne so horryble a bore. And
many one said that the bore was com*me* fro som*me* other
land, For none so grete / nor that ranne so fast sawe
they neuer. Thanne was eu*ery* man meruaylled / how 3

---

[2] Fr. *desjà.*   [3] Fr. *surprins.*   [4] Fr. *il avoit raison.*
[6] Fr. *comment.*

the Erle taryed so longe. and they went to the yate
for to see if he cam*me*, & abode hym þer a longe space.
and eu*er* cam*me* folk that said as the other had sayd /
4 and that they lay all that nyght in the sayd Forest, For
they had lost theyre way. Thanne was all the peuple
of Poyters woofull & heuy for loue of theyr lord, that
taryed so longe / and specyally the Countesse, the said
8 Erlis wyf. but more woofull & heuyer they were
wit*h*in a lytel while after/.

but still no Earl
Emery,

whereat the
people mourn.

Cap. VIII. How the Erle Emery was brought vnto Poytiers deed within a Lyttere.

12 THystorye [1]telleth vnto vs, that so long they abode
at the gate with Raymondyn, that they sawe
commynge toward the Cite a grete multitude of peuple.
and as they dide approuch & cam*me* nygh, they herd
16 and vnderstod the piteous voyces of them, wherof they
were all meruaylled / and bygan many one to doubte
lest that they shuld haue hadd som trouble or som*me*
empeschement.[2] And so longe they abod, that they
20 whiche bare the corps of theire lord cam*me* vnto them,
sore lamentyng & piteously waylyng, sayeng to them
in this manere : 'wepe ye, and wepe ayen, & clothe
you all in blak, For the bore hath slayn our good lord,
24 the Erle Emerye.' And after the corps cam*me* two
hunters, that bare the grette bore. and thus they
entred into the Cite, makyng grete sorowe. And alle
the peuple of the Cite, seeyng theyre lord deed, by-
28 ganne pyteously to crye / sayeng in this manere : 'Ha /
ha, cursed be he of god that first anounced this chasse.'
The sorow & dolour was there so grete that no man sawe
²neuer no greter. And making suche sorowe cam*me*
32 vnto the Palleys / and there was the Corps leyed. And
bycause one oughte not to kepe ne mayntenne longe

¹ fol. 18 b.

A crowd is seen
approaching the
city gate ;

their piteous
voices make the
townsmen
marvel.

They arrive, bear-
ing their lord's
body ;

two hunters fol-
low, bearing the
boar.

The citizens,
weeping,

² fol. 19.

arrive at the
palace, where
they lay their
lord,

¹ Fr. *empeschement.*

and all the peo-
ple sorrow.

sorowe, I passe it ouer lyghtly. The Countesse & her
children made ouergrete sorow / and so dide the Barons
and all the Comynaltee of the land. And knowe ye
also / that so dide Raymondyn, as it foloweth./   4

Raymondin sor-
rows more than
any other.

Raymondyn made grete sorowe and greter than eny
other, and sore repented hym of hys mysdede,
And so moche / that yf it had not be the hoop & comfort of his lady, he had not mowe withhold hym self, 8
but þat he had sayd vnto them al hys anenture, for
cause of the grete contricion that he had of the deth of
hys vncle and lord. But I wil not spek long of this

The Earl's obse-
quy is done in
the Church,

matere. Soone thobsequye was doon moche nobly & 13
richely within the Chirche of our lady of Poytiers,
after the custome that was at that tyme, And ye muste
knowe that the good folk of the land that had lost þeir
lord were full of heuynes and of sorow / and they 16

afterwards the
boar is burnt.

fourthwith toke the said bore, and byfore the said
Chirch of our lady they brent it / And as it is wel
trouth that there nys so grete a sorowe, but that within

Four days after
the Barons try
to comfort the
Earl's family.

foure dayes[1] it is somwhat peased / the barons of the 20
land thanne yede and swetly comforted the Countesse
and her two children aftir theire power / and so moche
they dide that her grete sorowe was somwhat peased.
But þe sorowe of Raymondyn grew & wexed more and 24
more, as wel bycause of his grete mysdede / as for the
grete loue of whiche he loued hys vncle. It was thanne

Soon after the
Barons are sent
for, to do homage
to their new lord,

ordeyned & concluded by the Counseyll that alle the
Barons of the land shuld be sente fore, & boden to 28
comme at a certayn day for to doo theire homage to
theyre gracyous lord, the sone of the said late Erle.

[2] fol 19 b.
on knowledge of
which Ray-
mondin returns
to his land.

And assone [2]as Raymondyn knew of it, he toke hys hors
and alone yssued out of Poytiers and entred within the 32
Forest, for to goo & hold hys couenaunt vnto his lady./

[1] Fr. *trois jours*

Cap. IX. How Raymondyn retourned toward hys lady, and sawe a Chapell whiche neuer he had seen before./

4 THystory telleth to vs that so longe rode Ray- Raymondin rides to Coulombiers,
mondyn that he cam*me* into the Forest of Cou-
lombyers, & passed thrugh the lytel toun*e*, & went vpon
the mountayne and yede so longe that he p*er*ceyued
8 the medowes whiche were vnder the roche, that was
aboue the Fontayne of Soyf, and sawe a hous made of where he sees a new chapel,
stone in a maner*e* of a Chapell. And knowe ye that Ray-
mondyn had be there many [a] tyme, but neu*er* tofore
12 he had seen it / and went neuer to hit; And before the
place he perceyued many ladyes, knyght*es*, & Squyers and knights and ladies.
whiche made to hym grete feste and praysed hym
gretly. Wherfor he m*er*uaylled gretly, For one of them
16 said to hym*me*: [1] ' Sire, alight & come toward my lady [1] fol. 20.
that abydeth aft*er* you wi*th*in her pauyllon or tent*e*.' He is asked to dismount,
' By my feyth,' sayd Raymondyn / 'hit plaiseth me wel
so for to doo.' Soone he descendid from hys hors &
20 yede wi*th* them, which conueyed hym toward the lady
moche honourably. And thanne the lady cam*me* to
mete hym, & toke hym by the hand and ledd hym and is led by his lady to a tent.
into her tente, And satte both vpon a bed [2] of parement
24 moche ryche / and all the other abode wi*th*out. Thanne
byganne the lady for to raisonne [3] wi*th* Raymondyn, &
said to hym in this maner*e*: 'My dere frende, wel I
wote that wel ye haue hold [4] alle that I introduysed, or
28 taught you of, And therfore fro hens fourthon I shall His lady ex-
presses confi-
dence in him,
trust you the more.' 'Lady dere,' sayd Raymondyn /
' I haue founde so good a bygynnyng [4] in your word*es*,
that nothing ye shall com*m*ande to me that humayn
32 body may or oughte to comprehende or vndertake /
but that I wyl & shal doo it after your playsire.'
'Raymondyn,' said she / 'for me ye shall vndertake and he in her.

[2] Fr. *couche*.   [3] Fr. *à arésonner*.   [4] Fr. *tenu*.

no thing, but that of it ye shal comme to your wor-

A knight an-
nounces dinner ;

ship '.' Thenne camme there a knyght whiche kneled
before her / and after his reuerence made / dressed hys
wordes toward her, & said: 'My lady, al thing' is 4
redy / ye shal comme whan it playse you.' And the
lady ansuerde & said / 'Couere your heed, fayre sire.'
Thanne the lady & Raymondyn wesshe theire handes
& sette them at a moche ryche table. and within the 8
sayd pauyllon were many other tables dressed, where

Raymondin mar-
vels at the great
company,

dide sette many knightes and ladyes / and whan Raymondyn saw this appareyll, he meruaylled moche / and
demanded of hys lady fro whens so grete a felawship 12
was comme vnto her. And to hys demande the lady ansuerd nothing'. Wherfore Raymondyn asked of her ayen,

1 fol. 29 b.

'My lady, fro ¹whens are comme vnto you so many

and asks his lady
whence they
come.

of gentyl men and ladyes !' ' By my feyth, Raymondyn, 16
my frend,' sayd the lady, 'it is no nede to you for to

She tells him
they are at his
service.

be meruaylled therof, For they be all at your commandement, & redy for to serue you / & many other
also that now ye see not.' Thanne held Raymondyn 20
hys peas / and so many courses & of dyuerse metes
were before them brought, that meruayll it was to see
it.   And whan they had dyned, they weshe theire
handes / and graces said & all thinges doon ' the lady 24

After dinner his
lady leads Ray-
mondin beside
the bed ;

toke Raymondyn by the hand & ledd hym beside the
beed, & euerychon voyded the pauyllon, and wheras
they lyst went, or wher they oughten for to haue goo,
eche one aftir theyre estate '.   28

THanne said the lady to Raymondyn: 'My frend,
to morowe is the day that the barons shal comme

where she tells
of the homage
that is to be done
to Earl Bertrand.

for to doo theire homage vnto the yong Erle Bertrand.
And know you, my frend, that there must ye be / & 32
shal doo as I shal telle you, yf it playse you so to doo /
Now vnderstand & reteyne wel my wordes. Ye shal

Raymondin is to
go to Poitiers,
but to let every
one do homage
before he does,

abyde þer vnto the tyme that all the Baronnes shal haue
doo their homages, and thenne ye shal putte your self 36

fourth byfore the said Bertrand, and of hym ye shal *and at last he is to ask from Bertrand a gift*
demande a yefte, for the salary & remuneracioun of
alle the *seruyse* that *euer* ye dide vnto his fader.   And
4 telle to hym wel, how that ye ne demande of hym
nothre toun*e*, ne Castel, nor other thing of no grete
value. and I wote wel that he shal acorde or graunt it
to you. For the baron*s* shalle counseylle hym for to
8 doo soo, And as soone as he shal haue graunted *your*
requeste / demande of hym to haue on this roche &   *of the rock, and as much land as a hart's skin can cover,*
about it / as moche of ground as the hyd or skynne of
a hert may comprehende./ and freely he shal gyue it
12 to you. In so moche that non*e* shal now lette nor
empesche you therof, by reason of [1]homage, nother by   *[1] fol. 21.*
charge of rente or other ordyna*u*nce, and whan he
shall haue graunted it to you, take þerof his *lettres*,   *and to get a charter for it, signed and sealed.*
16 vnder hys grete Seele, and vnder the seell*es* of the
peris,[2] or lord*es* pryncipal of the land. And whan
that al this ye shal haue doo / on the morow next
folowing after that / as ye shalbe comyng homward
20 agayn / ye shal mete on *your* way a good man, which   *Raymondin is to buy a skin of a man he will meet,*
shal bere wit*h*in a sac the skynne of a hert / and ye
shall bye it / and for it ye shal pay asmoch as the said
man shal aske you for it / and after ye shall make it
24 for to be cutte in the smallest and narrowe*st* waye that
is possible for to be cutte, after the maner*e* of a thonge.   *and have it cut into a thong, then get the land delivered,*
And after, lette *your* place be delyu*er*ed vnto you /
the whiche ye shal fynd all marked & kerued, and all
28 the trees pulled to the ground, there as it shal plaise
me for to be / And as for to bryng the two end*es* of
the sayd thong[3] of the hyd togidre about the said
place / yf it happe that greter ground may be com-
32 prysed wit*h*in it ye shall doo it to be leyd dounward   *and lay the thong down, when a fountain will spring out where the ends meet.*
vnto the valey / & there, at both thendes of the said
thonge or leder / shal spryng out of the roche a fayre fontayn*ne*, whiche in tyme to com*me* shalbe full necessary

      [2] *Fr. pers.*   [3] *courroie.*

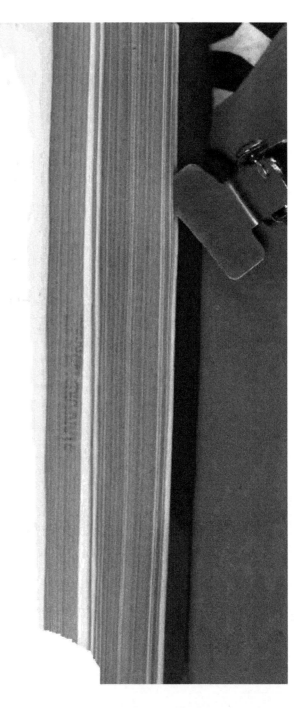

and conuenable. Goo þenne fourth, my dere frend /
and doo hardyly doubtles all that I haue said. For all
your werkes shalbe of good expedicioun, and without eny
trouble or lettyng / and on the mornne next after that 4
your yefte shalbe graunted and your lettres delyuered

to you, ye shall retourne hither to me.' Raymondyn
thanne ansuerde, 'My lady, after my power I shal
fulfylle al your playsire' / And thenne they embraced 8
and kyssed eche other / and toke leue one of other./
Here cesseth thystory of them / and begynneth for to

spek of Raymondyn, whiche toke hys hors, and rode
toward Poiters as ¹hastly as he myght./   12

*   *   *   *   *   *

Cap. X. How Raymondyn, after that the barons had doon theire homage vnto the yong Erle / demanded of the Erle a yefte, the whiche he graunted to hym./   16

THystorye telleth to vs, that Raymondyn rode so
longe that he camme vnto Poytiers, wheras he
founde many a high baron, which were comme there for
to make homage to the yong Erle Bertrand / and they 20
dyde grete honour and reuerence to Raymondyn, and
preysed hym right moche. And the next morow they

yede all togidre vnto Saynt Hylary of Poyters, where
the deuyne seruyse was doon right worshipfully, And 24
atte that seruyse was the yonge Erle reuested lyke a
Chanoyne, as theyre prymat or Abbot / and dyde hys
deuoyre as it apparteyned / and that of custome was

for to be doo. Thenne cam the barons ²tofore hym / 28

and there one after another, and eche one after hys
degre rendred to hym hys homage. And thenne,
after alle these thinges were doon Raymondin putte
hymself fourth before the barons / and with meke & 32
humble contenaunce or manere, said to them : 'Emong·

you, my lordes, nobles, Barons of the Countre[1] or Erle-dom of Poytwo, vouchesaf ye to here & knowe the requeste whiche I wyl putte & make vnto my lord

Raymondin tells the barons he intends to make a request to the Earl.

4 the Erle. and yf it seme you[2] to be lawfull & raison-nable / I beseche that it playse you for to pray hym to graunt it to me.' And the Barons ansuerd with right a good will, ' we shall doo it.' Thanne they altogidre

8 went before the Erle, to whom Raymondyn spake first moche humbly, sayeng in this manere: ' Right dere sire, humbly I beseche and requere you, that in remuneracion, or reward, of alle the seruyses that ever

12 I dide vnto my lord, your fader / on whos sowle god haue mercy, ye vouchesaf of your benigne & noble grace for to gyve to me a yefte, the whiche shall cost you but lityl. For knowe you, Sire, that I ne demande

16 of you neyther tounne, Castel, nor fortresse, ne nothinge of gretle valew.' Thanne ansuerde the Erle, ' yf it playseth to my barons / ful wel it playseth to me.' And the Barons said to hym in this manere: ' Sire,

He says he asks nothing of great value.

20 syn it is thyng of so lytyl valewe, as he speketh of, ye oughte not to refuse it to hym / For he is wel worthy therof, and wel he hath deserued it.' And the Erle said to them, ' Syn it pleseth to you for to coun-

24 seylle me soo / I graunt it ' / ' demande now,' said the Erles to Raymondyn, ' what ye wyl.' ' Sire,' said he, ' gramercy.[3] Other yefte I ne axe of you, but þat ye wyl gyue to me, about the fontaynne of soif that is

only as much land as a hart's skin can com-pass.

[4] fol. 22 b.

28 nygh to the roches & wodes / as moche of grounde as the hyde or leder of a hert shall mow comprehende or [4]goo aboute, bothe of lengthe & brede.' ' Forsouthe,' said þenne the Erle / ' this I ought not to refuse to you.

The Earl grants the request,

32 I gyue it to you,' said the Erle, ' freely, without rede-uaunce nor homage to be doon to me, nor to my successours for euermore.' Thenne Raymondyn kneled

[1] Fr. messeigneurs, nobles barons de la conté.
[2] Fr. se il vous semble.   [3] Fr. grans mercis.

& thanked hym ryght humbly / and requyred of hym

and gives letters of gift, lettres of hys gyfte, the which were graunted & made
in the best and moost surest wyse that could be
deuysed / and were Seelled of the grette Seal of the 4
Erle, by thassent and relacion of alle the Barons of

sealed by the Earl and Barons. the land / whiche also dide putte theire Seelles therto.
Thanne they departed fro the chirche of Saynt Hylary
of Poytiers, and yede fourth vnto the halle, where the 8
feste was grete and joyous, and swete melody was there
herd of almaner Instruments of Musyque. and of many

They hold a feast & dyuerse meets they were serued at the table.   And
after dyner the Erle gaaf grette yeftes / And wel trouth 12
it is, that it was sayd þerof many one, that among alle
the other Raymondyn was the moost curtoys / moost
gracyous, and of fayrest contenaunce.   And thus
passed the day tyl the nyght camme that euerychon 16

until they go to rest. went to take hys reste.   And on the mornne next they
roos and yede for to here masse vnto the Abbey of

At mass Raymondin prays for a good end to his enterprise. Montiers / and there Raymondyn prayed god deuoutly
that he wold help hym att his nede, and to brynge hys 20
enterpryse to a good ende, and to the saluacion of his
sowle & prouffyt of hys body.   And he abode within
the chirche, makyng hys prayers vnto thoure of
Pryme./   24

Cap. XI.   How Raymondyn founde a man
that bare the skynne or hyde of a hert /
and how he bought it /

1 fol. 22. [1]NOw telleth thystorye to vs, that whan Ray- 28
mondyn had herd hys masse, and that he had
ended his prayere / he went out of the chirche / and
at thyssue of thabbey byond the Castel he found a

Raymondin finds a man with a hart's skin to sell. man whiche bare within a sac vpon hys bak the hyde 32
of an hert, which man camme toward Raymondyn, and
said to hym in this manere. 'Sire, wyl ye bye this

hertis skynne that I haue with*in* my sack, for to
make good huntyng cordes for you*r* hunters.' 'By my
feyth,' said Raymondyn / 'ye / yf thou wilt selle it ;
4 and at one word[1] what shall I paye for hit ?' 'By my
feyth, sire,' said the man, 'ye shall paye to me for it
ten shelyng*es*, or ellis ye shall not haue it.' 'Frend,'
said thanne Raymondyn to the said man / 'bryng it   *which he buys*
8 home with me and I shall pay tho there.' And he   *for ten shillings,*
answer*d*, 'With a good wille.' Thanne he folowed
Raymondyn vnto his hous, and there he delyuer*d* hys
hyde / and Raymondyn payed hym for it. And anone
12 after, Raymondyn sent for a Sadelmaker,[2] to whom he
said : 'My frend, yf it plese [3]you, ye muste cutte this   *[3] fol. 22 b.*
hyde in fourme of a thonge, in the narowest & smallest
wyse that is possible to be doo.' The Sadler dide cutte   *and has it made*
16 it, and after they leyd it agayn with*in* the sac thus   *into a thong by a saddlemaker.*
cutte. What shuld I nowe prolonge the matere.[4]
It is trouth that they whiche were co*m*mytted for to
delyuer*e* to Ramondyn his yefte, rode, and Ray-   *Raymondin and*
20 mondyn with them, toward the fontayne of soyf, so   *the Earl's men ride to the foun-tain,*
long[4] that they cam vnto the roche that standeth ouer
the said fontayne, where as grett tranchis or keruyng[4]
was made with*in* the ha*r*de roche / and they fond[3] al   *where they mar-*
24 about it grete trees throwen doun to the ground[3],   *vel to find trees cut and rocks hewed.*
wherof they were gretly me*r*uaylled, For it was out of
mans mynde that euer trees were cutte there aboute.
Raymondyn, that thanne wel knewe that his lady had
28 wrought there, held hys peas. And whan they were
with*in* the medowe they toke the thonge out of the
sac /.

[1] Fr. *en ung mot.*   [2] Fr. *sellier.*
[4] *Que feroye ores plus long prolongation.*

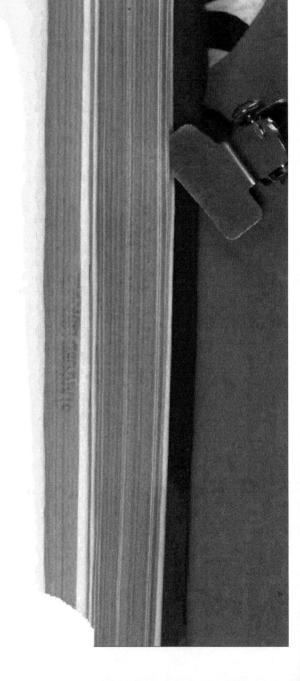

Cap. XII. How they that were ordonned cam*me* and delyuered to Raymondyn his yefte ./

[1] fol. 24.

The Earl's men are abashed at the length of the thong.

[1] WHan they that shuld delyuer the yefte saw the hyde cutte so smalle, they were of it alle 4 abasshed / and said to Raymondyn þat they wyst not what to doo / And there incontynent cam*me* to them two men clothed with cours cloth / the whiche said in this

Two men appear to help them;

manere. 'We are com*me* hither for to helpe you.' Thanne 8 they toke out of the sack the hyde and bare it vnto the bottom*me* of the valley, as nigh the roche as they

they set stakes to hold the thong;

coude / and there they dide sette a stake in the erthe, and to this stake they fasted the one ende of the hyde / 12 and as they went they sette stakes for to hold with the said thonge rounde aboute the roche / and whan they were com*me* ayen to the first stake, there was yet agrete remenant of the thong / and for to sette and fournysshe 16

It compasses the rock and part of the valley.

it they drew it dounward to the valey / and so fer they went with it, that they cam*me* to the ende of it. And ye must knowe that after that, it is said in the Countre, and as the very and true history witnesseth / 20

At the end of the thong a fountain springs furth.

there sprange at [the] ende of the said thong a fayr fontayn, the which rendred so moche of watre that a ryuere wexed or grew therof. Wherof many a mylle dyde grynde corne / and yet now grynden. Thanne 24 they that were there sent for to delyuere to Raymondyn

The men are abashed at the fountain and the great compass of the thong.

the place, were moche abasshed / aswel of the fontayne that they see spryng sodaynly before them, as of the grete compace of the ledder, whiche conteyned wel the 28 space of two mylles of grounde /

THistorye to vs recounteth that they whiche were ordonned for to delyuere the said yefte, as byfore is said, were moche abasshed whan they sawe the 32

[2] fol. 24 b.

watre spryng sodaynly & runne al along[2] fourth by the valey. And also they were meruaylled of the grete grounde that the thonge compassed. but neuertheles

they delyuered to Raymondyn the grounde that was
gyuen to hym after the texte or tenour of hys lettres.
And as soone as they had delyuered it, they wyst neuer
4 where the said two men that were comme there for to
helpe hem becamme, ne whither they were goon.

Thanne they departed alle togidre, for to haue retourned vnto Poyters, where as whan they were
8 comme, they dide telle and recounte vnto the Erle and
to his moder this meruayllous auenture. And thanne
the lady said to her sonne in this manere : ' Byleue thou
neuer of no thinge me / of that I shall say[1] / but yf
12 Raymondyn hath founde somme auenture in the Forest
of Coulombyers, For the same Forest is somtyme full
of moche meruayllous auentures.' And the Erle an-
ansuerd : ' by my feyth my lady / I byleue well that
16 ye say trouth / and long syn I haue herd say that
aboue the fontayne that is vnder the same roche,
men hath seen fall & happ many a wounder and meruayllous aduentures. but as to hym, I pray to god
20 that he may enjoye it to hys honour and prouffyt.'
' Amen,' said the ladye. As they spake thus togidre,
Raymondin arryued / whiche kneeled soone byfore the
Erle and thanked hym of the worship & curtoysy that
24 he had doon to hym. ' By my feyth, Raymondyn,'
said the Erle, ' ye thanke me of a lytil thing, but
betre I shall doo to you, with godis grace, in tyme to
comme.' ' Now, my frend Raymondyn,' said the Erle,
28 ' it is told to me of a grete and meruayllous auenture
whiche is happed as of present in the place that I
haue doon to be delyuered to you by my yefte. Wherfore I pray you that ye wil telle to me the pure & very
32 trouth of hit.' ' My feyth,' sayd Raymondyn. ' My
right dere lord / yf they that at [2]your commandement
haue delyuered the place to me haue not told you
of more than they haue seen / they haue doo wel.

[1] Fr. *Ne me croy jamais de chose que je die.*

They deliver the land to Raymondin.

The Earl's men return to Poitiers,

and recount to him the adventure.

The Earl and his mother speak of the marvels that have happened in the forest.

Raymondin arrives and thanks the Earl for his gift;

the Earl promises him more favours.

[2] fol. 25.

Neuertheless it is trouth that the space of grounde
compassed aboute with the hyde conteyneth two mylles.
And as for the two men whiche camme there clothed
with cours cloth, and haue holped for to compasse & to 4
mesuro the place / and also of the ryuere whiche
sourdred[1] sodaynly / of alle this, my lord, it is pure
trouth.' 'By my feith, Raymondyn,' sayd the Erle,
'ye telle to vs a grete meruaylle /. In good feyth, 8
Raymondyn, lyke as it semeth to vs and supposen, ye
most nedes haue founde som aduenture, and I pray
you that ye wyl declare it vnto vs, for to haue vs out
of the melencolye of it.' 'My lord,' said Raymondyn, 12
'yet haue I not founde but wel & honour / but my
ryght dere lord, I loue my self for to be & there to
dwelle more than in eny other place, bycause that it is
commonly renommed[2] auenturous and welhappy coun- 16
tre / and so I hope that god shall send to me some good
auenture whiche by hys plaisire shall be to me worshipfull & prouffytable bothe to my sowle and to my body.
And, my ryght dere lord, enquyre ye me nomore therof / 20
For certaynly, as of present, I can telle you nomore of
it /.' Thanne the Erle, that moche loued hym, held
therof hys peas, bycause that he wold not angre hym.
And this doon, Raymondyn toke hys leue of the Erle 24
and of his moder. And for as now I shall say no
more of them, And shall say how Raymondyn retourned toward his lady, where as he wyst that he had
lefte her /. 28

**Cap. XIII. How Raymondyn toke his leue
of the Erle of Poitiers & retourned toward
his lady./**

IN this partye, to vs telleth thistorye that Ray- 32
mondyn, whiche was moche enamoured of his

Marginal notes: Raymondin tells of the marvellous spring, and the compass of the thong. / and says that he loves to dwell by the fountain; / then bids adieu to the Earl, / and returns to his lady. / * fol. 23 b.

[1] Fr. est sours. [2] Fr. renommé.

lady, departed at this ooure fro Poytiers hastly al alone,
and rode tyl he cam*me* vnto the high Forest of Coulombiers, and descended fro þe hylle doun in to the valey
4 and cam*me* to the fontayne where [he founde][1] his lady,
that moche joyously receyued hym, and said to hym
in this man*ere* : 'My frend, ye begynne wel for to kepe
and hyde oure secretes : and yf ye perscuere thus, grete
8 wele shall therof com*me* to you / and soone ye shall see
and perceyue of it.' Thanne spake Raymondy*n* and
sayd in this man*ere* : 'Dere lady, I am & shalbe euer
redy for to doo aftir my power all your playsires.'
12 'In dede, Raymondyn,' said the lady / 'tyl ye haue
wedded me / ye ne may no ferther see ne know of my
secretes.' 'Lady dere,' said Raymondyn, 'I am alredy
therto.' 'not yet,' said the lady / 'For first ye must goo
16 vnto Poitiers for to pray the Erle and his moder and alle
your other parentes and frend*es*,[2] that they wil com*me*
and honoure you with their personnes at youre weddyng', in this place, on monday next com*myng*'. to
20 thende that they see the noblesses that I think and
purpose for to doo for to enhaunce you in honour &
worship / and that they take no suspecion but that ye
be maryed after your estate and degree. And wel ye
24 may tell to them that ye shall wedd the doughter of a
kinge / but no ferther ye shall not dyscouere of it. and
therfro kepe you as dere as ye haue the loue of me.'
'Lady dere,' sayd Raymondyn, 'doubte you not therof.'
28 'Frend,' sayd the lady, 'haue ye noo care that for what
folke that ye can bryng' / but that they all shalbe
wel and honourably receyued & wel lodged and wel
festyed / bothe of delycyo*us* meetes and drynkes, and
32 of allman*er* athing' acordyng / as wel to them as to
theire horses. Therfore, my frend, goo surely and be
not doubtous of nothing'.' They thenne kyssed eche
other / & Raymondyn departed fro the lady / of whiche

[1] omitted in MS. Fr. *où il trouua*.

His lady joyously
receives him ;

but tells him,
that he can know
no more of her
secrets until he
marries her,
which he pro-
mises to do
at once.

[2] fol. 26.

His lady tells
him to go to
Poitiers and in-
vite the Earl and
his friends to the
wedding,

and to tell them
that he is to
marry a king's
daughter.

Raymondin goes to Poitiers, thistory sylenceth   and bygynneth to spek of Raymondyn which goth toward Poytiers./

NOw telleth to vs thistorye that so longe rode
Raymondyn after that he was departed fro his 4
where he finds the Earl with many of his barons. lady that he camme to Poiters, wher he fonde the Erle
and his moder & grete foyson of Barons with them,
whiche were right wel glad of his commyng, / and demanded of hym fro whens he camme. And he ansuerde 8
to them that he camme fro his dysporte. And after that
they had spoken longe tyme of one thing and of other,
Raymondyn yede byfore the Erle & kneled & sayd to
hym thus : 'Right dere lord, I moche humbly besech 12
you, on alle the seruyses that euer I shall mow doo to
Raymondin invites the Earl to his wedding at the Fountain of Soyf; you, þat ye vouchessaf for to doo to me so moche of
honour as to comme on monday next to my weddyng,
to the fontayn of Soyf. and that it playse you to 16
1 fol. 26 b. bryng thither with [1]you my lady your moder, and
alle your barons also.' And whan the Erle vnderstode
The Earl is abashed at not being taken into confidence before. hym he was moche abasshed. 'How,' said the Erle,
'fayre Cousyn Raymondyn, are ye as now so straunged 20
of vs that ye marye you without that we know therof
tyl the day of weddyng? For certayn we gyue vs
thereof grette meruaylle, For we wende yf your wylle
had be to take a wyf to haue be they of whom ye 24
shuld first haue taken counseyll.' Thanne ansuerd
Raymondin, 'My right dere lord, dysplayse you nat
But Raymondin says that love has done what it listed with him. therfore, For loue is of so grete puyssaunce that she
maketh thinges to be graunted and doon as it playseth 28
to her, and so ferfourth I haue goo in this matere that
I may not flee it ; but neuertheles all were it soo that
I myght doo soo yet by myn assent I shuld not be
They ask his lady's lineage, fro it.' 'Now thanne,' said the Erle, 'telle vs what 32
she is and of what lynee.' 'By my feyth,' said Ray-
mondyn, 'ye demande of me a thing to the whiche I
which he can not tell. can not gyue none ansuere, for neuer in my lyf I ne dide
enquyre me therof.' 'Fersouthe,' sayd the Erle, 'it is 36

grett meruaylle. Raymondyn taketh a wyf that he
knoweth not, ne also the lynage that she commeth of.'
'My lord,' said Raymondyn, 'sith it suffyseth me as
4 therof, ye oughte wel to be playsed, For I take no wyf
that shall brawle or stryue with you / but only with
me / and I alone shall bere eyther joye or sorowe for
it, after that it shall please to god.' 'By my feyth,'
8 sayd the Erle to Raymondin, 'ye say right wel / and
as for me I ne wil kepe you therfro / but sith it is soo,
I pray to god deuoutly that he wil send you peas &
good auenture togidre / and right gladly we shall goo
12 to your weddyng', and with vs shall comme thither
my lady and many other ladyes and damoyselles of
our baronye.' And Raymondyn ansuered, 'My lord,
right gretly I thanke you, & as I byleue, whan ye
16 shalbe there and shal see the lady / ye ¹shalbe pleased
of her.' And thenne they lefte to speke of this matere,
and spake of one thing' and of other so long, that tyme
of souper camme. And notwithstanding, the Erle
20 thought euer on Raymondyn and his lady, and said
in hym self that somme Fortune he had fonde at the
fontayne of soyf./

I N this manere thoughte longe the Erle, so moche
24   that the styward² cam and said to hym: 'My
lord, all is redy, yf it plese you for to comme.' 'For-
south,' said he, 'it plaiseth me well.' Thanne they
weshe theyre handes, sette at the table / and wel they
28 were serued. And aftir souper they spak of many
materes, & after they went to bed. On the morowe
erly, the Erle aroos & herd his masse and made the
barons to be manded & boden for to goo with hym to
32 the weddynge of Raymondin / and they camme incon-
tinent. And the said Erle sent hys message for the
Erle of Forestz, whiche was brother to Raymondyn.
In this meane while³ made the said lady alle redy in

Side notes:
This abashes the Earl.

The Earl wishes Raymondin good luck,

and promises to attend the wedding;

¹ fol. 27.

but ever wonders about Raymondin and his lady, and their fortune.

After mass the Earl bids his barons to the wedding,

and sends word to the Earl of Forests.

¹ Fr. maistre d'hostel.   ² Fr. demantiers.

the medowe vnder the Fontayne of Soyf, and suche
appareill was there made, so grete & so noble, that for
to say trouth / nothing acordyng for suche a Feste
fawted ne waunted there, but honourably might a 4
kinge with alle his estate haue be receyued therat. The
sonday camme that alle made them self redy for to
goo to the fontayne of Soyf, at the weddynge of Raymondyn. The night passed & the day camme. And 8
thanne the Erle with hys moder / her ladyes & damoyselles / and with alle the barons, ladyes, & damoyselles
of the lande ; toke hys way toward the fontayne. And
as they rode thither the Erle enquyred of Raymondyn 12
the estate of hys wyf, but nothinge he would telle [1] to
hym therof. Wherof the Erle was sorowfull, And so
longe they rede talking togidre that they camme vpon
the hille, where they sawe the grete trenchis or keruyng 16
in the harde roche that sodaynly were made / and the
fontayne also whiche scurdred[2] & sprang ther haboundauntly. Thenne meruaylled therof euerychone, how so
sodaynly that might haue be doo. And they yede 20
fourth and biheld dounae toward the medowe and
sawe grete plente of fayre & riche pauillons or tentes,
right high[3] so grete, so noble, and so meruayllously facyoned that euery man awondred therof. and 24
namely,[4] whan they dide see & perceyued so grete
company of noble folke, as of knightes & squyers, that
went vp & doun in the medowe and without, for to
goo fetche suche thinges as neded to the festa. And 28
also might they see there right grete foyson of ladyes
& damoyselles richely apparayled & arayed, many
horses, palfreys, & coursers were there. There might
they see kychons & Cookes within, dressing meetes of 32
dyuerse maneres. And ouer the fontayne they sawe a
fayre chappel of our lady & ymages within right
connyngly kerued & entaylled, and of almener of

[2] Fr. sourdoit.   [3] Fr. si treshault.   [4] Fr. par especial.

ornamentes so richely ordeyned, that neuer so grete
richesse they had seen before that tyme in no churche,
wherof they meruaylled moche, and said oon to other.
4 'I ne wot what it shall befall of the remenaunt, but here
is a fayre bygynnyng⸱ grete, & shewyng⸱ grete noblesse
& worship.' /

Cap. XIV.   How the Erle of Poytiers camme
8   to the weddyng of Raymondyn, acompayned
of alle the Barons in hys land.

N O[w] telleth to vs thystorye, that whan the
Erle & hys folk were descended doun fro the
12   montayne / an auncyent knyght, nobly &
richely clothed and arayed, whiche rode on a fayre
palfray, and had in hys felawship xxiiij⸱ʰ men of worship richely & nobly aourned² & wel horsed / camme
16 gladly & with mery contenaunce toward the Erle.
First he mete with the Erle of Forest & with Raymondyn & theyre felawship, for they rode before.
And whan he perceyued Raymondyn, whiche wel he
20 knew among⸱ other / he yede tofore hym & made to
hym honour & reuerence, and his brother Erle of
Forest he salued moche honourably, & theyre felawship
also.   And shortly to spek, this auncyent knight
24 receyued them worshipfully, sayeng⸱ to Raymondin in
this manere : 'My lord, I pray you that I may be ledde
before the Erle of Poitiers yf it playse you, ²for I
desyre to spek with hym.'   And so Raymondyn made
28 hym to be ledde vnto the said Erle.   And whan
thauncyent knight camme before the Erle, he salewed
hym swetly, sayeng⸱, 'my lord, ye be welcomme.' And
the Erle ansuerd / 'and ye are wel mete with me. nowe
32 telle ye to me why ye dide axe aftir me.' Thanne said
the knight thus to the Erle : 'Sire, My lady Melusyne

Side notes:
¹ fol. 25.

An ancient knight comes to meet the company,

and salutes them.

He asks Raymondin to lead him before the Earl of Poitiers,
² fol. 25 b.
which Raymondin does.

² Fr. *aourné.*

The ancient
knight, on behalf
of Melusine,
thankes the Earl
of Poitiers for
his presence.

of Albany recommendeth her to you as moche as she
may ,' and thanketh you of the gret & high honour
that ye doo vnto Raymondyn your Cousin & also vnto
her whan ye vouchesauf of your grace to comme hither 4
for to bere vnto them felawship att their wedding'.'
'By my feyth,' said the Erle, 'In this cas ,' as ye may
telle to your lady , is no thankes to be had, for I am
holden for to do vnto my Cousyn all worship & honour 8
possible to me to be doo.' 'Sire,' said thauncient
knight, 'ye say full curtoisly / but my lady is sage for
to knowe what she ought for to doo ' and toward you
she hath sent both me and my felawship also.' 'Sire 12
knight,' said the Erle, 'this playseth me wel. but knowe
ye that I wende nat to haue found lodged so nygh to
me so noble a lady as your is, ne that had so many of
noble folk with her as she hath.' 'Ha, sire!' sayd the 16
knight, 'whan my lady wil she may haue of knightes &
squyers more than she hath now with her / for she ne
dare doo ,' but to commande.' And thus talking one
to other, they camme vnto the pauyllon. And the 20

The Earl 's
lodged in the
richest pavilion
he ever had seen,
1 fol. 22.

and the rest of
the company
after their estate.

Erle was lodged there within the moost riche lodgys
that euer he had seen before. After every man was
lodged honourably after his estate ' & they [1] said that
within theire owne places at hom they were not so 24
wel lodged. Theire horses were lodged within the
grett tentes ,' so at large & at theire ease / that no
palfrener was there but that he was full wel playsed.
And alle they meruailled fro whens so moch of goode 28
and suche plente of richesses might comme there so
haboundauntly. '

Cap. XV. How Raymondyn and Melusyne were wedded togider. ,

32

The Earl of Poi-
tiers' moder and
other ladies
arrive,

Fter them camme the Contesse moder vnto the
said Erle, and blanche, her doughtir, and
with them many ladyes & damoiselles. And

thanne Melusyne, sage & wyse, sent toward her
pauncyent knight, that had hold companye to the
Erle, and also with hym she sent many ladyes [1] and
4 damoyselles of high and noble Estate that moch
honourably salued and honoured the Countesse and
her doughter / and ledde them to be lodged in a fayr
pauillon made of riche cloth of gold, richely set with
8 perlys & with precyous stones. And, shortly to spek,
they were alle so wel & so rychely lodged that moche
they meruaylled of the grete riches that they see
within the pauyllon. And there was the Countesse
12 receyued with moch grete and melodyous sowne of
almaner instruments and alle they in her companye
were honourably lodged. And whan the Countesse
had rested a lytil while, and that she was arayed with
16 her ryche rayments / also her doughtir Blanche.
Knyghtes & Squyers / ladyes and damoyselles of her
companye went into the chambre of the spouse, the
whiche Chambre was fayrer and passed of ryches alle
20 the other chambres, but whan they sawe Melusyne, &
perceyued her ryche tyres / her riche gowne, alle set
with precious stones & perlys / the coler that she had
about her nek, hir gerdell & her other rayments, that
24 she had on her, they all meruaylled gretly / and
specially the Countesse, that said / consideryng that
grete estate / Neuer had I wende ne supposed that no
queene ne Emperesse had be in alle the world, that
28 might haue founde suche jewellis so riche & so grete in
value. What shuld I make long plee / the Erle of
poiters and one of the moost hygh barons, that is to
wete, the Erle of Forest, addressed and ledde the
32 spouse vnto the said Chapelle of our lady, which was
so rychely aourned, & arayed so nobly that wonder it
was to see / as of parements & ornaments of cloth [2] of
gold, purfeld and sett with perlys and precyous stones,
36 so wel wrought and so connyngly browded, that

[1] fol. 29 b.

and are wel-
comed by the
ancient knight,

and so richely
lodged that they
marvel much.

The Countess
and her daughter
are richly
dressed,

and go to Melu-
sine's chamber,

where they mar-
vel much at her
rich array.

The Earls of
Poitiers and
Forest lead
Melusine

[2] fol. 29.

to the richly
adorned chapel,

meruaylle it was to loke on.   fayre ymages straungely
kerued / as of Crucifixe & figure of our lady, all of
pure and fyn gold / and bokes were there, so wel
writon and so riche that in alle the world rycher bokes 4
might nat haue be.   And there was a bysshop that
wedded them & songe masse before them.

where the wedding takes place.

Cap. XVI.   How they were worshipfully serued at dyner. /   8

After diuine seruice

AFtir that the deuyne seruyse was doon they
rested them, and soone after the dyner was
redy within a moche riche and grete panyllon
in the myddes of the medowe.   Eche one satte there 12
aftir hys degree. and serued they were of dyuerse &
good meetes, and of many and dyuerse wynes, and
haboundaunce of ypocras [1] was there.   There serued
the squyers richely clothed one lyke another, whiche 16
were grete in nombre.   They were serued alle in plat
of pure gold & syluer, wherof alle the companye was
meruaylled.   And assoone as one messe was taken fro
the table, the othe[r] messe was redy.   And so of 20
dyuers meetes they were serued many a cours moche
honourably.

the company dine.
[1] fol. 30 b.
They are serued by squires,
and eat off gold and silver plate
divers meats.

Cap. XVII.   How after dyner the Knightes & Squyers Jousted.   24

After dinner

ANd after that they had dyned, and the tables
were take vp & graces said, and that they were
serued with ypocras & spyces. the Knyghtes and
Squyers went & armed them and lept on horsback. 28
And thenne the spouse & many other ladyes were sett
vpon the scaffold or stalage.   Thanne byganne the
Joustyng ' the Erle of Poytiers jousted moche wel
and so dide the Erle of Forest and alle theire knightes 32
and [2]squyers. but the Knyghtes of the spouse dide

the knights and squires arm and leap on horse-back.
the ladies go to the scaffold.
Jousting begins.
[2] fol. 31.

meruaill, For they ouerthrew bothe knightes and horses
vnto the grounde. Thanne camme there Raymondyn
that satte on a fayre & strong courser, alle in whyte,
4 & at hys first cours he ouerthrew the Erle of Forestz,
his brother / and so valyauntly he demened hym self
that there ne was knight on both partyes but that
he redoubted hym. And thann the Erle of Poitiers
8 seeyng his appertyse of armes meruaylled what he
was / and dressed hys sheld, & holding the speere
alowe ranne ayenst hym / but Raymondyn that knew
hym wel distourned hys hors and adressed his cours
12 toward a knight of Poitou and suche a strok he gaaf
hym, that both man & hors ouerthrew to the erth.
And shortly to spek Raymondin dide that day so wel
that euery man said that the knight with the white
16 armes had jousted right strongly. The night camme
and the justyng ended. Wherfore eche of them went
agayn in to theire pauyllons where they toke alitil
reste / but soone after was the souper redy. And
20 thanne they yede in to the grete tente / and after they
had wasshen they set them at table & wel and richely
they were scrued / and after souper were the tables
take vp / and they wesshed theyre handes. & graces
24 were said. This doon the ladyes wente asyde pryuely
and toke other gownes on them & camme agayn for to
daunse. The feste was fayre / and the worship was
there grete / so that the Erle and alle they that were
28 comme with hym meruaylled gretly ¹of the grette
ryches & honour that they sawe there. And whan it
was tyme they ledd the spouse to bed / moch honourably within a wonder meruayllous & riche pauyllon.
32 And there the Erles of Potiers and of Forests betoke
her vnto the ladyes handes. And thanne the Countesse of Poitiers and other grete ladyes had the spouse
to bed, and dide endoctryne her in suche thinges that
36 she oughte for to doo / how be it that she was ynough

Sidenotes:

Melusine's men being victorious.

Raymondin over-throws the Earl of Forest, and demeans himself so that all are afraid of him.

The Earl of Poitiers runs against him,

but Raymondin turns aside and fells a knight of Poitou.

Every man praises the prowess of Raymondin.

They have supper in the great tent,

then they have a dance.

¹ fol. 31 b.

They lead the spouse to bed,

the Countess tells her what to do,

but feels she
knows every-
thing.

The ladies wait
for Raymondin.

who is speaking
with the Erles.

purveyed therof, but notwithstandyng she thanked
them moch humbly therfore. And when she was abed
the ladyes saide there was tyme that Raymondin
camme, whiche was yet talkyng of one thing and of 4
other with the Erle of Poyters & with his brother,
whiche thanked Raymondyn of þat he first dide jouste
with hym. 'By my feyth,' said the Erle of Poytiers,
'myne Cousyn of Forestz, ye haue longe syn herd say / 8
how somtyme the loue of ladyes cometh peyne &
traueyll to the amerous louers, and deth to horses.'
'My lord,' answerde the Erle of Forestz, 'my brother
shewed it wel this day to me.' And Raymondyn, that 12
was somwhat ashamed said in this manere: 'Fayre
lordes, speyk of the loue and gyue not to me so
moche praysing. For I am not he which I mene[2] that
dide soo. For I am not he that bare the whyte armes / 16
but fayne I wold that god had sent to me the grace to
A knight sent by
the ladies
doo so wel.' And as thoo wordes camme there a knight,
whiche by the ladyes was sent thither / and said to
them: 'Faire lordes, Jape not ouermoche. For knowe 20
¹ tit. 22.
ye wel that as now on other thing he most think.'
'By my feyth,' said the Erle of Poytiers, 'ye say trew as
I byleue.' And yet agayn said the knight: 'my lordes,
comes for Ray-
mondin, and tells
him that all is
ready, whereat
the company
laugh.
come of & berynge with you Raymondyn. For the ladyes 24
axen after hym / for his partye is al redy.' And þerof
bygynne they to lawghe and said that he muste haue
witnes therof / and that they byleued it wel.

Cap. XVIII　How the bysshop halowed the 28
bed wheron Raymondyn and Melusyne
laye.

Raymondin is
led to the bridal
chamber and
brought to bed.
AT thoo wordes they went and ledde Raymondyn
in the pauylion and soone he was brought to 32
bed. And thanne camme there þe Bysshop that had

¹ Fr. frapper du plat.　² Fr. je ne soye mie celluy que.

spoused them and dide halowe theire bed. and after
that euerychon toke his leue / and the courteyns were
drawen aboute the bed. And of this matere recounteth
4 no ferther thystorye, but speketh of the other, of
which som went to bed, ¹and som went agayn to the
daunse and ellis wher them lyste for to goo. And
after thystory I shall speke of Raymondyn and of the
8 lady, how the[y] gouerned them bothe togidre. and
what wordes they had among' them two as the[y] laye
togidre.

THYstorye telleth to vs in this partye that whan
12 they euerychon departed and goon out of the
Pauyllon and the stakes of hit joyned & shette, Melusyne spak and said to Raymondyn in this manere:
'My right dere lord and frend, I thanke you of the
16 grete honour that hath be doo to me at this day of
your parents & frendes / and of that also / that ye kepe
so secretly that which ye promysed me at oure first
couuenaunte,² and ye moste know for certayn that yf
20 ye kepe it euer thus wel, ye shalbe the moost mighty &
moost honoured that euer was of your lynage. And ye
doo the contrary, bothe you & your heyres shall fall
litil & litil in decaye & fro your estate. Ne of the
24 land that ye shall holde & possesse, that tyme ye hold
not your promysse / yf it be so that ye doo it, whiche
god forbede, hit shal neuer be aftir possessed ne holden
alle holl by you ne by your heyrs.' And thanne to her
28 ansuerd Raymondyn: 'My right dere lady, doubte
you not of hit, For yf it playseth to god / that shall
neuer befall by me.' And the lady ansuerd to hym in
this maner: 'My right dere frend / sith it is soo that
32 so forfourth I haue putte my self I most abyde the
wylle of god, trustyng euer of your promesse. Kepe
you thanne wel, my fayre frend & felawe that ye
³fawte not your Couuenaunt. For ye shuld be he,

² Fr. *conrenant.*

then the bishop hallows the bed, the curtains are drawn,

¹ fol. 22 b.

and the company retires.

After the tent is closed

Melusine thanks her lord for his friends' presence at the wedding,

and for him keeping his promise,

and foretells honour to him and his if he remains faithful, but woe if he be false;

³ fol. 23.

after me, that moost shuld lese by it.' ' Ha / Ha, lady
dere,' said Raymondin, ' therof ye oughte not to be in
doubte / For that day, faylle to me god, whan I sawte
of Couuenant.'[1] ' Now my dere frend,' said the lady, 4
' lete vs leue our talkyng therof. For certaynly as for
my part there shal be no sawte. but that ye shal be
the moost fortunat & happy that ever was of your
lynee, and more puyssaunt thanne any of them shalbe / 8
without it be for sawte of your self.' And thus lefte
they theyre talkyng'. And as thystorye reherceth,
was that nyght engendred or begoten of them both
the valyaunt Uryan. whiche aftirward was kynge of 12
Chipre, as ye shall here herafter.

Cap. XIX. How the Erle of Poytiers and the Erle of Forests / the barons and ladyes, toke theyre leue of Raymondyn and of 16 Melusyne. /

[2] THystorye telleth to vs in this partye that so longe
abode these two louers, beyng abed, that the
sonne was hye. Thanne aroos Raymondyn and made 20
hym redy, and yssued out of the Pauillon. And as
thenne were alle redy, both therles of Poyters and of
Forests waytyng aftir Raymondyn, whiche they ledd to
the Chapell and there they herde their masse deuoutly / 24
and after they retourned vnto the medowe, where the
feste & reuell bygan of new, moche grete. but therof
we leue to speke. and shall say of the Countesse &
other ladyes, which aourned & made redy Melusyne. 28
And after they yede and ledd melusine moche honourably vnto the Chapel [3]forsaid. And there they herd
masse. thoffertory of whiche was grete and riche.
And after that the deuyne seruyse was doon, they 32
retourned vnto the Pauyllon. What shuld I make

upon which Raymondin pledges himself again to keep the covenant.

They beget that night Uryan, afterwards king of Cyprus.

[2] fol. 33 b.

When the sun is high the lovers rise.

Raymondin dresses and goes with the Earls to mass,

after which the feasting and revelling begins again. The ladies dress Melusine and go with her to mass.

[3] fol. 34.

---

[1] Fr. couuenant.

long tale herof; the feste was grete and noble, and
lasted XV dayes complete & hole. And Melusyne   Melusine gives
gaaf many grete yeftes and jewels both to the ladyes   great gifts to the company,
4 & damoyselles, also to knightes & squyers. And after
the feste the Erle, and the Countesse his moder, and
alle the barons, ladyes, and damoiselles of theire felawship, toke leue of Melusyne, whiche conueyed the said   and conveys the
8 Countesse and her doughter vnto & byonde the litil   Countess and her daughter beyond
tounne of Coulombiers. And at departyng Melusyne   Coulombiers,
gaf to the Countesse a fayre & moche riche owche of
gold, in value vnestymable. and to blanche her
12 doughter, a gerland all set with perlys with saphirs   and gives them
rubyes and with many other precyous stones in grete   rich jewels.
nombre. And alle they that sawe the said owche and
gerland, meruaylled gretly of the beaulte goodnes &
16 value of it. And ye moste knowe, that so moche gaf
Melusyne bothe to more & lesse, that none there was
at the feste / but that he preysed gretly Melusyne of
her yeftes. and alle abasshed & meruaylled they were   All the company
20 of her grete ryches. and they alle sayd that Raymondyn   are abashed at the richness of Melusine's gifts,
was grotly mightily and valiauntly marryed. And after   and say that Raymondin has
that all these thinges were doon and perfourmed, Me-   married well.
lusyne toke leue of [1]the Erle and of the Countesse   [1] fol. 34 b.
24 moche honourably, and of alle the Baronye. and with
a fayre and noble compayny retourned to her pauillon.
And Raymondin conueyed euer the Erle. And as
they rode on theire way, the Erle of Poytiers said to   As Raymondin
28 him in this manere: 'Fayr Cousyn telle me, yf ye   accompanies the Earl of Poitiers,
goodly may, of what lynee or kynred is your wyf /   the Earl asks the lineage of his
how be it that thauncyent knight dide thanke us of   wife,
thonour & worship that we bare to you by hys lady
32 Melusyne of Albanye. but yet I demande it of you /
bycause that we gladly wold knowe the certaynte of it.
For of asmoche that we may perceyue by her estate &
behauyng, nedes it muste be, that she be yssued &
36 comme fro moch noble ryche and mighty lynee. And

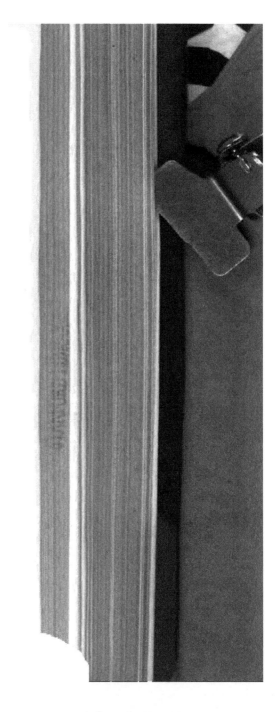

the cause whiche moeueth vs for to desyre and be
willing to knowe it / is bycause that we doubte to haue
mesprysed anenst thonour that apparteyneth to be doo
vnto her noble & goodly personne' / 'But my feyth,' 4
said the Erle of Forest, ' al thus was my wylle to have
said soo.'

Thystorye saith that thanne Raymondin was
gretly wroth, whan he herd the requeste 8
that the Erle of Poytiers, his lord, made
vnto him / and also likewyse the erle of
Forest hys brother. For he loued / doubted and
preysed so moche his lady / that he hated alle thinges 12
whiche he demed desagreable to her. Not withstanding he ansuerd to them full softe & fayr : ' By my feyth,
my lord / and you my brother, ¹playse it to you to
knowe / that by rayson naturel fro whosoever I hyd 16
my secrete / fro you I ought not to hyde it / yf it were
suche thinge that I knew of, or might say. and therfore I shall answere to you, to that ye haue demanded
of me / after that I knowe of it. Ye thanne muste 20
knowe, that neuer I ne demanded ne dyde enquere me
so fer of it / as now redyly ye haue demanded & enquyred of me, / but so moche I knowe, and may wel
say of her, that she is a kyngis doughter, mighty & 24
high terryen, And by the state, behauyng, & gouernement that ye haue seen in her, ye may perceyue
ynough, that she nys ne haue be norysshed in mendy-
cite or pouerte / but in superfluyte of honour & largesse, 28
and among plente of goodes. And I requyre you as to
my lordes and frendes, that ye ne enquyre nomore
therof. For none other thinge ye ne may knowe
therof by me. and suche as she is, she playseth me 32
wel, and am right wel content of her. And wel I
knowe that she is the rote of alle myn erthly goodes
present & to comme.' Thenne ansuerd the Erle of
Poytiers : ' By my feyth, fayr Cousin, as for my part I 36

think not to enquere of you nomore therof, For as ye
haue putte vnto vs wysely the high honours, riches,
man*er*es, and behauying of my Cousin, your wyf, we
4 oughte to conceyue of our*self*, that she is of noble birth
& extraction, and of right high and mighty lynee.' 'By
my feyth, my lord,' said the Erle of Forest, 'ye say
southe. and of my part I thinke nat to enquyre, ne

8 demande of hym eny ¹thing more therof / how be it

that he is my bro*þ*er.   For certaynly I hold hym right
wel ensuered *þ*erof aftir myn aduys.' But, helas! he
aftirward faylled Couen*aunt*. wherfore Raymondyn lost

12 his lady, and also the Erle of Forest toke deth therfore
by Geffray with the grete tothe, Whereof it shal be
spoken herafter more playnly. Raymondyn thenn*e*
toke leue of the Erle, & of his brother, and of the
16 barons, and retourned to the fontayne of Soyf. And
also the Erle of Forest toke leue of the erle of Poytiers,

of hys moder, and of hys sustir, and of aH the barons
right honourably, and *þ*anked them alle of thonour
20 that they had doon to hi*m* at hys brothers weddyng.
And thanne therle of Potyers, his moder, and hys
Suster, wi*th* alle theire felawship & meyne retourned
to poitiers, and euery one of the Barons retourned to

24 their Countrees. but there ne was none of them / b*u*t
that he merueylled & gretly wondred of the grete riches

that they had seen at the wedding of Raymondyn.
And here resteth thystorye to spek of them / and shal
28 spek of Raymondyn & of his lady, how they were
after the departyng* of theire parents and frendes. /

Thystory recounteth to vs that whan Raymondin
was retourned toward his lady / he founde the

32 feste greter than it was before / and also greter plente

of noble folk than neu*er* was there before. Alle whiche
folke yede, & said to hym with a high voyce: 'My
lord ye be welcomme as he to whom we are ser*u*aunts,

36 & whom we wyl obey.' And *þ*is said the ladyes as

wel the lordes. And thanne Raymondin ansuerd to

¹ fol. 36.
which Raymondin thanks them for.

Melusine takes him apart,

and thanks him for his demeanour to his brother and the Earl,

and promises to make all goods to abound.

She next day sends away many of her people.

When the feast was over

Melusine got a great many workmen,

who felled the trees and cleaned the rock,

on which they prepared a foundation,

where they builded so quickly that every one wondered;

² fol. 36 b.

but no one knew whence the workmen came.

The fortress was strongly built with two double walls and wards

them, 'gramercy of the ¹honour that ye proffre to me.'
And there thanne camme Melusyne, who moche
honourably sayd to hym : ' welcomme be ye ' / and had 4
hym apart, & reherced to hym word by word alle the
talking that was betwix the Erle and hym. and also
what his brother, Erle of Forest, had said, And yet
said the lady to hym : ' Dere frende Raymondin / as 8
longe as ye shal contynue soo / alle goodes shall
habounde to you. Fayre frende, I shall to morowe
gyue leue to the moost partye of our folk that ben here
comme to our feste.   For other thinges we must 12
ordeyne.' Raymondyn ansuered : ' ladye, so as it shall
playse you.' And whan the morowe camme Melusyne
departed her folke / grete quantyte went theire way /
and suche as she wold abode there. And now resteth 16
thystory of the thinges byfore said. and begynne to
treate how the lady bygan to bylde the noble fortresse
of Lusignen. /

IN this partye telleth thenne thystory that whan the 20
feste was ended and that suche as she wold were
goon / she anoone aftir made to comme grete foyson of
werkmen / as massons, Carpenters, and suche that can
dygge & delue. Whyche at her commandement fylled 24
dounne the grete trees, and made the roche fayre and
clene.   There Melusyne sett euery man to werk. eche
one dide his Crafte. they encysed the roche & made a
depe & brode foundement. and in few dayes they 28
brought the werk so ferfourth / that euery man wondred
of suche a fayre and stronge bylding so soone doon.
And euery Satirday Melusyne payed truly her werkmen / and meet & drynk they had ²in haboundaunce. 32
but trouth it is / that no body knew from whens these
werkmen were. and wete it that soone was the Fortres
made up / not only with one warde / but two strong
wardes, with double walles were there, or oon coude 36

have comme to the stronge donjon of it. Round about
the walles were gret tours machecolyd, & strong pos-
ternes / and also barreres or wayes gooyng out fourth
4 encysed and kerued within the hard roche. The Erle
of Poytiers / the barons and alle the peple meruaylled
moche of the said werke that so soone was doon, so
grete, so stronge, & so fayre. Then the lady Melusyne
8 and her husband Raymondyn lodged them within it.
and anoone after Raymondin made to calle to a feste
there, alle the noble men therabout. There camme the
erle of Poytiers, both hys moder and hys suster / the
12 Erle of Forestz, the Barons & noble men of theire
landes, also of other countres and nacions. And also
there was so many laydes & damoyselles, that they
wel might suffyse att that day. There was jousting,
16 dauncyng, and grete joye made with frendly and
curtoys deeling. And whan Melusyne sawe tyme and
place conuenable, she presented herself before the two
Erles / barons and noble men, and humbly said to
20 them in this manere: 'My fayre and good lordes, we
thanke you moche of the high honoure that ye haue
doon to us now at this feste—and the cause why we
haue prayed you to comme I shal declare it to you.' /
24 'Lordes,' said the lady, 'here I haue assembled your
noble personnes, for to haue your Counseill
[1]how this fortresse shall be called. for that it be in
mynd how that it hath be happely bylded & made.'
28 'By my feyth, fayre Cousyn,' said the Erle of Poiters,
'we as in general sayen to you, as oure wylle is / that
ye your owneself shall / as right is / gyue name to it.
For emong we alle is not so moch wyt as in you alone
32 that haue bylded up & achyeuyd so strong and fayre a
place as thesame is / and wete it, that none of us
shall entremete hym to doo that ye spek of.' Thanne
said Melusyne: 'Dere Sire, Wylfully and for the nones
36 ye haue kept þis ansuere for to jape with me, but what

therof is, I requyre and pray you that therof ye telle to
me your entenc*i*on.' 'Certaynly, dere Cosyn,' sayd the
Erle of Poytiers, 'none of us alle shal medle w*ith* all .
byfore you.   For by reason / sethen ye haue so moche 4
doon as to haue achyeued & made the moste strong
and fayre place that *ever* man sawe in this Countree /
ye owe to gyue name to it *your* owne self after your
playsire.' 'Ha / ha, my lord,' said Melusyne, 'sith it ne 8
may none otherwise be, / and that I see your playsire
is that I gyue name to it, hit shalbe called after myn
owne name, Lusygnen.' 'But my feyth,' said the Erle,
'the name setteth full wel to it for two causes, First 13
bycause ye are called Melusyne of Albanye, whiche
name in grek language is as moch for to say / as thing
me*r*uayllous or com*m*yng fro grete merueylle, and also
this place is bylded and made me*r*uayllously.   For I 16
byleue not other wyse / but that as longe as the world
shal laste [1]shall there be founde & seen som*m*e Wonder
& me*r*uayllous thinge.'   Thanne they alle ansuerd in
this man*er*e : 'My lord, no man in the world might gyue 20
betre name, that bettre shuld sette to it than she hath
doo after manere of the place / also aftir the interpretyng
made by you of her owne name.' and on this oppynyon
& worde were alle of one acorde.   Whiche name 24
w*ith*in few dayes was so publyed, that it was knowen
thrugh alle the land. and yet at this day it is called
soo.   They soone aftir toke leue, and Melusyne and
Raymondin also gaaf hem dyuers & riche yef*tes* at 28
theire departyng.   And herafter sheweth thystory how
Raymondin and Melusyne / right wysly, mightily and
honorably lyued togidre. /

A fter the feste was ended, Melusyne, that was grete 32
with child, bare her fruyte unto þe tyme that
alle wymen owen to be delyured of their birthe. and
thanne she was delyuered of a man child, whiche was
moche fayre, and wel proporcyoned or shapen in alle 36

but the Earl
replies, that as
she has built the
best castle in the
land, she must
name it.

Melusine then
names it Lusig-
nan.

Which the Earl
says is a good
one, because it
means 'marvel-
lous' in Greek.

[1] fol. 37 b.

All the company
think it a good
name.

And it was pub-
lished abroad,
and even unto
this day the
castle is so
called.
The company
breaks up,
taking with them
many rich gifts.

Melusine has a
son,

hys membres / except his vysage that was short and
large / one ey he had rede, and the other blew.   he
was baptysed, & named was Uryan, and wete it that
4 he had the gretest eerys that euer were seen on eny
child of hys age / and whan they were ouergrowen,
they were as grete as the handlyng of a fan. Melusyne
þenne called to hym Raymondin, and to hym she said
8 in this manere : ' My ryght swete felawe & frend, I
wold not see thyn owne herytage to be lost / which by
raison thou oughtest to haue by vertue of ¹patrymonye,
for Guerrende Penycence and all the marches aboute
12 apparteynen to the & to þy brother / goo thanne
thither, and make the king of Bretons to be sommed
that he wyl receyue you in your ryght & enherytance /
shewyng to hym how your fader slew his nevew in
16 deffense & warde of hys owne body. For which
encheson doubting the sayd kyng / lefte the Countrey,
and neuer durst retourne / and yf he wyl not receyue
you to ryght, be not therof abasshed. For afterward
20 he shal be glad, & fayne when he shal mow doo it.'
Thenne answerd Raymondyn, ' there nys nothing that
ye commande me, but that I shall doo after my power.
For wel I considere & see that all your werkes ne
24 tenden but to wele & worship.' ' Frende,' sayd the lady,
' it is wel rayson, sith that all your trust ye putte on
me that I hold to you trouth. It is trouth that your
fader, by hys predecessors, oweth to haue many grete
28 thinges in bretayne, the whiche shulle be declared unto
you whan ye be there. It muste thanne be by you
understand, that Henry of Leon, your fader, that tyme
he was in Bretayn for hys worthynes, grete policye &
32 valiauntnes, and as he that drad no man that owed hym
euyl wyll, he was moche loued with the kinge there /
in so moche that the said kynge made hym hys
Seneschall & Captayn general ouer allo his men of
36 werre. This king of Bretons had a nevew / but no
MELUSINE.

Side notes:

fair of body, but
of short visage,
and one eye red,
and the other
blue.
He is named
Urian,

and he had ears
as large as a fan
handle.

Melusine tells
Raymondin of
his patrimony,

¹ fol. 38.

and bids him go
to the king of
Britain, to enter
into his inherit-
ance.

He promises to
go.

Henry of Leon,
Raymondin's
father,

was Seneschal
and Captain-
General to the
king of Britain,

F

who had a
nephew as his
heir.

1 fol. 28 b.

This heir was
made jealous of
Henry,

by mischief-
makers telling
him that Henry
was to take his
place;

and by Josselin
Dupont,

who told him
that letters of
grant had been
made secretly in
favour of Henry.

2 fol. 29.

child begoten of his body he had. Whyche nevew, by
the introduction of som, had grete enuye on Henry,
your fader. For to [1] hym they said in this manere:
"Ha! Ha! right-full heyre of Breytayne. Woo is us to 4
see your grete domage / that is / you to be putte doun
fro the noble enherytaunce of Bretayne. yf by fawte
& lak of courage ye suffre it, what shal men say?
þey poyntyng you with the fyngor shal sey, Loo, 8
yonder is the fole that for his feynted herte hath be
putte out of so noble enherytaunce as is the royame of
Bretayne." And whan he understode the said enjurous
wordes, he said : "Who is he that dare vsurpe & take 12
fro me my right, I knowe none / but that god wyl
haue me to be punysshed. and wel I wot, þat the
kinge, my lord & oncle, wyl not take ony other to be
hys heyer than my self." Thenne sayd one of them to 16
hym : "By my feyth, ye are [not] enfourmed in this
matere, For the kinge, your oncle, hath made &
ordeyned hys heyre, Henry of Leon, and as now
letters of graunt ben therof made." Whan the yong man 20
herd these wordes, he as wood wroth ansuerd to them,
"wete it for certeyn / that if I knew these wordes to
be trew, I shuld putte hastly remedy thereto / in so
moche that neuer he shold hold land ne no possession." 24
And thenne ansuerde to hym a knight named Josselyn
Dupont : "certaynly it is soo / and for we wold haue
none other to be kynge in brytaynne but you, after the
decees of þo kinge, we warne you therof. For this 28
hath the kyng your oncle doon secretly, for ye shuld
not knowe of it. and wete it that alle we that now are
here, were present whan that couenaunt was made.
aske my felawes yf I say trouth [2] or not." he demanded 32
of them yf it was so, And they ansuerd "ye."
'The yongman thanne said, "Fayre lordes, I thanke
you of your good wylle whiche ye shewe to me,
goo youre way. For wel I shall kepe Henry therfro." 36

They toke theyre leue, For they rought not for no
thing that might fall therof, so that they might see
your faders deth.   For enuyous and wroth they wore
4 that the kinge louyd hym so wel, and for nought sette
they were by hym. knowe ye muste, that on the
sonday next, in the morning, the kingis nevew armed
hym self / yede in to the wod of Leon Castel, and
8 there wayted tyl your fader passed by, whiche he
perceyued gooyng alone to hys dysport about hys
Castel of Leon / thinkynge on none euyl ne harme /
and sodaynly cryed on hym, " Now shalt thou dey, false
12 traytour, that fro me woldest haue and vsurpe myn
herytage " / and foynyng at hym *with* hys swerd, wold
haue ouerthrawen youre fader. but he glanched asyde /
and so the kyngis nevew / for he recountred ayenst
16 nothing, fell doun to the grounde, and the swerd
scaped fro hys hand that then *your* fader toke up, the
sayd neuew that sawe hys wepen lost, toke a lytil knyf
that he had and ranne ayenst hym / but *your* fader,
20 *with* the pomel of the swerd, gaaf to hym suche a
stroke on the heed / that notwithstanding hys yron
hat, he broke hys heed so that he fell doun deed, but
[1] whan he knew that it was he / he was sory and woo /
24 retourned home / toke all hys hauoyr and goodes
meuable, and came in to the Shyre that men now call
Forests, and grette help & comfort he founde in a lady,
of whyche as now I kepe me styl to spek ony ferther.
28 And after the departyng of her fro hym, he toke by
maryage the sustir of hym that thoo dayes gouerned
the erledome of Poytiers, on whyche he gate many
children of the whyche ye are one. /
32 ' **F**rend,' said Melusyne, ' now haue I deuysed and
reherced to you how your fader departed fro
Bretayn, and lefte hys landes and possessyons voyde,
without lord, whiche owen to be yours. You thenne
36 shal goo toward an vncle of yours whiche is called

The Sunday after hearing this, the king's nephew laid in wait for Henry,

surprised and attacked him,

but was killed by your father, Henry of Leon,

[1] fol. 39 *b.*

who was sorry, and left the country for the Shire of Forests, where he married.

Melusine tells Raymondin to go to his uncle,

Alain of Quingant,
and to tell him
the tale,

Alayn of Quyngant / and ye shal make you to be
knowen of hym / and he shal byleue you ynough of
aH that ye shall sey. he hath two wrorthy knightes
to hys sones, the whiche are grete men with the kinge, 4

and get one of
his sons to call
Josselin before
his king,
and there accuse
him of his deed.

and loueth hem weL by one of them, your Cousyns,
ye shall make Josselyn Dupont, that as yet is alyue,
to be called byfore the kyng, and there ye shalle acuse
hym of the treson by hym & other machyned / thrugh 8
whiche the kyngis nevew, willing to haue destroyed
your fader, was hym self slayn.   And ye muste knowe

Oliver Dupont
is to fight Ray-
mondin,
but he is to lose,
and he and his
father are to be
strangled,

1 fol. 40.

that on this quareH his sone, called Olyuer Dupont,
shall fyght ayenst you therfore.   but ye shall haue the 12
vyctory ouer hym / and bothe fader and sone shal be
condampned to hang and to be strangled.   For the
fader shaH [1] vttre and knowe alle the treson / and aH
your grounde and enherytaunce shalbe adiuged to you. 16

and Raymondin
is to get posses-
sion of his land.

And thus shall ye be putte in pacyfyque or peesable
possessyon of it by the Peerys or lordes pryncypal
of the land. Now my ryght swete frend & felawe,
douteles goo surely. For certaynly god shal helpe you 20
in all your juste & true dedes.'

Thanne ansuerd Raymondyn : 'Madame, I shall
      endeuoyre me to achyeue & fulfiH your com-
mandement.' Raymondyn toke leue of Melusyne / 24

Raymondin with
many men goes
to Brut Britain,

and acompanyed with grete nombre of knightes and
squyers, rode fourth so long on hys way, tyl they
came in Brut Brytayne, wher the peuple was abasshed
& moche wondred what suche grete nombre of 28

where they pay
their way.

straungers wold haue. But for they payed wel &
largely for that they toke, they were ensured that they
wold & sought but good. For thauncyent knight of
the meyne of Melusyne rewled and gyded them alle 32
in aH honour & goodnes. And for they were not so
vnpurueyed / but that with them they had armures,

The king sends
to learn

with them yf nede were to arme them with / the
kinge that knew of it, sent to them to wete what they 36

sought, whiche message demanded of Raymondyn yf hee
owed euyl wyll to the kyng & to hys royame. In this
messagery or embassade were sent two wyse knyght*es*,
4 whiche wysly enquered of Raymondyn as byfore is
sayd what he sought and what he wold. to whome
Raymondin full curtoysly ansuered thus. 'Fayre
lord*es*, ye shall tell to my liege that I come but [1] for
8 good and wele, and for to haue the lawful right in
hys Court of suche thinges as belongen to me, For the
whiche I shall presente myn owne personne byfore hys
mageste, the same requyryng of socour and help.' 'For-
12 south,' ansuerd the two knyght*es*, 'ye shalbe welcome
whan it shal playse you to do soo. and wete it wel that
the kynge, our liege, is rightwyse & juste / and nothing
as fer as right requyreth shal not be by hym denyed
16 by ony wyse. but telle vs yf it lyke you whither ye
are now bounde.' 'Certaynly,' said Raymondyn, 'I
wold I were at Quyngant.' Thanne answerd one of
them, 'ye are wel on the way toward it, and wete that
20 ye shall fynd there Aleyn of Leon, whiche shall make
you good chere. and also ye shall fynd there two
knyght*es*, men of wele and honour, and hold strayte
this way and ye shal not mys of it, and with your leue
24 we retourne on our way toward oure liege.'

Whanne these two knyght*es* were fer fro Raymondyn and hys felawship an halfmyle, they
byganne to say one to other: 'By my feyth, yonder
28 are gentyl and curtoys folk*es*, worshipfull & honourable. For certayn they come not into this land without it is for some grete matere.' and yet sayd, 'lete
vs go thrugh Quyngan ; and to aleyn we shall anounce
32 theyre comm*yng*.' they toke the way toward it, and
rode so fast that soone they came there where they
found Alayn, to whome they said & announced the
comm*yng* of Raymondyn [2] and of his men. Whiche
36 Alayn wondred moch of it. And thanne the trew

If Raymondin intends evil to him.

[1] fol. 40 b.

Raymondin tells the messengers that he comes to obtain his rights,

on which he is welcomed.

He tells them he is going to Quingant.

The messengers leave,

and on their way home praise Raymondin and his men,

and pass by Quingant, where they announce to Alain the coming of Raymondin's party.

[2] fol. 41.

Alain sends his
sons to meet and
attend to them.

man dide calle to hym hys two sones, of whiche one
was called Alayn & was eldest, and that other yongest
had to name Henry, and he sayd to them in this
manere : ‘My good children, lepe on horsbak and ryde 4
on your way to mete yonde straungers / receyue ye
them worshipfully, and see that they be wel and
honestly lodged. For it is told to me, that they be
six houndred horses or theraboute.’ but for nought he 8
spak. For thauncyent knyght of Melusyne was come

The ancient
knight gets a
stock of food,

before that / and seeying the toune was to lityl for to
haue herberowed so moche peple in it / had made to

and pitches the
tents,

be dressed tentes & pauyllons, and sent aboute in the 12
Countre for suche thinges that necessary were to them,

and pays well for
everything.

which he payed or mayd to be payd largely, in so moche
that more vytayll was there brought than þey neded of.
And thanne Alayn was all abasshed whan ho herd of 16
that grete hauoyr & appareyll that they made there,
and wyst not what therof he shuld thinke or say.

Now sayth thystory, that so long rode the two

The brethren
meet Raymon-
din,

brethern with theyre felawship togidre, that 20
they mete with Raymondin, & full curtoysly welcommed hym, and prayed hym by byddyng of Alayn,

and invite him
to the castle of
Quingant.

theyre fader, that he vouchesauf to comme and be
lodged within the Fort or Castel of Qyngant with 24
theyre fader, that shuld make hym good chere. ‘Fayre
lordes,’ said Raymondyn, ‘gramercy to your fader, and
thanked be you of your curtoysy that ye thus proffre

¹ fol. 41 b.

to me,¹ But at your requeste I shall goo toward your 28

The invitation is
accepted,

fader for to rendre to hym reuerence. For glad &
fayn I were to see hym, for the wele & honour that I
have herde say by hym.’ Contynuyng suche wordes

and they ride on
to the town,
where the
ancient knight
comes to them;

& oþer they rode tyl they came nygh the toun. And 32
thann came there thauncyent knight to Raymondyn,
and sayd : ‘Sire, I have made your pauyllon to be
dressed vp, and tentes ynoughe for to lodge you & al
your men, and thanked be god we are wel purueyed.’ 36

'Ye haue doo wel,' sayd Raymondin / 'goo and make
ye mery and chere my men, and loke not for me this
nyght, For I goo to the Fortresse with this two gentyl-
4 men.' And thenne departed he fro thauncyent knight /
toke with hym a few of hys moost famyler men, and
yede to the Fortresse wher the lord of the place aborde
for hym styll at the gate. Whan Raymondyn thanne
8 sawe hym as to hys lord and vncle he made reuerence
& salewed hym mekely. Wherto shulde I vse prolixe
or longe wordes of theyre acoyntaunce. but of the
faitt or matere whiche I owe to uttre and say, Lete vs
12 þenne say. Whan they had souped / wesshen & graces
said / the lord of the place toke Raymondyn by the
hand / had hym apart upon a bench / there to deuyse
both togidre, whyle that the other souped / the whiche
16 þe two bretheren chered & honestly seruyd. The lord
Alayn thanne wyse and subtyl, and that knewe moche
of wel and honour, bygan to raissonne with Raymondin
in this manere: 'Sir knight, grete joye I haue of your
20 commyng hither, For certaynly ye are full lyke to a
brother of myn whiche was valyaunt, full wyse and
worthy. he departed [1]fro this land xl. yere goon, for
a stryf that befell betwix the nevew of the kinge that
24 reygned at that tyme and hym, and wete it that this
is the iiij[th] kynge that haue reyned syn that tyme vnto
now. And bycause that, to me seemeth ye resemble
my brother, I am the more glad & fayn to see you.'
28 'Sire,' said Raymondyn, 'therof I mercy & thanke
you / and or I departe from you I shall make you certayn
wherfore and by what inconuenience the stryf that ye
spek of happed betwixt the nevew of the kyng and
32 youre brother. For wete it, that for none other cause
I come hither. but for to shewe publiquely the pure
trouth & certeyntee thereof.'

Whan Alayn herd these wordes he was moche
36   abasshed, and loked on Raymondyn moche

who asks how he
knows about the
strife.

ententyfly, and after sayd, 'and how shal that mowe be?
ye haue not yet the age of xxx yere / by you may not
be recounted the faytte, the trouth of whiche none
might neuer knowe. For whan the stroke of the 4
mysdede happed. my brother sodaynly departed / so
that I ne none other herd neuer syn whither he was

Raymondin asks
if any counseller
of the late king
yet lives,

become.' 'Sire, yf ye vouchesaf / telle mee yf there
is as now yet lyuyng eny man that had on that tyme 8
auctorite or rewle aboute the kingo that regned whan

and is told of one

the stryf befell.' 'By my feyth,' said Alayn, 'one and
no more I knowe, that had gouernaunce in Court that
same tyme, and he hym self vsurpeth & holdeth my 12
brothers landes as his owne enherytaunce. For the
kyng gaaf it to hym, for hys first begoten sone to

¹ fol. 42 b.

whose son was
lately dubbed a
knight;

enjoye it for euermore, the which ¹hys sone is now of
late dowbed & made knight.' 'For southe,' sayd thenne 16
Raymondyn, 'wel I wote hys name.' 'And how know
ye hyt?' said Alayn. 'By my feyth,' sayd Raymondin,

whereupon Ray-
mondin tells
their names to
be Josselin
Dupont the
father, and
Oliver the son,

'he is called Josselin Dupont / and hys sone hys named
Olyuyer.' 'Sire knight,' sayd Alayn, 'ye say trouth. 20
But telle me how ye this may knowe.' 'Sire,' sayd
Raymondyn, 'no ferther ye shall as now know therof.
but ye vouchesaf to come & your two sones with me,

and promises to
tell Alain more
if he will go to
court.

unto the kinges Court / wete it that I shall declare 24
vnto you the quarrell & stryf so clerly that, yf ye
euer loued your brother, Henry of Leon, ye shal be
thereof fayn & glad.' And thanne Alayn heryng the
name of hys brother called, he was more abasshed than 28
before. For he wend none other but that hys brother
had be long deed. And thenne he thoughte longe in
hymself or he ansuerd ony word.

Thus, as I haue sayd to you / moche long thought 32
Alayne, and aftir he ansuerd: 'Sire knight, I

Alain grants
Raymondin's
request.

graunt & acorde me to your requeste / sethen that here
I ne may knowe your wyll. For thernt I lang moche.
I gladly shall hold you company vnto the kynges 36

Court.' 'gramercy,' sayd Raymondyn, 'and wel I shal
kepe you fro dommage.' Wherto shuld I make long
proces, Alayn manded or sent for a grete foyson of hys   Alain sends for
his friends;
4 frendes, & made hym redy in grete estate for to goo to
the court. The kynge that knew theire commyng
departed fro Storyon, where he laye, & came to
Nantes. For the two knightes whiche the kinge sente
8 Raymondyn were retourned, & had recounted to the
kinge the ansuere of Raymondyn, and the maner of his
estate. And therfore the kinge was come to Nantes   the king comes
from Nantes and
and manded a part of hys baronye, For he wold not   sends for some
of his barony,
12 that Raymondyn shuld fynd hym vnpurueyd of men.
And amonge other he sent for Josselin Dupont for [1]to   [1] fol. 42.
haue his Counseyll on the demande that Raymondyn   and for Josselin.
wold make. For he was moche sage. What shuld I
16 saye more? thaunceyent knight came before & made   The ancient
knight prepares
to be dressed bothe pauillons & tentes & purueyed for   tents for Raymoudin,
all thinges necessary. Wherfore the folke of the
toune were moche abasshed of the grete appareyl that
20 he caused to be made / Thenne came Raymondyn,
Alayn, and bothe his sones, and descended into the
chief Pauillon, where they made them redy and arayed   in which Alain
and his sons
them full richely, for to goo toward the kinge / and   dress themselves
to go before the
24 after they departed fro the tentes, acompanyed with   king.
xl knightes wel horsed and honestly arayed that   They set out with
forty barons;
wonder was to see / and had his barons with hym. And
whan they come to the kinges place they descended
28 fro theire horses / and Raymondyn / Alayn and his
two sones entred within the halle, there the kynge
was acompanyed with his barons / made to the kinge   arriving, are
welcomed by the
reuerence / after siewyng, salewed the barons & lordes,   king.
32 the kinge welcommed & receyued þem joyously / called
to hym Alayn, and said to hym in this manere:

'It gyneth me grete wonder,' said the kinge to Alayn,   who asks Alain
about his friend,
'of this gracyous straunge knight, with whome   the strange
gracious knight.
36 ye are so acoynted / What he seketh in this land.' 'Ha /

Alain tells the
king that he
marvels at the
knight's sayings,

but believes that
all will be made
plain soon.

ha, sire,' ansuerd Alayn. 'I am an houndred tymes
more meruaylled of the wordes that he yestirday
shewed vnto me / than ye are of his commyng, but
soone shull be declared al that we lang aftir & desire 4
to knowe.' Thenne Raymondyn, dressyng hys wordes
to theldest sone of Alayn, sayd softly in this manere,
'Sire knight, say me of your Curtoysye, yf one called
Josselyn Dupont be now in this company or nat.' 8

Raymondin
learns that Jos-
selin is present,

1 fol. 43 b.

with his son
Oliver.

Thanne sayd Alayn, 'ye—and wold to god so that
the kyng shuld not be dyspleased that I had slayn hym.
For he enjoyeth [1] therytage that apparteyneth to one our
oncle which we shuld haue.' And after these wordes 12
Alayn sayd to Raymondin / 'it is yond auncient knight
that sitteth by the kinge. And wete it for certayn
that he is replonysshed with all falshed & malyce /
and yonder is his son Olyuyer that weyeth not an 16
ownce lasse in alt wykkednes & euyll.' 'By my feyth,
Sire knight,' sayd Raymondin / 'ye soone shal be
auenged of hym yf god wyl.' And lenyng theire
talkyng, Raymondin hadd hymself fourth before the 20
kinge, to whom he said in this manere : 'ha, high sire

Raymondin
addresses the
king, and praises
his Justice;

& mighty kinge, It is wel trouth that common renoumee
ranneth thrughe alle landes. that your Court is so
noble & so raysonnable that it may be called fountayne 24
of Justice & raison / and that none ne commeth to
your Court but that ye shew & gyue to hym good
Justice and raisonnable after the good right that he
hath.' 'By my feyth, sire knight,' said the kinge / 28

the king asks
why ?

'it is trouth. but wherfore say you so, fayn I wold wete
it.' 'Forsouthe, sire,' said Raymondin, 'for to vttre &
shew it vnto you / I am come hither / & for none other
cause. but, Sire, yf it plaise you / or I telle it you / 32
ye shalt promyse me that ye shall susteyne me ayenst
alle personnes after right & raison. For that / that I
shal say is in a part your wele prouffyt & honour.
For no kinge acompanyed of a traytour is not wel 36

lodged ne sure of his personne.' 'By my feyth,' said
the king, 'ye say trouth / say on hardily. For I swere
to you by all that I hold of god, that I shal doo to you

4 alle Justice & rayson after the good right that ye shall
haue / and that shal I doo doubteles / yf it were ayenst
my brother.' 'Sire,' said Raymondin, 'an houndred

thousand thankes & mercyes / ye say as a valyaunt kynge

8 & [1] trew man. For first were kynges stablysshed for

to rendre or yeld to euerbody juste jugement in alle
thinges.'

'Noble mighty kinge,' said Raymondin / 'it is wel
12 trouth that one, your predecessour kynge,
reyned somtyme moche mightily & valyauntly that was

in the tyme of Josselin Dupont and of Alayn, whiche
bothe are here now present before your majeste / this
16 kynge whiche I spek of, had a moche fayre & noble yong
man to his nevew. that tyme was in this Countre a
baron whiche was called Henry of Leon, the whiche

was brother to Alayn here present.' 'By my feyth, sire,'
20 said thanne Josselyn, 'he saith trouth. and ouermore

the same Henry of Leon slew the nevew of your predecessour by treson / fledd out of this land, and neuer
syn came hither ayen. And then the kinge seased
24 his landes and possessyons, and anoone after gaf them
to me.' The kinge thanne ansuered, 'we haue herd

ynoughe of this matere / but suffre this knight fynyshe
his raison which he hath bygonne.'
28 To this ansuerd Raymondyn, 'Sire kinge, he hath
wel raison to speke of hit, For ferthermore he
shal be constrayned to say / how be it that as now he
hath said amys & not trouth of that he saith that

32 Henry of leon slew the kinges nevew in treson, For he
knew wel why & wherfore it was, and there nys no
man lyuyng that can say the trouth of it but he alone,

For they that were of his acorde and conspiracion ben
36 al deed. Therfore sire kynge, vouchesaf to command

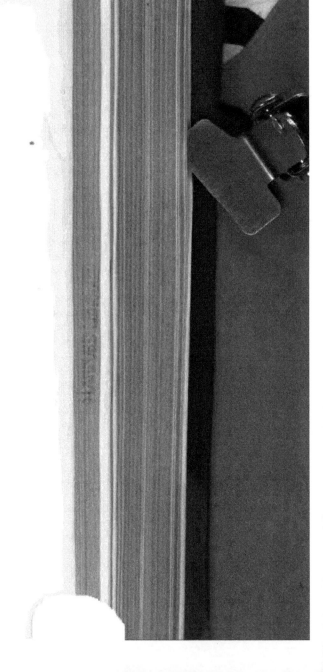

and asks the
king to bid Jos-
selin tell all.
   ¹ fol. 46 b.

This abashes
Josselin, who
asks if Ray-
mondin has come
to dishonour
him.

Raymondin tells
the king of the
treachery of Jos-
selin toward his
father, Henry of
Leon.

How Josselin
told the king's
nephew that he
was disinherited

because of
Henry,

* fol. 45.

hym telle trouth al on hye, that eueryone here may
¹ here it.'   And whan Josselin vnderstode that word,
he wexed sore abasshed; neuertheles, he ansuered in
this manere : 'Sire knight, are you come into this 4
land forto vndertake eny thinge in dyshonoar of me!'
And Raymondin ansuerd appertly : 'Fals traytour, he
fourueyeth nat that saith the playn trouth.'   Thanne
he said agayn to the kynge : 'Sire, it is wel trouth that 8
Henry of Leon was a moche valiant & hardy knight,
curteys and wel condicyoned, & moche was beloved
bothe of the kinge and of his nevew / and vsed the
kynge moche of his counseil, For he was he on whom 12
he trusted most.   It haped that dyuerse traytours beyng
that time about the kinge, of which Josselin here
present was one, as chef causer of the mysdede that
tyme perpetred or doon / came to said kingis nevew, 16
& to hym they said in this manere : "Gentyl Squyer,
alle we that are here byfore your presence ben sory &
woo of your grete dommage and shamfull losse whan
ye shall be dysheryted of so noble a land as is the 20
royame of Brytayne" / and he ansuered to them / "how
shuld that mowe be doo! the kynge hath none heyre
but my self."   "On my god," said thanne yond Josselin
to hym, " Wete it þat he hath made & stablisshed his 24
heyre, Henry of Leon, and I byleue that this Henry
hath enchaunted hym and the barons of the land also,
For therof ben lettres passed & sealled with theire
sealles annexed to the kingis grete seall / and al this 28
they all togider affermed on theire feyth for trouth."
" By my feith," said the squyer thanne / "here is grete
inconuenyence yf that be trew that ye telle me."   ²And
thanne Josselin with his complices alle with an acorde 32
sware yet ayen to hym that it was trouth.   Wherfore
the said yonge squyer was sory and woo.   Josselin
thenne seyyng that he byleued theire falsed to be
certayn, said yet agayn to the squyer in this manere : 36

" Yf in you lyeth so moch hardynes that ye dare vnder-   and urged him to avenge himself,
take to auenge the wrong doon to you by Henry of
Leon, We alle shal helpe you therto."   And the squyer   and promised to aid him.
4 answerd, "my courage and wylle ben agreed to do
soo."   Thenne said Josselin, "goo thanne & arme you
in a manner vnknowen, and we shall abyde you with
out the toune, and shall ledd you in to suche a place
8 where ye shal auenge you at your ease."   O noble &
mighty kinge, sethen I fynde now myself in Court of
right & iustice / and that I may see myn enemye, I
wyl no more be hyd, but lete euery man knowe that   Raymondin declares that he is the son of Henry, which abashes them all.
12 I am the sone of Henry of Leon.'   Thenne they were
alle abasshed of that word, but they held them styl /
and Raymondyn spake fourth in this manere./

' Sire kinge, it is trouth that my fader had take leue   He continues the story of Josse-lin's treachery ;
16   of the kinge, and was goon in to hys Countrey /
and was wonnt euery mornyng for to goo in a wode
nygh by his fortesse to dysporte hym, sayeng hys
matyns alone.   And this fals traytour Josselin, with his
20 complices, ledd the said kingis nevew and embusshed   how an ambush was laid,
them there.   My fader, that thoughte no harme, came
that same ooure / and whan Josselin perceyued hym
commyng he said to the squyer / "now it is tyme to
24 auenge you, For he is without eny armure or wepen /
he may not escape you / and yf we see that ye nede of
help [1] we shall helpe you."   The squyer, thanne esprysed   [1] fol. 43 b.
with euyl desire, departed fro them and ranne toward   and how the king's nephew tried to slay his father,
28 my fader and escryed hym to deth / and as he wold
haue thrested the swerd thrugh my faders body. my
fader glanched asyde / and as god wold he that fyersly
ranne fell to the ground.   My fader þenne toke the
32 swerde that scaped fro the squyers hand, and with the
pomel of it smote hym under the eere by suche   but was slain himself.
strengthe that the squyer fell doun ded.   And thenne
whan my fader saw hym lyeng on the ground deed he
36 dyscouered his face, and anone he knew hym, wherfore

How Henry fled
from the land on
recognising his
enemy, fearing
the king's ire;

which pleased
Josselin,

who thought he
would then be
able to rule the
king.

Raymondin
challenges Jos-
selin,

1 fol. 44.

his son Oliver,
and one of h s
friends;

but no one ac-
cepts the
challenge.

Alain, under-
standing now
who Raymondin
is,

embraces him.

he made grete sorow and was sory and woo / and after
the dede & euylhap, doubtyng the furour & yre of the
king, yede there hys hauoir was / toke it and fledd
with all from þis land.   And thanne Josselin the fals 4
traytour sayd to hys complices and felawes : " Now are
we come to our entencion & wylle.   For the kinges
nevew is deed, and yf Henry be take he may not scape
fro deth.   Now shal we gouerne and doo with the king 8
that we lyst after our guyse / lete vs not meue us tyl
he be ferre from vs / and after we shal take the corps
& putte it in a byere that we shal make with braunches
& leues, and so we shal bere it toward the king, to 12
whom we shal say that Henry of Leon slew hym in
treson." Ha / ha, noble king, all euen so as I say, dide
that yonder fals traytour / and yf he say nay / here I
presente & cast my gage of bataill agenst hym.   And 16
bycause, sire kinge, that I wil lete euery man knowe
that I doo vndertake þis not for auarice / but for to
kepe my right and enherytaunce / and for to declare,
manyfeste, and ¹shewe the vylonny and euyl treson 20
that this fals traytour Josselin and hys complices dyde
to Henry of Leon, my fader, for to haue hym out of
conceytte, and to be putte fro the kingis Court, I
besech your highnes that he may take hys sone Olyuer 24
and another yet of his frendes / and I shal fight ayenst
them thre without fawte, prouyded alwayes the noble
and juste jugement of your Court / one after another' /
and sayeng these wordes he kyst his gage.   but there 28
was none that spake or ansuerd ony word.   And whan
Alayn and his two sones vnderstode alle that Raymondyn had said / what for joye to see theire faders nevew
and Cousyn to them / and what for pyte to here telle 32
the traysen so machyned ayenst theyre faders brother
& vncle to them / ranne to kysse and embrased
Raymondyn.

Whan the king of the Bretons sawe that no body
ansuerd to these wordes so proferid in hys
presence / sayd al on high that euery one there might
4 here hym, 'how now, Josselin, are ye deef? / I now perceyue wel & see that the prouerbe that is said commonly
is trew / that is / "that olde synne reneweth shame,"
For this knight straunger bringeth you tydynges,
8 moche straunge and a wonder medecyne fro ferre land /
aduyse you of that ye shal ansuere.' Thanne ansuerd
Josselyn to the kyng: 'Sire kinge, I am not he þat
from hens fourth oweth to ansuere such thinges. And
12 also wel I byleue that he saith it but in jape & sport.'
Thanne ansuerd Raymondin, 'the mocke fals[1] traytour
shal tourne on the. I now requyre you, noble king,
that this matere may be discuted / lete him haue as
16 raison requyreth for his treson / and I to be punysshed
yf in eny poynt forsayd [I] haue myssaid or mesprysed.'
Thenne said the kinge, 'doubt not of it, For so shal
I doo. Josselyn,' said the kinge, 'ye muste ansuere to
20 this quareH & acusacion.' Whan thenne his sone
Olyuyer herd what the kyng said to his fader / he
ansuerd to his wordes: 'Sire, that knight is so sore
adrad that he trembleth for fere / he weneth as me
24 semeth to take the cranes flighing, by my feith he
shall wel fayH & mysse of that he hath said, For my
fader is a true man in aH his dedes / and I vouchesauf
& graunt the bataiH as he hath ordonned / and there
28 is my gage / he shal be wel happy yf he dyscomfyte
me and another of my lynage suche as I shaH chese. /'

Whan the king herd that word he was moche
wroth, & ansuerd in this manere / 'that shaH
32 nat happe in my Court as long as I shaH lyue þat one
knight alone shal fyght ayenst two for oo maner
quareH / and grete shame is to you / only to haue
thought it in your herte / and wete it / that by
36 semblaunt ye shew nat your fader to haue good quareH.

The king orders
Josselin to de-
fend himself,.

who says that
he belieues that
Raymondin is
joking.

[1] fol. 46 b.

Raymondin
denies it,
and asks the
king to bring
the matter to
an issue.

In answer to
the king, Josse-
lin's son Oliver
agrees to fight
Raymondin,
helped by
another of his
lineage.

The king is
wroth at the
proposal to pair
two knights
against one.

and gives Ray-
mondin choice
of a day of
battle;
Raymondin
desires to fight
now,

And fro this ooure fourthon I gyue you journey of
batayll at the requeste of the knight straunger on suche
day that he shall assigne.' 'By my feyth,' said thenne
Raymondin, 'I am euen now redy therto, for myn 4
armures are not ferre. and thanked be your highnesse
an hondred tymes of your lawfull graunt.'   There had
ye herd grete rumoure made on all sydes, for all said,
'yonder is the moste valyaunt knight that euer we sawe 8
requyryng his ryght.' but what so euer was woofull
therof, Alayn of Quyngant & his two sones were fayn
& glad that so shuld be doo / & said to Raymondin,

1 fol. 47.

and is en-
couraged by
Alain and his
sons.

'Fayre Cousin, be not ¹abasshed of nothing in the 12
world.   take boldly the bataill for you, and for us
both ayenst that same fals traytour / For yf god wil
we shall soone haue worship therof.' 'Fayre lordes,'
said Raymondin, 'take who wil bataill for hymself. 16
For the same I shal haue for my part, and doubte you
not but that I shal bring it to a good & worshipful
ende god before with the good right that I haue
therto.'   20

The king, know-
ing the might of
the parties,

Whilles the rumour was among the folk, the
kinge, moche wyse & subtyl / for that the
parties were of grete & high parentage & lynes /
doubtyng of some grete inconuenience that might happe 24
emong them / commanded sodaynly the gates to be
shette that none might entre ne yssue / & ordonned
men armed to kepe euery man therfro. and aftir callid
his Conseill apart / shewed to them and reherced all 28
the quarell. and they counseilled hym of that was

makes arrange-
ments to prevent
disorder,

nedefull to be doo. Thanne retourned the kinge vnto
the halle, where he made to be commanded by hym,
that none there, on peyne of deth, should be so hardy 33
to spek ony word but þat he were commanded.   The

and declares the
quarrel to be one
of life and death
on both sides.

kinge thenne spak & said, 'now, fayre lordes, ye muste
vnderstand how this quarell is now not litel, for it is
for lyf or grete dyshonour for euermore to the one 36

partye. and wete it for certayn that I ne owe ne also
wyl not refuse ryght to be doo in my Court. Olyuier,'
said the king, 'wil you deffende your fader of this
4 treson?' 'Sire,' said he / 'ye certaynly,' / . and thenne Oliver under-
takes to fight.
the king ansuerd / 'the lystes ben alredy dressed, and
therfore I ordeyne the batail to be to morow exploited. The king ap-
points next day
for the battle,
And wete it / that yf ye be dyscomfited & ouercome,
8 bothe your fader and ye shul be hanged. and not lesse and tells that
the loser shall be
hanged.
shal haue your partye aduerse, yf the [1] cas myshappeth 1 fol. 67 b.
to hym. Make you thanne redy toward / and gyue in
oure hand hostages & pledges / and first your fader
12 shall abyde.' and thenne the king made Josselin to be
ledde in to pryson in a stronge toure. and thanne said
the king to Raymondin, 'Sire knight, whome shul ye Pledges are
taken from the
combatants,
gyue vs for hostage?' Alayn and his two sones came
16 thanne fourth & said, 'sire, we pledge hym.' 'By my
feyth,' said the king, 'it suffyseth vs wel. and therfore
ye shall not hold pryson. For wel I wote that the
knight had not emprysed the batail without he wold
20 perfourme it.' And thus departed bothe parties fro the and both parties
leave the king.
presence of the kinge. and Raymondyn with hys folk,
acompanyed of hys vncle & Cousins, yede toward his
pauillons, and aboute euen tyme he went in to the
24 chirch Cathedrall, and there he watched, making hys
prayers to god with grete deuocyon / And Olyuer also
came to hys hous with grete foyson of them of hys
lynee, and made his hors & harneys redy. On the The combatants
pray and hear
mass.
28 morowe they herd masse, and after armed them / and
the king and the Barons of the land were sette on the
scafoldes rounde aboute the listes / and gardes to the On the morrow
the lists are
guarded,
champ or feld were ordeyned, and the Chayers sette.
32 And about the coure of pryme came Raymondin with and at noon Ray-
mondin appears
richly armed and
well mounted,
with his com-
panions, and
enters the lists;
fayre felawship, armed moche goodly & richely / the
spere on the rest, and on hym hys cote of armes,
browded with syluer & azure / and entred the lystes
36 vpon a grete destrier wel harneysed vnto the nayle of
MELUSINE.   G

and makes rever-
ence to the king
and barons;

the foot / as for gage of bataille / and there he made
reuerence & salewed the king & the Barons.   ' By my
feith,' said eueryone / ' it is long syn we sawe so fayre
man of armes ne of so fayr contenaunce / he hath not 4
beste werke that hath such[1] a man in hand to jouste
or fyght with hym.'   Thenne descended Raymondin
fro the destrer as appertly as he had be vnarmed, and
sette hym in the chayer abydyng after his aduersary. 8
It is trouth that long after that came Olyuer, right
wel & nobly armed, and sett on a moche ryche
destrier / and wel he semed man of grete fayttes / and
so was he / & before hym came Josselin, his fader, on 12
a palfray, and made reuerence to the kinge & hys
barons.   Moche semed Josselin abasshed as thanne /
For that euery man said he had euyl cause.   What
shuld I make long tale / the holy Euangiles were there 16
brought, wheron Raymondin swore that Josselyn had
euyl cause, and that he had doon the treson as he had
byfore declared / and after he kneled & kyssed the
book, and sette hym self ayen on the chayere.   And 20
after Josselin sware, but he stakered, and so timerous
he was that he coude not touche the boke / and also
Olyuer, which knew wel the trouth of all, swore full
feyntly / and that doon he sette hym self agayn in his 24
chayere.   and fourthwith a herault cryded with an high
voyce on the kingis byhalfe / that none, on peyne of
deth, shuld be so hardy to speke ony worde ne to make
eny signe or token that eny of the Champyons might 28
vnderstand or perceyue.   And thenne eueryman voyded
the place, saaf only they that were stablisshed to the
garde of the champ & Josselin.   And anoone Raymondyn lepte on horsbak moch appertly and toke hys 32
spere, and on the other syde Olyuer had hys destrier
redy, and lept on lightly, and toke hys spere with
sharp yron / and thenne cryded a herault thryes. ' lete
ranne your horses & [2] doo your deuoyre.'   36

1 fol. 48.

dismounts and
waits for his
adversary,

who at last
appears nobly
armed with his
father.

Raymondin
swears the
justice of his
cause on the
Gospels,

and likewise
Josselin and
Oliver, but very
timorously.

A herald pro-
claims that no
signs are to be
made:

the lists clear.

A herald shouts
' Do your duty'
to the combat-
ants.

2 Fol. 48 b.

Here saith the veray hystory, that whan the cry was made Raymondin had leyed the ende of hys spere to the grounde alonge the hors nek, and
4 thryes he made the signe of the crosse. and while he dede so hys enemy ranne at hym, and with hys spere hytte Raymondin on the brest or he was ware of hit moche redely, For dooyng so he putte to it alle his
8 strengthe & myght, but Raymondin bowed neuer therfore / and the spere of Olyuer brak in to pieces, and with that strok the speere of Raymondyn fell to the ground. 'Ha, traytour,' said then Raymondyn /
12 'thou folowest wel the right euyl lynee of whiche thou yssued. but that may not auaylle the.' and toke the sterope that hynge at sadelbowe, that had thre poyntes wel assured, eche of them seuen ench long. and at
16 retourne that Olyuer supposed to haue doo, Raymon- dyn smote hym on the helmet with the sterop that oo poynte of it entred & perced the helmet so that the nayl of the vmbrel brake, and the vysere hing at oo
20 syde / and the visage of Olyuyer abode all dyscouered, wherfore he was moche agast and abasshed. Neuerthe- les he drew out hys swerde & wel shewed contenaunce of a knight that lytil redoubteth hys enemye. and so
24 they faught long space togidre and gaaf eche other grete strokes / and there might men see grete appertyse of armes. At last Raymondin alighted on foot and toke vp hys spere that laye at ground & came with
28 grete paas toward his foo mortall, whiche the best wyse that he coude dystourned fro Raymondin that he made to goo after hym alonge the Champ. For he dide with hys hors what he wold,[1] and by that manere dooyng
32 he supposed to haue made Raymondyn wery that nedes he muste reste hym, and so the day shuld be soone passed. But Raymondin whiche that perceyued, yede & apperly to[ke][2] hys hors that he ledde with one hand, &

Raymondin, his spear couched,

making the sign of the cross, is struck fiercely on the breast by Oliver's spear;

but he does not bow; Oliver's spear shivers, and Raymondin's falls,

Upon which Raymondin breaks Oliver's helmet with his stirrop;

his visor falling discovers his face.

They continue to fight fiercely with swords

until Raymondin alights from his horse and takes his spear, and goes to attack his foe,

who runs away from him.

[1] fol. 49.

Raymondin then, leading his horse

[2] Fr. prinst.

G 2

toke the spere at other hand / and softly one pas after another came towarde hys enemye. And whan Olyuyer sawe hym come, perceyuying his manere he wist not how ne in what manere Raymondyn wold assayll

hym / and sodaynly spored his horse, wenyng to haue come & hurted Raymondyn as he had doon byfore.

but Raymondin kyst at hym yet ayen the sterop by grete anger, and hitte Olyuyer hors at foreheed with 8 suche strength that the chaunfreyn entred deep within the hors heed, so that it bowed the legges behind to therthe. Olyuyer thanne sporid his destrier, but as the hors redressed hym, Raymondyn with hys spere 11

smote Olyuyer at right syde of hym, so that he ouerthrew hym to therthe, and so wonderly a strok he gaf hym betwix the mayll panser & the Corset that the spere heed entred deep in hys body / and ar he might 16 be delyuered Raymondyn cast on hym so many strokes that he might no more meve hym self, and by force

plucked the helmet fro the heed of hym, and putte hys knee on his nauell, and the hand senester at hys nek, 20 and held hym in suche destresse that by no manere waye he might not meue hym.

Thystory telleth in this partye that Raymondin held Olyuyer as aboue is said long espace of 24 tyme, and whan he sawe that he had the best ouer

hym he drew a knife[1] that heng [2] at his right side and said to hym, 'False traytour, yeld thyself vaynquyssed,

or ellis thou art but deed.' 'By my feith,' said Olyuyer, 28 'I have leuer dye by the hand of suche a valyaunt knight as ye be than of another.' Raymondyn thanne

toke grete pite on hym and demanded of hym, vpon parel of the sowle of hym / yf he nothing knew of 32 the treson that Josselin his fader had doon / and he

ansuerd nay, and he was not yet borne þat tyme that this treson happed. and how be it that it plaised. to

---

[1] Knight in MS. Fr. version *coustel*.

god that Fortune were as thenne contrary to hym,
nowithstanding yet he held his fader for a trew man /
lawful and not gilty of that same dede. And thanne

4 whan Raymondyn, that wel wyst the contrary, herd
hym, he was sorowful & woo, and bete hym so moche
on the temples with hys fust armed with his gantlet
that he made hym so astonyed that he ne saw ne herd

8 ne wyst what he dide to hym / And thanne stode
vp Raymondin and toke hym by the feet and drew
·hym vnto the lystes, And syn he putte hym without
fourth / and retourned & came before the scaffold of

12 the kinge, the visere lyfte on hye, & said : 'Sire, haue
I doo my deuoire, For yf I haue eny thing more to doo
I am redy to it to the regarde of your Court &
ordynaunce!' 'By my feyth,' said the king, 'sire knight,

16 ye haue quytted your self full wel.' And the king
þenne commanded that Josselin and his sone shuld be
bothe hanged, and they to whom the king comanded
this execucion to be doo wente soone, & without delay

20 they seasid Josselin, who anoone cryed to the king
piteously for mercy. And þen the king yede and said
to hym that he shulde [1]telle the trouthe of the quarell,
and peradventure he night haue grace.

24 Thenne said Josselin, 'Sire, to hyd the trouth it
auaylleth not / haue pite on me yf it plaise you,
For certaynly it was doon in the manere & fourme as
the knight hat purposed & said / and wete it þat my

28 sone Olyuyer was not yet borne.' 'By my feith, Josselin,
said the kinge, 'here is grete falshed, and yf it ne had
be goddis playsire that ye shuld be therof punysshed,
he had not lefte you lyue so long in this world. and

32 as to my part, ye shall not fayll of the punycyon.'
Thanne he said all on high to them that were ordeyned,
that anoone bothe fader & sone shuld be hanged. And
thenne came fourth Raymondin & said to the king :

36 'Sire, I thanke you as I may of the good justice that ye

Raymondin
pleads for Oli-
ver's life, as he
is brave and
valiant,

and free from
the guilt of the
treason;

and for Josselin's,
because he is so
old, desiring only
that he should
make restitution
of the estate,

the money to be
used to found a
priory.

¹ fol. 50 b.

But the king
orders them to
be hanged,
and restores
Raymondin his
estates, and gives
him all Josselin's
land,
for which Ray-
mondin does
homage.

Raymondin is
feasted by the
king of Brut
Britain,

haue doon to me / but, sire, I moued with pite requyre
you of your mysericorde to be shewed on Olyuer. For
seeyng his valyauntyse & worthynes, also consideryng
that he is not gilty of the treson it were grete dommage ₄
of hys deth. For yet shall he mow doo wel. And as to
the fader, for this that I see hym olde & feble / of my
part, sire king, yf ye vouchesauf to graunt hym grace
therof I shuld be fayn & glad, soo that I haue myn ₈
herytage to my behouf, and that the prouffytes &
fruytes that he hath leuyed & receyued of it, syn he
had therytage in hys handes, be by extimacion reualued
in money. that same payment to be by you, sire king, 1₂
ordeyned to edefye or bigge a pryorye, & monkes
therin to be rented with reuenues & possessyons after
the quantyte of the said money to þe regarde of you
and of your Counseill. the said monkes to pray for the 1₆
sowle of the kinges nevew perpetuelly.' The kinge
thanne said to his barons, 'Fayr¹ Sires, here ye may
see the free courage of a knight that prayeth to me to
respyte hys enemys fro deth. but by the feyth that I 2₀
owe to god Josselin nor his sone shal neuer doo treson
ne cause no man to goo out of my land as exiled.' and
fourthwith he made them to be hanged, and rendred to
Raymondin his enherytaunce and al Josselyn's land 2₄
with all. Wherof Raymondin thanked hym moche
humbly and made to hym his homage. After byganne
the feste to be moche grete, and held the king grete &
noble Court open to al men, & was moche glad of that 2₈
he had recouered & goten so noble a knight in his
land. but for nought he made joye, For soone ynoughe
he shall see that Raymondyn had no grete wylle to
abyde and dwelle in Bretayne, for moch longed to hym 3₂
the sight of Melusyne.

Now in this parte telleth thystorye that Raymondyn
was moche wel festyed of the king of the brut
Bretayne that held grete & honourable Court for loue 3₆

of Raymondin, and the barons of Bretayne made grete
joye for his commyng, and specyally his vncle Alayn
and hys two children, & they of his lynage. And
4 thanne came Raymondin to the king and said to
hym thus : ' Sire king, I pray you & beseche that ye
vouchsaf to graunte & acorde that I gyue the Baronye
of Leon that was to Henry my fader, on whos sowle
8 god haue mercy, to Henry my Cousyn / and so the
land shal bere the name of his ryghtfull lord / and
you the name of your liege man, For he is of the
right lynee.' ' By my feyth,' sayd þe kinge, ' sire, sith
12 it playseth you thus wel it plesoth vs so to be.' Thenne
the kyng called Henry, For he loued hym wel and said
to hym : ' Henry, receyue the name of the baronye of
Leon, which your Cousyn gyue you, and make homage
16 to me therof ' / and so he dide · and thanked moche the
king & Raymondyn.[1] And this doon Raymondin
called to hym Alayn his Cousyn : ' I gyue you the
land that the king hath gyuen me that late was
20 longyng to Josselin Dupont, and make your homage to
the king ' : / and he thanked hym moche humbly · and
knelyng made hys homage to the kinge that moche
joyfully receyued hym to it. But the Barons of the
24 land byganne thanne to make rumour among them and
said : ' By my feyth, this knight is not come into this
lande for couetyse ne auarice. But only he hath putte
his lyf in grete auenture & parel for to conquere his
28 heritage. Whan so soone he demysed hymself therof.
it muste wel be that grete ryches he hath some where ' /
Thanne came thauncyent knight to Raymondin. and
when Raymondin sawe hym he said to hym that he
32 shuld delyuere hym self of that his lady had commanded hym / and he ansuerd, ' my lord, therfore
I am come toward you.' and thanne he presented
fro hys lady to the kyng a grete Coupe of gold sette
36 with many precyous stone. and after gaf to all the

Side notes:

and made welcome by the barons.

Raymondin asks the king to allow him to give his barony to his cousin Henry,

which request is granted.

The barony is given, and Henry does homage for it.

[1] fol. 51.

Raymondin gives the confiscated lands of Josselin to Alain, who does homage to the king for them.

The barons of Britain wonder at the riches of Raymondin, who gives away the land just won.

The ancient knight brings gifts from Melusine for the king and the barons,

Barons in the forsaid name many ryche jewelles.
Wherof all were meruaylled of whens might come
such a riches / and all they said that Raymondin
muste be moche riche & mighty in some other Coun- 4
tree. Wherfore the feest was greter than afore. And
Alayn and his two sones demened suche joye that
none shuld mow think it. but yet duryng theirs joye
was on other syde made grete sorow of the parents 8
& frendes of Josselin that had not forgeten þe deth of
hym / as herafter ye shal here reherce.   [1]And here
resteth thystorye to speke of this feste & folowyng
the matere saith how Melusyne gouerned her self while 12
that Raymondyn was in his vyage.

who rejoice
much, and keep
up the feast;

but all the time
much sorrow
prevails among
Josselin's
friends.

[1] fol. 51 b.

Thystory telleth vs that whiles Raymondyn was in
bretayne, Melusyne made to be byld up the
toune of Lusynen, and walled it with strong walles & 16
toures one nygh another,[2] and deep diches dide doo
make about it. A toure she dide to be made betwixt
the Fortresse & the tounne walled with a wall of xx
foot thikk. This toure was ouer hye / and ordeyned 20
men that shuld be styl both day & nyght, at leste one
vpon the vpermost batelments of it with a trompe in
his hand, that shuld blow at euery tyme he perceyued
& sawe men othre on foot or on horsbak togidre aboue 24
the nombre of xx[u] commyng toward the said toune
or Castel / and that same toure she called the tromped
toure. Now retourneth thistory to spek of the kyng
& of Raymondin, and of the feest & chere that euery 28
one made to Raymondin.

In Raymondin's
absence Melu-
sine builds Lu-
signan, and walls
it;

also builds a
high watch
tower, with walls
twenty feet
thick.

IN this partye reherceth thystorye that moch was
the feest grete at Nantes · and the king honoured
moche Raymondin, and there jousted gentilmen one 32
ayenst other byfore the ladyes & gentyl wemen wher
Raymondin bare hym full valiauntly & goodly that
euery man spak wele of hym, sayeng that he was

The feast con-
tinued at Nantes.

[2] + Fr. pour deffendre a concent tous les archiers.

worthy to be lord of a grete land. And moche were
they abasshed of the grete riches that they sawe euery
day about Raymondin / but who someuer made feest
4 for Raymondyn, the Chastelayn of Ardaħ, that was
neuew to Josselin Dupont, made aħ the contrary. For
he sodaynly sent to alle the parentes frendes and
affyns of Josselin, letyng ¹them to knowe how it was
8 of theire frend Josselyn, and that they shuld be at a
certayn day that he assigned to them at a certayn
retrette that was within the forest of Guerrende that
was of his owne. And whan they vnderstode the
12 deth of Josselin þey were sorowfuħ & woo, and assembled them togider about ii C men of armes, and
pryuely yede & came to the said retrette, where the said
Chastelayn had manded them to come. And thanne
16 the Chastelayn in the moost secrete wyse that he coude,
departed fro the kinges court without leue of the king
ne of the Barons / but there he lefte thre squyers of
his for to loke & aspye whiche waye Raymondin shuld
20 take, and that they shuld anounce it to hym to the
retrette beforsaid. So long rode the Castelleyn that
he cam to the retrette where he found them of his
lynage, and he reherced to þem aħ the manere of
24 thaduenture / and how Josselin & his sone were
hanged / and asked of them what they thoughte &
proposed to doo / yf they shuld auenge them on
Raymondin that was causer of it / and to them grete
28 blame & shame for euermore was bycause of hym
imputed / or elles to lete hym goo free. Thenne
ansuered for al the lynage an vnwyse & hasty knight
that was sone to the Cousyn of Josselin. 'cousyn
32 castellayne, we wol that ye wete & knowe that thus
shal nat this oultrageous werk be lefte. For we alle
of one accorde & wylle wil putte hym to deth that
to vs hath doo suche vitupere & dyshonour.' 'By
36 my feith,' said thanne the Castellayne, 'I hold & repute

(side notes)

while Josselin's nephew advised his kindred of their loss,

¹ fol. 52.

and summoned them to a retreat in the forest of Guerrende,

They assemble two hundred strong,

and are informed of the mishap by Josselin's nephew,

and are asked if they intend to avenge themselves.

They declare they will put Raymondin to death;

fol. 52 b.

upon which the
nephew promises
to assist them,

by spying which
way Raymondin
leaves the
country.

the wele & honour wel employed that Josselin dide [1] to
you in tyme passed.   And anoone I shall putte you in
the way and place where we shal wel acomplisshe our
wylle on hym that suche shame hath doon to vs.   For 4
by what someuer side he yssueth out of Bretayne he
may not scape fro vs.   For therto we haue good
wayters, & espyes that soone shall anounce his way
to vs whan tyme shalbe.'   And they answerd alle with 8
an voys /—'Blessed be you. and wete it that whatsomeuer fall therof / this enterpryse shalbe brought to an
end, and we shal slee that false knight that hath imposed to vs alle vylonnye & shame.'   And here spekeþ 12
no more thistorye of them, and retourneth to spek of
the king & of Raymondyn. and how he departed fro
the king moch honorably.

The feast con-
tinued fifteen
days longer;

Thystory saith that the feest dured wel xv dayes & 16
more. the king of Bretons & hys baronye made
grete honour to Raymondyn in so moche that I can

then Raymondin
took leave,

nat reherce it.   Raymondin thanne toke leue of the
king & of his Barons and humbly mercyed the king 20
of his good justice that he had doon to hym in his
noble Court, and departed fro them moche honourably.   And wete it that bothe the king & many his
barons were sory for his departing.   And thus Ray- 24

and accompanied
with Alain rode
to Leon,

mondyn acompanyed of his vncle Alayn his two sones
& all theyre meyne rode toward Leon.   But it is
trouth that þauncyent knight was departed & goon

where the
ancient knight
had already pre-
pared for them.

byfore / and had doo sette vp bothe tentes & pauillons 28
and all other thinges necessary he ordeyned & made
redy.   And thanne Raymondin / hys vncle with his

[1] fol. 53.

two [1] sones and the moost nere of his kynne to hym
lodged them togidre in the Castel. and the other 32
herberowed them in the toune.   Whan the peple of
the Countre knew the commyng of theyre owne lordes
sone they were joyfull & glad, and made to hym many
fayr presentes after the vse & custome of the Countre / 36

—

as of wyn, of bothe fleʃh & fyʃʃhe, hey & ootys, and of
many other thing*es*, and they were fayn & glad sith it
playsed not Raymondin to abyde & hold the land, that
4 they were befall in the sayd lynee of theire lord, ånd
that they were quytte & exempted fro the subgection
& boundage of the lynee of Josʃellin. Raymondin
thanne þanked them curtoysly of theire presentes &
8 yeʃt*es*. commanded & prayed them that they wold be
true & feythfull subgets to Henry hys Cousin to whom
he had gyue the land. and they anʃuered that þey
shuld doo soo.   Of them resteth thistorye, and speketh
12 of the spyes that wayted there / of whicħ one went to
the retrette where the Castellayne of Arualł · and the
lynee of Josʃelin were all redy / and the two other spyes
abode for to knowe what way Raymondyn shuld hold · /
16 I N this partye telleth to vs thistory that Raymondin
departed fro Leon, and toke leue of al hys parents
& frend*es* there, & went to Quyngant where the festa
was grete, and there after the feeste was ended Ray-
20 mondyn wold haue take leue of hys vnclo Alayn & of
all his lynage / but they dide putte the moost remedy
they coude for to hold hym there a seuen*e* nyght more.
·Wherfore Raymondyn obtempering to them / ye /
24 ayenst his entent & courage [1]fullfylled theire willes.
And in the meane while cam*e* to Henry hys Cousyn, a
man that told hym that as he passed fourth by the said
retrette where the Castellayne of Arualł was wiŧ wel
28 two houndred men in armes, that they abode for some
folke to whom they owed no good wylle. but he told
hym not whom they aspyed & watched for. And
whan Henry understode this he toke a squyer of his
32 and bad hym goo thithor & knowe what it was. and he
that was moche dilygent dyde so that he knew the
moost parte of theyre purpos and entent & what
nombre þey were.   Soone after he retourned to Henry
36 and reherced to hym all that he had found, and that

that fiue or six
hundred men are
assembled.

Henry enjoins
silence on the
spy,

and tells his
brother what he
has learnt.

¹ fol. 54.

The brothers
gather four hun-
dred men of
arms,

and accompany
Raymondin
when he leaves
Quingant,

until they ap-
proach the forest
where Josselin's
kindred are hid.
Josselin's
nephew, the
Chastellain of
Arvall, learns
from his spies
the approach of
Raymondin;

they were wel fyue or six houndred fighting men.
And this tydinges herd / Henry deffendid to the
messanger moche expresly that to no body he shuld
spek of it. And soone he called his brother Alayn 4
and some other of the moost noble of hys lynage and
reherced to them alle this werk. 'By my feyth,' said
they, 'we ne cannot thinke what they entende to doo,
but that they wold auenge them on Raymondin our 8
Cousyn or ellis to meve werre ayenst vs for the said
quarelle, but alwayes it is good to be purueyed of
remedye · lete vs therfore send for alle our frendes and
kepe vs secretly togidre tyl we see what they haue 12
purposed to doo / to thende yf they come on vs that
they fynde vs not discouered & vnpurueyed · also yf
Raymondin departeth that he be not surprysed of
them / and yf they entende to doo hym euyl / it is 16
but for to take the lyf ¹fro hym.' 'By my feyth,' said
the other, 'that is trouth. Now lete vs hye & delyuere
vs that our mandement be doo of light & secretly.'
And so did they / in so moche that within the second 20
day after / they were gadred togidre about foure
houndred in nombre men of armes what of theyre lynee
and what of theire affynyte & alyed / & made them
to be lodged in a wod so that few men knew of it. It 24
happed thanne that Raymondyn wold no lenger abyde /
and toke leue of Alayn hys vncle þat abode styl at
Quyngant moche wooful & sory of hys departyng /
and hys two sones companyed hym & conueyed with 28
grete foyson of theyre lynee. And neuer wold lete
hym goo byfore, but made theyre men to be on eche
side of hym, and so long they rode that they approched
the Forest where the Castellayne and his felawship 32
were in his retrette which Castellayn knew by his
spyes the commyng of Raymondyn & his men and
told it to hys parents sayeng in this maner: 'Now shal
be seen & knowen who euer loued Josselin and Olyuer 36

hys sone. For here we may putte to deth alle the
lynage of hym self þat to vs hath doon suche a shame.'
And they ansuered to hym that none shuld scape, but

4 alle shuld be putte to deth. But as the prouerbe saith,
' Such weneth to auenge his shame that encreassith it ' /[1]
and so it was of the Castellayne & hys parents. In this
meane while came þauncyent knight to Raymondin

8 and said to hym in this manere : ' Sire, ye[2] myster wel
for to [3]be armed gooyng thrugh the Forest. For the
lynage of Josselin that ye haue dystroyed loueth you
not, and they might bere bothe to your personne and

12 to your felawship & meyne grete dommage yf they
found you vnpurueyed / and my herte gyueth me that
soone we shall fynd hem ' / and Henry & Alayn his
brother and all theire lynage were armed all redy, and

16 had sent all theire meyne byfore to make embushe
within half a mylle fro the retrette. Thenne whan
Raymondyn / had commanded hys men to take theire
armures on hem & sawe them of his lynage that were

20 alle armed, ho- ne wyst what say but þe two brethern
his cousyns told hym how they had sent in embusshe
byfore wel iiii. C. of their men for to kepe hym fro hys
enemyes / and they reherced to hym all the trouthe.

24 ' By my feyth,' said Raymondin, ' curtoyse oweth not to
be forgeten / and for it shal not as to my parte fro hens
fourthon. For yf in tyme to come ye haue nede of
me / I am he that shal at al tymes be redy after my

28 power to fulfylle your wille.' And so longe they rode
that they entred the Forest /.

Thystorye saith that the Castellayne was in his
retrette and abode for the spye that last he

32 had sent to wete whan Raymondyn shuld entre the
Forest. the whiche exploited so that he came nigh
Raymondin / and thanne he lightly retourned toward

and on him tell-
ing his men, they
promise to put
Raymondin and
his kindred to
death.

[3] fol. 54 b.

The ancient
knight warns
Raymondin of
his danger,

who, seeing his
cousin's men all
armed,

thanks them,
and promises
to help them
should they ever
want him.

---

1 Fr. *Tel cuide venger sa honte qui l'acroit.*
2 Fr. *Et bien mestier.*

The Chastellain, hearing from his spy of Raymondin's appearance, cries on his men to follow him.

¹ fol. 55.

They mount, and are allowed to pass by the men of Henry of Leon, who are hidden in the forest,

until they meet Raymondin.

They run upon Raymondin's men;

and when Raymondin comes in sight,

the Chastellain and his three cousins attack him.

the retretle and to the Castellayn he said : 'Sire, ye may see hym come yonder.' And whan the Castellayn vnderstod hym he bygan to crye *with* a hye voys / 'on horsbak, & who that eu*er* loued Josselin & his sone 4 lete hym ¹folowe me.' Thanne styed eu*er*y man on horsbak / & they were so encressyd in nombre that they were wel viii C & moo fighting men, and rode fourth in ordynaunce ayenst Raymondin, and passed 8 by the embusshe that Henry and his parents had sent. whiche lete them passe fourth with*out* they discouered themself. and soone after þey rode after them. So longe rode the Castelayn & his folke that they per- 12 ceyued nygh them þe foreward of Raymondin. but abasshed he was whan he sawe them armed gooyng by ordyn*au*nce / though they were but a few seruaunts and a C. men of armes / they ²escryed them to the deth / 16 And whan they vnderstode it they yede apart & made to blowe theire trompettes and ranne vpon Raymondyns folke whiche were sore dom*m*aged or he coude come to helpe them, the whiche rode as fast as the hors 20 might walope, and hauyng the spere on the rest launched among his enemyes / and the first that he encou*n*tred he ou*er*threw hym doun to therthe & aftir drew out high [his] swerde and smote trauersing here 24 & there and in a lytel tyme he moche dommaged hys enmyes. But whan the Castellayn saw hym he was full woo & sory / and he shewed hym to thre hys Cousyns sayeng / 'loke yonder is the knyght that 28 hath shamed all our lynage / yf we had o*ur* wylle of hym all the other shuld be soone ou*er*come & vayn- quysshed.' thanne þey spoored theire horses, and all foure ranne ayenst hym / and wit*h* theire speeris 32 recountred hym, soo that they ou*er* threw bothe man

² Fr. *et leur escriwient : A mort à mort, mal acointastes celluy qui nous a fait la honte et le dommaige de Josselin notre cousin.*

& hors [1] to the erthe and passed al foure fourth. But   [1] fol. 55 a.
whan Raymondyn saw hym ouer thrawen he spooryd
hys hors, and the hors that was swyft and strong
4 releuyd hym on hys knees and soo fourth on his feet
so pertly þat Raymondyn neuer lost sterop fro the
foot ne swerd fro the hand. And thanne he tourned
toward the Chastellayn & so mightily smote hym on   Raymondin
8 the helmet with hys swerd that he so stakerid that he   smites the Chastellain,
lost bothe steropes / and as Raymondyn passed by
hym he hurtelyd hym soo with the sholder that he   and fells him.
fell doune to the erthe / and the pres came there so
12 grete that he was sore tradde with hors feet. Thenne
begane the bataill grete & fell and sore dommaged
were bothe partes. And thanne came there also   Assistance comes
thauncyent knight and Henry & Alayn hys brother,   in the persons of Henry, Alain, and the ancient
16 and foughte strongly ayenst theyre enemyes. There   knight,
Raymondin made grete fayttes of armes and sore
dommaged hys enemys. but the Chastelayn was had
out of the pres and hys men toke hym another hors.
20 Thanne toke the party aduerse, herte & courage &
stoutly fought they ayenst Raymondyn & his folke.
and there were many one slayn of both sydes. And
wete it that Raymondyn & his folke susteyned heuy
24 weyght. For hys aduerse party was moch strong &
moche wel they fought & valyauntly. but the em-   and the ambush
busshe of Henry came by the bake syde on them and   of Henry;
assaylled them on all sydes so that þey wyst not
28 what they shuld doo / how they shuld defende them
self nor where they shuld flee / Thenne was the   and routs the
Chastellayn taken & brought before Raymondin / and   Chastellain's companions,
he commanded thauncient knight to kepe hym. And   who are all taken
32 in conclusion all the other were soone after outhro   prisoners or slain.
take or deed. And this doon they came to the retrette
where Raymondyn said to hys parentes : 'Now lordes
I owe wel [2] to loue and thanke you of the grete   [2] fol. 56.
36 socoure that ye haue doon to me this day. For

Raymondin
thanks his
kindred for their
help;

certaynly I wote that yf it had not be the he
god and of you this traytour had putte me to de
treson, now haue regarde what best is for to
'Sire,' said Henry, 'as your wyl shall graunte we
assent therto.' 'I shall saye you,' said Raymo
'what we shal doo. lete vs take and assemble a

who propose
to take the
Chastellain, and
all others of
Josselin's
kindred to the
king of Brut
Britain for judg-
ment.

lynee of Josselin to-gidre / and bothe the Chaste
and alle the other his parents we shall sende t
kinge. Whiche hauyng regarde to theire grete fa
and treson shal punysshe aftir his good wylle.'
other thanne said / ' forsouthe, sire, ye say wel.' Tl

The prisoners
who are not Jos-
selin's kindred
are hung,

were chosen out all the prysonners that were n
the lynage of Josselin. and att yate of the said re
some were hanged / some at wyndowes & son

and the Chas-
tellain and the
rest are taken
bound before the
king.

batelments of it. And the Chastellayn and all
parents there were bounde bothe hand & fee
traytours and prysonners. the whiche Alayn
panyed with thre houndred spere men lede them
the kinge. and first Alayn presented to þe king

Alain tells the
king the treason
wrought,

Chastelayne of Aruall as he that had conspir
machined that treson / and al other after. and to
rehered Alayn all how it was happed. and how
mondyn recommanded hym to his good grace /
that he wold not be dysplaysed yf he had take v
aunce on hys mortal enmyes that wend to
murdred hym with treson, and that he sent to hyn

and says that
Raymondin has
sent the Chastel-
lain and his
kindred to
receive punish-
ment.

Chastellayn chief causer and other his complices f
knowe by them the trouth of the faytte and fo
punysshe them at his plaisure and wylle / 'And I

[1] fol. 56 b.

The king asks
the Chastellain
why he has done
such a shameful
deed.

Chastellayn,' said the kinge 'haue ye be so [1]hardy to
suche treson and so shamefull dede for the raisonn
justice that late we dide in our reaume / seeing &
considering the grete treson that Josselin your v
knowleched & confessed to haue doo?' 'By god,'
the king, ' ye were therof surquydous,[2] & it is wel i

[2] Fr. monlt oultre cuide.

yf euyl is comme to you therof.' 'Ha, noble kinge,'
said thanne the chasteleyn, 'for your pite lete falle   The Chastellain
your mysericorde on me caytyue personne. For the   begs for mercy,
4 grete sorowe & woo that I had of the dyshonour that
Raymondin had doon to our lynage hath caused me
to doo soo.'

   'By my feith,' said the king, 'it is euyl companye of
8 a traytour / and good it is to shette the stable
before the hors be lost, wel I wyl that ye knowe that
neuer ye shall haue suche purpos as to wyl slee no
gentylman with treson, For neuer I shall ete tyl that ye   but the king says
12 be hanged with your vncle, for ye shall hold hym   he will not eat
felawship, and also all them that are of your cohortacion.'   till they be hung.
The kinge made to be take alle them of hys cohorte or
company, and were all hanged / and the Chastelayn he   which judgment
16 sent to Nantes, and there he was hanged nyghe to his   is executed.
vncle Josselin & Olyuyer hys Cousyn. And thus kepte
wel the king of Bretons Justice in his time regnyng in
Breytayne.

20 Here sayth thistory that whan Alayn was retourned
to Raymondin unto the retrette, and that he
hadd to hym and to the other reherced this þat the
kyng had doon / they said that the kyng had doo right   Raymondin
24 wel as a valyaunt & lawfull justiser shuld doo. Thenne   praises the king's
called Raymondyn to hym Henry Alayn & other of his   justice,
lynee and said to them in this manere : 'Fayre cousyns
& good frendes, I enjoyne & charge you that ye doo   and asks his
28 edefye or bigge a pryorye with viii monkes, and that   cousin to build
ye reueste them with rentes and reuenues such that   a priory for
honestly & goodly they may lyue on for euermore /   eight monks,
they to pray there for the sowle of ¹my fader / for the   ¹ fol. 57.
32 kingis nevew sowle and for the sowles of them that are   to pray for the
slayn & ded in this quarell.' And they alle said 'they   souls of those
shuld soo doo. And Raymondyn prayed them to   killed in the
recommande hym to the kingis good grace to hys   quarrel.
36 barons and to Alayn their fader. And thanne he toke

Raymondin
parts from his
cousins, who

return to their
father.

leue of them / and they were sorowfull of theire
departement / and also of this that he wold nat lete
them goo no ferther with hym. They retourned to
Quyngant. And Raymondin yede on his way and 4
cam to guerrende · and wel he was there festyed and
worshipfully cheryed of them of the tonne. And here
resteth thistorye of Raymondyn · and shall recounte
how Henry & Alayn toke leue of theyre lynee and cam 8
ayen to theyre fader.

Henry and Alain
tell their father
the news,

This historye saith in this paas that Henry and Alayn
toke leue of theyre lynage & came to theire
fader and recounted to hym all thaduenture of the 12

and how they
have to build a
priory.

Chastellayn, how they were departed fro þeyr cousyn,
and how he hadd commanded & charged them to
fownde a pryory. 'By my feith,' said þeire fader. 'Alayn,

The father is
glad to hear of
the clearance
of Josselin's
friends,

now is the land wel clene delyuered of the lynage of 16
Josselin ; god on theyre sowles haue mercy, how be it
they loued vs neuer. Now fayre sones I shall saye
you what ye shal doo. First ye shal goo to the kinge

and advises his
sons to ask land
from the king to
build the priory.

& requyre hym that it plese hym to gyue you a place 20
for to edefye the Pryorye / and telle hym the maner
how ye be commanded of your Cousyn to fownde it.
and I byleue he shal gyue you a good ansuer.' And
they said that thus shuld they doo. And thanne they 24
departed fro theire fader, and so long they rode that
they camme to Vannes and founde the kinge departed

¹ fol. 57 b.

& was goon to ¹Sassymon for to dysporte hym at

They set out to
the king,

Chasse. And they mounted on horsbak and came to 28
the gate and passed & entred the Forest and rode so
long tyl they came to the Castel. and founde the kyng
goon to the park to the chasse / and the two bretheren

and find him by
a tree in the
forest of Sassi-
mon, waiting
for a hart ;
but hide them-
selves till it is
captured.

yed after & founde the king nyghe a grete tree by a 32
staung where he abode aftir the herte that houndes
chassed. Thenne the two bretheren drew them self aparte
bycause they wold not lette the kyng to see the dysporte /
who perceyued them wel² & coude them good thanke 36

² Fr. leur en sceut moult bon gré.

therfore. and not long after þe herte came that ranne
in to the staung / and there he was take by chaas of
dogges / and was hadd out of the watre / and the
4 curee made & gyue to the houndes as custome is to
doo.   Thenne Henry and Alayn his brother drew them
self byfore the king and salewed hym moche honourably / and made wel theire message as theyre Cousin
8 had charged them.   And the king welcommed hem &
moche enquyred of them thestate of Raymondin and
they told hym alle that they had seen of hit / and
after they recounted to hym how he enjoyed & charged
12 them to edyfye & make vp a Priorye of eyghte monkes.
them to reueste & empossesse with landis, reuenues &
rents, they to syng & pray therfore for the sowle of the
kingis neuew / for Henry his faders sowle, and for the
16 sowles of alle them that had receyued deth in this
quarelle.   Also how at hys instaunce they shuld pray
hym for a place where they shuld edefye the said
pryorye.   ' By my feith,' said the king.   ' the requeste
20 is wel lawfull & raysonable. and euen now ¹I shall
lede you to the place where I wyl that it be fownded
and made vp.'   Thanne they came out of the wareyne
and came all by the walle to thende of the clos. and
24 thenne said the king : ' Fair lordes, make here to be
edyfyed a Pryory & take asmoche of grounde as ye
lyketh / and I gyue liberte & habaundonne you the
forest for to cutte there the wode. and whan the
28 monkes shal be stablysshed there, I enlyberte &
habaundonne it to them for theire vse and to alle
thider commyng & dwelling.   And I graunte to them
the fysshing in the see that is nygh to this place a
32 quarter of a legge, and to take in the Forest birdes. &
wild beestes for theire lyuyng & sustenaunce of theire
houshold · and also I gyue to them all the landes erable
that are her about half a legge' / and of alle this he
36 made & gaf to them good & suffisaunt patents. and of

Side notes:
They come out
and salute the
king,

are welcomed,

and tell him of
Raymondin and
his will about
the priory ;

and ask for land
to build it on.

¹ fol. 56.

The king leads
them to a spot,

where he gives
them as much
land as they
require ;

and grants to the
monks the right
of fishing, hunt-
ing, shooting,
and wood cutting
in the forest ;

and gives some
arable land, all
on good patents.

all these graunts & geastes the two brethern thanked
the king moche humbly whiche made massons, carpenters, & other, to come, and in short tyme they made
the chirche & the priorye. and there they stablysshed 4
whyte monkes. vnto the nombre of VIII. religious
personnes, the whiche bere on theire vtterist habyte a
crosse of Azure / and enpossessed them wel for theire
sustenaunce & cotidiane lyuyng / as now yet is.   And 8
now resteth thystorye to spek of the king of Bretons
and of the two bretheren. and retourneth to recounte
how Raymondin gouerned hym self syn after.

Now telleth thystorye that so long abode Raymon- 12
din in the land of Guerrende [1] that he peased
and acorded togidre two barons of the lande that long
byfore hated eche other to deth.   In so moche that he
made them to be good frendes togidre, and theire 16
Countrees in peas and rest.   And after he toke his leue
of the barons & of the peuple, which sorowed moche
for his departing. and so long he rode that he came
into the land of Poytou, wher he found many grete 20
forests vnhabyted / and in some places he sawe many
wyld bestes, as hertes, hynd, & roo, wyld bores, and
other beestes ynough. and in other places many fayre
playnes & champaynes. many fayre medowes & ryuers. 24
' By my feyth,' said thanne Raymondin, ' it is grete pyte
& dommage that suche a commodyouse Countre is nat
enhabyted with peuple.' and many a fayre manoyr and
places were on the ryueres there that soone might be 28
redressed as hym semed whiche had be ouerthrawen in
tyme of warre.   And thus rydyng fourth he came to
an auncyent Abbey called Maylleses, and therein were
comprised thabbot and an houndred monkkis, beside 32
the Convers. and there herberowed Raymondyn for the
grete playsaunce that he toke of it. and þer he dwelled
thre dayes and thre nightes. and gaf to the chirch
there many fayre jewelles.   After he departed and 36

came rydyng tyl he aprouched & came nygh Lusynen. and first he perceyued & sawe the tromped
toure and the new toune, and thenne he supposed not
4 to be there as he was. For he knew not the place for
cause of the said toure & toune new made of late, and
moche he meruaylled whan he herd [1] the sowne of the
trompes within the toure /.

8 In this part saith to vs thystorye that whan Raymondin came aboue Lusynen, & he perceyued
the toune walled round aboute with strong walles and
fortifyed with deep dyches & grete. 'how,' said he to
12 thauncyent knight, 'What may this be; mesemed
right now that I was forwayed of my way to come to
lusygnen / and yet me semeth soo?' thenne began
thauncyent knight to lawhe. And Raymondin said
16 to hym: 'How, sir knight, jape you with me / I telle
you for certayn yf it were not the toure and the toune
that I see I shuld haue wend to be this nyght in
Lusygnen.' 'By my feyth,' said thatancient knight,
20 'soone ye shal fynde yourself there yf god wyl with
grete joye.' Now I shall sey you some of Raymondyn's
seruaunts were sent before by thauncyent knight to
anounce Melusyne the commyng of Raymondin. and
24 how be it she byleued them wel / she made no semblaunt þerof / but soone she caused the peuple to be
redy for to goo & mete with Raymondyn. and she her
self, acompanyed with many ladyes & damoyselles,
28 yede to mete & welcome hym wel horsed & arayed
honorably and rychely. Thenne Raymondin loked
fourth byfore hym and sawe the peple commyng fro
the valey vpward ayenst hym two & two togidre in
32 fayre ordynaunce, wherof he moche meruaylled. and
whan they aproched they bygan to crye with a high
voys, 'ha, ha, dere lord, welcome may you be.' And
thenne Raymondin knew som of them that were comme
36 [2]ayenst hym / and demanded of them, 'Fayre lordes,

and continues
his journey to
Lusignan, but
does not recog-
nize it, because
of the new tower
and town built
by Melusine.

[1] fol. 59.

He expresses
his doubts to the
ancient knight,

who tells him
he'll soon be
home.

Melusine,
advised of Ray-
mondin's arrival,
makes herself
and people ready
to meet him.

Raymondin sees
them,

and hears them
cry 'Welcome';

[2] fol. 59 b.

fro whens come you?' 'My lord,' sayd they, 'we com
fro lusynen.' 'thenne,' said Raymondin, 'is Lusynen
ferre hens?' They thanne, seeyng that he myaknewe
the place for cause of the new toune & toure / said: 4

'My lord, ye be at it, but ye mysknowe the place
bycause that my lady syn your departyng hath doo
made and byld this toun & that high toure. and
yonder ye may see her commyng ayenst you.' Thenne 8

was Raymondin moche abasshed / and said not all
that he thoughte. but when he remembred how she
dyde doo make the Castel of Lusynen in so short tyme
he gaf hym self no meruayll yf she had doon soo. 12

Thenne is come to hym Melusyne that honorably welcommed hym, sayeng in this manere: 'My lord, I am

right fayn & glad of that ye haue so wel wrought
& doon so honourably in your vyage. For al thinges 16
haue be reherced to me alredy.' And Raymondin
answerd to her: 'Madame, it is by the grace of god
and of you.' And talking togidre of this matere they

entred Lusynen and alighted. Ther was the feste 20
grete that lasted eighte dayes, And was there the Erle
of Forest that said to Raymondin, 'ye be welcome.'
And after the feest they departed fro Lusynen and

came to Poytiers toward the Erle that receyued þem 24
benygnely, and demanded of Raymondin where he had

be so long. and he recorded to hym alle his auenture.
And shortly to say, the Erle Bertran was therof joyful

& glad. ¹ And that doon, the brethern toke leue of 28
hym / and the one yede toward forests, and Raymondin

toward his wyf & lady, which thenne was grete with
child, and bare her terme / the which expired, she

made a fayre child that was her second sone / he was 32
soone baptised and imposed to name Edon,² and hadd
an eere greter without comparyson than that other
was / but all hys other membres were replenysshed

² Fr. *Odon*.

with beaute, the which Edon had syn to hys wyf the
Erle of Marchis doughtir.   And of hym resteth
thistorye / and speketh ferthermore of Melusyne & of
4 Raymondyn her lord.

he was after-
ward married
to the daughter
of the Earl of
March.

Thistorye sayth & certifyeth that whan the lady
had ended the terme of her childbed, and that
she was releuyd / the feste was made grete / and many
8 noble men, ladyes, and damoyselles were there, the
whiche, after the feest full honourably toke their leue
& departed.   And that same tyme the lady Melusyne
bylded bothe the Castel & toune of Melle.   Also she
12 dide doo make Vouant & Mernant.[1] and after she
made the bourgh & toure of saynt Maxence, and bygan
the Abbey there. and moche good she dide to poure
folk.

Melusine gives a
feast.

builds the castles
and towns of
Melle and Max-
ence,
and begins the
abbey there.

16 The second yere after folowyng she hadd a sone
that was named guyon, & [he] was a moche fayre
child / but he had an ey higher than that other.   And
wete it that Melusyne had euer so good nouryces, and
20 had so grete care for her children that they mendid
& grewe so wel that euery one that saw them meruaylled.   [2] And that tyme Melusyne bigged & fownd
many a fayre place thrughe the lande of Poytou unto
24 the duchie of Guyenne.   She bilded the Castel and þe
burgh of Partenay so strong and so fayre without
comparyson. after that she dide doo make þe Toures of
Rochelle & the Castel also, & bygan a part of the
28 toune, and thre leghes thens was a grete toure & bigge,
whiche Julius Cesar dide doo make, and men called it
the Egles toure, bycause that Julius Cesar bare an Egle
in hys banere as emperour.   That toure made the lady
32 to be walled & fortyfyed round aboute with grete
toures machecolyd, and made it to be called the Castel
Eglon.   And afterward she edefyed Pons in Poytou
and fortyfyed Xaintes[3] that was called at that tyme

Melusine has
her third son
Guyon, who has
one eye higher
than the other;

her children are
so well tended,
that they grow
so that folk
marvel at them.

[2] fol. 60 b.

She builds much
in Poitou: the
castle and town
of Parthenay,

and of Rochelle.

She fortifies the
Eagle's Tower,
said to have been
built by Julius
Cæsar.

She builds Pons,
fortifies Saintes,

---

[1] Fr. *Waviront et Mermant.*   [3] *Saintes.*

Lynges / and after she made Tallemounte and '
mondois and many other tounes & fortres.   And
& acquyred so moche Raymondin thrugh the po
& good gouernaunce of Melusyne, what in Bret
what in Gascoynne & in Guyenne as in Poytou
no prynce was about hym / but he doubted to dys
hym.

Soone after Melusyne was delyuered of her fo
man child, whiche hight Anthony, none i
was seen before that tyme.   but in his birth he br
a token along his chyk, that was the foot of a
wherof they that sawe hym wondred, & moche
abasshed.

Here saith thistorye, that the vij^th yere after I
syne bare the fyfte child, of whiche at th
of ix monethes she was delyuered, & was named
nald.   none fayrer child might men see, but he
borne only ¹with one eye / but it was so brigl
so clere that he sawe the ship thre kennynges ferr
the sea, that is, one & twenty leghes ferre / and I
wyse on erthe, whatsoeuer it was.   That same Antl
was full gracyous & curteys, as ye shal here in thys
herafter.

Ferthermore saith thistory, that the eight
Melusyne childed the vi. child, that was a s
and had to name Geffray, Whiche at his birth bro
in hys mouthe a grete & long toth, that apy
without an ench long & more / and therfore
added to his propre name Geffray with the g
toth.   and he was moch grete & hye, and wel for
& strong, merueyllously hardy & cruel, In so m
that euery man fered & dradde hym whan he wa
age / he made in his tyme many wonders & meruey
as heraftir ye shal here in thystorye.

Thystorye sayth that the ix^th yere after Melus
had a sone, that was the vij^th, & hight F

mond, that was fayre ynoughe, but he had on hys nose[1] a top of heeris, and in his tyme he was moche denonte. and afterward, by thassent of bothe hys

4 fader & moder, he was made monke in the abbey of Maylleses, of whom ye shall here herafter thystorye.

In this part sayth to vs thistorye that Melusyne was two yere without birth of child, but true it is that

8 in the xj[th] yere she had her[2] x[th] sone, and was grete merueyllously / and he brought at hys birth thre eyen, one of the whicñ was in the mydel of his forhed, he was so euyl & so [3]cruel that at the foureth yero of

12 his age he slew two of hys nourryces.

THe veray hystory saith that so long norysshed Melusyne her children, that Vryan, whiche was theldest & first born, was xviij yere old. he was grete

16 and fayre, & wonderly strong, and made grete appertyse in armes, so that euery man & woman had pyte of hys dyfformytee; for his vysage was short & large, hys one eye was red & the other blew, and hys eerys were as

20 grete as the handlynges of a Fan. and Edon his brother was of xvij yere of age. and Guyon had of yeres xvj, and loued Eche other wel Vryan & Guyon / and so pert & swyft they were, that alle thoo that sawe

24 them gaf hemself grete wonder & meruayñ. they were beloued of all the nobles of the land, & made many faytes & appertyses of armes in Joustes, tournoyeng, & in Lystes.

28　　It happed that same tyme that two knyghtes of Poytou came fro Jherusalem agayn / and recounted there as they passed, how the sawdan of Damask had besieged the king of Cypre in hys Cite of Famagoce, &

32 that he held hym therin in grete dystres. and þat same kyng ne had to hys heyre but only a doughter, whiche was moche fayre. and these tydinges were

Side notes:
tuft of hair on his nose,

and became a monk in the abbey of Mailleses.

Her tenth son Horrible had three eyes, one in the middle of his forehead,

[2] fol. 61 b.
and was very cruel.

Melusine's eldest-born Urian is now eighteen, and is fair and strong,

though his face is strange, and his ears large.

Edon is seventeen,
Guyon is sixteen;
Urian and Guyon love one another much.

Two Poitevin knights return from Jerusalem,

and tell of the Sultan of Damascus besieging the King of Cyprus; and in what distress the king is, and how his heir is a daughter.

[1] Fr. une petite tache vellue.
[2] Fr. hvitiesme, and so in Harleian MS. 418.

Urian hearing
the tale, speaks
to Guyon,

¹ fol. 62.

and proposes to
him to do some
deeds of arms.

The knights
from Jerusalem
are sent for,

and are ques-
tioned about
where they have
been.

Urian expresses
his surprise that
they did not stay
and help the
Christian king.

They explain
that it was im-
possible to enter
the town,
as it was be-
sieged by
eighty thousand
pagans.

ferfourth brought in the land, that Vryan knew of it
and he thenne said to his brother Guyon: 'By my
feith, fayre brother, it were grete almese to socoure that
kyng ayenst the Paynemys. We ben al redy eyght
bretherne. the land of our fader may not remayne
without heyre, though we were bothe deed. Wherfore
we owe the more to enterprise ¹vyages, and see wher
we may doo some faytes of armes, to be therwith en-
haunced in worship & honour.' 'By my fayth,' said
Guyon, 'ye said trouth. but what cause you to say
soo, seeyng that euer I am redy to doo as ye wyl doo?'
'Southly,' said Vryan, 'ye say full wel. Lete we send
for the two knightes that be come fro the holy vyage,
to be ensured of them more playnly of the trouth.'
they sent to the two knightes that they wold come &
spek with them, the which gladly dyde so. And
whan they were come, the two brethern welcommed
& receyued them goodly. and aftir they bygan
tenquyre of them the manere of theire vyage / of the
vse & maneres of the land where they had be. and
they said to them the playn trouth. 'We vnderstand,'
said Vryan, 'that ye haue passed thrugh an yle wher a
king cristen regneth, which is oppressid ouermoch of
the paynemys / & wonder is vs that ye abode nat in
the werre with that Cristen kyng, for to help &
comforte hym, ye that are so renoumed, Worthy and
valyaunt knightes, consyderyng as it semeth to vs that
alle good cristens are hold & bound to helpe eche
other specyally ayenst the paynemys.' To this ansuered
the two knightes: 'By my feith, gentil squyer & lord,
wel we wyl that ye knowe that yf by eny manere we
myght haue entred the toune without deth, & saf,
gladly we had doo so as ye say. but wel ye wote that
two knyghtes may not susteyne & bere the weight
ayenst wel Lxxx. or houndred thousand paynemys,
that thenne had besieged the toune wherin the said

king was. For ye oweth to wete that [1]wel fole is he
that fighteth ayenst the wynd, wenyng to make hym
be styll.' 'By my feyth,' said Vryan, 'your excusac*i*on

4 is good & iuste. but tell me yf men myghty to reyse
& lede wit*h* them a xxij^{ti} or xxv^{ti} thousand men of
armes, myght doo eny faytte there to help & socoure
the sayd kyng?' Thenne ansuerd one of the knight*es*:

8 'By my feyth, sire, ye / seen & considered that the
Cite is strong, and the kyng wit*h*in valiaunt, hardy &
worthy fighter of his personne / and he is acompanyed
with many good men of armes, & the toun wel

12 vytaylled / and yet ther be many Fortresses where they
of Rodes come to refresshe themself, of the whiche
the kyng & they in the Cite haue grete recomforte /
and wete it that moche easely & wel they might goo

16 thider / and wold to god suche a felawship as ye spek
of wer redy, and that my felawe & I shuld take
thadue*n*ture wit*h* them.' 'By my feyth,' said thenne
Vryan, 'my brother & I shall receyue you, & lede you

20 thither, god before, and that shortly.' And whan they
vnderstode hym say soo, they were moche glad, sayeng
that yf they soo dyde, hit moued them of valyaunt
courage & grete noblesse of herte. Here resteth thistorye

24 of these two knight*es*, and yet ferther speketh of Vryan
& Guyon.

Cap. XX. How Vryan & Guyon toke leue
of bothe theyre fader & moder, and of the
28 help that they had of þem.

[2]In this partye sayth thistorye that Vrya*n* and his
brother Guyon cam to Melusyne theire moder,
and to her said Vryan in this manere: 'Madame, yf

32 ye vouchesaaf, it were wel tyme that we shuld go
fourth to our vyage, for to knowe the Countrees ferre
& straunge, Wherby we may acquyre honour & good

Sidenotes:

[1] fol. 62 b.

Urian asks if a force of twenty-five thousand men would be any use to succour the town?

the knights think so.

Urian promises to lead them there,

for which the knights thank him.

[2] fol. 63.

Urian and Guyon ask Melusine to let them go abroad to seek their fortunes,

renommee in straunge marches, to thend that we lerne
& vnderstand the dyuerse langages of the world. Also
yf Fortune and good auenture wyl be propyce &
conuenable to vs, we haue wel the wyll & courage to 4
subdue & conquere Countrees & land*es* ; For we considere & see that alredy we be eyghte bretheren / and
are lyke, yf god wyl, to be yet as many moo in tyme
com*m*yng. and to say that your land*es* & possessions 8
were parted in so many partes for our sustenaunce &
gouer*n*ement / he that shuld enheryte the chyef lyflod
shuld not be able to kepe no grete houshold, ne to be
of grete estate, to the [1]Regard of the high blood & 12
grete noblesse that we com*e* of / also consideryng as
now your grete estate. Wherfore as to my brother & I
my self, we quytte o*u*r parte / except alonely your
good grace, thrugh thayde that ye now shall doo to vs 16
for our vyage, yf god wyl gyue vs grac*e* to acomplysshe.'
' By my feyth, children,' said thenne Melusyne, ' your
requeste is caused of grete worthynes and courageous
herte, and therfore it oweth not to be refused ne gayn- 20
sayd. and vpon this matere I shall entreate your
faders, For w*ith*out hys counseyll I owe not to accorde
your requeste.' Thanne fourthw*ith* came Melusyne to
Raymondin / and shewed hym the requeste & wyll 24
of theire two sones; the whiche ansuerd & sayd, ' By
my feyth, madame, yf it lyke you good they doo soo, I
assent gladly therto.' ' Sire,' said Melusyne, ' ye say
wel; and wete it that they shal do no*þ*ing in theire 28
vyage but that it shall tourne to theire grete lawde
& hono*u*r, yf god wyl.' Then came ayen Melusyne to
her two sones, and thus she said to them : ' Fayre
children, thinke from hensfourthon to doo wel; For 32
your fader hath graunted youre requeste, & so doo I.
and care you not for no *þ*ing, For w*ith*in short tyme
I shall ordeyne & purveye for your faytte w*ith* goddis
grace & help / in such wise that ye shall konne me 36

Margin notes:

because there are eight sons, and

if the lands are divided, the estates would not be great.

[1] fol. 63 b.

Melusine promises to ask their father's permission,

who assents gladly.

Melusine tells them that their father has granted their request, and so has she ;

and promises to provide an outfit for them.

good gree & thanke therfore. but telle me whether &
to what part of the world ye wyl & purpose to goo, to
thende I purvey of suche thinges that shalbe necessary
4 to you therfore.' Thanne ansuerd Vryan : 'Madame,
wel it is true & certayn that we haue herd certayn
tydynges that the kyng of Cypre is besiged [1] by the
Sawdan within hys Cyte of Famagoce / and thither, yf
8 it playse god, we entende & purpose to go for to ayde
& socoure hym ayenst the fals & mysbyleuers paynemys.' Thanne gan say Melusyne, 'herto muste be
purueyed / As wel for the see as for the land ; and
12 with goddis grace, my dere children, I shall ordeyne
therof in suche manere that ye shal be remembred of
me : and this shal I doo shortly.' The two bretheren
thenne kneled doun byfore theyre moder / and thanked
16 her moche humbly of her purveyaunce & good wylle.
And the lady toke hem vp, and sore wepyng she
kyssed them bothe, For grete sorowe she had in her
herte / though she made withoutfourth chere of theire
20 departyng. For she loued them with moderly loue, as
she that had nourysshed them.

Thystorye sayth that Melusyne was full curyous
and besy to make al thinges redy þat were
24 necessary to her sones for theire vyage. She made
Galeyes, Carrykes, and other grete shippes to be
vytaylled & redy to sayll / and þe nauye was so grete
in nombre that it was suffysaunt for foure score thou-
28 sand men of armes to sayll in. And in the meane
while the two bretheren sent for the two forsaid
knightes, & said to them that they shuld be redy to
meve fourth shortly, as they had promysed to them.
32 And they ansuered : 'Lordes, we be all redy. and
many gentylmen that we knowe ben shapen & redy to
go with you in your felawship, and we alle be desyrous
to serue you and to doo your playsir.' 'By my feyth,'
36 said Vryan, 'right grete gramercy to you. We shall

[1] fol. 64.

They tell their
mother they
intend succour-
ing the King of
Cyprus,

so she promises
to provide what
is necessary for
sea and land.

They thank her ;

and she, weeping,
kisses them both,

for she loves
them with
motherly love.

Melusine pre-
pares galleys,
carracks, and
other ships, and
victuals them,

enough for
eighty thousand
men of arms.

The Jerusalem
knights are sent
for,

and tell the
brothers they are
ready to go with
them.

¹ fol. 64 b.

The armament ready, Melusine appoints four barons to look after her two sons.

¹lede them wel, yf god wyl and you also.' Now thenne, shortly to saye, Melusyne dyde so moche that al was redy, and had foure Barons to whome she betoke the kepyng & gouernaunce of her two sones, and ¹ had grete foyson of gentylmen knightes & squyer, vnto the nombre of² two thousand Vᶜ men of armes, & fyue houndred archers / and as many men with crossebowes.   And thenne the vytaylles, artylery, harneys & ² horses were charged in to the vessdles, an syn mounted the men into the same.   There were seen baners & standarts / and the sowns of trompes & tambours and of many other instruments was herd, that euery one ⁱⁱ enjoyed that sawe it / And the two brethern toke leue of þeire bretheren and frendes, & of the peple of the land, that moche tenderly wept for theire departyng. And Raymondin & Melusyne conueyed theire children ⁱⁱ vnto the see; and whan they come there Melusyne drew hem apart, and said to them: 'Dere children, vnderstand this that I wil tell you & commande.' /

The men and stores are put on board the fleet;

the banners are waved, trumpets sounded, and every one enjoys the scene.

The brethren bid their friends farewell,

and are accompanied to their ships by their parents.
Melusine draws them apart,

and gives them each a magic ring,

'Children,' sayd Melusyne, 'here be two rynges ⁿ that I gyue you / of whiche the stones ben of one lyke vertue. and wete it that as long that ye shall vse of feythfulnes, without to think eny euyl, ne doo trychery or hynderaunce to other / hauyng alwayes ² the said rynges & stones vpon you, ye shall not be dyscomfyted ne ouercome in no faytte of armes, yf ye haue good quarell. ne also sort or enchauntment of art Magique, ne poysons of whatsomeuer manere shul ³ not lette ne greve you / but that assoone as ye shall see ³them they shall lese theyre strengthe.' and she delyuered to eyther of hem one / and they thanked her moch, kneelyng to therthe. And yet said Melusyne ³ to them in this manere : 'My dere & beloued children, I wol & charge you that wher so euer ye be, ye here the deuyne seruyse or euer ye doo eny oþer werk.

which, whilst they wear it and remain true,

they will never lose in a good quarrel,

nor be hurt by magical arts or poison.

² fol. 65.

The brothers thank their mother,

who advises them always to hear divine service before doing any work;

² Fr. *quatre mille hommes d'armes;* no particulars given. ³

also that in all your affayres & dedes ye clayme & ^{to call on God} calle thayde & help of our Creatour, and serue hym diligently, and loue & dredde hym as your god &

4 your maker. and that allwayes ye honoure & worship with all your power holy chirch, beyng her champyons, the same to susteyne & withstand ayenst alle her euyl wyllers. Help ye & counseylle the pouere wydowes,

8 nouryshe or doo to be noryshed the pouere orphenyns, both faderles and moderles / and worship al ladyes / gyue ayde and comforte vnto alle good maydens that men wol haue dysheryted vnlawfully. loue the gentyl-

12 men, and hold them good companye. / be meke, humble, swete, curtoys & humayne, both vnto grete & lease. and yf ye see a man of armes pouere, & fall in decaye by hap & fortune of juste werre, re-

16 fresshe hym of some of your goodes. be large vnto the good folke / and whan ye gyue eny thing, lett hym not tary long for it; but wel loke & considere how moche & why / and yf the personne is worthy to

20 haue it, and yf ye gyue for playsaunce, loke & kepe wel that prodigalite or folysshe largenes surpryse you not / so that after men mocke not with you. For they that haue wel deserued to be of you rewarded

24 shuld not be wel apayed ne ¹content therof / and the straungers shuld mocke you behinde your backe. and kepe ye promyse, or behighte no thing but that ye may fournysshe & hold it. and yf ye promyse eny

28 thing, tary not the delyueraunce of it, For long taryeng quenchith moch the vertu of the yefte. kepe wel ye rauyshe no woman / ne be coueytous of other mens wyues, of whom ye wil be loued and hold for your

32 frendes. believe not the Counseyll of none / but first ye knowe his manere, deeling & condycyons. also beleue not the counseyll of Flatterers, and enuyous, & auarycyous / ne suche putte not in none office aboute

36 you, For they cause rather to their maister dyshonour

Marginal notes:

- to call on God for help, and to serue and fear Him;
- to honour and sustain holy Church;
- to help widows, orphans, and ladies;
- to frequent the company of gentlemen;
- to be courteous to all;
- to help the unfortunate;
- to be thrifty;
- ¹ fol. 63 b.
- to keep promises;
- to abstain from ill-using women;
- to beware of flatterers and envious persons;

& shame, than ony worship or prouffyt.   kepe wel ye
borow nothing but that ye may yeld it ayen / and yf
for nede ye be constrayned for to borow / as soone as ye

to pay loans;   may / make restitucion of it / And þus ye shal mowe
be without danger, & lede honourable lyf.   And yf
god graunte that Fortune be to you good & propyce in

to govern well;   subduyng your enmyes & theire landes, gouerne wel
your folke and peuple after the nature & condycion
that they be of.   and yf they be rebell, kepe wel that

to keep all their privileges intact;   ye surmounte & ouercome hem without to lesse any
suche ryght that longith to your lordship & seignourye /
and that ye euer make good watche vnto tyme ye hem
vaynquysshed at your wylle.   For yf ye ouertradde
your self / nedes ye muste rule your self after theire
wylle.   but alwayes kepe wel, whether they be euyl &

never to inflict unreasonable taxes;   hard, or debonnaire, that ye ne haunce & sette new
customes that be vnraysonnable / and of them take
only your dute and ryght, without to retayll þem

[1] sol. 84.   [1]without and ayenst raison.   For yf the peple is
pouere / the lord shal be vnhappy / and yf werr came
he shuld not mowe be holpe of them att hys nede /
wherfore he might fall into grete daunger & seruytude.
For wete it wel / that a flyes of a yere is more
prouffytable / than the flyes þat is shorne twyes or
thryes in a yere.   now, my children, yet I deffende &

to beware of the advice of exiles;   forbede you that ye byleue not the Counseill of none
exilled and flemed fro his land, in this that may touche
the hynderyng or dommage of them that haue exilled
hym / yf there nys good, right & lawfull cause / and
ye to haue good reason to help hym, For that shuld
mowe lette you to come to the degree of worship &
honour.   And aboue all thinges I forbede you pryde /

to be just;   and commande you to doo & kepe justice, yeldyng
right aswel to the leste as to the moost / and desyre
not to be auenged at vttermost of all the wronges don
to you by some other / but take suffisaunt & raysonn-

able amendes of hym that offreth it. Dyspreyse not
your enmyes though they be litel, but make euer good
watche. and kepe wel as long ye be conqueryng, that
4 atwix your felawes ye mayntene nat yourself as lord
& aire / but be commyn & pryue bothe to more &
lesse / and ye owe to hold them company after the
qualite & vocacyon that they be of, now to one & now
8 to other. For al this causeth the hertes of creatures to
drawe vnto the loue of them that are humayn, meke &
curteys in theire dignite & seignouryes. Haue an
herte as a fyers Lyon ayenst your [1]enemyes / and shew
12 to them your puyssaunce and valyauntyse. and yf god
endoweth you with some goodes, departe som of it to
your felawes after he hath deserued. And as to the
werre, byleue the counseyll of the valyaunt & worthy
16 men that haue haunted & vsed it. Also I defende
you that no grete treatee ye make with your enmyes,
For in long treatee lyeth somtyme grete falshed. For
alwayes wyse men goo abacke for to lepe the ferther ;
20 and whan the sage seeth þat he is not able to resyste
ayenst the strengthe of his enemyes, he seketh &
purchaceth alwayes a treatee, for to dyssymyle vnto
tyme he seeth hymself mighty ynough for them / and
24 thanne anoone of lyght they fynd waye & manere
wherby the treatees ben of none effect ne value.
Wherfore loke ye, forbere not your enemyes there, as
ye may putte them vnder your subgeccion with honour.
28 And thenne yf ye shew them fauour & curtoysye, that
shal tourne to your grete honour / and leue ye to doo
for them by treatee or appoyntement. For though no
falshed or decepcion be founde in none of bothe sydes /
32 yet shuld mow some men say or thinke that ye
somwhat doubted them / how be it, I say not that
men owe to reffuse good traytee, who that may haue
it ' / Thus, as ye here, chastysed & endoctryned Melu-
36 syne her two sones, Vryan & Guyon, whiche thanked

MELUSINE. I

Side notes:

to be watchful
of enemies, no
matter how
small ;

to be on familiar
terms with their
men ;

to have a lion-
heart towards
their enemies ;
[1] fol. 66 b.

to share their
spoils with their
men ;

to make no long
treaties,

for they are
liable to be am-
biguous.

her moche humbly. and thenne she sayd : ' Children,
I haue sent gold & syluer ynoughe in to your ship for
to hold & maynten your estate, and to pay therwith
your men for foure yere. [1] And haue no doubte or 4
care for bred, byscuyte, Freshe watre, vynaigre, Flesh
salted, fyssh ynough, & good wynes suffysaunt to long
tyme, For therof ben your shippes wel fylled & purueyed. goo thanne fourth on your waye, vnder the 8
sauegarde of god / who kepe you / lede & retourne you
agayn with joye. and I pray you that ye thinke &
remembre what I haue sayd to you, to fulfyll it after
your power.' /   13

Cap. XXI. How Uryan & Guyon tooke leue of theire moder Melusyne and entred theire ship. /

Thenne they toke leue of theyre fader and moder 16
and entred theire vessell. This doon, the
ancres were had in, & the saylles haled vp, the
patrons made theire recommendacions to god as cus-
tomed it is, to [2] that by hys benygne grace he wyl 20
graunte to them good ryuage, and accomplysshing of
theyre vyage without lettyng or empeschement. The
wyndes were for them propyce & good / and in short
tyme they were ferre cast on the see so that they were 24
out of sight / ·

Thanne departed Raymondyn & Melusyne, and
theyre meyne with them, and came to the Castel
Eglon. And here resteth thystorye of them, and re- 28
tourneth to spek of Vryan and Guyon hys brother, and
of theyre felawship that saylled on the see, holding
theire way toward Cypre. /

Thystory sayth that whan Uryan and Guyon were 32
departed fro Rochelle they saylled long on the

see, and passed by many yles, & refresshed them in
many places; and so long they rowed þat they sawe till they see
two galeys being
chased,
many vesselles that chased two galeyes / and thenne
4 the Patron shewed them to þe two brethern / and they
ansuered, and demanded of them what was best to doo.
'By my feyth,' sayd the Patron, 'it were good we send
a galeye to wete what folke they be / and in the meane
8 while we shal make our men to take theyre armes &
harneys on them at al auauntures.' 'By my feith,'
said Vryan, 'that I vouchesaf' / and they dide soo.
And thanne the galeye departed abrode, and saylled They send to
see who are in
them.
12 toward the straungers / and escryed þem, & demanded
of them what they were, and they ansuerd, 'We The messengers
find the galleys
to be from
Rhodes,
be two galeyes of Rodes that haue be found of the
paynemys that foloweth & chaceth vs, and we see wel
16 ye be Cristen, and so are all [1]they that come after [1] fol. 68.
you.' 'By my feyth,' sayd they of the galeye, 'we
ben as ye suppose and saye.' 'By my heed,' said one
of the patrons of Rodes galeyes / 'goo & haste your
20 felawship, For ye haue found fayre auenture. yonder and that the
vessels that chase
them are the
Sultan's of De-
mascus, who is
on his way to
Famagosse, to
fight the King
of Cyprus.
be of the sawdans folke that goo to the siege of Famagosse / and who might dystroye them, he shuld doo
grete socoure to the king of Cypre / and to the sawdan
24 of Damaske grete dommage.' Whan thenne they of
the galeye herd this / they sodaynly retourned &
announced it to the two bretheren / and to theire folke On hearing this
news, Urian and
Guion prepare
their ships to
fight,
whiche anon yede vp to the Castels of theire shippes,
28 and clymed vp to the toppes of them, hauyng speere &
darts, stones, & wild fyre alredy / also bowes & arowes
in theire handes / gonnes & pouldre to shote with.
There bygan tompes to blowe vp, & rowed mightily and row towards
the paynim
Sultan.
32 toward the paynemys. And whan the Infideles &
paynemys perceyued so grete nombre of shippes rowyng
toward them they ne wyst not what to thinke, For The Infidels,
surprised at the
numbers of the
Christians,
they had neuer supposed that so grete puyssaunce &
36 strengthe of cristen men had be so nygh them / · but

alwayes they putte hem self in aray gooyng abacke,
but oure galeyes aduyronned them round about on al

sydes, and bygan of al partes to shutte theire gonnes.
And whan the paynemys sawe this / and that they 4
myght not flee, they toke a vessel whiche they had
take fro them of rodes, and had cast the folke that was

upon which the
paynims try to
send a fire-ship
amongst them,

in it into the see / and fylled it with wode, oyle, &
talowe, and with sulphre & brymstone. and whan they 8
sawe our folk approched nygh them they sette it

afyre. and whan the fyre was wel kyndled [1] they lefte
it behynd them to mete first with our folke / but as

god wold they were warned therof & kept / themself 12
wel therfro / and assaylled theires enmyes at the other
syde right vygourously. There was grete shotyng of

crosbowes & gonnes / and soone after our folk entred
byforce and strengthe of armes the shippes of the 16

paynemys / and fynally they were take & dysconfyted,
and putte to deth. and our folke gate there grete good
whiche the two brethern departed, and gaf to theire
felawes and to them that wer within the two galeyes of 20

They row to
Rhodes, where
they refresh
themselves,
and give the
captured ships
to the Rhodians.

Rodes / and syn rowed & saylled both so long that
they arryued in the yle of Rodes. And there they
refresshed them, & gaf to the brethern of the religyon
the fustes & galeyes that they had taken vpon the 24
paynemys, and they soiurned there foure dayes. And

the maister of Rodes prayd them that they wold come
into the Cite / and they dide soo / and were there

honourably receyued / and the said maister demanded 28
them of the cause of their commyng. And the two
brethern told hym that they were come forto socoure

the king of Cypre / And he asked them full humbly of
what land they were, and what they were / and the 32

They answer,
and ask the
Master of Rhodes
to help them to
assist the King
of Cyprus.

two brethern told to hym all the trouth. Thenns made
the maister to them greter chere than tofore / and said
to them that he shuld send for som of his bretheren / &
that he shuld goo with hem to helpe & socoure the 36

king of Chipre. And the two bretheren thanked hym
moche humbly therefore. /

4 Now sayth thystorye that so long abode, & soiourned the two brethern at Rodes tyl the
maister had assembled his folke, and vytaylled & laden
with good [1]men of armes, & archers six galeys, &
saylled with Uryan & Guyon so long that they arryued
8 nygh to the yle of Coles, & apperceyued grete lyght.
Thenne the grete maister of Rodes that was in Uryan's
galeye, said to the two bretheren : ' Sires, in good feyth
it were good & wel doon to send a Caruell vnto yonder
12 yle, to knowe & aspye what folke is there.' ' I vouchsaf it,' said Vryan. The Rampyn then, or Caruell,
saylled thither, & arryued in to the said yle, & some
of þem descended & founde many grete fyres & lodgis,
16 and by thexperience that they sawe, they extimed them
þat had lodged there to the nombre of xxx thousand
men / and that they myght wel haue dwelled þer foure
or fyue dayes. For they found without the lodgys grete
20 foyson of oxen hornes & of other bestes. And then
they came ayen in to theire Vessell, and retourned
toward our folke / & recounted to them the trouth of
all that they had found. ' By my feith,' said thenne
24 the maister of Rodes, ' I wene they be paynemys that
are goyng toward the sawdan at the siege, and that
they whiche ye haue dyscomfyted were of theire felawship, & abode for them in that same yle' / and for
28 certayn they were soo / and of them they sayled &
rowed fourth tyl they sawe an abbey on the see coste,
where men sought & worshiped saynt Andrew / and
men saith that there is the potence or cros wheron the
32 good thef Dysmas was crucefyed whan our lord was
nayled to the Cros for our redempcion. ' Sire,' said
the maister, ' it were good that we should entre that
lytil hauen Vnto tyme that we had sent to Lymasson
36 for to knowe tydinges, & for to wete yf they wyl

The Master of
Rhodes arms six
galleys,

[1] fol. 62.

and sails with
the brethren to
Coles, where
they see lights.

Men are sent in
a carvell to spy,

and discover a
camp of thirty
thousand strong.

They return with
their news,

The Master of
Rhodes believes
it to be a camp
of paynims,
friends of those
just defeated in
the sea-fight.

The company
continues their
voyage till they
come to an
abbey on the
coast.

: fol. 69 b.

receyue vs for to putte our nauye in ¹surete within
theyre clos.' 'Maister,' said Uryan, 'let it be doon in

They put into the
harbour,
and send a
message to the
Abbot,

the name of god after your playsire.' Thenne they
arryued, and entred the port or hauen / and sent 4
wordes to thabbot ther, that they shuld not doubte, For
they were theire frendes. And the maister of Rodes
with other went thider. And whan thabbot & monkes
knew the tydinges and the commyng of the two 8

who is glad to
hear of their
arrival.

brethern, they were joyous & glad, & sent some of
theire bretheren to Lymas to announce & telle þe socours
that was arryued at theire porte. Thenne whan a
knyght, Captayn of the place, herde these tydinges he 12

The Captain of
the place rows
to our folk,

was fayn & glad, and made fourthwith a galyotte to
be shipped redy, and came toward our folke, and
demanded after the lord of that armee /. and he to

sees Urian,
Guion, and the
Master of
Rhodes,

whome he asked it lede hym where Uryan / Guyon 16
his brother / the master of Rodes, & many other barons
were in a ryche pauyllon, that they had don to be
dressed on the streyte of the porte / and shewed to
hym Vryan that satte on a couche with hym his 20
brother, and the maister of Rodes. And whan he saw

and is abashed at
Urian's appear-
ance.

hym he was abasshed of the valeur & of the grete fyerste
of hym, & neuerþeles he yede & salued hym honourably, and Vryan receyued him goodly & benyngly. 24
'Sire,' said the Knight, 'ye be welcome in to this
land.' 'Fayre sirs,' said Vryan, 'moche grete thankes
to you.' 'Sire,' said the knight, 'it is don me to
vnderstand that ye departed fro your Countrie to 28
thentent to come ayde & help the king of Cypre.'

Being assured
that Urian has
come to help the
King of Cyprus,
he promises to
open the country
to him, and

'By my feyth,' said Uryan, 'it is trouth.' 'Then, sire,'
said the knight, 'it is reson that al be open byfore you,
where ye wyl by all the royalme of Cypre, thrugh all 32
tounnes, Cites, & Castels there as ye shal be please to
goo, but as to the same, which is to my ryght redoubted
lord the king of cypre, hit shal be soone appareylled &

give his vessels
anchorage.

open to you, whan it shall lyke you, & also the porte 36

to putte your vessels [1]in sauete.' 'By my feyth,' said   [1] fol. 70.
Uryan, 'ye say right wel, & gramercy to you. Sire
knight, it is tyme to meve, For my brother and I haue
4 grete langyng to approche nygh the paynemys / not for
theire prouffyt, but for theire dommage, if it plaise god
that we so doo.' 'Sire,' said the knight, 'it is good
ye doo to be had out some of your horses as many
8 as it lyke you / and take som of your men with you,
and we shall goo by land.' 'By my feith,' sayd Uryan,
'ye say right wel' / and thus it was doon / and Uryan
made some of hys men to be armed, vnto the nombre   Four hundred
                                                    of Urian's barons
12 of foure hundred gentylmen of the moost hye barons, go ashore, armed
                                                    and horsed,
knightes & squyers. and he himself, & his brother
armed them and mounted on horsbak / and the banere
dysployed, rode fourth in moch fayre ordynaunce / and
16 the maister of Rodes & the other shipped them on the
see & rowed toward the porte. And Vryan and his
felawship rode with the said knight that guyded hym   and ride to the
                                                      town;
so long that they came & entred in to the toune, and
20 were right well lodged. And then came the nauye,   the ships mean-
                                                       while row to the
& arryued to the porte, and the horses were all had out harbour, and the
                                                       horses and men
of the shippes, and the folke descendid to land, and   land.
lodged them in þe feld without the toune within
24 tentes & pauyllons / and they that had none, made
theire lodgis the best wyse they coude. and was moche
grete playsaunce to see thoost whan they were alle
lodged. The moost hye barons lodgyd them within
28 the toune / and the nauye was draw, & had in to the
clos in sauete / and they committed good folke to   Guards are set
                                                    to defende the
deffende & kepe it, yf Sarasyns or paynemys came   navy against the
                                                    Saracens.
thero for to doo som euyl. Now shal I leue to speke
32 of Uryan, & shal say of the Captayn of the toune
that moche wel aduysed thoost and the maynten of the
folke, & moche preysed it in his herte / and said wel
they were folke of faytte [2]and of grete enterpryse, whan   [2] fol. 70 b.
36 so few peuple enterprysed for to haue the vyctory ouer

the sawdan, that had with hym more than houndred
thousand paynemys. And for to say trouth, Vryan
had not yet comprised the men of the maister of Rodes,
eyghte thousand fyghtyng men / and therfore the 4
knight mervaylled, and held it to grete audacite &
hardynes of herte, and to grete valyaunce. And whan
he considered the grandeur & the facion of Vryan, &
the fyerste of hys vysage, and also of guyon hys 8
brother / he said to his folke / 'thoo same are worthy
for to subdue & conquere all the world.' and he said
to hymself, þat god had sent hem thither of his benyng
grace for to socoure the kyng, and for to enhaunce the 13
cristen feyth, and that he shuld lete it to be knowen to
the kynge by certayn message.

Thystorye sayth that the knight made a lettre, the
tenour of whiche conteyned al the matere of 16
Uryan, & of his brother, of theire men, & of theire
commyng, and how the two bretheren had to name,
and of what countre they were / and syn he called one
hys nevew, & said to hym in this manere, 'ye muste 20
bere this lettre to Famagosse, and gyue it to the kyng' /
and whatsoeuer it happeth that god forbede, but al
good to you, nedes ye muste doo it.' 'By my feyth,
sire,' said he / 'ye shall putte bothe the lettres & 24
myself in grete jeopardye & auenture, For if by some
myschief, as it happeth ofte, wherof god preserue me I
were taken of our enmyes, of my lyf is nothing / and
ye wote it wel / but for the loue of you, myn vncle & 28
of the kyng, to doo hym comfort, & to gyue hym herte
& hoop to be putte & delyuered fro hys enemyes, & fro
the mortal parel wherin he is now, I shall putte myself
in aduenture / and I pray [1]to god deuoutly, that it 32
please hym of his benigne grace to lede me gooyng &
commyng in sauete.' / 'Thus owe men to serue theire
lord,' said the Captayne, 'and yf god wyl ye shalbe wel
rewarded therof.' and anoone he toke the lettre, & 36

[1] Add. 71.

delyue*r*ed it to his nevew / þat mounted on horshacke,
& rode fourthon his way.   But as for now I shall reste
of hym / and I shal retourne there I lefte to spek of
4 Vryan / and shal say howe he gouerned hymself whiles
the messager yede toward the king*. how wel he knew
nat of it. /

Thystory saith that Vryan called to hym the maister
8   of Rodes and the Captayn of the place, and demanded of them thus : 'Fayre lorde*s*, is the sawdan
somewhat yong, ne of grete enterpryse' / and they ansuerd, 'that ye for certayn' / 'and how,' said Vryan,
12 'was he neu*er* byfore this place to make warre than
now?' / they ansuerd that, 'nay' / 'and what thenne,'
said Vryan, 'hath caused hym to passe the see now?
sith he is man of enterpryse, I m*er*vey#t that so long
16 he held hym styl, seeyng ye be his nigh neygbours,
and also that he hath so grete puissaunce, as it is told
me.' 'By my feyth, sire,' said the Captayne, 'it is
veray & trouth that *our* kyng hath a moch fayr dough-
20 ter of the age of .xv. yere, the which the saudan wold
haue had by force / and *our* kyng wold not acorde her
to hym w*ith*out he wold be baptysed. And wete it
that eu*er* here tofore we had trewes togidre of so long
24 tyme that no mynde is of þe contrarye.   and whan the
sawdan hath seen that *our* king wold not graunt to
hym his doughter, he sent ageyn to hym the trewes
with a deffyaunce or chalengyng, and was re*d*y on the
28 see with a .C. & fyfty thousand paynemys, and came &
made soone his harneys to be had out on erthe, & wente
and layd siege tofore Famagoce, where he found ¹ the
kyng all vnpurveyed of his baronye, that knew not of
32 his commyng / but syn there be entred moche folke
w*ith*in the Cite ayenst his euyl gree, & there is now
fayre scarmysshing where grete losse hath be on both
partes / and syn the paynemyes haue refresshed them-
36 self twyes of new folke, in so moch that they ben yet

The Saracens are a hundred thousand strong; but they had some vessels,

wel a .C{th} / but at this last vyage they haue lost a
parte of theire shippes & of theire folke, which they
abode fore in the yle of Coles, For one of our galleyes
of the blakke hylle that pursuewed them told it to vs, 4
& how they chaced two galleyes of the hospytal of

as was learnt from one of our ships, who saw them pass, chasing two Rhodian galleys,

Rodes / and wete it that þey ne wote not where they
bycame syn, For they taryed after wel by the space
of six dayes in the said yle / but whan they sawe that 8
they came not, they departed thens & came byfore

but saw no more of them.

famagoce at siege.' 'By my feyth, sire,' sayd the
maister of Rodes, 'this might wel be veray trouth. but

The Master of Rhodes tells the Captain of Urian's victory, which explains their non-appearance.

see here my lord Vryan and hys brother, that shuld 12
wel ansuere therof, For they haue be all dyscomfyted
& slayn by theire strengthe & valiauntis, and they haue
gyuen to vs theire fustes & their nauye.' 'In good
feyth,' sayd the knight, 'that playseth me wel, and 16
blessid be god therof.' 'My lord,' said the Captayn,
'now haue I recounted to you why the werre is meued,
and wherefore the sawdan of Damaske hath passed the

Urian, learning that love has made the Sultan fight,

see.' 'In the name of god,' said Vryan, 'loue hath 20
wel so moche & more of puyssaunce than of suche
enterpryse to doo. And wete that syn the sawdan is

says that he is the more to be feared, because love is so powerful that it makes even cowards brave,

enterprysed of force of loue, the more he is to be
doubted / For veray soth it is / that loue hath so moche 24
of myght that it maketh coward to be hardy and to
doo right grete enterpryse / & that byfore he durst not
passe. And therfore thenne it is all certayn to this,
that the sawdan is hardy & enterprenaunt [1]the more 28

[1] fol. 72.

he doth hym to be doubted / but alwayes be doo the
wylle of god. For we shall departe hens to the playsire

and states that next day, after divine service, he will set out in quest of him.

of god to morow by tymes after the deuyne seruyce
for to goo & vysyte them.' And then he made to be 32
cryed & proclamed with the trompette that euery man
shuld make redy hys harneys. and they departed after

At the third sound of the trumpets they march.

the thirde sowne of the trompette in goodly & fayre
ordynaunce, eucrone vnder his banere / and bade them 36

to siew the vanward / and so they dide.   here I shall
leue to spek of them / and shall retourne there as I
lefte to speke of the Captayns nevew that moche
4 strongly rode toward Famagoce / and so moche exployted his way that he came about midnyght to the
Cornere of the wode, vpon a lytil mountayn, & loked
doun into the valeye, and then he bygan to perceyue
8 & see the oost of the paynemys, where as was grete
lyght of fyres that were made by the lodgys; and he
sawe the Cite so aduyronned al about with paynemys,
that he ne wyst which way to draw for to entre the
12 toun. and there he was long tyme in grete þoughte.
It happed that about the spryng of the day foure score
basynets, straungers of dyuerse nacyons, yssued out at
a posterne of the Cyte, & commevyd al thoost by
16 manere of batayll / and that same ooure the watche
departed, & the moost part of them was retourned to
theyre lodgis / and they entred in the oost with some
of them that had watched without they were ware of
20 hem, & supposed they had be of theire companye, and
came nygh to the tente of the sawdan / and thenne
they bygan to launche & smyte with speeres & with
swerdes on al the paynemys that they mete & re-
24 countred / and cutted cordes of pauyllons to grete
desray, & made moche horryble occysyon & slaghtir
of paynemys after the quantite ¹that they were of.
Thenne was al the host afrayd, and bygan to crye alarme
28 & to harneys / then bygan thoost to take on them theire
armures.   And whan the cristen men sawe the force &
strengthe of theire enemyes that bygan to ryse, they
retourned with a lytel paas toward the Cite, fleeyng &
32 castyng to therthe al that they recountred on theire
waye.   And whan the messanger sawe so grete affraye
& noyse he cam at al auenture & broched hys hors
with the spoorys, and passed without fourth the lodges
36 thrugh out all the oost of þe paynemys / and he had

¹ fol. 72 b.

The Captain's nephew, that carried the letter to the king,

arrived at the city of Fama-gosse, sees it surrounded with paynims, and does not know how to enter it.

At the spring of day, eighty basinets leave the city,

and when the paynims' watch-men are in their tents,

the basinets fall upon the paynims, cut their tent ropes, and slay many of them.

But on the host of the Saracens arming,

they run back towards the city

The messenger seeing the ad-venture, spurs his horse, rides to the basinets,

not goo long when he found hymself atwix the Cite &
them that so had commoeuyd thoost, as said is. And
then he knew them soone ynough that they were of the
garnyson of the Cyte, and escryed them, saying : 'ha,
ha, fayre lordes, thinke to doo wel, For I bryng you
good tydynges ; For the floure of the noble cheualry
of Crystyante cometh to socoure & helpe you / that is
to wete the two damoyseaulx of Lusynen, that haue
dyscomfyted alredy a grete part of the Sodanis folk
vpon the see / and they bryng with them wel eyght
thousand men. And thenne whan they understode
hym they made hym grete chere and were ryght joyfull,
and entred the toune ayen without eny losse. wherof
the sawdan was moch wofull & angry. And then he
came & bygan the scarmoushe before the barers &
many paynemys were there slayn & dede / and they
of Cypre made theire enemyes to recule abacke with
strengthe / and the saudan made the trompetts to
sowne & call the retrette whan he sawe that he myght
doo none other thing. And þen came the said mes-
saunger byfore the kynge, & made the reuerence on
hys vnclis byhalue, and presented the *lettre.* And the
kyng receyued hym moche benyngly, & tok away the
wax and opend the *lettre* & sawe the tenour [1]of hit. /
and syn heued vp his handes joyntly toward heuen, &
said : 'ha, a veray gloryous god, Jhesu Criste, I þank
regracye & mercye the ryght deuoutly & humbly of
this, that thou hast not forgoten me that am thy pouere
creature and thy pouere *seruaunt,* that haue long tyme
lyued here within this Cite in grete doubte & feere, and
in grete myserye of my poure lyuyng and my folke also.'
And thenne he made to be announced in al the chirches,
that they shuld ryng theire belles, & that processyons
shuld be made with crosses & baners, and with torches
brennyng, lawdyng & preysyng the creator of creatures,
prayeng hym moche humbly that he of his mercyfull &

benynge grace wyl kepe & preserue them fro the hand*es* and God thanked and prayed to for help.
& daunger of mysbyleuers paynmys.   And thanne by-
gan the ryngyng to be grete, & was the joye ryght
4 grete whau the tydyng*es* of the socours commyng to
them was knowen of aH.   And whan the paynemys
vnderstode the gladnes & joye that they of the cyte
made, they were moche abasshed why they made & The paynims are abasshed at the rejoicings of the Christians.
8 demened so grete feeste.   'By my feyth,' sayd the
saudan, 'they have herd some tyding*es* that we wote
not / or ellis they doo so for to gyue vs vnderstandyng
that they haue folke ynoughe & vytaylles also for to
12 deffende & withstande ayenst vs.'   And here resteth
thystorye of the soudan & bygynneth to speke of
Ermyne the kingis doughtir of Cypre, which herd The King of Cyprus's daughter, Er-mine,
there as she was in her cha*m*bre the tydyng*es* of the
16 socours that the children of Lusynen brought wit*h*
them.   and the mayde had grete langyng & desyre to
knowe the veray trouth of aH.

T he hystorye saith to vs thus / that whan the
20 damoyselle knew of the socours & help that soone
she sent for hym that had brought the tyding*es* [1] therof, [1] fol. 73 b.
and he cam*e* to her in hir chambre & made to her on hearing of the help, sends for the messenger, and questions him.
the reu*e*rence.   'Frend,' said Ermyne, 'ye be wel-
24 come to me; but now teH me of your tyding*es*.'   and
he recounted to her al that was of it.   'Frende,' said
the mayde, 'have ye seen that folke that co*m*meth to
socoure my fader?'   'By my feyth, ye,' said the mes- The messenger tells of the men who have come to succour the king:
28 sanger, 'they are the moost appert in armes, and the
fayrest men that eu*er* entred in to this land, and the
best arayed & purueyed of aH thing*es*.'   'Now teH us,'
said the damoyselle, 'of what land they are, & who is
32 the chief Captayn & lord of them.'   'By my feyth, my
damoyselle, they be of Poytou, and lede them two
yong & fayre damoyseaulx brethren, that be named of of the captains of them, Urian and Guion,
Lusynen, of whiche theldest is called Vryan, & that
36 youngest Guyon, which have not yet berde fuH growen.'

'Frende,' said the damoyselle, 'be they so fayre damoy-
seaux as ye say?' 'By my feyth,' said the messager /
'the eldest is moche grete & hye, strong & of fayre
behauyng & maynten, but hys vysage is short & large 4
in trauerse / and hath one eye redde, & that other ey is
perske & blew, and the eerys grete to merueyll. and
wete it wel that of membres & of body he is the fayrest
knight that euer I sawe / and the yongest is not of so 8
hye stature / but he is moche fayre & wel shapen of
membres, & hath a face to deuyse, except that one of
his eyen is hyer sette than the other is. and seye alle
that see them, that they be worthy & noble to conquere 12
& subdue vnder them all the world.' 'Frende,' sayd
Ermyne, 'shall ye goo agayn soone toward them.' And
he ansuerd, 'my damoyselle, assoone as I may haue tyme
& place conuenable & propyce for to yssue & go out of 16
the Cite, and that I see I may goodly escape fro the
paynemys.' 'Frend,' said the damoyselle, 'ye shal on
my behalue salue the yong brethern, and ye shall delyuere to the eldest this ouch, [1]and telle hym bere it 20
for the loue of me / and this ryng of gold with this
dyamond ye shal take to þe lesso, and ye shall salew
hym moche on my byhalf.' And he ansuered, 'my
damoyselle, I shall doo it righte gladly.' He thanne 24
departed fro her & came to the king that had doon
writ his ansuere in a lettre, and made grete foyson of
men of armes to arme them redly, and them made he
to yssue couertly out of the cyte and entred in to the 28
oost / and or the oost were armed they adommaged
them sore. And þen yssued paynemys out of theire
tentes without eny aray, that rechaced them vnto the
barrers, where they had grete scarmusshyng & fyers, 32
and many men slayn & wounded of bothe partes. All
thoost arryued where the scarmusshing was / and ther
whyles was the said messanger putte out of the Cite
att another gate, a bow shotte fro al the oost, so that 36

and of their
looks.

[1] fol. 74.

Ermine sends an
ouch to Urian,
and a ring to
Guion, by the
messenger,
and bids him
salute them on
her behalf.

The king gives
the messenger
an answer to
the letter he
brought,

and to divert the
attention of the
enemy, orders
another sortie.

Upon which the
messenger goes
out at another
gate,

he was nat perceyued.   And thenne he rode hastly   *and rides to his uncle.*
toward hys vncle. For moche he langed that he myght
there be arryued for to shew hym aH the tydying*es*.

4 And dured not long the scarmoushe, For the sawdan   *The Sultan soon orders his men to retreat.*
made it to be cessed, For he sawe wel that he shuld
more lese there than wyne.   Now I shal leue to speke
of this forsaid matere / and shaH retourne to speke of

8 Vryan & of his brother.

In this parte telleth thistory that Uryan dide hys   *At the spring of the day, Urian commands his host to prepare to march.*
trompettes to be blowen at the spring of the day,
& roos & com*m*anded eu*er*y man to appareyH hym,

12 and put saddell*es* on theire horses / and soone after the
two brethern herd theire masse, & semblably dyde the
other prynces & barons / and after the masse Vryan
made to crye, that who wold drynk ones shuld drynk,

16 and that ootis shuld be gyuen to the horses, and that
at the other tyme that the trompette shuld be blowen,
eu*er*yman shuld be redy that was of the [1]Vanwarde.   *[1] fol. 74 b.*
And they beying in such estate, the Capteyns nevew   *At that time the messenger returns from the king.*

20 arryued there, and delyuered the *lett*re to hys vncle,
that the kyng had taken to hym / and the Captayn
toke & kyssod it fourthw*ith*, opend it, and sawe by the
tenou*r* of it how the kyng com*m*anded hym to putte   *The Captain reads the answer, which commands all the land to be given in charge of the brethren, Urian and Guion,*

24 bothe the fortresse and the toune at the wyH & commandement of the two bretheren.   Also that he shuld
com*m*ande to aH good tounnes, Castels, Fortresses,
portes, hauens, & passages that they shuld gyue them

28 entre & soiourne, and that they shuld obey to them.
And whan the Captayn sawe & vnderstode aH þe sub-
stance & matere of it, he shewed the *lett*re to Vryan, & to   *to whom the letter is shown.*
guyon hys brother, the whiche redde it ; & when they

32 knew the tenou*r* of it they called to them the captayn,
the maister of Rodes, & the two knightes, that had
anounced to them thauenture of the siege, and redde
to them the *lett*re on hye.   'Thenne,' said Uryan to the

36 Captayn, 'we thanke moche the king of the worship

Urian thanks
the Captain for
the king's inten-
tions,

that he doth to vs / but as to vs, our entencyon is not
to entre in to thoos tounes ne castelles, yf we may
goodly passe without fourth, For we thinke to kepe the
feldes, yf god wyl, & make good werre ayenst the 4

and asks what
force the
Cyprians have
in all their
fortresses;

sodan, but telle vs what nombre of men may ysaue out
of all your garnysons the Fortresses alwayes kept / and
wete it þat force is to vs to knowe it / and yf they be
men of whom we dare trust and be assured / For god 8

because he
wishes to fight
the Sultan, and
end the war.

before we tende & purpose to gyue batoylle to the
Sawdan, & to putte to termynacioun, & ende this warre.
For therfore are we come hither.' 'By my faith,'

The Captain
says that would
be hard to do,
because the
paynims have
one hundred
thousand men.

said the Captayn, 'that shal be hard to doo, For þe 12
paynemys are in nombre wel C^{XCL} and more.' 'Care
you not, therefore,' said Vryan, 'For we haue good
right in oure caas / they are come vpon vs without

[1] fol. 76.

Urian replies
they have a good
cause,

cause / and though we had goon on them [1]vnto theire 16
owne lande, we ought to doo soo, For they are enemyes
of god / and doubteles though they be of grete nombre
to the regarde of our felawship / yet one grayne of

that victory lies
not on the side
of numbers,

peper alone smertith more on mans tonge than doth 20
a sacke full of whette / ne victorye also lyeth not in
grette multitude of peuple / but in good rule & ordyn-

and that Alex-
ander fought
the world with
twenty thousand
men.

aunce.   And wel it is trouth that Alexander, that subdued so many & dyuerse landes, wold not haue with 24
hym aboue the nombre of xx^{ti} thousand fyghtyng men
for one journey ayenst all the world.   And thanne
whan the Captayne herd hym speke so valyauntly, he

Which speech
cheered the
Captain,

held it to grete wele & valeur, and thoughte he was 28
wel able & worthy to conquere & subdue many landes,

who promised
a company of
eight thousand
men;

and said to hym in this manere : 'Sire, I shall enforce
your oost with foure thousand fighting men, and of two
thousand brygandyners & crosbowes, & other.' 'By 32

which Urian says
is enough.

my feyth,' said Vryan, 'that is ynoughe / now doo
that we may haue hem to half a journey nygh oure
enemyes,' and he ansuerd there shuld be no fawte of
it.   And then came there the Captayns nevew, and 36

kneled byfore Vryan & Guyon, and said to them in
this man*e*re : 'Noble damoyseaulx / the moost fayre
mayde / & the moost noble that I knowe salueth you

4 bothe, and sendeth you of her jewels' / and thenno he
toke the ouche of gold that was sette wit*h* many a ryche
& precyo*us* stone / and said thus to Vryan : 'Sire, hold
& receyue this ouche of Ermynes byhalf, doughter to

8 my liege lord the kyng', that requyreth & beseche*þ* you
to were it on you for her sake.' Vryan toke it joyously, and made it to be attached & sette it on his
cotte of armes, and said to hym : 'My frende, right

12 grete thank*es* & thousand me*r*cys to the damoyselle
tha so moche hono*ur* sheweth to me / Wete [1]it that I
shall kepe it moche dere for her sake / and gramercy
to you messanger & brynger of it.' And after he pre-

16 sented and toke to Guyon the ring on the forsaid
damoysellis byhalf / and that she prayed hym to bere
it for the loue & sake of her / And guyo*n* ansuerd that
so shuld he doo, and putte it on his fynger / and

20 thanked moche the damoyselle / and *þe* messager also /
and the brethern gaf moche ryche yeft*is* to the same
messager. And soone after the trompette blew, and
eueryman putte hym self fourth on hys way. and

24 there myght men be seen in fayre & good ordyna*u*nce.
And the Captayn sent to all the Fortresses & tounes,
and made to yssue out & assemble togidre all the men
of armes / and wel were of them aboue the nombre

28 that the Captayn had sayd to the two bretheren fyue
hondred more. Vryan thenne lodged hym and hys
felawship on a lytil ryuere / and on the morne erly
they departed, and went fourth tyl they came a lytil

32 byfore mydday, in a fayre medowe, nygh to a grete
ryuere / and there were foyson of trees / also there was
a quarter of a leghe thens a grete bridge, where they
muste passe / and fro that bridge vnto Famagoce were

36 but seuen leghes / and there made Vrya*n* hys folke to

MELUSINE.   K

The messenger
presents Urian
with the ouch
from Ermine,

who takes it
joyfully, and
attaches it to his
coat of arms,

[1] fol. 75 b.

and says he will
keep it for her
sake.

Guion is pre-
sented with the
ring, and puts it
on his finger.

The brethren
give rich gifts to
the messenger.
The trumpets
are sounded,
and the men get
under arms.

The captain
assembles from
the fortresses
the company he
promised,

and Urian
marches his
army within
seven leagues of
Famagosse,
nigh a great
bridge,

be lodged, and said he wold abyd þere the said Captayn
and his men that he shuld bring with hym.   There
they laye that nyght, and abode tyl the morne noone.
but alwayes some knightes were goon for theire dys- 4
porte vnto the said bridge, and aspyed there about xv
men of armes that were descended therat / and had
theire speeris in theire fystes, and the salades after the
guyse that they armed them in that Countre / and of 8
anoþer syde they sawe come about foure houndred
men ¹of armes, that peyned them self moche for to
passe ouer for to greve them of the other side / thanne
came one of our Knightes that ascryed them, & de- 12
manded of them what they were / and one of them
answerd, 'we are Cristen / and they that ye see at the
other side of the watro are paynemys, that come for
fourrage about the Countre / they haue mete & faught 16
with vs, and they haue slayn wel an C good men that
were of our felawship.'   'Now, fayre lordes,' said oure
knyght, 'yf ye can hold you, ye shal soone haue socours
& ayde.'   And thenne the knight broched hys hors, 20
and waloped toward hys felawes, and recounted to
them shortly all thauentura.   And whan they vnderstode this they hastly came to the oost, and mete
with xxᵘ crosbowes men, to whom they bade they 24
shuld hye þem toward the bridge for to help the xv
men of armes that were there ayenst thenmyes.   And
whan they vnderstode this they walked fast, & cam
nigh to the bridge, and sawe thre cristen that were 28
ouerthrawen on the bridge by strokkes of spearys.
'Fourth,' said then one of them, 'we tary to longe /
perceyue you not how this Dogges oppressen vylaynly
these valyaunt & worthy crystens!' / and anone they 32
bended þeir crosbowes, & shot all at ones / and ouer-
threwe doun on the bridge fro theire horses with that
first shotte xxiiᵘ paynemys.   Whan the mysbyleuers
paynemys sawe this they were sore abasshed, and 36

withdrew themself somwhat backward fro the bridge.
Thenne yede the cristen men, and releuyd vp their
felawes that were ouerthrawen on the bridge / and
4 thenne they made grete joye & toke good herte / and
the [1]Crosbowe men shote so ofte & so strong, that
there ne was so bold a paynem that durst putte his
foot on the bridghe / but made to come there theire
8 archers, & thenne bygan the scarmusshing strong &
grete and moche mortal. but betre had be to the
paynemys that they had withdrawe them self apart,
For the knightes came to the oost and reherced to
12 Uryan the tydinges therof, the whiche moch appertly
armed hymself, and made hastly a thousand men of
armes to take theire harneys on them, & rode forth
toward the bridge / and ordeyned another thousand
16 men of armes, & C crosbowe men to folowe hym, yf he
nede had of them / aud commanded that all the oost
shuld be in ordynaunce of batayll, & betoke it to the
kepyng & gouernaunce of guyon his brother, and of
20 the maister of Rodes. Uryan thanne made the stand-
arde to passe fourth rydyng in batayll moche ordyn-
atly / and was Vryan before, hauying a staf on hys
fyste, & held them wel togidre, and so vnyed, that
24 one marched nothing afore that other. But or they
were come to the bridge there were come eight thousand paynemys, that moche strongly oppressed our
folke, and had putte them almost fro the bridge. but
28 anoone came there Vryan, whiche alyghted / toke hys
speere, & so dyde hys folke moche appertly / and
made hys banere to be dysployed abrode / and were
the crosbowe men on bothe sydes of hym vpon the
32 bridge / and then they marched fourth, and bygan to
oppresse and rebuke sore the paynemys, and made
them to withdrawe bakkwarde. And there Vryan
cryed 'Lusynen' with a hye voys & lowde, and yede
36 & marched ayenst hys enemys, hys banere euer byfore

[Side notes:]
and rescue some of their friends on the bridge from the paynims,

[1] fol. 76 b.

who retire to bring up their archers.

Urian hears of the skirmish,

and rides with a thousand men to the bridge,

leaving his host in charge of Guion.

Eight thousand paynims come against him, who at first press his company,

but are at last repulsed.
Urian crying 'Lusignan!' rushes with his men against the enemy,

1 fol. 77.

hym. [1]and hys men after that assaylled the fals dogges
moche asprely, Whiche of the other syde bygan to
launche & to smyte. Uryan smote a paynem on þe
brest with hys speere so demesurably, that hys spere 4
apered at back syde of hym. they medled them
fyersly togidre. but at last the paynemys lost the
bridge, and many of them fell doun in to the rynere.
And thenne passed the crystens the bridge lyghtly / 8
and there bygan the baytayll moche cruel, For many
were there sore hurte & slayn on both partyes. but
euer the paynemys were putte abak, & lost moche of
ground. Vryan made to passe the horses, for wel he 12
perceyued that his enemyes wold mounte on theire
horses to putte them self to flyght. Thenne came the
arregarde that asprely passed ouer the bridge / and
whan the paynemys perceyued them they were sore 16
affrayed / and who that myght flee, fledd toward theire
folke that lede theyre proye, oxen, kyn & shep, swynes
& othre troussage. Uryan than lepte on horsback, and
made hys folke to doo soo, & commanded the arrer- 20
garde that passed them ouer the bridge, that they
shuld folowe hym in fayre ordynaunce of bataylle /
and so they dyde / and Uryan & hys folke chaced the
paynemys that fledd sore chaffed & aferd, For al they 24
that were by Uryan, & they of hys felawship atteyned,
were putte to deth / and endured the chasse with grete
occysyon & slaghter þe space of fyue ooures & more.
And thenne the paynemys ouertoke theyre folke, & 28
made them to leue behynd them alle theyre proy,
& came vpon a grete mountayne toward Famagoce /
and þer the paynemys reassembled, & putte them self
in [2]ordynaunce. but there came Vryan & his folke, 32
theire speris on theire fystes alowe / at that recountryng were many one slayn & wounded sore, of one
syde & of other / the paynemys susteyned the stoure
strongly, For they were a grete nombre of folke. but 36

drives them over
the bridge,

presses them
hard,

and gets his
horses over
the bridge.

His rear coming
up frightens the
paynims,

who flee toward
their friends.

Urian's com-
pany chase the
pagans,

kill many,

and cause them
to leave their
spoil.
The paynims
rally with their
friends upon a
mountain,

2 fol. 77 b.

Uryan assaylled them vygourously / and so moche he
dide there of armes that all were abasshed, and had
grete wonder of it. Then came thither the arregarde
4 that was of a thousand men of armes, & C crosbowe
men which entred, & marched sodaynly vpon theyre
enemyes, & faught so strongly that the paynemys were
putte abacke, & lost ground. and so fyersly was
8 shewed there the cheualry & hardynes of Cristen folke,
that soone they had the vyctory, and putte theyre
enmys to flight, of whiche lay dede on the place foure
thousand & more, without them that were slayn at for-
12 sayd bridge / and the chasse endured vnto nygh the
oost & siege of the paynemys. Thenne Vryan made
hys folke to withdrawe them, and ledd with them the
proye that the paynemys had lefte behynd. And
16 thus within a short while they eslongyd ferre one fro
other / and our folke retourned to the bridge / and the
paynemys went fourth to theire oost cryeng alarme.
Wherfore euery man went to harneys, & yssued out of
20 theire tentes / and thenne one of them recounted to
the sawdan all thaduenture þat happed to them. And
whan the sawdan herd of it, he wondred moch who
might haue brought þat folke, that so grete harme &
24 dommage had born vnto hym. Thanne was there grete
affray in thoost, & grete noyse of trompettes. Wherof
they of the Cite merueylled what thing it might be, &
armed them self / and eueryone was in his garde / and
28 there [1]came to the gate one of the knightes that were
at forsayd brydge. whiche had putte hym in auenture
to passe thrugh all thoost, and knewe the convyne[2] of
one parte & of other, also the grete fayttes of armes that
32 Vryan had don / he escryed hye with a lowde voys /
'open the gate! For I bring you good tydynges.' And
thenne they demanded of hym what he was / and he
ansuerd, 'I am one of the knightes of the fortres of the

[margin notes:]
but Urian and
his guard

again put them
to flight,
and slay another
four thousand
of them;

after which
Urian retires
with the booty.

The paynims
alarm the
Sultan,
who is surprised,
and wonders who
can have so de-
feated his men;

he sounds his
trumpets,
which alarm the
people in Fama-
gosse, and they
arm themselves.
[1] fol 78.

A knight of
Urian's arrives
at the town,

and tells them
that he brings
good tidings;

[2] Fr. convyne

being led before
the King of
Cyprus,

he recounts the
victory.

The king is glad,

and sends the
knight to his
daughter,

² fol. 78 b.

who asks about
the battle,
and Urian.

The knight says
Urian is the
bravest and
strongest knight
he has ever
seen.

blak mountayne.' And thanne they opened the gate,
and he entred, and they ledd hym toward the king,
that soone knew hym. For other tyme he had seen
hym. The knight then enclyned hym before the 4
king, and made to hym the reuerence / and the kinge
receyued hym moche benyngly / and demanded to hym
som tydynges; and he rehersed to hym worde by word
all the faytte / and how Vryan dyde, & had rescued 8
the proye / also of thauenture of the bridge, and alle
other thinges, & how hys entencion & wylle was for to
gyue batayll to the sawdan, and to reyse the siege / &
that shortly / · 'By my feyth,' sayd the kyng, 'that 12
man ought me god wyll, for to rescue my land of the
fel & cruel dogges paynemys / and for the holy feyth
crysten to susteyne & enhaunse / and, certaynly, ¹I
shall to morne doo fele to the sawdan þat my socour 16
& help is nygh redy to my behauf & playsire, & that
I doubte hym not of nothing.' 'My frende,' said the
kyng to the knyght, 'goo & say these good tydynges to
my doughter.' 'Sire,' said the knight, 'right gladly.' 20
Then came he in to the chambre where the mayde
was, and ²moche humbly salued her, and rehersed to
her all the auenture. 'How, sire knight,' said she,
'were ye at that bataylle?' 'By my feyth, damoyselle,' 24
answerde the knight, 'ya.' 'And how,' sayd she, 'that
knyght that hath so straunge a face, is he such a fyghter
as men saye?' 'By my feyth, my damoyselle, ye
more than a houndred tymes / For he ne dreddeth no 28
man, al be he neuer so grete & so pusyssaunt. And
wete it what that men saye to you of hym / he is one
of the moost preu & hardy knightes that euer I sawe in
my lyf.' 'By my feyth,' sayd the damoyselle, 'yf he 32
had now hyerid you for to preyse & speke wel of hym,
he hath wel employed hys coste.' 'By my feyth, my
damoysolle, I spake neuer with hym. but yet he is betre

¹ Fr. *Je ferai demain sentir.*

worthy than I telle you.' Then she ansuered to the
knight, [1]'goodnes & bounte is betre than fayrenes &
beaulte.' And here leueth thystorye to speke of the
4 mayde / and retourneth to Vryan, þat abode at the
bridge, and founde þys oost lodged at this syde of the
bridge / And also the Captayne þat had brought the
men of armes, that he leuyed fro the garnysons & for-
8 tresses vnto the nombre of V^ML men of armes, with
two thousand V. C. crosbowe men / and also there were
many footmen / And þey were alle lodged in the
medowe at the other syde of the ryuere. Where
12 Vryan found his pauyllon dressed vp / and the other Urian rests that night in his tent.
that had be at the pursyewte & chaas of the paynemys,
they lodged þem that nyght the best wyse they coude,
& made good watche. And here resteth thystory ther-
16 of, and bygynneth to speke of the kyng of Cypre, that The King of Cyprus was glad at the victory,
was moche joyous & glad of the socours that was
come to hym / and regracyed deuoutely our lord of
it / and in that party passed the nyght. But who
20 someuer was glad that was Ermyne, For she coude not and his daughter Ermine thought ever of Urian,
by no manere in the world haue out of her thoughte
Vryan, [2]and desired moche to see hym for the well [2] fol. 79.
that it was said of hym / in so moche that she said in
24 herself, that yf he now had the vysage more straunge & his strange visage, and his bravery,
more contrefaytte than he had ' yet he is wel shappen
for his proesse & bounte to haue the doughtir of the
moost high kynge in the world to hys paramour. And
28 so thoughte the damoyselle al the nyght on Vryan,
For loue by hys grete power had broughte her therto. because love by its great power had hold of her.
Here resteth thystorye to speke of her, & bygynneth to
speke of the kyng her fader.
32 The hystorye recounteth here, that on the morne In the morning the king w. a host
at the spryng of the day, the kynge had hys
folke all redy, & yssued out of the Cyte with a thousand
men of armes, and wel a thousand of Crosbowemen;

---

[1] Fr. Amy, bonté vault mieulx que beaulté.

went out of the
city and fought
the enemy,

giving no
quarter.

The paynims
come in great
force,

and the King of
Cyprus shows
great bravery.

² fol. 79 b.

The Sultan,
bearing a
poisoned dart,
comes with a
great company,
and seeing the
king, strikes him
on the left side
with it,

which causes the
king great
anguish. He
pulls out the
dart, and throws
it at the Sultan,
but missing him
it kills a paynim
warrior.

and some brygandyners were embusshed at bothe
thendes of the barrera, for to helpe & socoure hym yf
he were to moche oppressyd by the paynemys. And
þen the king entred in to thoost, & bare grete dommage 4
to hys enemys. For he had commanded vpon peyne
of deth that none shuld take eny prysoner, but that
they shuld putte all to deth / and this dide he for
cause they shuld not tende to the dyspoylle & proye, 8
and that at laste he myght gader them ayen togidre for
to withdrawe them without ony losse. And then the
oost began to be mevyd / and who best coude of the
paynemys cams to the medlee. And whan the king 12
perceyued that they cam with puyssaunce, he remysed
hys folke togidre, and made to withdraw them al the
lytil pas, and came behynde, the swerd in his fyst.
And whan he sawe a knight approuche, he retourned 16
& made hym to recule abacke. but yf he atteyned
hym, he chastysed hym so that he no more had
langyng to siew[1] hym. And there the kynge dide so
wel & so valyauntly, that euery one sayd he was 20
moche preu & worthy of his hand / and there ne ²was
so hardy payneme that oo stroke durst abyde. Then
came the Sawdan with a grete route of paynemes,
armed on a grete hors, that held a dart envenymed. 24
And thanne whan he aspyed the king, that so euyl
demened his folke, he cast at hym the darte yre, &
hytte hym at the synester syde, in suche wyse that he
perced hym thrugh & thrughe, For hys harneys coude 28
neuer waraunt hym / And soone after the kyng felt
grete anguysshe, and drew the dart out of hys syde,
and supposed to haue cast it agayn to the Sawdan / but
the Sawdan tourned hys hors so appertly that the dart 32
flough besyde hym, & smote a payneme thrugh the
body in suche wyse that he fell doune dede. And
whan the sawdan, that ouermoche had auaunced hym

[1] Fr. suyrir.

self, wende to haue retourned, the kynge smote hym
with his swerd vpon the heed of hym, that he ouerthrew hym to therthe.   Thenne cam the paynemes
4 there so strong that they made the kynge & hys folke
to withdraw backe / and then*n*e was the sawdan
redressed & remou*n*ted agayn vpon a grete hors.   And
thenne was þe prees grete, and the paynemes were
8 strong / in so moche that they made the kyng & his
folke to withdrawe vnto theire barrers.   Thanne bygan
the Cypryens, that kept the passage there, to shote &
to launche on the paynemes so strong that they dyed
12 the place *with* the blood of theire enemyes.   but so
strong were the paynemys, that they gaynstode the
crysten / and also the king had lost moche of hys
blood, & wexed feble, and hys folke bygane to be
16 abasshed.   And how be it that the king suffred moche
dolour & peyn*e*, neuertheles he resioysshed moche hys
peuple & encouraged them, and so moche they dide
that the fals paynemes might gete nothing on them /
20 but that they lost twyes ¹asmoche more / and was
the scarmusshing moche fyers & peryllous.   And thus
the kyng of Cypre, by hys valyaunce & noble herte,
recomforted his folke.   and though he felt grete peyne
24 & woo, he full wel remysed hys folke into the toune.
And it was grete meruaylł how so grete a lord, wounded
to the deth, myght sytte on horsbake / but the stroke
was noþing mortalł but for the venyme.   For the dart
28 was envenymed / and wel it appered w*ith*in a lytil
tyme after, For he deyde of that same stroke.   but for
certayn he had the herte so full of valiauntnes, as the
faytte shewed it, that he ne daynet not make signe
32 of eny bewayllyng before his folke, vnto tyme that one
of the barons perceyued alł his senyster syde dyed w*ith*
bloode / the whiche Baron sayd to the king: 'Sire,
ye abyde to long here / come & make your folke to

The Sultan, advancing too near the king, is overthrown by him,

but is rescued by his people,

who at last drive the Cyprians back;

but these shoot so well that many paynims are killed.

The king now begins to be faint from loss of blood.

His people are abasshed, but, encouraged by him, they fight well, and slay many more of their enemies.

¹ fol. 94.

At last he conducts his folk to the town, still on horseback. Though suffering from the poisoned wound,

he makes no sign of pain, but a baron seeing the blood on his side advises him to withdraw.

For the nyght approucheth / to thende that your
enmyes putte not them self thrughe the medlee emong
vs.' The kyng, whiche felt grete sorowe, answerd to
hym thus : 'Doo therof after your wylle.' This knyght 4
thenne made a houndred men of armes, that were
reffresshed, to come before the barryere, & made to
bygynne ayen the scarmusshing with an C crosbowe
men ; and so were the paynemes sette abacke, wherof 8
the sawdan was full of grete anger, and escryed to
hys folke : 'fourth lordes & barons, peyne your self
to doo wel, For the tonne shalbe oures this day : hit
may not escape vs.' And thenne enforced ayen the 12
medlee. And there ye had see wel assaylled &
ryght wel deffended, of that one part & of that other.
But whan the kinge of Cypre sawe that the paynemes
strengthed them soo, he toke courage grete, & ranne 16
vpon them vygourously / and there he suffred so moche
peyne þat all the synewes[1] of hys body were open,
wherof, as some [2]sayen, his lyf was shorted / and by
that same enuahisshing were putte aback the paynemes, 20
& many of them wer slayn & sore wounded. The nyght
thenne approuched, and was nygh / and grete harme
& losse was there of both partes. but alwayes the
paynemes withdrew them vnto theire oost, For the 24
king encouraged hys folk soo that they ne doubted no
stroke nomore than yf þey had be of yron or of stele.
And whan the paynems were departed, the kinge &
hys folke retourned in to the toune. And whan they 28
knew the euyl auenture of theire king, they beganne to
sorowe & to make grete dueil. And the kynge, that
sawe this, sayd to them : 'My good folke, make no
suche waymenting' ne sorowe, but thinke wel to def- 32
fende you ayenst the Sawdan / and god our sauyour
shalbe at your ayde & helpe, For yf it playse hym I
shall soone be heelid.' Thenne was the peuple peased

This baron with
some archers
continues the
fight,

which makes the
Sultan angry,
who calls on his
people 'to do
well,'

upon which
they fight
vigorously.

The king, though
in great pain,
comes to the
rescue,

[2] fol. 86 b.

and the paynims
are driven back;

afterwards the
king and his
people return
to the town,
where they learn
of the king's
wound; at which
they mourn.

The king en-
courages them,

and tells them
he may soon be
healed,

[1] Fr. *vaines*.

ayen. but neuerþeles, the kyng that said suche wordes
for to resioysshe hys peuple, felt in hym self that he
coude not escape fro deth. . And thenne he commanded

4 to his folke they shuld make good watche, and gaf
hem leue, & came to the palleys, and there alyghted
& yede in to hys chambre / And thenne came hys
doughter, that somwhat had vnderstand of hys mys-

8 auenture. but whan she perceyued that hys harneys
was all rede with bloode, and sawe his wounde, she
fell doun in a swoune, & lay as she had be deed.
Thenne commanded the kynge that she shuld be borne

12 in to her chambre / and so it was doon. After the
Cyrurgiens came to see the kingis wounde, and was
leyed on his backe along his beed / and they told hym
that he was saaf fro parell of deth, and that he shuld

16 not be abasshed. 'By my feyth,' said the kynge, 'I
wote wel how it is with me / the wylle of god be duo /
hit may not be kepte so secretly but that it shalbe
¹knowen thrughe the Cyte.' And thenne byganne þe

20 sorowe moche grete among the Cytezeyns & peple of
the Cyte, and more without comparacion than it was
byfore. But here resteth thystorye of the kynge & of
the siege / and shal speke of Vryan and of his brother,

24 and how they exployted afterward. /

In this parte, saith thystorye, that on the morow
erly, that was thursday, was Vryan after hys masse
herde byfore hys tente / and there he made come,

28 one aftir other, all the Captayns & chieftayns with
theire penons & standarts, and theire folke vnder them
al armed of all pieces, for to behold & vysyte theire
harneys, yf eny thing' wanted / as wel the straungers /

32 as hys owne folke / and beheld wel the mayntene &
contenaunce of them. And after this was doo he
made them to be nombred / and they were founde by
extymacion about ix. or ten thousaund fyghting men.

36 Thenne said to them Vryan : 'Lyste, all fayre lordes,

but at the same
time he knew
he was near
death.
The king orders
good watch to be
kept;

is visited by his
daughter,

who faints at the
sight of his
wound and the
blood on his
armour.

The surgeons
tell the king he
is safe;

but the king says
he knows well
how it is with
him.

¹ fol. 81.

The people of
the city mourn
for their king.

In the morning
Urian hears
mass,

reviews and
numbers his
men,

finding between
nine or ten
thousand in all.

He addresses
them.

' It is their duty to maintain the faith of Christ, who died for them,

even at peril of life,

though our enemies are ten to one against us.

Alone, Christ fought for our redemption.

² fol. 81 b.

If you die, salvation and Paradise awaits you.

Soon I will march;

but if there be any whose heart is not steadfast, let him withdraw,

for one coward has often spoiled a great undertaking.'

we are here assembled for to susteyne the feyth of Jhesu
cryste, of the whiche he vs alle hath regenered and
saued / as eche of vs knoweth wel ynoughe how he
suffred cruel deth for the loue of vs, to thende he
shuld bye vs ayen fro the peynes of helle. Wherfore
lordis, seen & considered in our hertes that he hath
doon to vs suche a grace, we ought not to reffuse the
deth, or such auenture as he shal gyue vs, for to 8
deffende & susteyne the holy sacrements that he hath
admynystred vs for the saluacion of our sowlis /
though that we now haue adoo with strong partye.
For our enmys ben tene ayenst one to the regarde of 12
vs / but what therof we haue good ryght, For they
are come to assayll vs without cause vnto our right
herytage / and also we ought not to resuyngne no
dylaye therfore. For Jhesu Criste toke alone the warre 16
for our redempcion, And by hys deth alle good folke
that kepen his comman²dements shal be saued. ye
oughte thenne to vnderstand all certaynly, that alle
thoo that shull dye in this quarelle, mayntenyng & 20
enhaunsyng the feyth, shal be saued, & shal haue the
glorye of Paradys / And perfore, fayre lordes, I tell you
in generall that I haue entencyon, god byfore, to meue
presently for to approche our enemys, and to fyght 24
with them as soone as I may. Wherfore, I praye you
frendly, that yf there be ony man in this place that
feleth not his herte ferme & stedfaste for to withstande
& abyde thauenture, such as it shal playse to god to 28
send vs / that he withdrawe hym self apart fro other,
For by one only Cowarde & feynted herte is sometyme
lefte & loste al a hoole werke. and wete it that, al thoo
that wyl not comme with theire good wyll, as wel of 32
my folke as of other,³ I shall gyue them money

³ ' Wha will be a traitor-knave ?
  Wha can fill a coward's grave ?
  Wha sae base as be a slave ?
    Let him turn and flee !' (*Scots wha hae.*)

ynoughe & syluer for theyre sustenaunce & fyndyng
for to passe ouer the see ayen.' After these wordes he
made hys banere to be dressed a bowe shote fro the
4 valey, vpon the mounteyne, and ordeyned hys brother Urian gives Guion his banner,
Guyon for to hold & bere it / and after he said, al on
hye, in heryng of hys folke / 'All they that entenden, and calls on all who want to avenge Christ's death,
& haue deuocion for to auenge the deth of Jeshu
8 criste, to thenhaunsyng of the holy feyth cristen, Also
to ayde & helpe the kynge of Cypre, lete hym with- and to help the King of Cyprus, to come under it,
drawe hym self vnder my banere / and they that ben
of contrary wyll, lete them passe ouer at the oper syde and march across the bridge.
12 of the bridge.' Thanne whan the noble hertes herde
hym saye thoo wordes. they held it to grete wysedome The noble hearts heard him,
of hym, & of grete prowesse & worthynes, & went alle and were glad, and marched under his banner.
in a companye togider vnder his banere, wepyng for
16 Joye & for pyte of the wordes that Vryan had said /
ne none delayed ne taryed for nothing, but yede all
vnder hys banere, as said is / Thenne was moche
gladde Vryan, and joyous, and anone he made his The trumpets are sounded, and the march begins;
20 trompettes to be blowen vp, and all was troussed[1] &
putte them self on theire way. And thanne the
[2]maister of Rodes, and the Captayne of Lymasson   [2] fol. 82.
putte them self assembled togidre, and rode in fayre
24 batayll, And said wel that ayenst Vryan and his folke
no man shal endure / And thus they rode tyl they
came nygh to the mountayne / and as half way to the they come to a mountain,
place where the batayll had be the day byfore. 'By
28 my feyth, lordes,' sayd Vryan, 'there nygh that yond
ryuere were good that we went to be there lodged tyl and halt for refreshment,
we were refresshed. And in the meane while we shal and to hold council.
see and aduyse how we shall for the moost surest way
32 hyndre & adommage our enmyes' / And they answerd
that so was good to doo. They went thenne all togider,
to thende they were not founde abrode, & lodged pem
self there. Now leueth here of them thystorye / and
36 bygynneth to speke of the Sawdan. /   [1] Fr. *troussé*.

Thystorye

On the Sultan's spies telling him the state of the city,

and of the secour coming, and of the illness of the king,

he orders an assault.

The townspeople defend themselves by shooting stones, pitch, hot oil, and overturning the enemy's scaling ladders.

The Sultan urges on the assault,

² fol. 82 b.

and promises the first man that enters the city his weight in s.lver.

They attack vigorously, and are pelted with logs of wood, burning oil, molten lead, quick lime, sulphur, and brimstone on fire,

and are obliged to retire,

Thystorye sayth that the Saudan had hys espyes withín the Cite, whiche aspyed secretly þe Convyne of them of the toune. Wherby he knew that socours & help came to the kyng / and also how the kyng was sore wounded, wherof the people was gretly troubled. Thanne had the sawdan cause to do assayll the toune / and he made to blowe trompettes whan þe sonne was vp, and ordeyned his batuylles, and his Crosbowes & paueys,¹ and came vnto the dyches & barryers. There bygan the scarmusshing outrageously fyers / they shotte with Crosbowes demesurably of one part & of other. There were many paynemes slayn, For they withín the toune shotte many gonnes,² & cast vpon them fro the batalments of theire walles grete stones, pyche & grece brennyng hoot, and reuersed them fro the ladders vnto the botome of the dyches. Thenne came the Sawdan fourth, cryeng with a high voys, 'Now, lordes, deffende yourself worthily, & late vs take toune or ony socours come to our enemyes, For on my god Machomete, he that first shall entre the toune, I shall gyue hym hys pesaunnt or weyght of syluer in suche estate as he entre in to it.' Who thenne had see them assaylle & cleme vp to the walles, and putte them self in parellous passage, he shuld haue be meruaylled. But they that were vpon the walles withín, fourth cast on them ⁴grete logges of wode, brennyng oyle, lede molten / tonnes & barels full of vnquynched lyme, and vesselles full of flaxe grecyd with oyle and mixtyouned with brymstone and sulfer, al ardaunt & brennyng / so that magre them they were fayn to relenquysshe the place, and to remounte at another syde of the wall : and there

4
8
12
16
20
24
28
32

¹ Fr. *pavilliers.* ² Fr. *gros canons et d'esprin galles.*
⁴ Fr. *pierres, pieux agus, huilles chaudes, plong fondu, poinsons plains de chaulx vive, tonneaux plains destouppes engressées et ensouffrées tous ardens.*

abode many paynemys al brent and sore hurt. And
thanne the Sawdan made thassawte to be strengthed
with new folke / but they within forth deffended them
4 ful valyauntly as preu & hardy. Also they were more
vygourous of herte, for that they knew theire socours
commyyng, that was nygh. Here I shall leue of þis
matere / and shal say how Vryan dide, whiche had
8 sent hys espyes to knowe how it was of the siege / And
they reported to hym how the saudan gaaf grete &
contynuel sawtes to the Cite / and that without shortly
it were socoured, they were within in grete daunger /
12 and how the kynge was syke & sore wounded. Whan
vryan and Guyon vnderstode these tydynges, they were
within them self wel angry and fylled with sorowe /
but no grete semblaunt they made of it, to thende
16 theire folke shuld not be of lesse courage therfore. /

Cap. XXII. How the Sawdan was slayn byfore Famagoce.[1]

[2]In this parte sayth thystorye, that whan Vryan herde
20 the tydynges forsaid, he made to sowne his trompettes, and made thoost to be armed, and departed it
in foure bataylles; wherof of the first batayll he hymself was conductour, hys brother lede the seconde, the
24 maister of Rodes was Chieftayn of the iii[de]; And the
foureth was conduyted & lede by the Captayn of
Lymas. And he made to abyde in the valey all the
sommage, and mad it to be kept with a houndred men
28 of armes and fyfty cros bowemen. And after they bygane to mounte the hille, And fro thens they sawe
how the paynemes assaylled moche strongly the Cite.
And thenne Vryan said to his folke / 'Lordes, that
32 folke is of grete nombre / but no doubte they be oures /

---

[1] Famagusta (named by Augustus after the battle of Actium,
Fama Augusta), on the west coast of Cyprus, south of the
ancient Salamis, the only harbour in the island.

Sidenotes:

many burnt and hurt. The Sultan renews the assault, but the townsfolk, knowing of the soccours, fight vigorously.

Urian's spies tell of the assault on Famagosse, and the sore need of the King of Cyprus,

at which he sorrows, but dissembles his grief.

[2] fol. 83.

Urian sounds to arms, and marches his host in four battalions,

leaving the baggage with a guard in the valley.

At the hill they see the battle, and the great number of the pagans.

They march
forward; the
paynims at first
take them for
friends, but
recognising
them, are sore
afraid.

Urian's batta-
lion enters the
fight;
two other bat-
talions march
forward between
the enemy's
watch and the
city.

But Urian's
battalion falls
on them before
they have time
to do so,

and god before they shalbe dyscomfyted by vs / and
that right soone.   goo we thenne ayenst theire oost /
and so fourth without dylayeng to them that sawten
the Cite.   ¹and I wene with goddis grace that they 4
shal not endure long ayenst vs.'   And they answerd,
'that good it was for to doo soo.'   Thenne he wold
descende the mountayne and haue passed at back syde
of the oost; but whan they supposed to haue passed 8
fourth, the paynemes perceyued that they were not of
theire folke / they cryed alarme and were sore aferd.
Thanne sayd Vryan to the Captayn, that with all his
bataill he shuld entre thoost to fight ayenst them that 12
were there.   There bygan a mortal medlee, And Vryan
and the other two batayllee yede ferther, & putte them
self atwix the watche & them that assaylled the Cite /
and so long they sawted, that alle they that kepte theire 16
lodgis and of þeire watche were slayn and dystroyed,
and incontynent all the foure batayllee in fayre ordynaunce marched fourth toward the other that strongly
assaylled.   But one came to the sawdan, and said to 20
hym how the tentes & pauyllons were take, and alle
they that kepte them slayn / 'and they that haue doon
þat faytte, ye may see them commyng hitherward, the
moost strong and fell folke that euer I sawe ne herde 24
speke of.'   The saudan thanne loked abacke, and sawe
baners & standarts and hys enmyes commyng in fayre
ordynaunce / and so nygh togider that they semed not
in nombre to be as moche by the half as they were. 28
Thenne was the Saudan abasshed and wood angry / and
made to sowne hys trompette to withdrawe & assemble
his folke togider.   But or they were half assembled,
Vryan came first with hys batayll / and with a grete 32
courage ran vpon them moche asprely, And þer began
thoccysyon & slaghter moche grete / but for certayn the
gretest losse tourned on the paynemes, For ²they had
no leser for to putte them self in aray of baytaylle, and 36

were sore wery of thassawte / & none of them were
vnder his banere whan Vryan and his folke ranne vpon
them, whiche were aspre & harde and full wel wyst
4 the crafte of armes, wherfore many of the paynemes
putte them self to flight. But the sawdan, that was ful
of grete courage & of grete vasselage, realyed his folke
about hym, & delyuered & gaf ryght a grete sawte to
8 our folke moche proudly. There were many men slayn
& sore wounded / and made hym self to be redoubted
and dradde, For he held a two handes ax / and smote
with at lyfte syde and at the ryght syde that none
12 myght susteyne hys strokes that were about hym.
But whan Vryan perceyued hym þat so sore demened
his folke, he was full woo, and said in hymself, ' By my
feyth, it is grete pyte & dommage that yonder Turcke
16 byleueth nat on god, For he is moche preu & valyaunt
of his hand ; but for the dommage that I see he doeth
on my folke, I ne haue cause to forbere hym any more /
and also we be not in place where grete & many wordes
20 may be holden.' Thenne he braundysshed hys swerd
and with a fyers contenaunce rane vpon the Saudan /
And whan he sawe hym commyng he refused hym not,
but toke his ax and wende to haue smyten vryan withal
24 vpon the crosse of the heed / but Vryan eschiewed
the stroke ; the ax was pesaunt and heuy, and with that
vayne stroke it scaped fro the Saudans handes. And
thanne Vryan smote hym vpon the helmet a grete
28 stroke with all his might / and was the sawdan so sore
charged with that stroke that he was so astonyed and
amased that he neyther sawe nor herde, and lost the
brydel and the steropes, and the hors bare hym where
32 he wold. And Vryan [1]pursiewed hym nygh, and yet
agayn atteyned hym with his trenchaunt swerde betwix
the heed & the sholders, For his helmet was all vnlaced
and his hawtepyece fell of with the forsaid stroke,
36 wherfore with his second stroke vryan made hys swerde

MELUSINE.   L

kills many of
them, and puts
others to flight.

The courageous
Sultan rallies
his people,
and assaults the
Christian folk
severely.

Urian seeing the
bravery of the
Sultan,

regrets he be-
lieves not in
God ;

but because of
the damage he is
doing,

rides against
him,

stuns him,

[1] fol. 84 b.

to entre in the sawdants flesshe, in so moch that he detrenched & cutte the two maister vaynes of his nek, and fell douns fro hys hors to the erthe. And there was so grete prees of horses of one parte and of other, 4 that the stoure of batayll was there so aspre and so mortall that hys folke might not help hym / and lost so moche of hys blood that he most there deye in grete dystres & sorowe / And soone after that the paynemes 8 knew that the saudan was deed they were affrayed and moche abasshed, and neuer aftir they fought with no good herte. Thanne Vryan and his brothir Guyon esprouned themself there, & faught so strongly, gyuyng 12 grete & pesaunt strokes, that wonder it was to see. And wete it wel þat bothe Cypryens & Poytevyns dide so valyauntly that in short space of tyme they dystroyed theyre enmyes, whiche were all slayn or take. And 16 thenne Vryan & his folke lodged them self in the paynems lodgys / and was the sommage of the cristen sent fore / and the gardes and kepers of it, fayne & glad of the vyctory, came & brought it in to thoost and lodged 20 there / And the two brethern made the Butyn or conqueste to departe & deele so egaly after euery man had deseruyd & was worthy, þat none there was but he was full of Joye & content of it / And here resteth 24 thystorye of Vryan / and shal speke of the capytayne of Lymas,[1] that soone came to Famagoce.

In this parte telleth vs thistorye that after þe dyscomfyture of the batayll the Captayne ²departed 28 fro the two brethern, with hym xxx knightes of grete affayre, and came to the Cite, where the yates were opend to hym gladly, and entred and found the folke by the stretes, of whiche some made grete feeste, for 32 þat they sawe them delyuered of theires enemyes, and blessid the heure that euer the children of Lusignen were borne, and the heure also whan they entred the

[1] Fr. *Lymasson* :—Limassol, on S. coast of Cyprus.

land. And some folke made grete sorowe, grete wepynges, sore lawmentyng, and grete bewaylling, for
theire kynge þat was wounded to the deth. Wherfore
4 he wyst not what to thinke, For he knew not yet þe
kyng was hurt. And so moche he exployted that he
came to the palleys, and there he alighted, where he
found the peuple wel mate[1] / and he demanded of them
8 what they ayled, and yf they wanted of eny thing. 'By
my feyth,' said one of them, 'ye / and that ynough;
For we lese the moost true & valyaunt man that euer
was borne in this royalme.' 'How thanne,' said the
12 Captayn, 'is the kynge syke?' 'Ha / a! sire,' ansuered
to hym a knight, 'knowe you no more of it? We dide
yssue yesterday, and enuahysshed our enmyes / and
at retourne of it the sawdan smote our king with a
16 venymous darte, by so that no remedye nys founde
therto / For we supposed euer that these two damoyseaulx had come to our ayde & help at that day,
And wete it that the kingis doughtir demeneth suche
20 heuynes & sorowe, that grete pyte it is to see, For
almost two dayes are passed that she ete no manere of
mete / woo & euylhap shalbe to vs yf we lese both our
king & our damoyselle & lady, For yf that happed the
24 land were in grete orphanite of bothe lord & of lady.'
'Fayre lordes,' said the Captayne, 'all is not yet lost
that lyeth in parell. Haue lost[2] in our lord Jhesu Criste,
and he shall helpe you. I pray you lede me toward
28 the king.' 'By my feyth' / said [3]the knight, 'that
shall soone be doo, For he lyth in the next chambre,
where euery man may goo as he had no harme / He
hath alredy made hys testament, & hath ordeyned &
32 bequethed of hys owne good to his seruaunts, so that
euery one is content / and he is confessed & hath receyued our lord, and he is admynystred of all his
rightes & sacrements.' 'By my feyth,' said the Cap-

but find the folk weeping.

The Captain of Lymas proceeds to the palace,

where he learns that the King has been mortally wounded by a poisoned dart.

and that the King's daughter is sore depressed and will not eat.

The Captain asks an audience with the King,
[3] fol. 85 b.
who lies in the next chamber. It is granted.

[1] Fr. mat.   [2] Fr. fiance.

On entering,
the Captain
makes his rever-
ence, and is
welcomed by the
King,

tayne, 'he is thanne in good caas / and he hath doon as
a wyse man oughte to doo' / And thenne he entred in
to the Chambre & enclyned hym self byfore the kyng
that leye on his beed, and made to hym the reuerence. 4
'Captayne,' said the kinge, 'ye be right welcome /
and I thanke you of the good diligence that ye haue
doo to haue accompanyed these two noble men by
whome my land is out of the subgection of the pay- 8
nemes, For I had no more puyssaunce to gouerne my

who asks him to
bring Urian and
Guion, as he
desires to reward
them for the help
they have given
him.

folke ne my land / I pray you that ye goo & telle
them on my behalf that þey vouchessaf to come &
see me or I be deed, For grete wylle I haue to make 12
satisfaction to them to my power of the loue & curtoysye that they haue shewed to me; And also I haue
grete desyre to see & speke with them, for certayn caas
whiche I wyl declare vnto them.' 'My lord,' said the 16

Captayne, 'gladly I shall doo your commandement.'
'Now gooth thenne,' said the kynge, '& lete hem be to
morne with me by the houre of pryme.' The kinge

and the King has
the great street
of the city
decorated.

thanne commanded that the grete strete where they 20
shuld passe shuld be hanged richely vnto the paleys,
and dyde doo make grete appareyl ayenst theire
commyng. And here resteth thistory to speke of the
king / and retourneth to saye of the Captayne.   24

Thistorye saith that so fast rode the Captayne that
soone he came to the oost, and alighted at the

[1]tente of the two brethern, that moche humbly receyued
hym. And thenne he recounted to them how the king 28
was sore hurt / and that affectuelly he prayed them
that they vouchessaaf to come toward hym, so that he
might thanke them of the noble socours that they

and tells how the
King wishes to
reward them.

had doon to hym, and to make satisfaction to them of 32
theyre peyne & dyspens to his power, and also for to
speke with them of other matere. 'By my feyth,' said

Uryan, 'we are not come hither for to take sawdees[2]

[2] Fr. souldoier pour argent.

ne for no syluer / but only to susteyne & enhaunse the

that his only de-
sire is to support
the Catholic
faith,

catholique feyth.   And we wol wel þat euery man

knowe that we haue hauoyr & syluer ynough for to pay

and that he has
treasure enough;

4 our folke / but alway we right gladly shall goo toward

hym.   And wete it that I purpose to goo toward the

king in suche a state as I departed fro the batayll ; For

yf he vouchesaaf I wyl receyue of hym the ordre of

he will however
go to the King
to be knighted.

8 knighthode for the valyaunce & honour that euery man

sayth of hym.   And ye, Captayn, ye may goo and telle

hym that to morne at that houre he hath poynted

bothe my brother and I and the maister of Rodes, god

12 before, we shal be toward hym, and a houndred of our

moost high barons with vs.'   Thenne toke leue the

Captayne and came to the Cite, where he was receyued

The Captain re-
turns to the King,
who is still alive
and pleased to
see him,

moch honourably / and soone he came to the paleys,

16 where he fonde the kynge in also good poynte as he

lefte hym.   And there was his doughter Ermyne, that

was full of sorowe for the euyl of her fader / but

that notwithstanding she recomforted her self moche of

as is his daugh-
ter, when she
learns that the
brethren are
coming to the
city

20 this that men said to her, that the two damoyscaulx

shuld come there.   And wete it that she moche desyred

to see Uryan.   And thenne the Captayne salued the kyng.

'Ye be right welcomme,' said the kinge / ' what tydinges

1 fol. 86 b.

24 bryng you of youre [1]message / shal I not see that two

gentil damoyseaulx ?'   'Sire, ye,' said the Captayne /

The Captain
delivers his
message,

'they and houndred more with them / and playse you

to knowe that they wil haue no recompense of you /

28 For as they saye they be not sawdyours for siluer / but

þey name them self sawdyours of our lord Jeshu criste.

And so moche, sire, hath told me Uryan / that to

morne, god before, or it be fullysshe pryme, he shal

32 come toward you in suche a poynt & state as he

came fro the baytaylle ; For he wyl receyue thordre

of cheualrye and to be dowbed knight of your hand.'

'By my feyth,' said the kyng, 'I lawde our lord Jeshu-

for which the
King thanks his
Saviour.

36 Criste, whan before my dayes be termyned, it playseth

hym that I make & dowbe knight one so valyaunt &
hye prynce / and wete it I shal therfore deye betre at
ease.' And whan Ermyne herd of these tydinges she
had so grete joye therfore in her herte, that she coulde 4

not holde her contenaunce no manere / but therof she
made no grete semblaunt, but shewed to haue grete
sorowe woo in her herte. She tekp thenne, lyue of

her fader / and sore weping kyssed hym moche swetly / 8
and she went into her chambre / and there she bygan
to bewaylle her self sore / one houre for the doulour &
woo that she had for her fader / and another houre for

the grete joye & desyre that she had of the sight of 12
Vryan, whos taryeng enjoyed her moche / & moche
long she was in thoughte so argued and vexed therwith
all, that all that night she coude not slepe /

In this parte saith thistory, that on the morne erly 16
the king commanded that all noble and vanoble

shuld make theire houses to be appareylled ¹& hanged
without forth euery one after his power, for to make feste
& honour at the commyng of the two brethern and of 20
theyre folke / and that at euery corner of a strete shuld
be trompettes and other dyuerse Instruments of musyque
making grete melodye / And for certayn the peuple endeuoyred them self wel / ye / more than the kynge had 24
commanded to be doo. What shuld I make long pro-
logue / the two brethern within pryme came mounted
moche nobly vpon two grete coursers / and Vryan was

al armed, euen so as whan he came fro the batayll, 28
the swerd naked in his fyst. And Guyon, hys brother,
had on a gown of fyn clothe of damaske, rychely
fourred / and byfore them rode thretty of the moost
hye barons in noble aray / and nygh to them was the 32
maister of Rodes and the Captayn of Lymas. And
after the two bretheren came & folowed nygh thre
score & ten knightes and theire squyers & pages in her
companye / and in fayre aray they entred in to the 36

Cyte.   There had ye seen the feste begynne moch The welcome is
grete / and the trompettes & menestrels dooyng theire great, what with
crafte / And thrugh the stretes had ye sene folke of
4 grete honour that were moche wel and richely clothed,
whiche cryed with a hye voys / ' ha / a welcomme be ye, shouting, decor-
prynce vyctoryous, of whom we hold and are all sus- press of people.
cited of the cruel seruytude & boundage of thenemyes
8 of our lord Jeshu Cryst.'   There had ye see ladyes &
damoyselles at wyndowes in grete nombre / and thauncyent gentylman & burgeys were merueylled of the The townsfolk
grete fyerste of the noble Vryan, that was al armed, Urian's fierce-
12 the vysage dyscouered / a grene garland on his hed, ness,
an the swerd in his fyst.   And the captain bare byfore hym hys helmet on a tronchon of a spere.   And
whan they perceyued his fyers visage [1]they said be- [1] fol. 87 b.
16 twene them self togidre / ' that man is able and shappen and say he is
for to subdue & putte vndre hym all the world.'   ' By all the world.
my feyth,' said the other, ' he sheweth it wel, For he
is entred into this toune lyke as he had conquerd it.'
20 ' In name of god,' said other / ' the rescue of the daunger of whiche he hath kept vs fro is worth & ynough
for a conqueste.'   ' Certaynly,' said other, ' thaugh his
brother hath not so fyers a face, yet he semeth to be
24 man of wele & of faytte.'   And so talkyng of one thing
& of other they conueyed þem vnto the paleys, where At length the
they alighted.   And here resteth thystorye to speke at the palace,
ony more of the peuple / and bygynneth to speke how alight.
28 the two brethern came byfore the king /

Cap. XXIII.   How Vryan & Guyon came
byfore the kinge, he beying in his bed syke.

[2]Thystorye sayth now that the two breþern moche [2] fol. 88.
32 honourably came & made the reuerens to the They make rever-
kinge / and the kinge receyued them joyously / and who thanks them
thanked them moche gracyously of theire ayde & socours/ have given him,

and said to them / that after god / they were they by
whom he & al his reaume was suscited fro the moost

cruel passage, & more fel þan eny deth, For yf they
had not be, the paynemys had dystroyed them all / 4
or had constrayned to be conuerted to theire fals lawe,
whiche had be to vs wers & heuyer than ony deth cor-
porall. For they that to it had consented with herte,
they had had for euermore dampnacion eternel / ' And 8
therefore,' said the kyng, 'it is rayson that I rewarde

you to my power, For I haue none other wylle than to
endeuoyre me þerto / how be it certayn that I may
not acomplysshe to the regarde of the grete honour 12
that ye haue me shewed / but lowly & humbly I beseche you to take in worthe my lytil puyssaunce.'

' By my feyth,' said Vryan, ' of this ye ought not to
doubte / For we be not come hither neyther to haue 16
of you gold nor syluer / ne of your tounes, castals, ne

landes / but only to seke honour and for to dystroye
thenemyes of god, and to exalte the feyth catholical /
and I wil, sire, that ye knowe that we hold our peyne 20
wel employed, yf ye vouchesaaf to doo vs so moche of
honour that ye wyl dowbe my brother & me knightes
of your hand.' ' By my feyth,' said the king, ' noble
damoyseaulx, in asmoche as I am not worthy to acom- 24

plysshe your requeste, I consent to it / but first shall
the masse be said.' ' Sire,' said Vryan, ' tha me semyth

wel doon.' And thanne the chapellayne ¹was soone
redy. And thenne Vryan, hys brother, and all other 28
deuoutly herde the messe & the seruyse deuyne, And
after the deuyne seruyse Vryan came tofore the king.
And thenne he drew the swerde out of the shede &

kneled doun byfore the kyng, where he laye, and sayd 32
to hym in this manere : ' Sire, I requyre you, for alle

the salary of my seruyce that I haue doo or may doo
in tyme to come, that ye vouchesaf to dowbe me
knight with this swerde / and so shull ye haue wel 36

rewarded me of all that ye say that my brother & I
haue doo for you and for your realme ; For of the hand
of a more valyaunt knyght and noble lord, I ne may
4 receyue the ordre of knighthede / than of yours.' ' By
my feyth,' said the kinge / ' damoyseau, ye shew me
more honour than ye owe me / and ye say moche more
of me than euer I deserued. but sene I considered
8 that grete honour is to me to dowbe you knight, I am
agreable therto / but after that I haue acomplysshed
your requeste, ye shall couuenaunt with me yf it
playse you to graunte me a yefte, the whiche shal not
12 tourne you neyther to preiudice ne dommage, but only
to your ryght grete prouffyt & honour.' ' By my feyth,'
said Uryan, ' I am redy therto to acomplysshe your wille
& playsire.' Thenne had the kynge grete joye, and
16 dressyng hym to sytte vp, and toke the swerde by the
pomel that Uryan toke hym, and therwith dowbed hym
knyght, sayeng, in this manere / ' In the name of god,
I adoube you & admytte you into thordre of a knyght,
20 prayeng god to putte from you all euyll.' And þenne
gaf hym the swerd ayen, and thus makyng his wounde
opend, and out of it ranne blood thrugh ¹the wraper,
wherof Vryan was sory & woo, and so were all other
24 that sawe hym ; but thenne the kyng layed hym self
ayen along in his bed sodaynly, and said he felt none
euyll. And after he commanded two knightes that
they shuld fetche hys doughter / and they dide soo /
28 and brought her at mandement of her fader. And
whan the kyng sawe her, he said thus / ' My doughter
thank & remercye these noble men of thayde and socoure that they haue doon to me & to you bothe, and
32 also to all our realme, For yf had not be the grace of
god & theire strengthe & puyssaunce we had be all
dystroyed, or at leste exilled out of our land / or ellis
vs to haue be conuertid to theire fals lawe that had be
36 wers and more importable to vs than to suffre deth

Before knighting
him the King
gets Urian to
promise to give
him a gift, the
giving of which
will not impover-
ish Urian ;

then in the name
of God, the King
dubs Urian
knight.
The exertion
opens the King's
wound,

¹ fol. 80.

but he is eased
by laying down ;

then he sends for
Hermine,

and bids her
thank the
brethren ;

temporall' / And thenne she kneled byfore the two

which she does
much humbly,

bretheren & salued them, & thanked moche humbly
And wete it that she was in suche manere commouyd[2]

and is overcome
by her feelings of
sorrow for her
father and love
for Urian.

as she had be rauysshed, and wyst not how to hold 4
contenaunce, what for the woo & sorowe that she had
at her herte of thanguysshe that her fader felt / as of
the thoughtes that she toke for Uryan, in so moche
that she was as a personne that is awaked newly fro 8
her dreme.   But thenne vryan, that wel perceyued that

Urian seeing her
emotion,
raises her,

she had her spiryte troubled, toke her vp ryght swetely,

and bows to her.

and enclyned hymself byfore her, makyng moche
reuerence eche of them to other / and where as they 12

The people say
that were Urian
to marry their
lady, they would
have no fear for
the pagans.

of the countre said / 'yf this noble man had take
oure damoyselle to his lady wel it shuld come to passe,
For thenne we shuld drede neyther paynems nor man
that wold doo vs hurt.'   And thenne called the kyng 16
his doughtir, and to her said thus : 'My doughtir,

2 fol. 89 b.

sette you here [1]by me, For I deme that ye shall not

The King tells of
his approaching
end,

long hold me company.'   And she thanne wepyng satte
herself by hym.   And thanne all they that were there 20
bygan to sorowe & wepe for the pyte they had of the
kyng, And also of the sorow that they sawe the virgyne,
his doughter, made so pitously.

Thystory telleth vs that the kyng was sorowfull 24
    whan he sawe hys doughter take such heuynes,

and seeing his
daughter's grief
tries to console
her,

and thenne he said amyably : 'My doughtir, lete be
your heuynes and your grete doulour that ye take, I
pray you, For that thing that may not be amended it 28
is folye to make therof grete sorowe / notwithstandyng
it is raison naturel that eueryche creature be sorowfull for hys frend & neyghbour whan that he lesith

by promising to
provide for her.

hym.   but, and it playse god, I shal puruey for you 32
so that ye shal hold you content, or I departe fro this
mortal world, and so shall all the baronye of my
realme' / And þenne bygan the mayde to wepe more

Fr. *esmeue.*

haboundauntly than she dide to fore, And also all the
barons demened suche woo & sorowe that it was pyto-
ous for to see / but vryan and guyon were sorowfullest
4 of all.   and the kyng perceyuyng theire doulour, he
said to them : 'Fayre doughter, and you, vryan and
guyon, this sorowe is not necessary to you, For therwith I preuaylle not nor you neyther in no manere /
8 but it augmenteth my doulour, wherfore I you com-
maude that ye cesse of this heuynes yf ye loue me,
and to haue me yet with you here alyue a lytil space
of tyme.'   And thenne they bygan to cesse theyre
12 doulour in theire best manere, for the wordes that the
kyng to them said.   And ouer that spake the kynge
hym self dressyng to vryan, and thus said : 'Sire
knyght, thankyng be to you, ye couenaunted with me
16 a yefte whiche I purpose now to take / and þat shal
neyther touche your cheuaunce nor honour.'   'By ¹my
feyth,' sayd Vryan, 'demande what it playse you, For
yf it be of that thing wherof I haue power I shal fulfyll
20 it voluntarily.'   'Gramercy sire,' sayd the kynge, 'wete
it that by this that I shal demaude of you, shal retourne
to you a noble thing.   Now, sire knight, I pray you
that it may playse you to take my doughter in mary-
24 age, and all my royalme with her / And fro this tyme
fourth I gyue you full possessyon therof to doo therwith your prouffyt' / And wel veray & trouth it is that
he had doo brought there the crowne / and with these
28 wordes he took it, & said / 'hold, Vryan, ne reffuse
not my requeste that I desyre of you.'   Thenne were
the barons of the land so joyous that teeris fel fro
theire eyen for pyte & joye that they had therof.   And
32 whan Vryan vnderstode these wordes, he called a lytel
remembraunce / and wete it wel he was sorowfull &
dolaunt therof.   For he was wyllyng to seke the straunge
countrees of the world and poursiewe for honour.   But
36 alwayes for as moche as he was accorded with the kynge

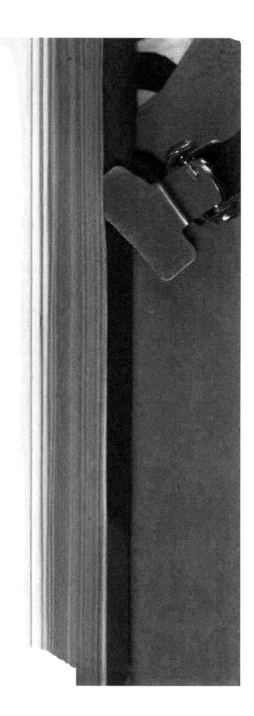

of the yefte, he wold not gaynsaye it / And whan the
barons sawe hym so pensefull they cryed al with a hye
voyce ryght pyteously / 'ha / a then, noble man, wilt
thou reffuse the kinges requeste?' 'By my feyth, lordes 4
& barons,' said Uryan, 'no more shal I doo.' Thenne
enclyned Uryan byfore the kyng wher he laye, and
toke the croune and putte it in Ermynes lap, sayeng /
'Damoyselle, it is your, and sith it hath fortuned thus 8
with me, I shall you helpe to kepe it my lyf naturel,
yf it playse god ayenst al them that wold vsurpe it or
putte it in subgeccion.' Thenne was the kinge joyful
and glad, & so were al the barons. And after he dide 12
make come the archebysshop of the Cite that assuryd
them togidre. But Ermyne ¹said she wold see first
the termynacion of her faders syknes or she shuld
procide ony ferther. Thanne said Vryan, 'damoyselle, 16
sith that it playseth you to doo so I am agreable therto.'
Thenne was the kyng woofull & dolaunt, and said :
'Fayre doughter Ermyne, ye shew wel þat lytel ye loue
me, whan that thinge which I desire moost to see afore 20
myn ende ye ne wyl acomplysshe. Now wel I see
that ye desyre my deth.' Whan þe mayde vnderstode
hym she was ryght dolaunt & sorowfull / and wepyng
kneeled byfore the king, hir fader, and said in this 24
manere : 'My right redoubted lord & fader / there nys
thing in the world that I shuld reffuse you vnto myn
owne deth / commande you me your playsire.' 'Ye
say now,' said the king, 'as a true doughtir ought to 28
say, that is wylling for to kepe her fader from wrathe
& fyre. I now thanne commande you that ye leue
your sorowe, and lete this halle to be dressid and with
ryche clothes hanged, and make the masse to be said / 32
and aftir the deuyne seruise do make the tables to be
couered, and after dyner make here byfore me the feste
as that I were now on my feet ; For wete it wel / that
shal helpe & comforte me wel.' And thenne they all 36

endeuoyred them self to fulfyll this that he com-
manded.   Thenne was the masse said, and sate them After mass the
company dine,
self at dyner / & Ermyne was sette at a table that was
4 layed byfore her faders bedd / and Vryan with her,
And Guyon serued Ermyne of mete.   Thanne had the
king grete joye, but he made betre semblaunt than his which pleases
the King,
herte was of power, For certayn what chere that he
8 made he felt grete peyne & grete dolour, For the venym though he is in
great pain from
his wound.
that was within the wounde caused grete putrefyeng &
rotyng of his flesshe / but for to rejoye the baronnye
he made no semblaunt of no sorow ne [1]douleur / and [1] fol. 91.
12 after dyner bygan the feest, and lasted til nyght came.
The king thanne called to hym vryan, and said, 'Fayre
sone, I wyl ye wedde my doughter to morne, and I The feast over,
the King tells
Urian that he
wishes him to
wyl delyuere vnto you the Crowne and Ceptre of this marry Hermine
16 realme, For wete it I may not long be alyue.   Wher- the next day,
fore I wil that alle the barons of þis land make theire and to have the
Barons make
homage to you byfore my deth.'   'Sire,' said vryan, homage to him.
'sith that playseth you / your wylle & myne be one' /
20 And there was Ermyne present þat refussed not to
fulfylle her faders wyll.

Cap. XXIV.   How Vryan espoused Ermyne, doughter vnto the kinge of Cypre.

24 ON the morne next, about the hooure of tierce, was In the morning
the spouse appareylled & rychely arayed, and the
chappell nobly hanged with riche cloth of gold, And
the Archebysshop of Famagoce espoused them there. the marriage
takes place,
28 And after came Vryan before the kyng [2]that toke the [2] fol. 91 b.
Crowne, and ther withall crouned vryan, that moche Urian is crowned,
of thankes rendred to the kynge therfore.   Thenne
called the king to hym all the barons of þe lande / and
32 commanded them to make theire hommage to kyng and the Barons
of the land
render homage
Vryan, his sone / and they voluntarily dide soo.   And to him.
the masse than bygan, and after it was doo they satte

at dyner / and syn bygan the feste right grete, and endured tyl euen / and after souper begane ayen the
feste / and whan tyme was the spouse was lede to
bed / and anone aftir Vryan layed hym self by her / 4
and the bysshop came & halowed the bed / And so
thenne all departed / some went to bed / and some retourned ayen for to daunce.   And Vryan laye with his
wyf, and her acqueyntaunce toke curtoysly & wel / 8
And on the morne they came ayen tofore the kynge /
the masse anoone was bygone.   And thither was the
queene conueyed & lede of guyon her brother, and by
one of the moost highe barons of the lande.   12

In this parte sheweth vs thistorye, that on þe next
morne after about the hooure of pryme, kyng vryan
acompanyed with the baronnye of poytou and of the
royalme of Cipre, came byfore the king and enclyned 16
hym self & salued hym right humbly. ' Fayre sone, ye
be welcome,' said the kyng. ' I am full joyouse of your
commyng / make my doughter to come, so shul we
here the deuyne seruyse.'   Thenne came his doughtir 20
Ermyne, wel nobly acompanyed of many ladyes &
damoyselles / and she come byfore her fader & salued
hym full humbly.   Thenne said he to her : ' My wel
beloued doughter, ye be welcome.   I am right wel joy- 24
ous whan god hath don to me suche a grace, that I have

purueyed you of so hye a prynce & worthy knyght to
your lord / and wete it that therfore I shal dey more
easely sith that you and al my land is out ¹of the 28
daunger of the paynemes, and no doubte ye haue to
your protection and wraunt a prynce worthy & valyaunt,
that right wel shal kepe and defende you ayenst all
your euyl willers, and in especial anenst thinfideles & 32
enemys of Ieshucrist.'   And with that worde the Chape-

layn bygan the masse.   And whan the masse was
celebred & said, the kyng callid to hym Vryan &
Ermyne, & to them said in this manere : ' My fayre 36

children, ryght affettuously I pray you that ye thinke
to loue, kepe, and honoure wel eche other / and to hold
& bere good feyth one to other, For nomore I may
4 hold you companye. Now thanne I recommande you
to the blysfull kyng of heuen, prayeng hym deuoutely
that he gyue you peas & loue togidre, and honourable
lyf & long.' And with these or semblable wordes he
8 shette hys eyen and departed fro this mortal lyf so
swetly that they supposed that he had be aslepe /
But whan they were certayn of his deth the douleur
& sorowe bygan to be grete. Thenne was Ermyne had
12 in to her Chambre, For she demened such sorowe that
grete pite it was to see. The kynge thenne was buryed
and his obsequyes doon ryally, and in the moost honourable guyse that coude be deuysed after the vse and
16 custome of the land. And wete it that all the peple
was sorowfull & dolaunt; but they took comfort of
this, that they had founde & recouered a lord ful of so
grete prowesse as Vryan was / and lytel & lytil cessed
20 the lawmenting & heuynes. And soone after yede
Vryan thrugh al his realme to see and visite the places
& fortres / and betoke one part of his folke to Guyon,
his brother / and another part to the maister of Rodes,
24 and made them to be shipped on the see, for to wete &
knowe, for to here & knowe yf they shuld here ony
tydynges that paynemes were on the see for to lande in
his lande. 'For wete it wel,' said the king vryan,
28 'that we purpose ne think not to abyde ¹vnto tyme
they fetche vs, For we shall & god before goo & vysyte
them within short tyme, after that we haue ouerseen
the rule & gouernaunce of our land.' And forasmoch
32 departed Guyon & the maister of Rodes, & rowed on
the see with thre thousand fyghting men. And here
leueth thistorye of them / and bygynneth to shewe how
Vryan & Ermyne went and vysited theire land.

the dying King
gives his blessing
to his children,

and then departs
this mortal life
in peace.

Great sorrow is
felt by all,
especially by
Hermine.

The King is
buried,

and the people
seeing the
bravery of their
new lord, cease
their lamenting.

Urian visits the
towns of his
realm,

and sends some
of his men
to learn tidings
of the pagans.

1 fol. 92 b.

Urian and his
wife are well
received in their
land,

Thystory saith that king Vryan, with Ermyne hys
wyf, yede & vysited theire land al about, and
full gladly & honourably they were receyued in euery
burghe, toune, & Cite where they passed / and grete 4
yeftes were presented to them / And wete it that Vryan
purueyed ryght wel to all hys fortres, of all suche
thinges that were necessary for the werre yf some
thing befell in tyme to come. And for trouth euery 8

and his subjects
marvel at his
strength.

one was meruaylled of his heyght, of his fyersnes, &
of his puyssaunce & strengthe of body. And wel said
the men of the Countree, that ferdfull & daungerous
thing was to cause his wrath & anger. And thus went 12
Vrian fro place to place thrughe his royalme. And

He reappoints
honest officers,

suche officers that made rayson & kept justice, he lefte
them in their offices stil / but to al oþer that oþerwyse
dide than right requyreth, he purueyed of remede by 16
good & meure deliberacion of his counseill. And com-

and commands
Justice to be
well kept.

manded euery one to make raison & Justice in al tymes,
as wel to the leste as to the moost, without to bere eny
fauour to ony of eyther partye / and yf they contrary 20
did to this hys wyll, he shuld punyssh them so cruelly
that al other shuld take ensample therby. And thene

Afterwards the
King and Queen
return to
Famagoce.

he, his lady, & his folke retourned to Famagoce / and
the quene was grete with child / And now resteth 24
thystorye of them, and speketh of Guyon and of the
maister of Rodes, that rowed on the see by the Costes
of Surye, of Damask, of Baruth, of Tupple, & of
Danette, for to knowe yf paynemes were on the see 28
or not.

¹ fol. 93.

Guion and the
Master of
Rhodes
searching on the
sea for the
pagans,

¹Now saith thistorye, that so long sailled & rowed
the Crystens on the see, that they sawe aprouch
as of a leghe nygh to them a certayn quantite of shippes, 32
but by liklyhode they might not be grete nombre.
Thenne they sent a Galleye toward our folke that al
redy were in ordynaunce to wete what they were / but
the galey came so nygh that the cristens, our folke, 36

toke it / and by them knew and vnderstode almaner of

Oure folke thanne halid vp saylles hastly,

and saylled anone toward theire enmys. And whan the

4 paynemes perceyued them they were moch abasshed,

and gretly aferd, and wend wel to haue withdraw them

self in to the hauen of Baruth / but our galeyes ad-

uaunced them, and ran vpon them by al sydes. There

8 was grete occysion / and shortly to say the paynemes

were dyscomfyted, and their nauye take / and all were

cast onerbord or slayne. And the nauye was full of

grete goodes. And after our barons putte them self in

12 the see ayen for to haue retourned in to Cypre. but

by fortune & strengthe of wyndes they were cast to

Cruly[1] in Armanye. And whan the king of Armanye,

that was brother vnto the kinge of Cipre, knewe theire

16 commyng, he sent anone for to wete what folke they

were / And the master of Rodes said to them that

came to wete what they wer: 'Telle the kyng that it

is the brother of Vryan of Lusynen, kyng of Cypre,

20 that hath trauersed the see for to wete & knowe yf

paynemes were on it in armes, for to haue come vpon

the Cypryens for cause of the saudan that hath be

dycomfyted & slayn, and al his folke at the grete batayll

24 of Famagoce.' 'How,' said they of Armanye, 'is there

ony other kyng in Cypre than our kingis brother?' 'By

my feyth,' said the maister of Rodes, 'ye / For the

king [2]was wounded with a dart enuenymed by the

28 sawdans hand in so mortal a wyse that he is deed

therof, and he beying yet alyue, he gaf his doughtir in

maryage to Vrian of Lusynen, that slew the saudan

& dyscomfyted all his folk.' Whan they thanne vnder-

32 stode hym, they yede & denounced it to theire kyng,

which was sorowfull of the deth of his brother. but

not withstandyng, he came toward the see syde with

a grete company, and entred in to the vessell where

Marginal notes:

take a galley and learn the pagans' whereabouts.

They set out for the fight, and gain a victory,

and set sail for Cyprus;

but are driven by wind to Cruly in Armenia.

The King of the land sends to know who they are,

and is sent word that it is the brother of the King of Cyprus.

The King of Armenia asks if there is a new King in Cyprus,

[2] fol. 93 b.

and the Master of Rhodes relates how Urian became King there.

<hr>

[1] *Truli* in Fr. ed. Afterwards spelt *Cruli*.

MELUSINE.

M

Guyou and the maister of Rodes were in. And whan
guyon wyst of his commyng he went ayenst hym, and
eche to oþer made grete reuerence. Thenne said the
king to the grete Pryour of Rodes, 'Maister, sethen 4
this yong damoyesau is brother vnto my nyghtis lord,
I were vncurteys whan he is arryued in my land, yf I
receyued hym not honourably as to hym apparteyneth.

And of this I pray you, that ye vouchssaf to pray hym 8
on my behalf, that it playse hym to come in to our
paleys, and we shal doo to hym the best chere that we
can.' 'By my feyth,' said the grete Pryour / 'that
shal I doo gladly.' Thanne he spak therof to guyon, 12
whiche answerd to hym right gladly, 'I wold doo a

greter thinge yf it lay in my power for the kyngis sake.
For good feyth & rayson requyreth it.' And thenne
they went togider / and guyon lede with hym a fayre 16
companye of knightes / but alwayes they had theire
cotes of stele on þem, and were in right good aray, as
folke vsed to the faytte of armes. And here speke I
no more of þem, And shal speke of Florye the 20
doughter of the kynge of Armanye. /

This historye sayth that the kynge of Armanye had a
doughter, and none other children / but here.
[1]And the quene, his wyf, was deed / and wete it þat 24
this kyng and the kyng of Cypre had to theire spouses
the two susters that were doughters to the kyng of
Malegres / and eche of them gate a doughtir on their
wyues / of the whiche Ermyne that Vryan spoused 28
was one / and that other was the pucelle florye of
whome I haue bygonne to traytte. She was that tyme

at Cruly ryght glad & joyous of the commyng of
the straungers. She appareylled and arayed her self 32
moche richely, and so dide all her damoyselles. Soone
after came the kynge her fader / guyon / the maister
of Rodes, & theire felawship, and entred in to the
toune, and came to the palleys in to the grete halle. 36

And thenne Florye, that moch desyred theire commyng, came there, and humbled herself moche ayenst
her fader / and the kyng said to her, 'Cherysshe and
4 doth feste to this noble men, & receyue them honourably / and in especiall the brother of my nyghtis lord &
husband.' And whan the mayde vnderstode that, she
was full glad & joyous. She thenne came to guyon /
8 toke hym by the hand swetly, & sayd : 'Sire damoy- She takes Guion
by the hand,
and welcomes
him to the land.
seau, ye be right welcoms in to my faders royalme.'
'Damoyselle,' sayd Guyon, 'gramercy to you.' There /
bygan thenne the feest right grete & fayre / and wel A fair feast is
served,
12 they were festyed, & seruyd with dyuerse meetes &
wynes / and betwix guyon & Florye were many honeste and Guion and
Flory have much
gracious speech
together.
& gracyous talkyng. and wete it for certayn yf guyon
had had leyser, he had dyscouered his thoughte to
16 her. but while they were in that grete solace & joye, a
galeye arryued to the port that came fro Rodes / and News comes from
Rhodes
they that were within were receyued honourably of
them of the toune / and joyful & right glad they were
20 whan they knew that theire maister was there. Wherfore one of them said to the peuple there, 'Sires,
vouchesauf to lede one of vs there ¹the lordes befor, ¹ fol. 94 b.
to aduertyse them of paynemes that ben vpon the see that the pagans
are at sea,
24 in grete nombre.' Thanne was a knight brought there
the maister of Rodes was / and said to hym, that
paynemes with grete nauye were passed byfore the yle with a great navy
sailing towards
Cyprus.
of Rodes / and had taken the wind & waye toward
28 Cypre / and how men said that the Calyphe of Bandas
with all hys puyssaunce & power was there. Whan
the maister of Rodes vnderstode these tydynges, he
went & told Guyon of it. Wherfore, guyon seeyng Guion, on learn-
ing this, bids
Flory farewell,
32 hym self as constrayned, humbly said to the pucelle,
'Damoyselle, right hertily I beseche you that ye
vouchesaf, sethen I moste departe your presens, to call and asks her not
to forget him.
me ofte in your remembraunce / For as to my part,
36 your vassall & seruaunt shal I euer be vnder the

standart of your gouernance.' Florye thanne knowyng
for certayn his soudayn departyng, her herte was fylled
with dueyl & sorowe / how wel she kept contenaunce
in the best man*er*e that she coude / and louyngly be- 4
held guyon, whiche toke his leue of her fader, that
conueyed hym to the see side, and grete peple wi*th*
hym.   There thenne entred guyon in to his ship, and
commanded the sailles shuld be had vp to the wynde, 8
that was good & propyce to them.   And wete that
Florye was mounted vp vnto the vppermost wyndowe
of an hye tour, and neu*er* departed thens tyl she lost
the sight of guyo*ns* vessel, prayeng god to preserue 12
hym fro*m* al daunger. /

Thystorye recounteth & saith here that the Caliphe
of Bandas, and the kinge of Brandymount in
tharse, that was uncle to the saudan of Damaske, herde 16
tydynges how the sawdan was slayn, and al his folke
putte to grete dyscomfyture in the yle of Cypre. Wherfore they beyng full sory therof assembled anons theire
power / and purposyng to auenge his deth entred theire 20
shippes, and toke theire way toward Cypre / and [1]they
supposyng the Cypryens had be wi*th*out king, hyed
them fast thitherward in suche man*er*e that they shuld
not be perceyued where as they shuld arryue. but þey 24
of Rodes perceyued them, and made knowleche þerof
vnto kyng Vryan, that alredy had assembled his peple,
and putte them in aray for to receyue the batayll. and
morou*er* had made good ordonnau*n*ce and gardes for the 28
portes, that assoone as they shuld perceyue them commyng to the hauen, that they shuld make a token of
fyre, wherby the Countrey might perceyue the commyng
of theire enmyes, and eu*er*y man to be redy in armes 32
thitherward / and so was the kingis proclamac*i*on
vpon deth. And wete it that the king kept the feldes
in the myddes of the portes of his royalme for to
be the sooner at the porte where the sarrasyns shuld 36

arryue to take theire landing / And the king made so
grete moustre & semblaunt that he gaf his peple so
grete courage, that with hym & his enterpryse they
4 durst wel fight with the Caliphe, and with his puyssaunce. It happned so, by the grace of god, that the
see was enragid thrugh the stormes and horryble
tempeste, that the sarrasyns were al dysmayed &
8 abasshed / and the tempeste casted them in suche wyse
here & there, that within short tyme they ne wyst
where eyghte of theire galeyes were become. And on
the morowe about the hooure of pryme, thayer was al
12 clere, and the wynd cessed, and the sonne shone fayre
& clere / thenne the grete shippes of the paynemes
held them togidre, & toke theire way vnto the port
of Lymasson. And of them I leue to speke / and shal
16 shew you of the viii vessels that were sparpylled by
the tempeste, and what way they held / and in thoo
vessels was all thartyllery of the paynemes, as gonnes,
bowes, arowes / ladders / paueys, & such habylements
20 of werre ¹as they had / and so it fortuned that guyon
and the maister of Rodes with theire puyssaunce recountred them, and perceyued eche other. but whan
oure peple knewe that they were sarasyns / and the
24 sarasyns knew that they were crysten peuple / they
bygane eche of them to lye and bord other with
shotte of gonnes & crosbowes / and whan they were
chayned togidre they threw darts as thikk as hayle
28 stones / and the batayll was so grete, hard, & stronge /
but guyon, the maister of Rodes, & theire puyssaunce
assaylled so manfully the paynemes that they knew
not to what part they shuld tourne them to defende,
32 For our peuple that were in the galeyes faught so
mightly that the paynemes were as dycomfyted. There
might men here them crye on theire goddes / nat that
withstanding they were dyscomfyte & slayne. And
36 thanne whan theire admyrall, that was maister of the

A storm causes
great damage to
the Saracen
fleet;

but on the mor-
row they sail
to the port of
Lymasson.

Eight galleys full
of stores, belong-
ing to the Sara-
cens, sparpilled
by the tempest,

¹ fol. 95 b.

were met by the
Master of
Rhodes,

who attacked
them, and fought
so well as to
defeat the pagan
sailors.

The admiral seeing he is defeated,

leaves the fleet in a boat accompanied with eight persons.

The Christians enter the enemy's vessels, and throw overboard or take prisoners the Saracens.

The spoils are divided,

Guion sending his share to Flory,

1 fol. 96.

and to her father the King of Armenia.

The King welcomes Guion's knight, who conveys the present, and Flory is very joyful, for she loves Guion much.

The King of Armenia learns from his Saracen prisoners that their comrades have gone to Cyprus,

artylery, sawe the dyscomfiture tourned vpon them /. he made to be haused a lytal galyote out of the grete galeye with viii hores / and so entred he and syghte personnes with hym of the secretest / and toke thauen- 4 ture of the wynd / & rowed so mightly that our peuple meruaylled þerof / but they made neuer semblaunce to pursiew them / but entred into the paynemes vessels, & bygan to cast alle onerbord. but they toke to the 8 nombre of ij C sarasyns prysonners / wherof guyon gaf oo hondred to the maister of Rodes to make them cristen, and also two galeyes / and guyon toke the other hondred sarasyns and two of the moost richest 12 vessels that they had wonne, and toke it to a knyght of Rodes / and thus said to hym, ' Conduyte me this two galeya, and þis houndred sarrasyns to Cruly, and recommand me to the kinge & his doughtir / and on 16 my byhalue ¹presente to the pucelle Florye this two vessels as they are garnysshed / and to the kyng the houndred sarasyns.' Wherof the knyght toke the charge & departed, & hasted hym tyl he came to the 20 Cite of Cruly / and dide his message as he was youen in commandement / and recounted to them the grete dyscomfyture and the valyaunt conduyte of guyon. ' By my feyth,' said the kynge, ' ye be welcome, and 24 thanking be to that noble damoyseau ' / And the pucelle was so joyous of these nouuelles that she had neuer in her naturel lyf so grete joye. For knowe ye wel she loued so entierly guyon þat all her joye was of hym. 28 The king thanne & his doughter yaf to the knight a riche jewel, wherof he thanked þem, and toke leue of them, & retourned hastly to Rodes. And anone, after hys departyng, the kyng of Armenye questyoned with 32 the paynemes where the armee of the Calyphe was / and they said in Cipre to reuenge the deth of the sawdan of Damaske that the Cipryens had slayn in batayll. ' Par ma foy,' sayd the kyng, ' as for you, ye 36

haue faylled of your enterpryse' / And thenne he commanded that they shuld be feteryd with yrons, and to
be putte in to parfounde pryson / and the two vessels
4 to be descharged, and all the goodes that were in to be
borne into the Castel. It is now tyme that I speke   as does Guion.
of guyon and of the maister of Rodes, that had ques-
tyoned the sarasyns wher the Calyphe purposed to
8 land / and they said in Cypre. Guyon thenne by
thauys and Counseyll of his barons for cause they had
many vessels & lytel nombre of peuple / commanded
that al thartylery that they had wonne shuld be putte   Guion ships the
                                                           spolis of the
12 into theire shippes / and also al other thinges that were victory,
of nede to them / and the remanaunt & the vessels also /
1 he gaf to the maister of Rodes that sent them to Rodes.   1 fol. 96 b.
And whan this was don they saylled, & hasted þem   and sets sail for
                                                       Cyprus.
16 toward Cypre. And here leueth thystory to spek of
them / and retourneth to speke of the galyote where
thadmyrall was in, where it became or toke porte. /.
Thystory sayth that the kyng brandymount & the
20 Calyphe of Bandas were sorowfull for þeir losse
& grete dommage / and so longe rowed thadmyral on   The boat contain-
                                                       ing the admiral
the see that he perceyued the port of Lymasson, &   and eight men is
                                                       rowed to Lymas-
sawe grete nauye byfore the toune. And whan he came   son,
24 somewhat nygh he herd shotte of gonnes & sowne of   where the sound
                                                        of battle is heard.
trompettes, and soone after he knew that it was þe
Calyphe of Bandas and his armee, & the puyssaunce of
kyng brandymount of tharse,2 that assaylled them of
28 the toune for to take it. But there was the Captayne
of the place & his peple3 wel paueysed, that valyauntly   The Captain of
                                                           Lymasson de-
deffended the porte in so moche that the sarasyns   fends his port
                                                         well, and the
gat there nought / but lost many of their men, and   Saracens wish for
                                                         their artillery
32 wysshed ofte aftir theire galeyes with theire gonnes &   from the eight
                                                           vessels,
artyllery that were sprad on the see by the tempeste /   which they think
                                                          are still at sea
they wyst not where. Thenne came to them thadmyral
that thus said on hye: 'By my feyth, Calyphe, woo

2 Fr. Tarche.   3 Fr. w. p]atout bons parars.

may be to you, For your nauye that I conduyted is lost
& take, For the Cristen recountred vs vpon the see, and
haue dyscomfyted vs / and none is scaped but only we
that are here / and at oo worde al is lost / for to hold 4
you long compte therof that shuld preuayll you nought.'
Thenne whan the Calyphe vnderstode hym he was sorowfull & dolaunt. 'By my feyth,' said he / ' lordis, here
ben heuy tydinges. For wel I see that Fortune slepeth 8
as to our help / and so hath he doo long / but fauourable & moche propice it is as now to crysten peple, For
wel it appereth presently by vs / and so dide but of
late by our Cousyn the saudan, the which & al hys 12
peuple also haue be slayn or dyscomfyte in the same
yle of Cypre.' Thenne said the admyral to hym : ' Sire,
yf ye anounce or shew se blauses of abasshement byfore your folke that shal   use them to be half dyscom- 16
fyte / and onermore knowe ye to this that I perceyue
of them of this porte d   ns, that they be not shappen
to lete you arryue d   e theire land without sore
fyghting and grete sawtes gyuyng. For they shew not 20
to be aferd of your puyssaunce. therfore I wold aduyse
& counsayll you, that we shall withdraw vs into the
hye see, & lete coule them self / and about the spryng
of the day we shalbe at a lytel porte that not ferre is 24
hens called the port of saynt Andrew / and there without ony deffense or gaynsayeng we may take land.'
And this they dide. And whan the Captayn of Lymasson sawe hys enmyes departe, he made a rampyn or 28
smal galeye to folow them of ferre, þat it coude not be
perceyued of them / and aspyed how at euen they
ancred aboute a myle nygh to saynt Andrews porte.
Thanne retourned the rampyn hastly toward Lymas- 32
son / and to the captayne recounted al that he had
seen / Thenne made the captayn fyre to be putte high
vpon the garde for manere of token / and whan they
of the nerest garde or watching place sawe the token of 36

(marginal notes)

fol. 97.

and that he
should withdraw
to the port of St.
Andrew,

where it will be
easier to land.

The Caliph gives
up the attack,
and sets sail for
St. Andrew,
followed by a
rampin from
Lymasson,
sent to learn the
movements of
the Saracens.

.rmy will
.urage ;

fyre / soone after fyre was made fro garde to garde, The alarm is given throughout Cyprus,
that knowleche was therof thrugh all the royalme.
Thenne euery man, what on foot & on horsbake, drew
4 them self to the place where kyng Vryan was, that al
redy had sent hys espyes to knowe wher the paynemes and spies are sent to learn where the Saracens will land.
shuld land, and manded to euery captayne they shuld
kepe & defend wel theire fortresses / 'For,' said he,
8 'yf it playse god none of them shal not repasse the see.
And here resteth the [1]hystorye to speke of kynge [1] fol. 97 b.
Vryan / and bygynneth to speke of the Caliphe. /

I n this partye sheweth thistorye / that the sarasyns
12 that were entred in to the see / as soone as þey The Saracens at daybreak weigh their anchors and land their men and artillery at St. Andrew.
apperceyued the day spryng, they deceueryd, & toke
vp theire ancres, and came al in oo flotte to the porte,
& there landed. And wete it wel, that they of thabbey
16 of saynt andrew perceyued them wel, the whiche immediatly made knowleche to Lymasson / and the Cap-
tayne of þe place gaf vnto the kyng' knowlech ther- Word is at once sent to Urian of their landing;
of / the which had grete joye therof / and fourthwith
20 bygan to apparayll hym to go to batayll. And the
Calyphe, hys enemy, made to be putte a land his
artylery out of the shippes / and dide make hys lodgis
therby, as it were half a leghe fro the port, vpon a
24 grete ryuere at a cornere of a lytel wode, to refresshe
hym & his peple also; and lefte foure thousand men
within the shippes, for theire sauegarde / and in the
meane saison guyon / the maister of Rodes, & theire
28 peuple arryued to Lymasson / where men said to them and Guion learns that their navy is unprotected,
how the sarasyns had landed / and how theire nauye
was a leghe fro saynt Andrewes porte. 'By my feyth,'
sayd Guyon, 'we shal thanne goo & vysyte them / For
32 who that might take them fro the sarasyns, none of
them shuld neuer retourne foot, in sury nor in tharsy' /
and in these wordes sayeng, they putte them in to the so sets out to capture the Saracen fleet,
see, & went lightly sayllyng', that they came so nygh
36 the panemes that they sawe the porte of saynt Andrew,

and the grete nombre of shippes that were there.
Thenne they putte themself in aray and in good ordynaunce / and this done, they rane vpon theire enemys
as thondre & tempeste, smyttyng⁴ vpon the shippes of 4
the sarasyns byforce of shotte so horrybly, that yl

¹ fol. 96.

bestade were the sarasyns, that wel happy was he ¹that
myght recouere the lande. And by that meane were

and succeeds,

the shippes take / and al the sarasyns that were take 8
were putte to deth. Thanne guyon sent to the abbey
foyson of them that he had wonne of the sarasyns /

taking many
prisoners,

and brought to Lymasson with them as many galeyes
& shippes as there were laden with the goodes of the 12
sarasyns, except suche as they brent. And þe other

Fugitives arrive
at the Caliph's
camp with news
of the defeat,

that escaped, came to thoost of theire lord, cryeng with
a hye voys alarme / and recounted & said how the
Cristen had by force & strengthe discomfited them. 16
Thenne was the oost gretly mevyd, & came to the
port who best coude, and fonde many of theire peuple
ded, and som were hyd in the busshes. And whan the

which makes
him doleful.

Calyphe perceyued & sawe this grete dommage, he was 20
moche dolaunt. 'By machomete,' said he to kyng

He says that if
the French
knights stay they
will do much
harm.

Brandymount, 'these Cristen that are come hither fro
Fraunce, ben ouermoche hardy & appert men in armes,
and yf they soiourne long⁴ here it shal be to our grete 24
dommage' / 'By machomet,' said the kyng Brandy-

King Brandy-
mount swears
he will remain to
be either victor
or conquered.

mount, 'I shal neuer deporte fro this land vnto tyme I
be al dyscomfyted, or þat I haue put them to flyght, &
brought to an euyl ende.' 'No more shal I doo,' ansuerd 28
Calipha. Thenne þey recouered there six of theire

The Saracens
save six galleys
from the fire.

galeyes, & eschiewed þem fro the fyre, and lefte in it
good wardes for to kepe them ; and after they retourned
to theire peple. And here ceasseth thystorye of them / 32
and retourneth to speke of Vryan /

Now sheweth thistorye how the kyng Vryan was
lodged in a fayre medow vpon a ryuere, in that
self place where the fourragers of the sawdan were 36

dyscomfyted at the brydge, as before is said. And had
sent his espyes to haue knowlege where his enemyes
had take theyre lodgys / And thenne came [1]the
4 maister of Rodes, whiche alighted byfore the kinges
pauyllon, whom he made reuerence moche honourably.
And the king, that was moche joyous of his commyng,
receyued hym benyngly, and demanded of hym how
8 guyon his brother dyde. 'By my feyth, sire,' said the
maister of Rodes, 'wel / as the moost assureat man that
euer I knew. Sire, he recommandeth hym to you as
affectually as he may.' 'Nowe telle me,' said the king,
12 'how ye haue doo syn that ye departed from vs!' And
the maister recounted hym fro braunche to braunche
all thauentures that had happed to them. 'By my
feyth,' said the kyng, 'ye haue worthyly vyaged; I
16 thanke & lawde my Creatour therof / and as for myn
vncle, þe kynge of Armanye, I am moche glad that ye
lefte hym in good prosperyte. but we moost haue
aduys of our Counseyll, to see how we may dystroye
20 the Sarasyns / and as touching me & my peple, I am
redy to departe for to approuche to them, For to long
they haue soiourned in our land without to haue assayed
vs. goo thanne toward my brother, and telle hym that
24 I departe for to goo ayenst the paynemes.' The maister
thanne toke leue of king Vryan, and hastly retourned
to Lymasson / and immedyatly the king & his peuple
marched fourth, tyl they came & lodged them a leghe
28 nygh to the Calyphes oost, vnknowyng the paynemes
of it. And the maister of Rodes came to guyon, and
told hym how the kyng was departed for to recountre
& fyght with the sarasyns; wherfore guyon commanded
32 his trompettes to blow, and departed fro Lymasson in
fayre aray; & came vnto a ryuere, and lodged hym
therby, vpon the which ryuere were the paynemes
lodged, & no distaunce or space was betwene them
36 & their enemyes, but a [2]high mountayne. And now

Urian sends spyes to find his enemies' camp.

[1] fol. 98 b.

The Master of Rhodes visits the King.

and tells him of Guion's bravery, and brings Guion's regards;

and also tells of their adventures.

Urian says he may have the advice of his council how best to overcome the Saracens,

and sends back the Master to Guion.

King Urian marches his people within a league of the Saracen host.

The master of Rhodes gives Guion the King's message,

and then Guion also marches his men near the Saracens.

[2] fol. 99.

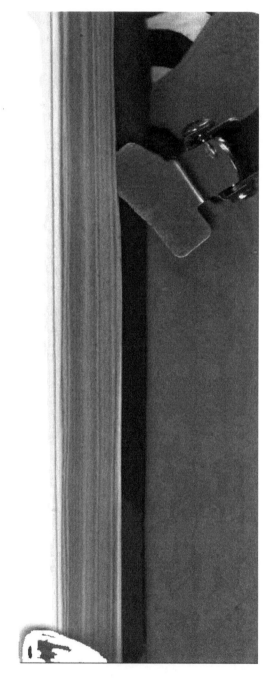

resteth thistorye of hym, and retourneth to speke of
Vryan his brother.

Thystorye sayth that kyng Vryan desired moch to
knowe where the sarasyns were lodged / also to
haue true knowlege of theire connyne; wherfore he
called to hym a knyght, that knew wel al the Countrey,
and said to hym : 'putte on your harneys, and take the
sureat hors that ye haue, and come alone here byfore
my pauyllon : and telle nobody of it / & ye shal come
with me there as I shal lede you' / and anone the
knight dide his commandement / and wel horsed &
armed retourned to hym byfore hys tente, wher he
fonde king vryan redy on horsbak, the which said to
some of his barons, 'Sires, meue not your self fro this
place tyl ye haue tydi   s of me / but yf I cam not
hither ayen / loke ye no that I shal lete you wete by
this knyght.' And they answerd that so shuld they
doo / ' but take good l   e,' sayd they agayn, 'where
ye goo' / ' be not in d   ibte therfore,' said vryan to
them / And thenne they departed; and Vryan said to
the knight, ' conduyte me now the surest waye that ye
can, tyl that I may see the porte where the sarasyns
landed.' And the knyght lede hym vnto the hylle
ryght high, & said : ' Sire, yonder is the porte that ye
desire to see.' ' And how,' said the kyng, ' it hath
be said to me that theire nauye was al brent, and yet I
see yonder some grete vessels ? Fro whens myght they
be come now ?' / and thenne behild the king' / at the
synester syde in to the founs[1] of the valey, and sawe
his brothers oost, that was lodged vpon the ryuere /
and at the ryght syde of the hille he sawe þe Caliphes
oost, that were in grete nombre. 'By my feyth,' said
the kyng, 'yonder is grete multitude of peple payneme / them I knowe wel ynough; but þey [2]of this
other syde I knowe not what they be. abyde me

4 a

to recon-

ith hitu,
own

The knight leads
the King to a
high hill,

where he sees
some vessels,

his brother's and
the Saracen host.

2 fol. 99 b.
He does not
recognize his
brother's army,

---

[1] Fr. *font.*

here, and I shall goo wete what folke they be, yf I
may.' The kyng thanne rode tyl he came nygh his
broþers oost, and founde a knight on his way, which he
4 knew wel; and anoon called hym by hys name, and
demaunded of hym yf his brother guyon was there /.
Whan the knight vnderstode hys wordes, he beheld
& knew hym, and soone kneeled byfore hym, say-
8 eng in this manere : 'My liege & souerayn lord, your
brother guyon is yonder with al hys peuple, and the
maister of Rodes also.' Thenne commanded hym the
kyng that he shuld goo to Guyon hys brother, and
12 telle hym that he shuld come & speke with hym
vpon the said mountayne. And the knight went &
tolde these tydinges to guyon; wherfor he, and the
maister of Rodes with hym, mounted on horsbak / toke
16 the way to the mountayneward, wher as Vryan retourned
to his knyght, whoms he said : 'Frend, wel it is with
vs, For that is my brother guyon which is lodged
yonder.' Thenne came þer guyon & the maister of
20 Rodes where the two bretheren made moche, eche of
oþer. The kinge after shewed to them thoost of theire
enemyes / and whan they sawe it / they said / 'we
wyst not them so nygh to vs.' 'Now,' said vryan,
24 'they may not escape vs, yf it be not by the meanes of
yonder galeyes,' wherof guyon was abasshed / 'For,'
said he / 'these deuels haue brought moo vessels, For
within these foure dayes last passed we toke & brent
28 al theyre nauye.' 'Thenne,' said the maister of Rodes,
'I suppose wel what that is / happely some of them
were not fonde, which haue eschewed that few shippes
fro the fyre.' 'By my feyth,' said the kyng, 'thus it
32 may wel be / but þerto ¹We most puruey of gardes,
For therby shuld mowe escape the chief lordes of
theire oost, that happly might adommage vs in time
to come.' 'How, sire,' said the maister of Rodes, 'it
36 semeth that ye haue dycomfyted them al redy, and

and so rides to it.

On the way he
meets a knight
he knows well.

The knight
kneels to him,
and tells him to
whom the host
belongs.

King Urian sends
for Guion,

who, accom-
panied with the
Master of Rho-
des, comes to the
King.

Urian says that
now the Saracens
cannot escape,
except by the
vessels.
Guion is abashed
at the Saracens
having vessels,
as he believed he
had burnt or
captured them
all, but the
Master says,
these are some
saved from the
fire.

¹ fol. 100.
The King orders
guards to be
ready to prevent
any one embark-
ing,

that it ne resteth more but to kepe the Calyphe and
brandymount, that they scape not at þat porte.' 'Certaynly,' ansuerd the kynge, 'yf they be nomore than I
see, we nede not so grete peple as god haþ leued vs.' 4
The kinge thenne commanded his knight, þat he shuld
goo to hys oost and make them to be putte in aray,
and that he shuld conduyte them vnto þe foot of the
said mountayne. The knight departed, & dide as it 8
was youen to hym in commandement / and al thoost
obeyed hym, and came in fayre aray & good ordynaunce vnto the hille. Also guyon went and made
hys peple to be armed, and brought þem at the other 12
syde of the ryuere, so nygh the paynemes oost that he
might wel perceyue theire manyere & contenaunce.
And the kyng commanded the maister of Rodes, that
he with all hys peuple shuld entre in to þe see / and 16
that they shuld trauerse, rowyng nygh the porte, to
thende yf the sarasyns shuld putte & withdraw them
self into theire shippes, that they might not escape /
'And I goo,' sayd vryan, 'putte my peple in aray, forto 20
gyue batayll to these paynemes.'

The kynge thenne came to his oost, and made his
archers & crosbowe men to marche & goo fourth ;
and after folowed the wynges. & the arryergarde came 24
after in fayre ordonnaunce / and assoone as þe sarasyns
perceyued them, they bygan alarme, and euery payneme
armed hym self / but or they were all armed, Vryan
sent vpon them a thousand good men of armes wel 28
horsed, that moche adommaged them, for they fonde
them vnpurueyed & out of aray. But notwithstanding,
they assembled them in batayll & aray. Thanne bygan
the stoure fyers & cruel. For there had ye seen arowes 32
flee as thykk as motes in the sonne / and after Vryan
and his auantgarde assembled to his enemys; and so
manfully they faught, that they made the sarasyns to
withdraw bakward. For vryan made there so grete 36

fayttes of armes, and gaf so pesaunt & horryble strokes Urian doing great feats of arms.
both to the lyft & right syde, that al them that he
recountred he smote & threw doun fro theire horses to
4 the erthe, in so moch that his enemyes fled byfore hym
as the partrych doth byfore the sperehauke. And
whanne the Calyphe of Bandas perceyued hym, he
shewed hym to kyng Brandymount, sayeng, 'yf we be
8 abasshed and yl bestad of this man only, al the other
shal preyse & doubte vs nought' / and sayeng these
wordes, he broched his hors with hys sporys that blood
rane out of bothe sydes / And know it wel, that this The Caliph, a strong man with sword and shield,
12 Caliphe was one of the moost fyers & strengest man
that was that tyme alyue / he casted hys targe behynd
his bakk / toke hys swerd, & rane vpon vryan, the runs upon Urian,
whiche he recountred / and by grete yre gaf hym so and gives him a heavy blow,
16 meruayllable a stroke vpon that one syde of hys
helmet, that hys swerd redounded vpon hys hors nek nearly killing his horse;
by suche myght that nygh he cutte his throtte of.
Thanne came kynge Brandymount vpon vryan, the King Brandymount rushes on him also,
20 which, seeynge his hors almost deed, stood vpon hys
feet, & lete goo hys swerd fro his hand, and embrased Urian d'smounts, and pulls the Saracen King from his horse.
his enemy; and by the strengthe of his two armes,
pulled hym from his hors doun to therthe. There was
24 ¹the prees grete, both of Sarasyns that wold rescue ¹ fol. 101.
theyre lord / and of cypryens also, that wold haue
holpen vryan theire kynge, to bryng hys enterpryse at
affect. The batayll was there mortall fyers & doubtous The fighting becomes fierce at this point;
28 for bothe partyes. but vryan drew a short knyff out of
the shethe that hanged at his lyft syde, and threstid it but Urian stabs his foe in the neck, and so slays him;
vnder the gorgeret thrugh brandymontis nek, and thus
he slewgh hym. Thanne stod vryan vpon his feet
32 ayen, and cryed with a high voys 'Lusynen, Lusynen' /
and the Poyteuyns that herd that, putte them self in
prees by suche vertu, gyuyng so grete strokes that the and his companions put to flight the Saracens,
sarrasyns that were about vryan lost & voyded the
36 place. Thenne was kyng vryan remounted vpon kyng

brandymontis hors, and pursiewed the Caliphe of
Bandas / and thus bygan ayen the batayll to be
reforced, in so moche that grete occyayon was don on

eyther partye.   And in that meane season came guyon 4
with his peuple, and courageously rane vpon þeire

enemyes.   And whan the Caliphe saw hym be surprysed on eche syde by his mortal enemyes / he with
xi departed in the secretest manere that he coude out 8
of the batayll, and fled toward the see / where the
admyrall of Damask was, whiche made them to entre
into a lytel galyote, in whiche he escaped, as byfore is
said / and soone aftir he made the nauye, that he saued 12

fro brennyng, to take vp theire ancres, & entred in
the see.   And here seaceth thystorye of hym, and
retourneth to speke of the batayll. /

I̅n this partye sheweth thystorye, & sayth þat whan 16
the sarasyns knew the deth of theyre kynge bran-
dymou*n*t[1] / and how the Caliphe on whos prowes &

strengthe was al theire hope & comfort [2] was thus de-

parted and fled, they were all abasshed, and bygan 20
strongly to breke their aray and to voyde the place,
puttyng themself to flight.[3]   What shuld I make you

long compte / the paynemes were putt all to deth,
what in batayll, what fleyng as drowned in the see. 24
And after the chaas, retourned kyng vryan and hys

barons to the paynemys lodgis, where they found in
their tentes & pauyllons grete riches.   And here thistorye cesseth of kyng vryan / and I shal shew vnto you 28

how the caliphe of Bandas dyde, the which swore by
his machomet & his goddes, that yf he myght euer come
to sauete in damask ayen, yet shuld he doo grete hynderaunce & enuye to the Cypryens.   But as he was 32
rowyng in the see / and supposed to haue escaped al

---

[1] Fr. *Brandimont de Tarse.*
[3] xviis. viiid. is noted in margin of MS.   If it is price of
copying up to this point, it would be about the rate of 1d. a
page.

parels / the maister of Rodes that kept the see and
wayted after hym, as aboue is sayd, perceyued the
sarasyns flote þat wold haue retourned to Damask / by-
4 gan to lye by them and sayd to his peuple in this
manere : 'Fayre lordes and knightes of Ieshu Criste, our
desyre and wysshyng is brought to effect, for knowlege we haue ynough that the valyaunt & redoubted
8 kyng vryan hath obtayned the vyctory vpon his enemyes & oures / yf we be now men of faytte & valyaunt,
none of them shal neuer see Damaske.' Who thanne
had seen the Cristen putte them self in aray, and theire
12 meruayllable shottyng with gonnes & arowes vpon the
sarasyns, he shuld haue be meruaylled / and syn oure
folke cheyned with them & casted darts & stones with
suche strengthe & might, that wonder it was to see.
16 The sarasyns defendid hem self [1]manfully / but at last
they were dyscomfyte. And the admyrall that sawe
the grete myschief þat fell on them hallid vp saylles /
rowed in hys galyote with eyght hores and so ho
20 escaped. And the maister of Rodes and hys peple
toke the galeyes of theire enemyes and all slew or
casted ouer bord / and brought them ayen to saynt
andrews porte. Thanne the maister of Rodes acom-
24 panyed with C knightes, bretheren of his religyon, went
toward king vryan & guyon his brother, and recounted
to them all theire good fortune. but sory was the king
that the Caliphe and the admyral were so escaped.
28 kyng Vryan thenne departed & dalt emong his peuple
al the proye of his enemyes that he had wonne / sauf
he reteyned for hym the artylery & some pauyllons &
tentes, and gaf them leue to retourne in to theire
32 Countrees. These thinges thus don, kyng vryan in
grete tryumphe & honour as vyctorious prynce, retourned to his cyte of Famagoce, accompayned of Guyon
his brother, of the maister of Rodes, and of al the
36 barons, wher the quene Ermyne receyued them right

MELUSINE.   N

Side notes:
but his fleet is observed by the Master of Rhodes, who is on the watch.

He is attacked,

[1] fol. 102.
and defeated,

but escapes with the admiral in an eight-oared boat.
The master of Rhodes captures the navy, slays or drowns all the Saracens, and takes the vessels back to St. Andrew's Port.

He recounts his victory to Urian, who is sorry at the caliph's escape.

Urian and his companions return to Famagoce.

honourably, thankyng god of the noble vyctorye that
they obteyned vpon his enemyes. /

Urian's wife
Hermine, being
with child, he
prepares to give
a feast,
Now sayth thistorye, that Ermyne was grete with
child & nygh her terme / and that vryan made
a feast to be cryed & proclaimed ; For he wold in tyme
of peas & rest haue festyed his barons of poytou and
al other prynces estraungers & other his subgects.
Eyght dayes toforne the feste, began grete multitude 8
of peuple to come to the Cite, wherof the kyng was
joyful, and made cryees vpon peyne of deth that none
shuld make derrer the vytaylles.   And trouth it was

but a fair son is
born three days
before the feast
is ready.
¹ fol. 109 b.
He is named
Henry.
that thre dayes tofore the feste the quene Ermyne 12
was ¹delyuered of a fayre sone.   Thenne bygan the
feste to wex grete / and the child baptised and named
Henry, bycause of hys auncestre hight Henry.   And
so encreased the feest in ryches & in yeftes.   And 16
there were some of the barons of poytou that toke
theire leue of the king' & of his brother, and of the
quene, for to departe, whom the kynge yaf grete yeftes
of riches.   And they were in nombre six knightes and 20
þeire companye, which putte them in to the see.   Now
wyl I cesse of them that are departed to the see / &
shal shewe of the feste that was ryght noble and sumptuous, but soone it was turned to sorowe, bycause of 24
the tydinges of the kingis deth of Armenye that came
to the Court. /

Twenty-one Ar-
menian knights
Thystorye sheweth all thus, whan the feest was at
best, there came xxi⁽ᵘ²⁾ knightes of the moost 28
noblest barons of the royalme of armanye, al clothed in
black / and it shewed wel by theire contenaunce that
come to Urian,
they were sorowful in herte.   And whan they cam tofore
the kyng' they dide theire obeyssaunce ryght nobly / 32
and the kynge receyued them with grete honour / and
with news of the
death of the King
of Armenia,
they said to him : ' Sire, the kynge of armenye, your
vncle, is passed out of this world, on whos sowle god

² Fr. xci.

haue mercy / and hath lefte to vs a ryght fayre pucelle
begoten of his body by lawfull maryage / and she is
alone hys heyre.   Now knowe ye thenne, noble kynge,
4 that in hys playn lyf he dide doo make this lettre, and
commanded vs to directe it to your noble grace / prayeng the same that the tenour of þe lettre ye vouchesaf
tacomplysshe.' 'By my feith, fayre lordes,' said Vryan /
8 'yf it be of the thing that I may goodly doo, I shal
fulfyll his wyll ¹right gladly.'   Thenne toke Vryan
the lettre & redd it, of the whiche the tenour was this :
' Ryght dere lord and right wel beloued nevew, I re-
12 commande me to you as ferfourth as I may / prayeng
you right hertyly to haue me to my ryght dere & beloued nyghte your wyf to be recommanded.   And
where by these my lettres I make to you the first re-
16 queste that euer I demanded of you / also consideryng
that it shal be the last / For certaynly at the makyng
of thees my present lettres, I felt myself in such poynt
that in me was none hope of conualescence nor of lyf.
20 I hertyly beseche you that ye haue it not in reffus nor
in dysdayne. It is so thanne that none heyre I ne
haue of my body, sauf only a doughter, the which
your brother guyon sawe but of late / whan he was
24 with me. Wherfore I pray you that ye vouchsauf to
entrette your said broþer in manere that it playse hym,
to take the cepter of my dignite ryall and my doughter
to hys lady, and thus to crowne hym self king of
28 armanye. And though she be not worthy to haue
hym to her lord, yet is she come of royal blood. consideryng thanne her consanguinite haue pite on her /
and yf that mouyth not you to compassyon / yet re-
32 membre that ye be champyon of Crist, exalting his
feyth. My royalme is now cristen, and hath be long
soo / Woo were to me / yf for wantyng of a preu &
valyaunt man it shuld retourne in to the paynemes
36 handes. Wherfore, noble kyng, haue regarde to this

fol 108 b.

that forsaid is,' &c. Whan vryan vnderstode the tenour
of þe lettre he was moche dolaunt of the kingis deth /
& mouyd by compassion & pyte, ansuerd to the [1]Arma-
nyens, sayeng in this manere: ' Lordes & barons, I shall 4
not fayll you at your nede, For yf my brother wyl not
accorde therto, yet shall I endeuoyre my self to gyue
you helpe, ayde, comfort, & counseyl, as ferre as my
power shal reche.' Thanne called he to hym guyon, 8
hys broþer, that thanne knew the kingis deth, wherof
he was sorrowfull / and vryan to hym sayd the wordes

He is offered
the hand of the
daughter of the
king of Armenia.

that here folowen : ' Guyon, receyue this yefte, For I
make you heyre of armenye and possessour of the moost 12
fayrest pucelle that is in all the land / that is my
Cousyn florye, doughter to the kyng of Armanye, which
by the wyll of god is passed out of this world /. and I
pray you that ye dayne to take this yefte, For it oughte 16
not to be refussed.' ' By my feyth, fayr brother and
my lord,' said guyon, ' I thanke you moche therof, and
hym also that is causer of hit, on whos sowle god haue

The Armenian
knights are joy-
ful, and kneel
before Guion
and kiss his
hands.

mercy.' Thenne were the knyghtes of armanye joyfull 20
& glad. And as soone as guyon had consentid therto,
they kneeled byfore hym & kyssed hys handes, after
the custome of theire land / And thanne bygan ayen
the feest greter than it was afore. And in that meane 24
saison the king dide doo make hys nauye redy, that

The navy is
prepared at Ly-
masson, and
Guion and many
of his friends
sail to Armenia,

was in to the porte of Lymasson, and in the vessels
he made to be putte grete rychesses / and guyon hys
brother, accompanyed with the maister of Rodes, & with 28
many barons of poytou and of Cypre, toke hys leue, &
entred in to the see & saylled so long that they arryued
in Armenye,[2] where they were receyued honourably.[3]

---

[2] Fr. Et tant allèrent, tant de jour comme de nuyt, qu'ils
apperceurent et virent la ballet du Crub, qui est la maistresse ville du royaulme d'Armanie.

[3] There is an omission here; the French version opens a
new chapter, entitled Comment Guion espousa la pucelle
Florie et fut roy d'Armanie, as follows:—Adonc l'ung des

There was guyon wedded with Florye / and after the
feste all the barons of the land came to Cruly & made
theyre homage to guyon, whiche crownned himself
4 king & regned honourably.   And after these thinges
doon the maister of Rodes & the barons of Poytou toke
theire leue of guyon, whiche yaf to them grete yeftes
of ryches, & they entred in to theire shippes and rowed
8 tyl they [1]cam at Rodes, where. as the said maister
festyed worshipfully the estraungers, and so dide al the
knightes bretheren of hys relygyon.   And at thende
of viii dayes the barons of Poytou entred agayn in to
12 the see, and in short tyme they arryued in Cipre, And
recounted to Vryan al the trouth of the fayt, and how
his brother guyon was honourably receyued in armanye / and how he had wedded Florye, and was crowned
16 kyng of the land & loued of al the peple' there,
wherof moche thankes rendred guyon to god.   Within
few dayes after many of the knightes of poytou toke
theire leue, and to them yaf vryan grete yeftes of
20 ryches / and sent word by them in wrytyng to his
fader & moder of al thestate & prosperous fortune of
hym & of hys brother.   And thus departed the barons
& entred in to theire shippes, whiche they fonde wel
24 purueyed of al that was necessary to them, and toke
theire way toward Rochelle in poytou.
    [2]Now sayth thystorye, that the barons of poytou
    sailled so long that they perceyued & sawe
28 Rochelle, where they arryued with grete joye / and

(marginal notes)
where he weds Florry.
The barons do their homage to him, and he is crowned, and reigns honorably.

His friends set sail to Rhodes,
[1] fol. 104.
where the Master entertains them,

and from thence to Cyprus, where they relate to Urian all the adventure.

Some knights of Poiton, after receiving gifts from Urian, and a letter for his parents,

set sail for Rochelle.

They arrive,

*barons d'Armanie parla moult hault addressant sa parole à
Guion, et dist : Sire, nous vous avons esté querir pour estre
nostre seigneur et nostre roy; si est bon que nous vous delir-
rons tout ce que nous vous devons bailler. Et voicz cy ma
damoiselle qui est toute preste de acomplir tout ce que nous
vous avons promis et au roy Urian votre frère. Par foi, dist
Guion, ce ne demourera mic à faire pour mey ;* and continues
then as above.
    [2] This begins a new chapter in the French version, en-
titled, *Comment les messagiers apportèrent les lettres à Raimondin et à Melusine de ses deux enfans qui estvient roix.*

and three days
after ride to
Lusignan,

where Raymon-
din and Melusine
receive them
with great joy.

They deliver the
letters from
Urian and Guion,

which please
their parents.

This year Mela-
sine builds the
Church of our
Lady and many
other abbeys.
    1 fol. 104 b.
and Odo marries
the daughter
of the Earl of
March.

Anthony and
Regnald, hearing
of the brothers'
success,

desire to follow
their example;

so they ask per-
mission to go out
into the world
to earn the order
of knighthood.

there they refresshed them self the space of thre dayes,
and after mounted on theire horses & rode toward
Lusynen, where they founde Raymondyn and Melusyne
and theire other children with þem, whiche receyued 4
them with grete joy.   And þenne they delyuered to
them the lettres of kynges Vryan & guyon theire sones.
And whan they herde & vnderstod the tenour of
them they thanked god of the good auenture that he of 8
his grace had youen to theire two sones / and yaf grete
jewelles & ryche yeftes to the barons that brought
tydynges of þem. And that same yere melusyne fownded
the chirch of our lady in Lusynen & manie other 12
abbeyes in þe ¹ lande, and endowed them with grete possessyons.   And thenne was the trayttee of maryage
made betwix Odon her sone and the Erle of marchis
doughtir, And was the feest grete & noble holden in 16
a medowe nygh to the Castel of Lusynen. /

   Thystorye sheweth here, that Anthony & Regnald
     were right glad whan they vnderstode the ty-
dinges of the fortune & noble fayttes of armes of theire 20
two bretheren / and that in so short space of tyme they
had sore adommaged the enemyes of god, and said one
to other, 'My ryght dere brother, it is now tyme that
we goo seke auenture thrugh the world, For here to 24
dwell ony lenger we may not acquyre nor gete honour,
as oure brethern Vryan & guyon haue don.' Wherfore they come to theyre fader & moder, and to them
said humbly in this manere, 'My lord and you my 28
lady, yf ye vouchsaf it were tyme that we went thrugh
the world at our auenture, for to gete & acquere
thordre of knyghthode as our bretheren vryan &
guyon haue don / how wel we be nat worthy to receuye 32
it so nobly nor in so noble a place as they haue doo /
but yf it playseth god our entencion is to endeuoyre
vs þerto.' Thenne ansuerd to them Melusyne theire
moder, 'Fayre sones, yf that playseth wel your fader, 36

I me consent to your requeste.' 'By my feyth, lady,'
said Raymondyn, 'doo your wyll therof, For what
someuer ye wyl I me consent therto.' 'Sire,' said
4 Melusyne, 'it semeth to me good that from hens fourth
they begynne to take on them som vyage for to knowe
the world & the straunge marches / also to be renommed
& knowen / and to knowe & discerne good from euyl.'
8 Thenne the two bretheren kneeled byfore theire fader
& moder, & thanked them moch humbly of the honour
that they promysed them to ¹doo. And here ceaseth
thystory to spek of them / and speketh of another
12 matere.

In this partye sayth thistorye, that in the marches
of Allemayne, betwene Lorayne & Ardane, was a
noble Countrey, the which was somtyme called the
16 Erledome of Lucembourgh, and now it is named a
duchye. In that same Countree was some tyme a lord
erle of the land, whiche after his decesse lefte a fayre
doughter his heyre / she was clepyd Crystyne, and her
20 fader was named Asselyn. Alle the barons of the land
made theire homage to her as to the rightfull heyre of
the lande. On that tyme was in Anssay a kynge
whos wyf was deed in her child bed at the birthe of a
24 doughter, whiche the fader made to be baptised &
named Melidee. Whan this kynge thanne herde how
the Erle of Lucembourgh was passed out of this world,
and that none heyre he had but a doughter, whiche
28 was the fayrest damoysell of all the land / he sent in
ambaxade to her the moost noble & secretest men of
hys Counseyll, to speke & treate the maryage of hym
with her. But the pucelle Crystyne wold neuer con-
32 sent therto / wherfore he wexed sorowfull in herte /
and sware god that outhre by force or by her wyll he
shuld haue her, whatsoeuer it might fall therof. Thenne
made he his mandement, & chalenged the mayde & alle
36 her lande. Whan thanne the barons & noble men of

Their parents
consent.

¹ fol. 106.

At the time
when the ruler
of Luxembourg
was a maiden
named Christine,

the wife of the
King of Anssay
died.

He wished to
marry again, and
made proposals
to Christine,

but was rejected.

In revenge he
swore he would
have her by
force, and chal-
lenged her and
her land.

the lande & all the commynalte wyst it / they said
& sware that syth theyre lady wold not haue hym to
her lord / they shuld shewe to hym that he dide wrong
to the pucelle and to them also. And immediatly they 4
garnysshed theire Cites, tounes, & Fortresses. ¹And
the moost part of the barons drew themself to the
toune & Castel of Lucembourgh with Cristyne, theire
owne propre lady. What shuld I make you long compte / 8
they were nat that tyme strong ne puyssaunt ynough for
to fyght ayenst the kyng of Anssay. For he came vpon
them with a grete puyssaunce of peple & moche adommaged the lande / and came al brennyng vnto byfore 12
the toune & Fortresse of Lucembourgh, where he layed
siege. And of faytte theire was grete scarmysshing and
grete losse of one parte and of oþer. It happed thanne
that one of the noblest barons of the land, the whiche 16
had be with Vryan at the conqueste of the royaume of
Cipre, and euer was with hym at all the baytaylles that
he had ayenst the paynemes / the whiche was come
ayen with the barons of Poytou vnto Lusynen / and 20
had receyued of Melusyne riche jewels & grete yeftes
of ryches / and sawe there Regnald and Anthony, that
were moche strong and grete, & of fyers & hardy
contenaunce / and wel it semed to hym that they 24
shuld ensiew the condicions & maneres of theire
bretheren, and theire high prowes & enterpryse / drew
the noble men of the land apart, and said to them in
this manere : ' Fayre lordes, ye may conceyue and wel 28
perceyue that we may not hold longe ayenst the puyssaunce of the same kinge. Wherfore yf it seme you
good, myn oppynyon were to see a remedy be had to it
rather to fore than to late, For good it is to shette the 32
stable or euer the horses be lost.' And they answerd,
' that is trouth / but we may not perceyue no remedy
therto without the grace of god be.' ' For southe,' said
the forsaid baron, ' Without godis grace none may but 36

lytel or nought doo, but with that it is good to take
ayde who that may [1]haue it.' 'Certaynly,' said the
barons, 'ye say right wel; yf ye thanne know some
4 gentylman worthy to haue our lady, and valyaunt &
preu to deffende vs ayenst our enemyes, lete vs knowe
hym. For ye be therto hold & bounden bycause of
your alygeaunce.' This gentylman thanne reherced to
8 them fro hed to hed how vryan & hys brother departed
fro Lusynen, and all thauenture of theire vyage / also
thestate of theire fader and moder / and ouermore, he
shewed to them the fayre maynten & countenaunce of
12 Anthony & Regnauld / and that he knew for certayn /
that who so went to seke & requyre the socours and
helpe of the two bretheren, they shuld come with
grete puyssaunce, whan they shuld haue knowledge of
16 the faytte. 'By my feyth,' said the noblemen, 'ye say
full wel.' Thenne they fourthwith went tofore Crystyne theire lady, and worde to worde they recounted
to her all this affayre. And she said to them, 'Fayre
20 lordes, I recommande you my land and yours / doo
what semeth you best to thonour of me and of you, for
the commyn wele of all my land. For wete it for
certayn, that for to dey or to be dysheryted, I shal not
24 haue the kyng of Anssay to my lord / how be it he is
better than to me apparteyneth, but for asmoche that
he wyl haue by force me & my land.' And they
ansuerd to her / 'doubte you not therof, my lady, For
28 yf it playse god, he shal not haue so moche of puys-
sance as long as we shall mowe stere our owne bodyes.'
'Lordes,' said she, 'gramercy.' And thenne they departed
thens. Thenne said one of the barons to the forsaid
32 gentylman in this manere : 'ye that haue putte vs in
this quarelle / say now what best is for to doo.' 'By my
feyth,' said he, 'yf it lyke you good, ye shall delyuere
me two of you to goo with me to Lusynen, to wete yf
36 we can fynde there [2]ony thing' to vs prouffytable.'

Two wise and
noble men are
sent as messen-
gers to Lusignan
with Urian's
knight.

Thenne they anoone chose among them, that is to wete,
two of the wysest & noblest men for to goo with hym.
And they departed about the first slepe, mounted vpon
good & lyght horses, and yssued out of a posterne, and 4
passed by that one side of thoost, so that they were neuer
perceyued / and hasted them self on theire way toward
Lusynen. And here cesseth thystorye of them, and
speketh of Meluysyne & her children, that is to wete, 8
of Anthony and of Regnald. /

During the great
feast, at which
Anthony and
Regnald dis-
tinguish them-
selves in
jousting,

Thystory sayth that the feste was right grete in
the medowe byforsaid / and men jousted there
valyauntly. but aboue alle the yonge squyers that 12
were there, Anthony and Regnald dyde best after the
sayeng & commendacion of the ladyes and gentyl
wymen that were there. And there were grete jewels
gyuen. but alwayes Melusyne thoughte to purueye to 16
thestate of her children, and made to them fayre robes
& ryche raymentes, and ordeyned and purueyed of men
to goo with them, and in especial wyse, and noble men
to endoctrine them, & shew to them the way of good 20
gouernaunce. Duryng yet the feste, came there the

the ambassadors
from Luxem-
bourg arrive,

ambaxatours of Lucembourgh / þe whiche made theire
obeyssaunce to Raymondyn & to Melusyne ryght honour-

and are wel-
comed.

ably, and also to alle the companye / And joyously 24
they were receyued / & soone was there knowen the
knight that had be with vryan at the Conqueste of

Urian's knight
is asked by
Anthony if he
will accompany
him and his
brother on a
voyage

Cypre. and he was honourably festyed, and of hym
demanded Anthony, for the wele that he herde saye of 28
hym, yf it playsed hym to goo with hym & with hys
brother Regnauld in som vyage where he purposed to
goo, & to thayde of god, he shuld be wel rewarded.
The knyght thanne demanded of Anthony : 'My lord, 32
& whither is your entencion for to goo?' And he

¹ fol. 107.

ansuerd : ¹' At our auenture there as god shal conduyt

in search of
honour.

vs, for to gete honour and cheualrye.' ' By my feyth,'
said the knyght, ' I shal telle you the fayrest and the 36

moost honourable auenture that eu*er* gentylman had

that aduentured hym self, and the moost honourable

enterpryse.' And whan the two damoyseaulx vnderstod

4 hym, they made moche of hym, & said in this man*ere* :

'Noble man, vouchesauf to vtt*re* to vs that noble

enterpryse that ye speketh of.' ' By my feyth, lordes,'

said the knight, ' in as moche that I were ryght joy*ous*

8 you to see enhaunsed in honour, also for to susteyne

ryght & reason, I shal ryght gladly shew to you aH the

matere therof.

' **R**yght dere lordes, it is trouth that aH thoo that

12 loue ryghtwysnes and that be wylling to gete

honour / they oughte to helpe and susteyne the wydowes

an orphenyns. And forasmoche, fayre lordes, it is soo

that in the marche of Lorayne & of Ardane is a moche

16 ryche & noble Countree that clepen the duchye of Lucem-

bourgh, the whiche duchye a noble man gou*er*ned long

as hys owne propre herytage / the whiche valyaunt man

passed to god but of late, and hath lefte a doughtir hys

20 heyre of the land / to the whiche right noble and fayre

pucelle alle the nobles and barons of the land haue as

now don theyre homage & obe*y*ssau*n*ce. And where

it is soo that the kynge of Anssay, knowyng the beaute-

24 fulnes of the mayde, and her grete & noble enheryt-

au*n*ce, hath demanded her by maryage / but that pucelle

reffused hym bycause he had be wedded tofore, & of

late he was wydower. Wherfore this kynge of Anssay

28 hath deffyed her and al her land, and supposeth to

haue her by force & ayenst her wylle / and he is entred

in to the land / and hath brent & slayn al byfore hym

vnto the toune & Castel [1]of Lucembourgh, where as

32 he hath now besieged the said lady, and hath sworne

that he shaH neu*er* departe thens vnto tyme he hath

his wylle of her, other by force or by loue. Wherfore,

lord*es*, me semeth that in aH the world nys more honour-

36 able a vyage ne more raysonnable than that same is,

The knight tells
of the fair ad-
venture,

and is asked by
the brothers for
full information.

He relates that

the Duke of
Luxembourg

left his daughter
his heir,

and owing to
her beauty and
riches she is
sought as wife
by the King of
Anssay, but be-
cause he is a
widower she has
refused him.

In revenge war
has been de-
clared, and the
king is trying to
get her by force,

[1] fol. 107 b.

and now he is
besieging her at
Luxembourg.

For alle thoo that loue honour & gentylnesse ought to

On hearing the story Anthony agrees to succour the maiden,

draw them self that part.' 'In good feyth,' said thenne anthony, 'ye say trouth / and wete it I shall shew this matere to my lady my moder, to see what ayde and 4 helpe my lord our fader and she wyl gyue vs / and how so euer it happeth, by thayde of god we shall goo and socoure the pucelle that the kynge of Anssay wyl haue by force, wherof me semeth that he is euyl coun- 8 seylled.' 'On my feyth, my lord,' sayd thenne the knight, 'yf ye vouchesauf to vndertake that vyage / I

and the ambassadors promise to conduct Anthony and help him all in their power.

& my felawes, two knightes that be here come with me, shal conduyte & helpe you of al our power.' And 12 þe two bretheren thanked them moche, & saide / 'no doubte we shal goo thither, yf it be the playsire of god' / And thenne they retourned toward theire moder / and the knight toward his felawes / and reherced to 16 them how he had exployted / and that no nede was to speke ne requere Raymondyn ne Melusyne therof. 'Now, veryly,' said the two barons, 'it is ryght wysly don of you / blessid be god therof.' /   20

Anthony and Regnald relate the tidings to their parents, and ask for help.

Here saith thistory, that Anthony & Regnald came to theire fader & moder, and denounced to them these tydinges, and requyred them of help & ayde tacomplysshe this enterpryse.   Thenne 24 spake Raymondyn to Melusyne, & said, 'Certainly,

Raymondin thinks it a good opportunity,
1 fol. 108.

lady, herto they may haue a fayre begynnyng' in armes. Wherfore I pray you that ye purueye for ¹them in suche wyse that we may haue therof honour & prouffyt.' 28 'For southe,' said Melusyne, 'Sire, for tacomplysshe

and Melusine promises to provide well for her sons.
She announces that any man prepared to serve under the brothers, should come to Lusignan.

your wylle, I shall endeuoyre me so diligently therto, that bothe you & they also shal be content.'   And thenne she made that ony man that wold take wages 32 vnder Anthony & Regnald of Lusynen, that they shuld come at a certayn day to Lusynen, and there they shuld be payed of þeir wages for one yere / and also she made it to be cryed al about the marches of poytou. /   36

IN this partye reherceth thystorye, that within the
day that Melusyne made to be cryed and anounced
the said wages,[1] were assembled many gentylmen in a
4 meddowe bysyde Lusynen ; and grete foyson men of
armes, to the nombre of foure thousand helmets and
fyue houndred, some archers & oþer crosbowe men /
and there were no pages, but al strong men / and were
8 al lodged in fayre tentes & pauyllons, and so purueyed
of all maner harneys & of al other thinges necessary to
þem, that euery man was content. And while Raymondyn & melusyne payed them theire wages, &
12 purueyed for al thinges that were nedefull to theyre
vyage / Anthony & Regnald araysonned & demanded
of the said knight and of his barons, hys felawes, of
the estate of the pucelle of the land / And they said to
16 them the very trouth / and were joyfull in theire hertes
of the grete apparayll that they sawe so soone redy,
For wel they had take in thanke half of the same to
socoure with all theire lady. Wherfor þey thanked
20 god & our lady his blessid moder, And sent fourth
with a messager toward the barons of Lucembourgh,
for to anounce to them the noble socours [2]that god sent
to them. Wherof they were joyful & glad. And aftir
24 the barons went & told to theire lady the tydynges, of
the whyche she was moch recomforted, and bygan
moche deuoutely to lawde god her creatour. And
whan the peuple knew therof, they had grete joye, and
28 thanked god, and made grete fyres, and cryed with a
mery voys, sayeng thus : 'Joye & victory to our
pucelle.' And whan theire enemyes withoutforth herd
them, they wondred moch, & went & denounced it to
32 theire kynge, wherof he was abasshed & pensefull.
And thenne came tofore certayn personnes, that said
to hym : 'Sire, doo make good watche, For they of the
toune awayte dayly for socours.' 'By god,' said the

On the day
appointed for
the meeting,

4000 helmets
and 500 archers
assemble.

They are well
armed ;

and are paid
their wages.

The barons
describe the state
of the land to the
brothers,

and send word of
the aid coming to
Luxembourg,

[2] fol. 108 b.

whereat the
barons, the lady
Christine, and
her people are
glad.

The king of Ans-
say is informed
of the rejoicing,

[1] waged in MS.

kinge, 'I ne wot nor may knowe by no manere fro
whens socours shuld come to them ; I doubte not / but
that I shal haue them at my wyll, other by strength
or by honger and for lack of meete.' And thus the 4
kyng of Ansaay assured hym self, But aftirward he
fond hym self deceyued. Now I shal leue of hym,
and shal retourne to speke of Melusyne and of her two
sones.   8

Melusyne thenne called to her Anthony and Regnald, her two sones / and to them she said in
this manere : 'Children, ye now wyl departe fro my
lord your fader & fro me / and happely we shal neuer 12
see you agayn. Wharfore I wyl teche & introdruyte
you for your wele & honour. And I pray you that ye
vnderstand & reteyne wel that I shall say, For that
shal be to you nedefull in tyme to come. First, ye 16
shal loue / doubte, & preyse god our creatour; ye shal
fermely, iustly, & deuoutly hold the commandementes
of our moder holy chirche / and stedfast shal you be in
our feyth catholical. / be ye humble & curteys to good 20
folke / fyers & sharp to the wicked & euyl folke / and
be ye [1]alwayes of fayre ansueryng, bothe to moost and
leste / and hold talkyng to euery one whan tyme
requyreth, without eny dysdayn / promyse ne be- 24
heyghte nothing¹ but that ye may shortly acomplysshe
it after your power; withdrawe not rapporteurs of
wordes toward you / byleue not enuyous / nor beleue
not to soone ne lyghtly / For that causeth somtyme 28
the frend to wexe mortal foo; putte not in office
auarycyous nor fel folke / acoynte[2] you not with
another mans wyf / departe or deele to your felawes of
suche thinges that god shal gyue you; be swete & 32
debonnaire to your subgects / and to your enemyes
fyers & cruel vnto tyme they be subdued & vnder
your puyssaunce / kepe your self fro auauntyng & fro

² Fr. acointez.

menace / but doo your faytte with few wordes this that   not to be given
to vain speaking
may be doo. Despyse neuer none enemy, thaugh he   Not to despise
their foes, but
be lytel / but loke wel about and make good watche /   ever to keep
good watch.
4 be not emonges your felawes as maister, but commyn
with them / and worship euerychon after his degre /
and gyue to them after your power, & after that they
be worthy. ¹gyue to the good men of armes hors &   To treat their
men-at-arms
8 harneys & syluer as rayson requyreth. Now, my   well,
children, I ne wot nat what I shuld more saye to you /
but that ye kepe euer trouthe in al your dedes &   and above all
to keep to the
affayres. Hold I I gyue eche of you a ryng of gold,   truth.
She gives them
12 wherof the stones ben of one vertue. For wete it that   each a ring,
which will pre-
as long as ye haue good cause, ye shal neuer be dys-   vent them ever
being defeated in
comfyted in batayll.' And thenne she kyssed them in   battle in a good
cause.
moderly wyse, whiche thanked her; and toke leue of   The brothers
take leave of
16 theire fader, that ryght dolaunt was of theire departyng.   their parents,
They made thenne theire troompettes to be sowned &   sound the trumpets,
blowen, and putte them self al byfore, & conduyted the
auauntgarde / and after folowed the sommage & the
20 grete batayll in fayre ²aray / and the arryergarde also   ² fol. 109 b.
marched forth in fayre ordynaunce. It was a good
sight to see the state of the vantgarde, whiche the two
bretheren delyuered to be conduyted to a noble baron
24 & valyaunt knight of poytou / and them self toke &
conduyted the gret baytayll / and by them rode the
ambaxadours of Lucembourg. And of the reregarde
were captayns the two knightes of poytou that ledd
28 vryan & guyon in to Cypre, and that first told to them
that the sawdan had besieged the Cite of Famagoce.
And to these two knightes Raymondyn & Melusyne
had recommanded the estate of theire two sones, Reg-

---

¹ Fr. *Donnez aux bons hommes d'armes, chevalx, cottes
d'acier, bassines, des premiers, et argent selon raison, et vous
se vous voies ung bon homme de la main qui vienne devers
vous mal restu ou mal monté, si l'appellez moult humblement
et luy donnes robes, chevaux et harnois, selon la valeur de sa
personne et selon le povoir que vous arez alors.*

nald & Anthony. And trouth it is, that on the first
nyght they lodged them nygh to a strong toune vpon
a lytel ryuere / and was that same toune named
Myrabel, þe whiche Melusyne founded / and that same
nyght bygan the two brethern to make good watche, as
they had be alredy in londe of enemyes, wherof many
gaf themself grete merueyll; but they durst not reffuse
it, For Anthony was so cruel that euery man dradde
hym. On the morowe next after the masse was doo /
the two bretheren made cryees vpon peyne of hors &
haryneys, & to be banysshed out of the felawship, þat
eueryman shuld ryde armed vnder his banere, in good
aray of batayll. none durst not refuse it / but thus was
it doo, Wherof they al merueylled. And in this manere
they rode by the space of ten dayes, & so long that
they cam in champayne / and many one were wery &
ennuyed of theire harneys / as moche for þis that it
was no nede / as bycause they were not acustomed of
it / and som spake therof, wherfor the knight that conduyted the vangarde cam to the two brothern, & thus
said to them: 'My lordes, the moost part of your
peuple is euyl apayed & content bycause that ye [1]con-
strayne them to bere theire harneys; For them semeth
no nede to doo soo tyl that they come nygh to the
marches of your enemyes.' 'And how, sire,' said
Anthony, 'thinke you not that the thinge which is
acustomed of long tyme be bettre knowen of them that
exercice it, & lesse greuable than that thing which is
newly lerned ?' 'By my feyth, sire,' said the knyght,
'ye say wel.' 'morouer,' said Anthony, 'It is bettre
for þem to lerne the peyne for to susteyne theire
harneys in tyme, that surely they may so doo at theire
ease, & to refresshe them surely for to essaye them
self, and knowe the manere how they myght easy
susteyn & suffre it whan nede shalbe. For yf they
muste be thaught of theire enemyes / theire peyne

Side notes:

and march that
night to Mirabel,

where they set
good watch.

Anthony orders
everyone to ride
under his banner
in battle array.

This wearies the
men,

and in ten days
the knight com-
manding the
vanguard

[1] fol. 110.
declares to the
brothers that
the people think
there is no need
to be so arrayed
till they are in
the enemies'
country.

But Anthony
replies that it is
best they should
learn themselves,

rather than that
their enemies
should teach
them.

Line numbers: 4, 8, 12, 16, 20, 24, 28, 32, 36

shuld be greter & doubteous / and ye wote ynough, that
who lerneth not his crafte in his youngthe, with grete
payns & harde it shal be for hym to be a good werke-
4 man in his old age.' 'Certaynly, my lord,' said the
knyght, 'ye saye the playns trouth of it, and your
reason is ful good.' And thenne he departed fro
hym, and anounced to many one this tayres, in so
8 moche that knowlech of it they had thorugh al thoost,
wherof every man held hym self wel apayed & content /
and al sayd that the two brethern might not fayll to
have grete 'welth, yf god wold send to them long lyf,
12 and that they shuld come to grete perfection of honour.

Thystorye sayth in this partye, that the same nyght
the oost was ledged vpon a ryuere that men
called aisne / and about the first slepe, the two brethern
16 made to be cryed alarme thrugh the oost right fersfully.
Thenne was there grete trouble, and in euery syde they
armed them, puttyng themself in fayre aray of batayll.
euery man vnder his banere byfore theire tentes. And
20 wote it wel, that it[1] was grete beaute to see the good
contenaunce & the noble [2]ordynaunce & fayre aray of
the men of armes, and of the two bretheren, that went
fro bataill to bataill / and there as fewte was of
24 ordynaunce, they redressid theire peple to it. And
the thre barons, embaxadours of Lucembourgh, behald
wel theire maner & contenaunce, & said that one to
that other : 'On my fayth, these two children ben wel
28 chappen to subdue & conquere yet a grete part of the
world / now wel may say the king of Anssay, that
dere he shall abye his folye & proude enterpryse, and
the dommage that he hath borne to our lady, & to
32 her land & subgetz.' In suche party they were long
tyme, tyl the espyes that secretly were departed fro the
oost to dyscouere & ouersee the Countre about, yf
enemyes were nygh / came agayn, & sayd that]ey

turned
he news
.o enemy
1 night.
4 it was
1 to be a
larm.

dns of
--d rear

he

-4

aspyed no personne; whero[f] al gaf them self grete
wonder of that alarme & affray, but at last it was wel
knowen that the two bretheren caused it. Thenne
came the two knightes, captayns of the arryergarde, 4
& also the Captayne of the vantgarde, to the two
bretheren, & said to them in this manere : ' My lordes,
grete symplenes it is to you thus to traueylle your
peuple for nought.' 'How,' said Anthony to them / 8
' whan ye doo make a new rayment, be it harneys or
clothing, make ye not it to be essayed, for to knowe yf
ony fawte is fonde in it, and to haue it mended & sette
as it shuld be !' / And they al ansuerd, ' For certayn, 12
sire, ye / and that is ryght.' Thenne sayd Anthony,
' yf I wold haue assayed my felawes to fore that it had
be tyme, for to knowe how I shuld fynd them redy at
my nede / sene & consydered that we approuche our 16
enemyes / to thend, yf ony fawte we had fond, to
haue purueyed of conuenable remedy therto, at our
lesse dommage / than yf in dede it had be.' Whane
they [heard[1]] that word / they ansuerd, 'my lord, ye 20
say but rayson' / and they wondred moche of [2]theire
gouernement, and of theire subtylte & wyt / sayeng
betwene them self / that they shuld yet come to grete
perfection. Soone after the day was come, the masse 24
was said and the trompettes sowned; at which sowne
the vantgarde marched fourth, and the sommage and
Cartes folowed / and after the grete oost deslodged, &
went so long by theire journeyes that they came & 28
lodged them vpon a ryuere named Meuse, vnder a Fortresse named Damcastel / And fro thens vnto the siege
tofore lucembourgh, were not past two days journey
for them. Thenne came the barons ambaxadours of 32
Lucembourgh to the two bretheren, & said : ' My lord,
we haue no more but xij leghis vnto the siege, it were
good that ye shuld refresshe your peple here vpon this

* fol. 111.

The next day
they marched to
Dam Castle,

which is twelve
leagues from the
besieged town.

The ambas-
sadors advise
the brethren
to halt and
refresh their
men.

---

[1] Word scraped out of MS.

fayre ryu*er* ; For here is good soio*u*rne & good abydyng' /
and also is good to take aduy*s* & Cou*n*seyl how ye wyl
doo.' /

4 Thanne ansuerd Anthony ryght boldly : 'By my
feyth, fayre lord*es*, thaduy*s* is ou*er*long take,
For assoone that my brother & I haue sent toward the
kynge of Anssay, yf he wyl not doo after o*u*r wyll, he
8 may hold hym sure to haue batayll / and the vyctory
shal send god to whom it playse hym / but what / me
semeth we haue good quarell, And therfor we haue
hope on o*u*r lord that he shal helpe v*s* / and also we
12 shal, or eu*er* we fyght, demande of hym ryght &
rayson / but it muste be aduysed who shal goo on the
message.' 'By my feyth,' sayd the Captayne of the
vantgarde, 'I shal be yo*u*r messanger, yf it please you,
16 and the gentylman that knoweth the Countre shal lede
me thither.' 'In the name of god,' said anthony /
'that playseth me ryght wel / but that shal not be tyl
myn oost be but thre leghes ferre fro them / to thende,
20 yf þe batayll muste be that we may be nere them for
to fyght, and haue thayde of the tou*n*e with vs.
[1]For yf he wyl the batayll we wold be alredy by
hym.' And thus they lefte to speke of this matere.
24 And on the mor*n*e erly, after that the masse was doo,
thoost marched, & passed the ryu*er*e vnder Damcastel
in fayre ordynau*n*ce / and so long they rode that they
arryued on an euen betwene vertone and Lucem-
28 bourgh, and there lodged them self. And on the
morow erly Anthony sent the Captayne of the vantgarde, and the said gentylman toward the kynge of
Anssay, to whom they said the word*es* that herafter
32 folowe. Then*ne* they hasted them so moche that they
came to the siege, and were brought as messagers
tofore the kyng', whom*e* they salued, & made reuerence as they oughte / and aftir the knyght captayn
36 said to hym in this man*er*e : 'Sire, hither we be sent

Side notes:

But Anthony declines to do so, and says he will send to the King of Anssay, and if he accepts not their terms they will fight,

The captain of the vanguard volunteers to be the messenger.

Anthony says he will send when they are as near as three leagues to the enemy.

[1] fol. 111 b.

In the morning after mass the army marches beyond Virton, and rests there.

Next morning Anthony sends the captain of the vanguard and the gentleman to the King of Anssay.

The captain, after making reverence to the king,

says he has been
sent to show the
outrage that has
been committed
on the noble
lady of Luxem-
bourg.

If the king will
make amends for
the wrongs he
has done and
depart, he can
do so : if not he
must fight.

The King of
Anssay mocks
the knight,

¹ fol. 112.

who now de-
mands a speedy
answer.

The king replies
that he cares not
a straw for the
knight's masters;
whereupon the
knight defies the
king on behalf
of his lords.

from our redoubted lordes, Anthony & Regnald, of
Lusynen bretheren, for to shew vnto you the fawte &
grete oultrage that ye doo to the noble damoyselle lady
of Lucembourgh / the which our lordes redoubted ⁴
mande, & lete you knowe by vs that yf ye wyl restablysshe the dommage, & to make raysounable & lawful
amendes of the Iniury & vyloanye that ye haue don
to her / to her subgets & to her propre enherytaunce, 8
and after to departe out of her land ye shal doo wel,
and they make them strong¹ to make your peas with
her / and yf ye wyl not so deele with her / theire
entencyon is for to take reparacion vpon you of the 1̈
dommages beforsayd by strengthe of theire armes & by
batayll. and gyue to vs an answere what your wyll is
to doo / and after morouer I shal telle you as I am
commanded to doo.' 'How, sire knyght,' said the 1̈
kyng¹, 'are ye come hither for to preche vs / by my
faith lytel or nought ye may gete here. For as to your
lettres ne to your preching¹, I shal not be letted of myn
entencion / but as long ye may preche as ye wyl, For I 2̈
vouchesaf. ¹For I take my dysport in your talkyng &
prechement. And also I trow that ye ne doo or saye
suche thinges but for dysport.' 'By my heed, sire,'
said the Captayne, that was angry / 'yf ye doo not 2̈
promptly & anoone this that our lordes mande by vs
vnto you / the dysport that ye speke of / shal hastly
tourne you to grete myschief & sorowe.' 'Sire knight,'
said the kyng¹, 'of menaces ye may gyue vs ynoughe. 2̈
For other thing¹ ye shal not haue ne withbere fro me,
For your maisters, nor your menaces I preyse not
worth a strawe.' 'Thenne, king¹ of Anssay, I deffye
you on my ryght redoubted lordes byhalf.' 'Wel 3̈
thanne,' said the kyng¹, 'I shal kepe me fro mystakyng
& fro losse & dommage, yf I may' / 'By ² my sowle,'
answerd the Captayne, 'grete nede ye shal haue to do

² MS. read *My.*

soo.' And wit*h*out ony moo word*es* they departed / And
whan they were out of thoost or siege / the gentylman
toke leue of the Captayn*e*, and secretly entred in to
4 the toun*s* for to recounte the tydinge*s* of the two
brethern / and whan he cam*e* to the gate he was
anon*e* knowen, and the yate was opened to hym, &
gladly he was welcommed of eu*er*yone / and they
8 demanded tydynge*s* of hym / whiche ansuerd*e* to them.

'Sire*s*, make good chere, For soone ye shal haue the
moost noblest socours that eu*er* was seen / and wete it
wel that the king*e* of Anssay abydeth so long*e*, that he
12 shal be certaynly othre slayn or take, & his peuple al
dyscomfyted, take, or putte to deth.' Thenne byganne
the joye to be so grete thrugh the toun*e* that they withoutforth herd the bruyt therof, and woundred moche
16 what it might be / and announced it to the kyng*e*.

'By my feyth,' said the kynge, 'they recomforte themself for the comⁱmyng*e* of thoo two children by whom*e*
that knyght hath deffyed vs, For ¹as I trow, they
20 haue herd*e* some tydynge*s* therof, and þerfor they make
suche joye.' 'In the name of god,' said an auncyent
knight, 'al this may be / but good were to take heede
therto / For there nys non*e* litel enmy, but we ought
24 to haue doubte therof. For I know them wel ynough
by semblau*n*t. For or eu*er* they com*e* hyther from
poytou we shold haue brought about a parte of ou*r*
wyH.' Now I shal leue to spek of the kynge / and shal
28 retourne to speke of hym that brought tydynge*s* of the
two bretheren in to the toun*e*. Whan the knyght
thann*e* was entred as byfore is said, he went fourth
vnto the Castel where the pucelle Cristyne was / and
32 after hys obeyssaunce don vnto her, he reherced to her
al the playn trouth of the mayntene & countena*u*nce of
the two bretheren / and he said to her / 'how Anthony
bare a claw of a Lyon in his face' / and shewed to her
36 hys grete fyerste & his grete strengthe / Also how

The captain and the gentleman leave the king. The gentleman secretly enters the town to give tidings of the brethren.

He tells the people that the King of Anssay will be either slain or taken, and his people overcome;

whereat they make a joyful noise.

The King of Anssay says they rejoice because of the succour of

¹ fol. 112 b.

the children who have defied him.

An ancient knight advises the king to take heed of the report.

The Luxembourg knight goes to the castle where the maid Christine dwells,

and describes Anthony and Regnald to her.

Regnald had but one eye / and the beaulte of theyre
bodyes & of theire membres / wherof she merueylled
moche, & said that it was grete dommage, Whan any
contreyfayture was in the membres of suche noble men. 4
And now cesse thystory to speke of them / and retourneth to tell of the captayns that retourneth to
thoost toward Anthony and Regnald. /

The captain
arrived at the
two brethren
and their host,
Thystorye sayth that so long rode the Captayne 8
that he came in to thoost of the two bretheren,
& recorded to them how he had fulfylled hys message,

and recounts the
king's proud
answer, and how
the knight left
him to go to
Luxembourg.
¹ fol. 118.
& recounted word by word the proude ansuere of the
king¹, and how he had deffyed hym in theirs byhalf / 12
and also how the knyght was departed fro hym, & was
gon to Lucembourgh to tell there ¹of theire commyng /
And whan the two bretheren herd hym they were full

The brethren
send word
through the host
that those who
have no will to
fight can go
home,
joyous / and soone made cryees thrughe theyre oost, 16
that al they that had no wyll for to fyght & abyde
the batayll shuld draw themself aparte, & gaf to them
leue to retourne agayn in theire Countrey / but they

but the host
cries, 'Let us
go forth upon
your enemies.'
escryed them self with an hye voys. 'Ha / a, franc 20
demoyseaux make your trompettes to be sowned, &
lete vs go forth vpon your enemyes / For we ben not
come in your companye / but for to take thauenture
with you suche as god shal send vs / Ha, lordes, goo we 24
& renne vpon our enemyes, For with goddes grace, &
with the good wyll that we be of, they shal soone be
dyscomfyted.' Whan thenne the two bretheren herd

The host marches
forward to a little
river,
the ansuerd of theire peple they were joyfull, and made 28
theire oost to departe, & came & lodged vpon a lytel
ryuere / and the vantgarde & the grete batayll lodged

where they rest,
sup, and appoint
a good watch.
togidre, bycause they might goo no ferþer / and they
soupped togidre, and after went to reste them, & made 32
good watche / and at day spryng they were al redy /

At day-spring
they are ready ;
200 men of arms
and 100 cross-
bowmen are left
to take charge of
the camp.
and lefte to kepe their lodgis two houndred men of
armes with an ₡ crosbowes / and thenne the oost in
fayre aray marched forth. There myght men see 36

baners & standarts in the wynd, and vnder them the
flour of cheualrye in good aray & fayre ordynaunce /
there had ye sene salades & helmets shynyng clere /
4 and harneys knokyng togidre that grete beaute it was
to see. They kept & marched nygh togidre, so that
one passed not that other. And Anthony and Regnauld
rode at the first frount, mounted vpon two grete horses
8 armed of all pieces. And ¹in that estate and aray they
went tyl they came vpon a lytel mountayne / and
sawe fro thens in the valey the toune & Castel of
Lucembourgh, and the gret siege that aduyrouned it
12 about. And wete it þat they of the siege had not yet
perceyued thoost of the two bretheren / but they were
all asured þat they shuld haue the batayll. Thenne
sent anthony foure houndred helmets for to scarmysshe
16 the siege / and the oost folowed with lytel paas
in fayr aray of batayll / And on the wynges of
thoost were knightes and Crosbowes in fayre ordynaunce. Now tell we of the foure houndred fyghting
20 men that went for to scarmyssh with them of the
siege. /

Thystory saith that the foure houndred fyghtyng
men entred vpon theire enemyes, and slew &
24 hew doune all that they recountred / And whan they
were come nygh to the kingis tente, they of the night
watche that were not yet vnarmed went ayenst them, for
the cry that they made that was 'Lusynen' / many sperys
28 were putte there all to pieces, and many one cast doune
to the ground / and the gretest dommage tourned vpon
them of the siege / but sodaynly the kyng armed hym
self, and putte hym vnder his banere byfore his tente /
32 and whiles they held foot alle thoost was armed, &
drew them toward the kyngis banere. And he demanded of them, 'Fayre lordes, what affray is this?'
'By my feyth,' said a knight, 'they are men of armes
36 that entred in your oost ryght fyersly, and they call

They march forth in good order; Anthony and Regnald in front on two great horses.
¹ fol. 118 b.
They come to a little mountain, from which they see the town and castle of Luxembourg and the siege around it. The besiegers do not see the relieving host.
Anthony sends 400 skirmishers in advance.
These knights slay all they encounter,
and come nigh the king's tent, which was defended by his night watch.
The king arms himself,
and asks his men what affray is this?
A knight answers that men of arms have

Lusynen, and they haue adommaged you sore / and yf
it had not be the nyght watche the losse had be greter,
For they haue faught with them valyauntly / and haue
made ¹them to goo back by force.' ' By my feyth,' said 4
the kynge / ' these damoyseaulx, in whos behalf I am
deffyed, haue not taryed long to come & bere dommage to me / but wel I think for to auenge me therof.'
Thenne is come Anthony and his batayll, which made 8
his trompettes to be sowned clerly. And when the
kyng perceyued them he came withforth the lodgis
in fayre aray & batayll ranged. And thenne the
bataylles recountred eche other / and archers & cros- 12
bowemen approuched & bygan to shoote, and there were
slayne & hurt many one of the kinge of Anssays party,
and neuertheles the grete batayll assembled togidre /
and there was grete occysion & fyers medlee. And 16
thenne anthony broched his hors with the sporys, the
spere alowed, & smote a knyght by such vertue that the
targe nor his cote of stele might not warauntyse hym,
but that he threw hym doune to therthe al deed. 20
And thenne he drew out his swerd, and smote on the
lyfte syde & on the ryght syde, gyuyng grete & pesaunt
strokes, in so moche that in a short while he was so
knowen thrugh al the batayll that the moost hardy 24
of them alle durst not abyde hym. Thenne came
Regnald mounted vpon a grete Courser callyng ' Lusygnen,' which made so grete appertyse of armes that alle
his enemyes redoubted hym. Thenne was the baytayll 28
fyers, cruel, and mortal on bothe partyes / but alwayes
the gretest losse & dommage tourned vpon the kyng of
Anssay & his peple, which was moche dolaunt & sorowfull, & envertued hym self strong, and made with his 32
handes grete vasselage / but al that preuaylled hym
nought, For the poytevins ²were ryght strong, hard, &
fel lyke lyons / and theire were the two lordes so
puyssaunt that none so bold was there that durst abyde 36

fol. 114.

fights

that the most
hardy dare not
abide him.

Regnald also
does great feats
of arms.

² fol. 114 b.

them.   Thenne sawe wel the kynge by the puyssaunce The King of
Anssay sees he
cannot with-
stand them.
& strength of the two brethern, that he myght no lenger
suffre theire force.

4 Cap. XXV.   How Anthony & Regnald dys-
    comfyted the kynge of Anssay tofore lucem-
    bourgh / and how he was take.

The kyng᷒ thenne, which was a valyaunt man & He encourages
his people,
8 strong᷒, cryed with a hye voys 'Anssay, Anssay,
lordes & barons be not abasshed, For the batayll is
oures' / and at his callyng᷒ his peuple toke courage, &
assembled them self ayen togidre about theire kynge, they rally and
again fiercely
attack the
Poitevins.
12 and made a fyers enuahye[1] vpon the poytenyns / there
was many man slayn / hewen & sore hurte with grete
doleur.   That mornyng᷒ was fayre & clere, & the
soonne shoone bright vpon the helmets / and caused
16 the gold & syluer ther on to [2]resplendysshe, that fayre [2] fol. 115.
it was to see.   And they of the toune that herde this The noise of the
battle is heard
by the towns-
folk, and by the
knight mes-
senger who is
with the maid
Christine.
grete affray, toke theire armes; & eche of them made
good watche, For they were ryght ferdfull & doubtous
20 of treson.   And the knyght which anounced to them
the socours of the two breþern was with the pucelle
Crystyne in a hye toure, & loked out at a wyndowe /
and he knew wel that it was Anthony & Regnald, that
24 were come for to fight ayenst the king᷒ and his peple,
& anon called with an hye voys, 'My lady, cōme He asks her
to look at her
champions,
hither & see the floure of knyghthod᷒, of prowesse &
hardynes / cōme & see honour in his siege royall, &
28 in his mageste / cōme & see the god of armes in
propre figure.' 'Frend,' said the pucelle / 'what is
that ye say to me?' 'I calle you,' sayd the knight,
'to come hither & see the flour of noblesse & of all
32 curtoysye, that fro[3] ferre land is come hither for to
fyght with your enemyes for to kepe your honour,

---

[1] Fr. *enuaye* = attack.   [3] *for* in MS.

n of your lande, & your peple / this are the two children of
Lusynen, that be cöme for to deffend you ayenst the
king of Anssay & all his puyssaunce, and to putte
theire honour & lyf in auenture for to kepe your 4
honour sauf.' Thenne came the mayde at the wyn-
ald
ghter dowe, & beheld the mortal batayll & horryble medlee /
sayeng in this manere : 'O Veray god, what shall doo
this poure orphenym / bettre it had be that I had 8
drowned myself, or that I had be putte to deth in
some other wyse, or elles that I had be deed whan I
yssued out of my moders wombe / than so many
creatures shuld be slayne & perysshe for myn owne 12
synne.' Moche dolaunt & heuy was the yong damoyselle of the grete myschief that she sawe, For in
certayn thoccysyon was grete on both partyes, For the
king recomforted his peuple by his wo[r]by conten- 16
aunce & valyaunt maynten ; For with his propre swerd
1. 115 a. he moch adommaged his enemys poytsuyns. [1] But
seeing
... made
lost, Anthony, seeyng the grete dommage that the kynge
bare vpon his peple / he was dysplaysed with, & sayd 20
resolves to fight
the King of
Anssay. in hym self : 'By my feyth, thy lyf or myn shal not
be long, For rather I wold dey than to suffre & see my
peuple so murdryd before me.' Thenne he sporyd hys
He rushes upon
the king,
smites him, hors / and fyersly as a lyon rane vpon the king. and 24
with his swerd of stele smote hym vpon the hyest part
of his helmet by suche strength & vertue that he made
hym to be enclyned vpon þe hors neck, so sore astonyed
that he ne wyst wheþer it was nyght or day, nor he 28
had no force ne power to helpe ne redresse hymself
vpward / and Anthony that this sawe, putte his swerd
in the shethe ayen ; & toke the king by the middes of
and casts him
from his horse. the body / drew hym fro the hors, & so rudely cast 32
hym to therthe that vnnethe hys herte brake within
He makes him
prisoner.
Four knights are
appointed to
guard him. his bely / and after toke hym to foure knightes, and
charged them on theires lyues that they shuld kepe
hym, so that þey myght ansuere hym of it. And they 36

said that so shuld they doo / and they thanne bonde
hym & lede hym out of the batayll, and called xxv[ti] *They lead him out of the battle.*
archers with them.   And after these thinges thus doon
4 Anthony retourned in the prees, callyng¹ 'Lusynen'
with a hye voys, & said : 'Now lordes & barons, gyue *Anthony now urges his men to give great strokes, and to spare none, and tells them he has made the king prisoner.*
grete strokes, & spare none, For the journey is ours
thankyng¹ be to god; For I haue take the kynge of
8 Anssay my prysonner, that so grete vylonny haþ don
to the gentyl pucelle Cristyne.'   Thenne was the
medlee rude & paryllous / and there dide the bretheren
so moche of armes, that al tho that saw them said that
12 they sawe neuer two so valyaunt knyghtes.   What
shuld preuayll you long compte.   ¹Whan the Anssays *¹ fol. 116.*
peuple knew that theire kynge was take, they neuer *The king's people give up hope after he is taken.*
syn made no deffense / but wer alle outhre slayne or
16 take.   And there gate the poytevyns grete conqueste &
noble proye, and lodged them self in the pauyllons &
tentes of the king of Anssay & of hys peple.   And
was the kinge brought in Anthonys tente, which a
20 lytel byfore was hys owne propre tente ; wherfore the *He is brought to Anthony, and confesses that 'that god doth, he doth anone.'*
king¹ myght not hold his owne tonge, but said : 'By
my feyth, damoyseaulx, wel sayth he trouth that sayth /
"that god doth / he doth anoone" / For this day, in
24 the mornyng, men had doo here within but lytel for
your commandement.'   'Sire,' sayd Anthony, 'your
folyshnes & synne is cause therof ; For tofore ye wold *Anthony tells the king that he is to blame for desiring to seize Christine,*
rauysshe by force the pucelle Crystyne lady of this
28 toune / but therof ye shall be payed after your
deserte, For I shal yeld your self vnder her subgection.'   Thenne whanne the kyng¹ vnderstode hym, he
was shamfast & woofull / and as dysolate & dyscomfyte,
32 full heuyly ansuerd in this manere : 'Sith now it is
thus vnfortunatly happed with me, rather I wyl dey
than to lyue.'   'Nay,' sayd Anthony, 'ye shal delyuere *and announces that he is to be delivered into her hands.*
your self / no doubte of / vnto þe mercy & subgection
36 of the pucelle.'

Cap. XXVI. How the kyng of Anssay was lede byfore the pucelle Crystyne.

¹Thenne called Anthony to hym the two barons, ambaxadours that were come to Lusynen, with 4 the said gentylman fro Lucembourgh and xx^u other knyghtes of poytou, and to them said in this manere :

' Now lede me this kinge tofore þe damoyselle Crystyne, and recommande vs moche vnto her / and that we send 8 her / her enemy prysonner, for to do with hym her wyll.' And thenne they departed, & lede the kinge as they were youen in commandement / and came to the toune, where they were wel festyed & honourably 12 receyued. And thenne the Citezeyns conduyted them towarð the pucelle, theire lady Crystyne, with grete joye. 'Noble lady,' said the messagers, ' the two yong damoyseaulx of Lusynen recommande them hertyly 16 vnto you, ²and send you this kyng^r your enemy prysonner, to doo with hym after your dyscrecyon &

wylle.' ' Fayre lordis,' ansuerð the damoyselle / ' herto behoueth gret guerdon / but I am not puyssaunt 20 ynough for to reward them as they haue deseruyd. I

pray to god deuoutely that of hys grace he wyl rewarde them to whom I am mocħ bonden / and I pray you, fayre lordes, that on my behalf ye wyl pray my two 24 yong lordes that they vouchesauf to come and lodge them self here within, & as many of theyre barons with them as it shal lyke them good. & in þe meane while men shal burye the deed bodyes, & the deed 28

horses shal be brent / and also they of my Counseyl shal take theire best aduys to see how I shal reward them of theire grete peyne & traueyl, that they haue suffred for me vnworthy þerof, and to recompense 32 them of theire grete expenses & dommages in the best

wyse that we can or shal mowe. And ye, kynge of Anssay, ye swere vnto vs by your ryalte that ye shal

not departe from hens without the wyll & gree of the
two noble damoyseaulx, that here haue sent you toward
me.   For yet so moch I knowe / thankyng to god /
4 that I shuld mysdoo to cast you in pryson / not for
your sake / but for loue of them that hither haue sent
you.'   Whan thenne the kynge vnderstode the wordes
of the pucelle, he ansuerd al ashamed, ' Noble damoy-
8 selle, I swere you on my feyth that neuer hens I shal
departe without your leue & theirs also ; For so moch
of wele / of honour & of valyaunture I haue sene in
them, that moche I desyre to be acoynted with them /
12 how be it that grete dommage they haue borne vnto
me & my men.'   And thenne the noble mayde made
hym to be putte into a fayre chambre & riche, & with
hym ladyes & damoyselles, ¹also knyghtis & squyers,
16 for to make hym to forgete his losse, & forto reioye &
haue hym out of melencolye.   And thus don, the
messagers retourned toward the tentes, & reported the
mandement & prayer of the pucelle Cristyne vnto the
20 two bretheren, whiche were counseilled to goo thither ;
and ordeyned the mareshal of the oost for to gouerne
theire peple vnto tyme that they came agayn / and
also he commanded hym to make the deed bodyes to
24 be buryed, & to make the place clene where as the
batayll had be.   Thenne they departed, accompanyed
with theire baronnye / and ayenst them came, in theire
best wyse, an houndred gentylmen / and also the
28 barons of the land mete with them, & made theire
obeyssaunce full honourably vnto the two brethern,
prayeng them yet agayn, on theire ladys behalf, that
they vouchesauf to come & lodge them in the toune /
32 And they ansuerd that gladly they wold doo soo.
Anthony was mounted vpon a grete Courser / and he
had on hym a jacke of Cramesyn velvet, all brouded &
sette with perlis, and held a grete vyreton in his hand.
36 And in lyke & semblable manere went hys brother

in the town until
the brethren are
satisfied.

This done
he is given a fair
chamber.
Knights and
¹ fol. 117 b.
ladies are sent
to keep him
company.

The guard of the
king returns to
the brethren,

who leave their
army in charge
of the marshal,

and accompanied
with their barons
go towards the
town.

Regnauld. And whan the barons of Lucembourgh
sawe the two brethern, they wondred mochᵭ of theire
fyersnes, gretnes & myght, and wel said that there
was no man that might withstand ne abyde .theire 4
puyssaunce / and moche they merueylled of the Lyons
claw that appiered in Anthonys cheke, & said that yf
ne had be that he were the fayrest man in the world /
and moche they playned Regnald of that he had but 8
one eye, For in al his other membres he passed of
beaulte al oþer men.

¹ In this partye sayth thistorye, that in noble estate &
fayre aray entred the two brethern in to the toune 12
of Lucembourgh ; & before them sowned trompettes in
grete nombre, with heraults & menestrels ; And Cyteseyns had hanged theire houses withoutforth toward
the stretes, with theire best & rychest hangyng clothes / 16
and the stretes where the said lordes passed were
couered on high with lynen clothes, that no rayne or
other fowll wedryng myght lette þeire entree within the
toune / and many noble & worshipful ladyes, bourgeys 20
wyues / damoyselles and fayre maydens, were in theire
best rayments, eche one after the state & degree that
she was of / lokyng out at wyndowes for to behold &
see the noble brethern & theire felawship.   24

Thystorye thanne sayth that the two bretheren departed out of theire tentes with noble companye,
as barons, knightes, squyers, & other gentylmen /
and as vyctoryous prynces rode full honourably vnto 28
Lucembourgh, and thrugḫ the toune, where as they
were behold with joyous herte of euery one, sayeng
that one to other : See yonder be two the fyers men,
bretheren that are to be redoubted / he is not wyse 32
that taketh noyse or debat with them / and they had
grete wonder of Anthonyes cheke / and also for certayn
it was a straunge thingᵗ to behold & see / but the grete
beaulte that was in his body caused that inconueny- 36

ence to be forgoten / And thus they rode toward the
Castel. The ladyes & damoyselles beheld them out of
the wyndowes / and said that they neuer sawe two
4 damoyseaulx of more noble affayre. And thenne they
came to the Castel, wher they alighted, and entred
fourthwith into the hall, where as the noble Crystyne
mete them at the gate, wel acompanyed of ladyes &
8 damoyselles in grete nombre, and of knightes & squyers /
and with a joyous contenaunce & gracyous maynten
honou¹rably receyued them & gretly festyed them.
The halle was hanged nobly with ryche clothes after
12 the vse of the land, and fro the halle they went in to
another chambre, moch noble & ryche, & þere the
pucelle Cristyne bygan to say to them in this manyere :
'My right dere lordes, I thanke you moch, as I may
16 of the noble socours & help that ye haue don to me / I
am not so moch worth as ye ought to be rewarded of /
not that withstanding I shall endeuoyre me therto / al
shuld I laye of my land in pledge this tene yere day.
20 And also, my lordes, of your noble grace ye haue sent
to me the king¹ of anssay, myn enemy, of the which
plaise it you to knowe that I am not she to whom
oughte þe punysshement of hym / but to you appar-
24 teyneth to doo therwith your playsire & volente, that
haue had the parel & peyne for to ouercome & take
hym your prysonner / wherfore after that right requyreth he is yours, & may doo with hym whatsoeuer
28 it plaise you / and I remyse hym in your pocession.
For as touching my persone I gyue hym ouer vnto you,
& loke not to medle ony more with him tofore you.'
'Noble damoyselle,' said thanne anthony, 'sethen it is
32 your playsire, we shal ordeyne wel þerof, in suche wyse
that it shal be to your grete honour & prouffyte / and
to hym grete shame & confusyon / no doubt of / And
wete it that my broþer and I are not come hither for
36 loue of your siluer, but for to susteyne rayson & right /

and because
they think all
noble men
should aid
widows and
orphans.

fol. 119.

He declines all
reward,
save the lady's
favour and good
grace.

Christine is
abashed,

and wishes to
pay the soldiers
of the brethren,

but her offer is
refused.

The steward an-
nounces dinner;

they wash,
and send for the
King of Anssay,

who sits down
to dinner with
them.

fol. 119 b.

also considered that alle noble men oughte to helpe &
ayde the wydowes, orphenynis, and the pucelles also.
And forasmoch also that we were truly informed, that
the kinge of Anssay made grete werre ¹anenst you & 4
your land wrongfully, wherfor no doubte of / of all
your goodes we wyl not take the value of one peny /
but alonly to be receyued in your noble fauour &
good grace, all vylonnye excepted.' Whan the pucelle 8
Cristyne vnderstode these wordes, she was abasshed of
the grete honour that the two bretheren dide vnto her /
not that withstandyng she ansuerd in this manere:
'For southe, my gracyous lordes, at lest it were no 1¦
raison, but that I payed wel your peple that be come
hither to take your wages as sawdoyers.' 'Damoyselle,'
said þenne Anthony, 'vouchsaf to suffre that we haue
said, For my lord our fader, & my lady our moder, 1¦
haue payed them alredy for a hole yere day, or euer
they departed out of our land / & yet it is not fullysali
a moneth complet syn that we departed thens; And
ouermore wete it that syluer & gold we haue ynoughe. 2¦
Wherfore, noble demoyselle, ye lese your wordes to
speke therof, For certayn it shal none other be' / and
she thenne thanked them in her best manere ryght
humbly.   2¦

Thenne came the styward, & enclyned hym tofore
the pucelle, & said: 'My lady, ye may wesshe
whan it playse you, For al thing is redy to dyner' /
'whan, my lordes,' she said, 'be redy þerto, I am 2¦
playsed.' Whom Anthony ansuerd: 'noble damoyselle, we be al redy whan ye vouchesaf to go therat.'
and thenne they toke eche other by þe handes & wesshe.
And Anthony desired the king of Anssay to be sent 3¦
for / and made hym sette first of all at the table / and
after the pucelle and syn Regnauld / and anthony satte
last. And nygh to them satte foure of the noblest
barons of the land. And along the halle were ¹other 3¦

tables dressed, wherat sette all other gentylmen, barons
& squyers, eche one after hys degree.   Of the seruyse
I nede not to hold you long compte, For they were so
4 nobly & haboundauntly serued, that nothing accordyng
to such a ryall feste they wanted of.   And whan they
had dyned they wesshe handes, and graces were said,
and all the tables voyded.   thanne said the king of
8 Anssay in this manyere : ' Lordes damoyseaulx, vouchesauf to here my wordes.   It is trouth that the wyll of
god & myn vnfortune hath brought me to that caas,
that by your valiauntnes & prowes I am & haue be
12 bothe myself & al my peple dyscomfyte, & ouer that ye
haue take me your prysonner / but I ensure you, consideryng your high prowesse, your bounte, & your
noble affayres, I am glad & joyous to fynde me now
16 with you, For I shal be the bettre therfore al my lyf
naturel ; and syth, fayre lordes, þat my presence & long
abydyng here with you may nought preuaylle to you /
humbly I besech you, as I best can, that it playse you
20 to putte me to raisounable raunson & payement portable to me, so that I be not al dystroyed nor dysheryted / thaugh it lyeth now in your power / but
haue pyte on me, & punysshe me not aftir the regarde
24 of my follysshe enterpryse / how be it þat rygour of
justice requyreth it.'   ' By my hed,' said Anthony,
' who that shuld punysshe you after the regarde of the
grete iniurye, vylonnye, & dommage that ye haue don,
28 and yet had purposed to do to this noble damoyselle
without eny lawful cause / ye were not puyssant to
make amendes suffysaunt therof / but for as moche that
ye knowleche your synne the lasse penytence shal ye
32 haue / and I wyl wel that ye knowe that my brother
& I be not come from our countre hither for hoop of
getyng of siluer vpon you nor vpon other / but for
desire & hope of getyng of honour & good fame or
36 renommee, without to haue ony wyll or appetyt to

MELUSINE.   P

Dinner over,
hands washed,
and grace said,

the King of
Anssay
declares himself
discomfited,

and beseeches
that a reasonable
ransom may be
named,

and prays that
he be not dealt
with according
to the extreme
rigour of justice.

Anthony answers
that he would be
unable to make
amends if he
were duly pun-
ished for the
wrong he had
committed ;

but as he and
his brother seek
honour and not
silver,

haue mortal rychesses. Wherfore, as touchyng our part, we [1]now remyse & putte you free quytte & at your lyberte / sauf that we taxe you to pay to this noble pucelle all such dommages that she hath had at your 4 cause / and þerof ye shal gyue good pledges or euer ye departe hens, And yet morouer ye shal swere vnto her vpon the holy Euaungiles, that neuer ye shal bere, ner ye shal suffre to be borne ony manere of dommage ne 8 dyshonour to the forsaid pucelle that is here present / but at your power ye shal gyue her ayde, help, & comfort at al tymes aneust all them that iniurye or dommage wold doo to her. And wel I wyl that ye 12 knowe that yf ye wyl not swere & accorde to that I haue said with your good wylle, I shal send you in to such a place, wherout the dayes of your lyf ye shal not escape. And whan the kynge vnderstode these wordes 16 he ansuered in this manyere. 'Sire, I am wyllyng & redy to swere that conuenaunt, yf the noble mayde be content of that ye haue ordeyned & said.' 'By my feyth,' said she, 'I consent me therto, syn it is my 20 lordes plaisure' / and yet morouer said Anthony suche or semblable wordes as folowen /

'Yet, sire, I haue not al said that ye muste doo, For ye muste doo founde a Pryoure of twelue 24 monkes & the pryour, in suche place there as my lady shal ordeyne / and ye shal endowe & empossesse them with rentes & reuenue conuenable for theire lyuyng & for their successours for euermore / the said monkes & 28 pryour to pray there for the sowles of them that haue be slayne of your part & of myn in this batayll.' 'By my feyth,' said thenne the king, 'I promyse you þat so shal I doo, and good pledges & hostages I shall gyue 32 you, & to my lady to be asured therof.' Thenne sware the kynge by hys feyth vpon the holy Euaungiles that he shuld hold & accomplysshe al that beforesaid is / & gaf & delyuered good hostages / & lettres patentes were 36

[1] fol. 120.

they gyve him liberty on condition that he pay Christine for all the cost his attempt has put her to,

and that he undertakes never again to injure her.

The king agrees to these terms,

and Anthony adds,

that the king must build and endow a priory for twelve monks,

who shall pray for the souls of those who have been slain in the battle.

The king swears on the Evangels to keep these terms;

therof made vnder hys seal, & the seales of all the
[1]barons of his lande. And that don, Anthony said
to the kynge / ‘ I now gyue you, and delyuere free all
4 the prysonners that we & our folke haue take, and your
tentes & pauyllons also / but the hauoir that is departed
amonges my felawes I may not it rendre or yelde to
you / And thenne he made to be delyuered to hym
8 foure thousaund prysouners or therabout, al men of
estate & faytte / And thenne the kynge enclyned hymself, & thanked hym moch therof. What shuld I
make long compte / the feste bygane sumptuous &
12 grete thrughe the toune of Lucembourgh, & specially
in the Castel / and eueryone spake of the grete noblesse
and curtoysye that Anthony & regnald his brother had
shewed to the king of Anssay /

and he and his
lords delivered
[1] fol. 120b.
letters patent
agreeing to the
same under all
their seals.

Anthony then
delivers four
thousand
prisoners to the
king.

There is a great
feast in Luxem-
bourg,

and all men
praise the
courtesy of
Anthony.

16 Cap. XXVII. How the kinge of Anssay
called to hym al the barons of Lucembourgh to Counseylle.

[2]Thenne called the king of Anssay all the barons of
20 the land to Counseyll, and said to them : ‘ Fayre
lordes, Whan the yron is hoot it moste be wrought &
forged; how be it thenne that I haue be yl wyller
bothe to you & to your lady / the tyme is now come
24 that I wold her honour and prouffit & youres also /
lyst & here, For god hath sent good auenture to you,
yf ye can take it in gree.’ Thenne said the barons :
‘ Now, sire, syth that ye haue entamed þe matere /
28 vouchesauf to declare vnto vs the sentence therof.’
‘ Ye moste,’ said the kynge, ‘ fynde the manere &
meane that Anthony take your lady to his wyf, and
he to be your lord, For thenne ye shal mowe saye
32 surely, þat no nede ye haue of none other / & none so
hardy were to take an henne from you ayenst your
wyll.’ And they ansuered thus : ‘ Sire, yf Anthonye

[1] fol. 121.
The King of
Anssay calls the
barons of Lux-
embourg to
council,

and advises
them to find
means to make
Anthony marry
Christine.

y they
glad to

wold do soo we were therof full glad & joyous.' 'Now
thenne, fayre lordes, lete me deale tharwith / and I
hope to god I shal brynge the matere to a good ende.
Abyde and tary here a lytel, & I shal goo speke with 4
hym.' Thenne came the kynge tofore Anthony, &
said : ' Noble man & curtoys damoysean, the barons of
this land desire & pray you, that ye, your brother, &
your Counseyll come and entre in to this chambre. 8
For they desyre moch to speke with you for your
prouffyt & honour.' 'By my feyth,' said anthony,
'ryght gladly.' And thenne he called to hym hys
brother & them of theire Counseyll / & syn entred in 12
to the chambre / and the barons of the land that were
there enclyned themself, & made grete reuerence to the
two brethern.   Thenne spake the kynge of Anssay, &
said : ' Fayre lordes, these two noble damoyseaulx are 16
come hither at your requeste & prayer / declare now
to them your wylle.' And they ansuerde to hym :
' Noble kinge, humbly we beseche you, that ye anounce

1 fol 121 b.

& shewe to them our entencion, that ye knows ¹wel 20
ynoughe.' 'By my feyth,' said the kyng', 'I wyl.'
And thenne suche wordes as folowen he bygan to say /
' Anthony, noble man, curtoys & valyaunt knight,

The King of
Anssay, in the
name of the
barons of Lux-
embourg says,
seeing that
Anthony and
his brother will
accept no gift
of Christine,

þe barons of this Countree haue had regarde to 24
the grete honour that ye haue borne & shewed to theire
lady, to her lande, & to them / also they haue considered how nought ye wyl take of theyre lady ner of
them / and for asmoche that they desyre your wele & 28
honour, they humbly beseche your good grace that it

will Anthony
grant them a gift
of a kind which
will not lessen
his possessions?

playse the same to graunte to them a yefte, the which
shall not lasse your good nor hauoyr / but shal rather
augmente your honour.' 'By my feyth, noble kynge, yf 32
it be of that thing' that I may recouere / touching myn

Anthony answers
he will, if it is
something he can
do honourably.

honour, I graunt it right gladly.' 'Certainly,' said the
king', 'theire requeste is thenne fulfilled, For they
desyre none other but your honour.' 'Now, sey thenne, 36

said Anthony, 'what they desyre of me.' 'Damoyseau,' said the kinge / 'they wyl gyue you the Duchesse
of Lucembourgh, þeire liege lady, to your wyf / reffuse

The king offers
the Duchess of
Luxembourg to
Anthony to wife.

4 not that noble yefte' /

When anthony vnderstode hym he stood penseful
long tyme / and syn said in this manere : 'By my feith,
fayre lordes, I supposed neuer to cõme vnto this

When Anthony
understands
the position,

8 countre for that quarrell ; but sethen I haue accorded
to you I shal not gaynsay it / lete now the pucelle be
sent for, For yf she be playsed therwith I consent me
þerto.' Thenne was the damoyselle fete thither by

he asks that the
maid should be
sent for, and says
if she agree, he
will consent.

12 foure of the noblest barons of the land, the whiche
recounted to her al the faytte, wherof she was ryght
glad & joyous / how wel she made of it no semblaunt.

Christine is told
what has been
done, and is
right glad.

And whan she entred in to the Chambre she made her

She enters the
chamber.

16 obeyssaunce tofore antony, & salued alle the barons
there / and as she beheld Anthony she bygan to wexe
in her vysage more rede than a rose / and thenne the
barons reherced & shewed vnto her all this affayre.

When she sees
Anthony, her
face becomes
redder than a
rose.

20 And whan the pucelle had herd them speke 'she
answerd to them in this manere : 'Fayre lordes, I rendred & yeld thankes & mercys vnto almyghty god, to
his blessed moder, and to you also, of the grete honour

¹ fol. 122.

24 that now happeth to me, For I pouere orphenyme am
not worthy to be addressed in to so highe a place as to
haue to my lord the flour of knighthode and the noblesse of alle the world / and of that other part, I

28 wote & knowe wel that ye whiche are my liege men,
that bettre knowe myn own affayres than I doo my
self / wold not counseylle me that thinge, but it were
to my grete prouffyt & honour. Wherfor I ne oughte

She declares
that though un-
worthy she is
ready to do their
pleasure.

32 nor wyl not gaynsey it / but I am al redy to do therof
your playsire.' /

Cap. XXVIII. How Anthony espoused Crystyne, Duchesse of Lucembourgh. /

¹ 'Forsoothe, noble lady,' said the Barons, 'ye say right wel & manerly.' What shuld I bring 4 forth prolixe or long talkyng ? For shortly to say, they were assured togidre with gret joye / and on the next morne after they were espoused & maryed togidre, & was the feste holden right grete & noble, and the peple 8 of the land was ryght joyous whan they vnderstode & knew therof / and þat same nyght lay Anthony with the noble mayde Crystyne, and gate on her a moche

valyaunt heyre, & was called Bertrand. The feste 12 thenne endured longe sumptuous & grete, & grete ryalte was seen there / and anthony gaf noble & ryche jewels / and receuyed the homages of the lordes & barons of the land. And the king of Ansaay yaf leue to his peuple 16 to retourne into theire Countrees / and abode with anthony with a pryuy² meyne for to fulfyll & accomplisshe that he had promysed at traytee makyng of

the peas. And soone after the duc Anthony with his 20 brother Regnald and tho king of Ansaay and tho baronnye, went thrugh the land to vysyte the tounes & fortresses & putte al thing in good ordonnaunce / in so moche that euery man said, that he was one of the 24 moost wysest prynce that euer they sawe / and whan he had vysyted all þe land he retourned to Lucembourgh, where the duchesse Cristyne receyued hym

right joyously / And thanne by thaduys of his Coun- 28 seill he adiousted to his armes the shadow or fygure of a Lyon, for cause of the duchery, wherof the lady Cristyne had oftyme prayed hym to fore. And thus they soiourned at Lucembourgh with grete dysport & 32 joye / tyl that a messager came fro the king of

Behayne there, whiche was brother to the king ²of

² Fr. privet maisgnés.

Anssay, and was besieged wit*h*in his toun*e* of praghe who is besieged by the Sarasins at Prague.
by the paynemes & sarrasyns.

Cap. XXIX.   How the kyng, of behayne
4   sent a messager toward the king, of Anssay
his brother. /

Thystorye sayth that a messager cam*e* to Lucem-
bourgh fro the kyng' Federyk of behayne, that The valiant King Frederick of Bohemia,
8 was moche valyaunt & a true man, whiche ryght strong'
susteyned the feyth catholicaH ayenst the Sarasyns /
It is so that the paynemes entred in to his land / and
seeyng hym self not puyssau*n*t ynoug*h* for to gyue unable to give battle to the Paynims, with- drew to Prague.
12 them iourney of batayH, drew hym self & his peple
wit*h* hym in to hys toun*e* of Praghe / and had this
kyng' Federyke but on*e* only doughtir to his heyre, His heir is his only daughter, Eglantine.
whiche was named Eglantyne / & certayn it is that he
16 was brother to the king' of ¹Anssay.   Wherfore he sent ¹ fol. 123 b.
a messager to Lucembourgh there as the kyng of Anssay He sent a letter to his brother, the King of Anssay,
his brother was at that tyme.   And shortly to speke,
the messager cam*e* & directed his le*t*tres to the king'
20 of Anssay, whiche opened & re*d*d it / by the tenoure of
whiche he vnderstode & knew the myschief where his telling him how matters stood.
brother was in / and sayd al on high in heryng' of
eu*er*yone there in this manere : 'Ha / a, Fortune, how The king after reading it com- plains against fortune,
24 art thou so peru*er*se & so crueH, certaynly² wel is he
deceyued *þ*at trusteth in the nor in thy *ȝ*eft*es* by no
man*er*e.   it hath not suffysed the to haue ouerthrawen
me fro the vppermost stepp of thy whele vnto the
28 lowest / but vtterly wylt dystroye me for eu*er*, whan my
brother, whiche [is] one of the moost trewest & valiaunt
kyng' in the worl*d*, thou wylt so dysempare & putte
out fro his roy*au*me, yf god of his grace purueye not of and tells Anthony that it is worse than ever with him,
32 remedy therto' / and thenne he retourned hym self
toward anthony, & sayd : 'Ha / right noble & valyaunt

² Fr. version reads : *Certes l'omme est bien deceu que en
toy ne en tes dons se fie en riens.*

rynes, it is now with me wors than euer was / For
your noble chenalrye & puyssaunce haue not only
mated me & made lose myn honour, but also ye haue
dyssemfyted with me the moost true & valiaunt kyng 4
that euer was of my lynes, & that more valyauntly
hath defended the cristen feyth ayenst thenemyes of
god. For Federyke, my brother, noble kyng of Behayne, beyng sore oppressed & besieged within his 8
toun of praghe by thinfideles & enemyes of god,
writeth[1] vnto me ful tenderly for help & socoure /
alas, now your grete fayttes in armes haue kept me
therfro, so that I may not help hym / how be it that al 12
this coometh thrugh   owne fawte & folyssshe enterpryse, For god hat. ̣ inysshed me haue ynough
than I haue deseruyd.' And thenne he bygan to make
suche sorowe that grete pite it was to see. / 16

[1]Thystorye sheweth in this partie that the duc
Anthony was ryght dolaunt & sorowful whan
he vnderstode the pyteous bewayllyng of the king of
Aussay, and said to hym in this manere: 'Sire, telle 20
me why ye demene & make such dueyl' 'By god,'
sayd the kynge, 'wel I have cause / loke & see what
the tenoure of this lettre specyfyeth.' Thenne toke
anthony the lettre and redde it al ouer, Wherby he 24
vnderstode & knew the grete myserye & myschief
wherin Zelodyus, kyng of Craco, held Federyk, kyng
of Behayne, besieged within the Cite of praghe. And
thenne the noble duc Anthony consideryng the grete 28
myschief wherinne the Cristen peple was hold by the
puyssaunce of the paynemes, his herte was al replenyssed
with pite, and said in hym self that yf he might the
Sarasyns shuld bye full derly the peyne whiche they 32
made the Cristen peple to bere / and he thenne said
to the kynge: 'Sire, yf I wold helpe you for to socoure
your brother, wold ye not be soone redy to goo thither-

[1] vnriteth in MS.

ward?' And whan the kyng⸱ vnderstod thoos wordes
he kneled doune tofore the duc, & said : 'Sire, yf ye
wyl graunte me so moche of your grace / I swere &
4 promyse you feythfully that I shall make Regnald your
brother kyng of Behayne after the decesse of my
brother, whiche is elder than I almost xxᵗⁱ yere. For
wete it that he hath none heyre sauf only a ryght fayre
8 doughter, whiche is cleped Eglantyne / and she is about
xv yere of age, & that pucelle shall I gyue, yf ye vouchesauf, to Regnauld your brother.' 'By my feyth,' said
thenne Anthony, 'and I accorde therunto. / goo thanne
12 hastly to Anssay and make your mandement, and be
with vs ayen within this thre wykes, and lodge your
peuple in yonder medowe, Where your tentes ¹as yet
ben, and in the meane season I shal sende for my men,
16 whiche are with a knyght of myn at the Leffe, where
men had doon wrong⸱ to hym.' And the king⸱ ansuerde,
'Noble & curteys lord, he rewarde you therof, that
suffred deth for vs and bytter passyon.' And thenne
20 he toke his leue of the duc and of the duches, of
Regnauld, & of all the baronnye there, & syn mounted
on horsback / and with his owne meyne rode tyl he
came in to his land of anssay, sorowful for his losse
24 & joyfull for the socours that the Duc Anthony promysed to hym, for to helpe his brother ayenst the
panemes & enemyes of god. /

The veray hystorye testyfyeth that so long⸱ rode the
28 kinge of Anssay that he came in his land, where
he was welcommed of his baronnye / and soone went to
vysyte & see his doughter Metydee, that was not yet
two year old / and syn retourned with his barons / to
32 whome he shewed al his affayre, and how he moste
go socoure his brother ; Also how Anthony & Regnald
his brother shuld helpe hym therto with al theire pus-
saunce. 'By feyth,' said thenne the barons, 'syth it is
36 soo that thoo two brethern medle with this enterpryse,

The king is glad, and says that if Anthony will go,

he will make Regnald king of Bohemia on his brother's death.

Anthony then asks the king to go to Anssay and to return with his people in three weeks.

¹ fol. 124 b.

The king thanks him,

and takes his leave.

He rides to Anssay, sorrowful for his losses, but glad that Anthony will help his brother against the Paynims.

The king arrives in his land, and visits his daughter Metydee.

He returns to his barons, and explains all his affairs.

The barons think that as the brethren of Lusignan

hit may not fare but wel. For ayenst theire puyssaunce
& worthynes may none withstand nor abyde / hast you
thenne to make your cryees & mandement, For we al
shall go with you.' Thenne made the kyng his oost 4
to be boden & sent for, & prayd al his frendes & alyes /
& within a lytel space of tyme he assembled about

seuene thousand fyghtyng men / and departed fro his
royalme, whiche he lafte in good gouernaunce vnder a 8
noble baron of the land. And syn dide so moche by
his journeys, that at thende of thre wykes he came &
lodged hym & his oost byfore Lucembourgh, ¹in the
medow where his tentes were lefte. And thenne were 13

also come the dukes peuple, that were in nombre
fyue thousand helmets and a thousand V.C. archers &
crosbowe men, beside them of the duchery, that were
in nombre thre thousand, of þe whiche anthony toke 16

with hym two thousand and the other he lefte behynd
for the sauegarde of the land / of þe whiche he ordeyned
chief captayne and protectour a noble baron of poytou /
and that was the lord of Argemount. /   20

Cap. XXX. How the duc Anthony toke hys leue of the Duchesse Crystyne, and went toward praghe with hys oost.

Now sayth here thystorye, that whan the Duc 24
Anthony toke his leue of the Duchesse hys wyf,
she was right dolaunt & sory in herte, how wel she
durst make no semblaunt / but she prayed hym to
retourne assoone as he goodly myght / and he said 28
to her that so shuld he doo / And, morouer, he said to

²her in this manere / 'Duchesse, take good heede of
your fruyte that groweth in your blood, and cheryssh
your self / and yf goddis grace gyue that it be a sone, 32
make hym to be baptysed & named Bertrand, For thus
is my playsira. Thenne they embraced & kyssed eche

other, takyng leue one of other / and syn departed the
duc & came to hys peuple, and made his trompette*s*
to be sowned. Thenne mounted spere men on hors-
4 back, and bygan*e* eu*er*y man to marche forth in fayre
aray. The vantgarde conduyted & lede the kynge of
anssay and Regnald wi*th* hym, whic̄ was mounted
vpon a hye Courser, armed of al pyece*s* except his
8 helmet, and held a grete staf in hys fyst, and putte
his men iu ordre ful wel, & semed wel to be a prynce
courageou*s* & of hye enterpryse / and after folowed the
Cartes, Charyots & bagage, & the grete batayH̄ / and
12 after siewed the ryergarde, whic̄ Anthony conduyted
in fayre ordyna*u*nce of batayH̄, For it was tolde hym
*þ*at in that countre were many theevys / but . the duc
Anthony manded, & sent word fro fortresse to fortresse
16 that yf they were so bold to take on hym or on hys
peuple ony thing*, that he shuld punysshe them in
suche wyse that other shuld take ensample therof.
And so he passed thruḡ aH̄ the Leffe / and no man
20 was so hardy that he durst take ony thing on hys oost.
It is trouth that on an euen he lodged hym tofore the
Cite Acon[1] with aH̄ hys oost / and the Citezeyns there
made & pr*e*sented to hym grete *y*efte*s* of ryches, wherof
24 he thanked them moche, and proffred to them his seruyse, yf they myster of it. And on the morn*e* after
the masse he deslodged, & so long· marched fourth on
his way w*it*h his oost, that he cam*e* & lodged vpon
28 the ryu*er*e of Ryn*e*, whic̄ is grete & meruayllo*u*s.
And [2]they of Coloyne made grete daunger to lete
passe the oost thrughe the Cite at brydge / wherof
anthonye was angry & dolau*n*t, and fyersly sent worde
32 to them how he had entenc*i*on to reyse the siege, that
the king· of Craco had layed, & sette with lx thousand
Sarasyns tofore the Cite of praghe, wherinne was in
grete oppression and dystres the king of behayne,

The army
marches away
to the trumpet
sound.
The vanguard is
led by Regnald
and the King of
Anssay;

then comes the
baggage in the
middle, as
Anthony was
told the country
was full of
thieves, and then
the rearguard
led by Anthony
in good order.

At last they
arrive at the
Rhine.

[2] fol. 126.
The men of
Cologne object
to the host pass-
ing through the
city.
Anthony angrily
tells them the
reason of the
expedition,

---

[1] Fr. *Ays*:—*Aix la Chapelle*, Ger. *Aachen*.

that they
s the
and who
d
and that they shuld send hym word yf they held with
the paymentes or not / and vpon that he shuld take
hys aduys what he shuld doo / and also that amonge
them he shuld fynd good passage, but not so short as 4
by theire Cite. And whan they of Coloyne understode this mandement, & were wel informed of the
grete prowes & fyernes of the two bretheren, they
were dredfull & doubtous. And soone after they sent 8
toward Anthony foure of þe notablest & moost worshipfull burgeys of the cyte, whiche come & mede to hym
ryght honourable and humble reuerence / and wondred
moche of hys fyernes and proude countenaunce / not 12
that withstanding, they said to hym in this manere:
'right high & myghty prynce, the Cilezeyns and commynalte of Coloyne haue sent vs toward your good
grace. And know ye þat gladly they shal suffre you 16
& al your oost to passe possibly thrugh the Cite, soo
that ye shal kepe & preserue them fro al dommage
that your pepie might bere vnto them.'   'By my
feyth,' sayd Anthony, 'yf I had be wyllyng to doo the 20
contrary of theire wyll, they shuld haue had of me

knowlege therof / and also I haue no cause to doo soo,
For I knowe not that they haue mysdoon to me of ony
thing, nor to the myn nother / How wel they cause 24
me to thinke other wyse / goo and telle to them, yf
they remember not of old some mysdede don to them
by myn auncestry, or of the Dukes, my predecessours,
wherof as yet they be ¹not pacyfyed & accorded / 28
that they wyl suffre me & myn oost passe surely / or
ellys to send me wordes therof.'   Whan they vnderstode hys wordes & knew his wyll, they retourned to
the Cyte, & announced to the Commynaltee the mande- 32
ment of the Duc Anthony. And they anone assembled theire counseyll, & the auncyent men / and
found that neuer they had no hate ne dyscorde with
the dukes of Lucembourgh, nother to theyre frendes 36

nor alyez / and that sethen he was so noble a man & so
valyaunt, they shuld lete hym passe, and al his oost
also.   And they remanded to hym theire wylle with

4 grete yeftes of ryches that they made to be presented
to hys grace / and purveyed for hys oost moch of
vytayll, as bred, wyne, and flesshe / & ootys for theire
horses / And whan the Duc vnderstode theire ansuere

8 & sawe theire grete yeftes, he thanked them moche /
and was joyous of that they of Coloyne wold be hys
frendes.   Wherfor he said to them, that yf they had
nede of hym & of hys powere, he was redy at theyre

12 commaundement / and they thanked hym ryght
humbly.   And the duc Anthony made to gyue to
them that had brought to hym the said presents of
vytayll, many ryche yeftes, that asmoch were worth, or

16 more than the presents & yeftes gyuen to hym by the
toune, For he wold not that thabytants of the Cyte
shuld suppose or thinke that he wold haue ought of
them for nought.

20 In this partye sheweth thystorye, how that same
   nyght soiourned the oost byfore Coloyne, & was
wel refresshed of them of the Cite & of theire vytayll.
For as the dukes commandement was / they were

24 departed in suche wyse tha[t] euery man there had
part therof.   And on the morne erly, [1]the Duc entred
into the Cite with hym, two houndred men of armes /
and made his cryees, vpon peyne of deth, that none

28 were so hardy to take ony thing of them of the toun ;
but he payed wel for after raison.   And soone after
passed the vantgarde in fayre aray ouer the bridge, and
so forth thrugh the Cyte.   And so passed al thoost,

32 and lodged them at the oþer syde of the ryuere of
Ryn / and it was about euen tyme, or euer al the
Cartes, Charyots, & bagage were past.   And that nyght
the Duc & grete part of his baronnye lodged within the

36 Cyte, where as grete honour was doon to them.   The

[1] fol. 127.

Side notes:
They agree to let Anthony and his host pass,

and send him many gifts for himself and victuals for his host.

When the duke understands their answer, he thanks them,

and gives them as rich gifts and presents as had been sent to him.

The host remains opposite Cologne for the night.

In the morning the river is crossed, and the host marches through the city.

The duke and his barons stay all the night in the city,

and give a great
copper, and great
gifts to the ladies
of the town.

duc Anthony bode at souper with hym all the ladyes
of the Cyte, & festyed them ryght honorably, & gaf
grete yeftes ar he departed in so moche that they of
the Cyte wysshed hym to be theire lord.   4

He leaves in the
morning, after
thanking the
townspeople,

In the morne the Duc toke his leue of them of the
toun / and thanked them moche of the grete
honour that they had shewed to hym & to his barons.
And they answerd all with one voyce : 'Noble Duc / 8
the Cite / we & all our goodes ben at your commandement more than to ony other lord that marcheth about
vs / and spare vs not of nothing' that we may doo for
you, For we be now, & shal euer be, redy to do you 12
playsure, ayde, & comfort at your mandement and first
callyng' / And he departed fro them, and went in to
his tente.   And on the morne as he came from the
masse, & commanded the trompettes to be sowned for 16
to departe & meve / there came fro the Cite foure

who offer him
aid.

As the duke
comes from them,

four knights and
five hundred men
arrive from the
city.

knightes wel mounted on horsbak, & armed of all
pyeces sauf the helmet, whiche alyghted byfore the
duckes tente with foure houndred men of armes, and 20
C crosbowe men in theire felawship.   These knightes
made their obeyssaunce / and syn sayd in this manere :
'Right noble & puyssaunt duc, the Cite & commynalte
of Coloyne recommande them to your good grace / 24
and where as þey haue sene so moche of noblesse &
curtoysye in you / [1]desyryng right affectuelly to be
frendes & alyez vnto you, they send you foure hondred
men of armes & an C crosbowes, al payed of theire 28
wages for tene monethis day, for to goo with you
where so euer it playse you to goo.'   'By my feyth,'
sayd Anthony, 'thankyng be to them, whome I am
moche beholden to / this curtoysye is not to be reffused / 32
& wete it I shal not forgete it / but remembre in tyme
& place.'   'Sire,' said one of the foure knightes, 'there
nys none of vs foure, but he knowe wel al the way fro
hens to Craco / and yf it mystier, we shal guyde & lede 36

[1] fol. 127 b.
The knights say
that the com-
monalty of
Cologne wish
to be his allies,
and ask him to
accept the help
of the five
hundred men
of arms.

One of the
knights offers to
guide the army
to Cracow.

you wel & surely thrughe all the passages & ouer al
the ryueres betwix this & that.' To that ansuerd the
Duc & said / 'this that ye say hurteth not our affayre,
4 and I gaynsay not your sayeng', whan tyme shalbe.'
Thenne he putte them in ordynaunce, and receyued
them vnder his banere. And þenne desloged the vantgarde, the grete batayll, & the ryeregarde, and marched
8 on theire waye in fayre aray so long', that they entred
in the land of Bavyere, nygh to a grete Cite named
Nuenmarghe, where as the Duc of Ode was with a
grete companye of peuple, For he doubted the kyng
12 Zelodus of Craco, that had besieged the kynge Federyke of Behayne, and held hym in grete necessite,
For he had with hym foure score paynemes / and the
Duc Ode was doubtous lest he shuld come vpon hym,
16 yf he subdued and dyscomfyted the kyng Federyke.
And therfore, he had assembled hys Counseyl to knowe
& see what best was to doo. /

Thenne cam to the Cite an auncyent knyght that
20 was of the Duc Ode, to whom he said after his
obeyssaunce made : 'My lord, by my sowle I come
from the marches of Almayne / but there is ¹commyng
a grete oost hitherward of the moost goodlyest men of
24 armes and best arayed that euer I sawe in my dayes /
but I wot not where they purpose to goo / but so
moche I know, that they draw them self hitherwarl.'
'By my feyth,' said the Duc, 'I gyue me grete wonder
28 what folke they may be, yf the king of Anssay had not
be of late dyscomfyted tofore Lucembourgh, I shuld
suppose that it were he that wold socoure his brother
Federyke ayenst the Sarasyns / and on my sowle yf it
32 were he I shuld goo with hym for to helpe his brother.'
'My lord,' said the knyght, 'it were wysely doo to haue
knowleche certayn what folke they be, ne yf they purpose other wyse than wele.' 'Sire knyght,' said thanne
36 the Duc, 'ye muste your self goo to knowe & reporte

The duke accepts
the company,
and puts them
under his banner.

The army
marches to
Bavaria, nigh to
Nuenmarghe,

where the Duke
Ode is taking
council what to
do about the
siege.

¹ fol. 128
An ancient
knight tells
Duke Ode of
the approach of
a great host.

The duke says
if it were the
King of Anssay
he would go with
him to help
Frederick.

The duke sends
the knight to
ascertain what
host it is.

the ouyrsyte of it, syr ye haue sene theʳᵉ'. And he
answerde, 'By my feyth, my lord, I am truly therto.'
And soone he departed, and so long he rode that he
perceyued theost in a valey by a ryuere. There he 4
saw grete companyes of goodyʳ men here & there,
some caryyng the harneys of hym ... other held theire
spere & shild and enayauntted them self that one on þat
other / some assayed theire harneys with shott, with 8
strokes of swerdes, and in many other appertyse of
armes they exercyted them self. 'By my feyth,' said
thenne the knight, 'there is fayre myystere and noble
enteynaunce of men of armes ... suche folke is to be 12
doubted and dredde.' Thenne he loked on the ryght
syde vpon a lytel mountayne & saw the grete batayll,
and saw the watche and the sewers al about the
oost. 'By my feyth,' said the knight that moche thing 16
had sene in his dayes / 'this ben ²worthy men of
werre and able to subdue ony lande.' And thenne he
entred in to theost ... and demanded after hym that had
the gouernaunce & gydyng of it ... And soone he was 20
brought tofore Anthony. And whan he saw the Duc
he was moche abasshed of his facion ... but alwayes he
salued hym ryght curteysly ... and syn said to hym,
'My lord, the Duc Ode hath sent me toward you to 24
wete of you what ye seeke in hys land / and yf ye thinke
or purpose other wyse than wele ; also what ye be that
conduyteth so fayre company of peuple that I see here
assembled. For he woteth wel that ye come not hither 28
with suche a felawship without it be for som grete affayre' / 'Frend,' sayd anthony / 'tell your lord that we ne
demande ought of hym, nor suppose not to dommage his
land in no wyse. Also ye may telle hym that it is the 32
kinge of Anssay / Anthony of Lusynen, Duc of Lucembourgh, and Regnald his brother, with theire puyssaunce that supposen to goo reyse the siege of praghe,
that the Sarasyns haue besieged.' 'Sire,' said thaun- 36

Marginal notes:

[How ... a right great host of men of ... him ... and not far for the gouernor. He is brought before Anthony.]

The knight says he is sent by Duke Ode to enquyre why the host had come into his land.

Anthony an-wers that he is the Duke of Luxembourg, and with him is his brother and the King of Anssay, and that they are going to rayse the siege of Prague.

cyent knyght, 'god graunte you good vyage.' And so
he departed and retourned toward the Duc Ode of
Bauyere, to whom he reherced as aboue is said, and
4 shewed hym the fyersnes and facion of Anthony, and
the contenaunce of his oost / sayeng¹ that they were
folke to be redoubted & dred². 'By my feyth,' said
thenne the duc Ode, 'It commeth of noble courage to
8 that two bretheren to haue come fro so ferre lande
for to seke auenture of cheualerye & honour, and also
for to come & gyue ayde & socour to kynge Federyke
anenst the enemyes of god / and I promyse god that
12 shal not be without me, For it shuld be tourned to me
to grete shame yf that I went not thither / seeyng that
he is my Cousyn, & that my land is so nygh his
royalme / and that the straungers come fro so ferre
16 for to ayde & helpe hym ayenst the paynemes.' And
thenne had the Duc Ode ¹made his mandement but of
late, and had assembled al redy foure thousand fighting
men. What shold I make long compte / thoost desloged
20 and passed³ byfore Murmych. And thanne the Duc
Ode yssued out of the toun with a fayre companye of
peuple, and came and presented hym self and al his
peple tofore the kinge of Anssay, Anthony / and his
24 broþer, whiche Joyously receyued them / and thus
marched thoost forth in fayre aray and good ordynaunce
by the space of six dayes. And now seaceth thistorye
to speke of them, and speketh of the king¹ Federyke
28 and of the siege. /

H ere sheweth thistorye how the puyssaunce of
Zelodyus, kyng of Craco, was ryght grete / and
the king Federyk durst not goodly haue yssued / but
32 alwayes he scarmousshed ofte with his enemys / and
almost dayly was at the barrers / the medlee was grete
& stronge / and there were within the toune about
a houndred helmets of Hongery, that were valyaunt
36 knightes & good men of werre / the whiche yssued /

The knight re-
turns, delivers
his message,
and describes
the host.

The King thinks
the brethren
courageous,

and resolves to
go with them

against the
paynims.
¹ fol. 129.

He assembles
four thousand
men,

and presents
himself with his
company to the
King of Anssay
and the brethren.

Frederick is
unable to cope
with Zelodius,

though he often
tries skirmishes.

ofte & dide grete dommage to the sarasyns.   It happed

on a mornyng erly that the paynemes gaf a grete sawte
to the toun / and the king Federyke with his peuple
yssued out vnto the barrers / and there the scarmyssh- 4
ing bygan grete & mortall / and so manfully faught
the kyng, that with the help of his men he gretly
dommaged his enemyes / and made them to cesse of the

sawte / & made them to goo back vnto theire lodgys. 8
And that tyme was the kyng of Craco mounted vpon a

grete hors, his banere to the wynd acompanyed with
xv M¹ sarasyns, and came in fayre ordynaunce to the

batayll.   There was many stroke gyuen & receyued / 12
and by force of armes the kynge & his peple was constrayned to withdrawe hym back vnto the barrers.
There was grete occyayon made, For horryble strokes
were gyuen of bothe sydes, and the king Federyke re- 16
comforted wel his peple, For he dide grete faytte of

armes of his owne handes.   And whan he perceyued
¹kyng Zelodyus that sore dommaged his peple, he
sporyd his horse and toke his swerd in his fyst / and 20

rane smyttyng on the lyft syde and on the ryght syde
vpon his enemyes tyl he made place, and came &

smote Zelodius vpon his helmet, by suche strengthe &
vertue that he made hym to enclyne vpon his hors neck 24
al astonyed / and lytel fayllcd that he was not ouerthrawen to the erthe, For he lost bothe the steropes /

but soone he was socoured of his men whiche redreced
hym vp ryght / and the king Federyk adreced hys 28
swerd vpon a payneme, & suche a stroke he gaf hym
that he slew hym therwith.   The kyng of Craco was
thenne redreced as said is / and he perceyuyng the kyng
Federyk / that hewed legges & armes, & casted to 32
therthe al that he recountred of the sarasyns / had
grete anger in his herte and came nygh at hym / and

with an archegaye or dart launched at hym, by suche
strengthe that the dart entred so depe into hys body 36

that the hed of it was sene at the back syde of hym. which pierces his body through and through.
That doon the kynge Federyk that felt the dystresse of
deth myght no more hold hym self up ryght, but fell He falls to the ground.
4 & reuersed deed fro his hors to the ground. Thenne
was his peple full heuy and dolaunt, and withdrew His people withdraw to the town and close their gates.
them self anoone, and reentred into the toune & shetted
the gates after them.   And thenne byganne the sorowe
8 to be grete in the town al about. /

Cap. XXXI. How the kinge of Craco dide do take the body of kynge Federyke that he had slayn and commanded it to be brent.

12 ¹The king of Craco thenne glad & joyous for cause of ¹ fol. 130.
kyng Federykes deth, commanded the corps to be Zelodius commands Frederick's body to be burnt.
brought byfore the gate, & there to be brent for to haue
abasshed the more þem of the Cite, seyng theyre king
16 in a fyre.   Whan the Cyteseyns & commynalte of The citizens of Prague are sorrowful for the death of their king.
praghe knew the deth of theire kynge / and the grete
tyrannye of Z[el]odyus, they made grete sorowe / but in
especial the pucelle Eglantyne, his doughtir, was sorow-
20 full in herte, and so pyteously bewaylled and lamented,
that grete pyte it was to here & see / sayeng such or
semblable wordes : ' Ha / god ! who might comforte me His daughter, the maid Eglantine, piteously mourns her father's death,
whan I see my faders deth byfore me, & the total dys-
24 comfyture of hys peple, & also the destruccion of my
self, For I see no way wherby myght come ony socoure
vnto me, For I haue herd say that myn vncle, the
kynge of Anssay, on whome I trusted more than to
28 all ²other men in the world, hath be dyscomfyted ² fol. 130 b.
tofore Lucembourgh.   Ha, veray god ! creatour of Creatures, I ne wote other reffuge for me for to escape the
tyraunt Z[el]odyus handes than the mercyfull bosom
32 of your grace to hyd me therin.   O ryght noble, ryght and calls on the Virgin Mary.
puyssaunt, & ryght excellent pryncesse ! virgyne &
moder of god ! Marye, my lady & maistresse / haue

Those who see
her grief are
full of pity.

The commonalty
propose to yield,

but two true
knights upbraid
them,

And advise them
to wait tidings
from the King
of Anssay:

and bid them
trust in Christ.

The people are
comforted and
refuse to yield,

¹ fol. 131.

whereat Zelodius
is angry.

He sorely as-
saults their city.

compassion on me! poure orphanyn & faderles.' Certaynly the pucelle Eglantyne bewayled, syghed, &
complayned so piteously that no persoone behekl her /
but they were of pyte constrayned to wepe how hard
that theire hertes had be, For in her anguysshe &
sorowe she made none ende, but euer she wept &
rendred teeris habundauntly. Thenne the communalten
of the toune, sore agast and timerous, were in propos
& wylle for to yeld the toun & themself ouer to the
kyng Z[el]odyus, but made them to be requyred & ad-
monuested¹ therof / shewing to them how they myght
not long endure nor withstand ayenst his grete puyssaunce / & that theire Catell & goodes shuld be saued
to them / but yf he toke theire Cyte byforce, he shuld
make þem bothe theire wyues & children to be brent
al to asshis, as theire kynge was. Wherfore the cyte
henge in balaunce to be delyuered & gyuen ouer to the
Sarasyns. But emonge other were there two good
men, true & auncyent knightes, that said in this
manere : 'False peuple, what wyl you now doo, yet is
not the messager come agayn that rode toward the
kyng of Anssay for socour, take courage & comfort
your self, For within short space of tyme ye shal here
good tydynges / thinke that ye be Cristen / & that
Criste shall helpe vs or it be long.' And whan they
herd hym so speke they were all recomforted, &
ansuerd to the paynemes ambaxatours that they shuld
neuer yeld them ouer vnto the last ²mans lyf of all
them. And whan the kynge Zelodyus knewe theire
wyll, he was wood angry & sorowful, & sware his
goddes that he shuld putte al on fyre. /

The kynge³ Zelodyus was mouyd to yre & grete
anger for thansuere of the commynalte of Pragh,
wherfor he scarmysshed them sore, & gaf grete sawtes
to theire Cite, but the noble and valyaunt men that

¹ Fr. faisoit remonstrer.　　　³ kynge of: MS.

were within deffended it strongly.   I wyl now retourne
to speke of the Duc anthony and of hys brother Regnauld, of the kynge of Anssay / and also of Ode, Duc
4 of Bauyere, whiche conduyted theyre oost, & marched
fourth hastly, For they had tydinges of the myserye
that they of the Cite were in / but nothing they knew
of the deth of kyng Federyke.   And on a thursday at
8 euen, they lodged themself nygh to a grete ryuere, a
leghe & a half fro the Cite of Praghe / and that same
euen was a knight of that same Countree that was in
theire felawship commanded that on the morne he
12 shuld anounce theire commyng to them of the Cite /
and he on the morne erly mounted on hys hors, and
toke his way toward the Cite / and after a grete sawte
was seaced for fawte of daylight, he cam vnto a lytel
16 posterne / and they of the garde there knew hym anone,
and lete hym eutre the toun / and as soone as he was
entred he rode softly along by the gardes, cryeng alowde
in this manyere : 'Lordes, deffende you wel, For here
20 commeth the floure of knighthode to your socours &
helpe with the kinge of Anssay, & anoone ye shal see
them bygynne the bataylle / and be a good chere, For
on my hed not one Sarasyn shall escape, but he be
24 deed or take.'   And [1] whan they vnderstode hym, they
bygane to make such a Cry, & so lowde, that it was
wonder to here sayeng : 'Lawde & thanking be to god
almighty þerof.'   And thenne they employed them self,
28 & defended so valiauntly, that no sarasyn durst no
lenger abyde nygh the wall a bowe shotte / & many
paynemes were thenne slayne, in so moche that the
dyches watre was as tourned & dyed with theyre blood.
32 And whan Zelodyus sawe the grete & courageous
deffense of them of the toune he was abasshed, &
meruaylled moche of theire joyful contenaunce. /

Thenne whan Zelodyus perceyued that his folke
36 withdrewe them self thus backward, he was

Side notes:

The relieving host marches hastily,

and arrives on a Thursday evening a league and a half from Prague.

A knight is sent to the city with the news of their approach.

He enters, and bids the lords fight well because of the succour that is near.

[1] fol. 131 b.

The people thank God for the good news,

and slay many Saracens.

Reginald is contented that the assault has failed.

Anthony and his host approchen.

They are the Saracens' camp.

Anthony maketh a halt, and ordereth archers to his wynges.

I fol. 122.

The paynims perceive their coming, and tell Zelodius.

He is wroth, and commandeth his men to assemble in battle array.

Anthony's host advances against the paynims.

The air is full of arrows.

Christians and paynims fight manfully.

somewhat & dolorust, & had grete mervaylle, why & wherfore they of the hooste were of so euyngreate deffemce more then in other sewtes tofore gyuen, / but anone after hys deière & sorowe encreased moch more, For Anthony approached in fayre aray. He, & Reynald hys brother, conduyted the first batayll; and the kyng of Anssay, & his Cousin the due of Baryene, helde the myer garde. There had ye seen fayre companye of gentilmen in good aray, / the heaumes & standartes dysployed / helmets & salades wel garnysshed with fyne gold & syluer, which resplendysshed full clere, / And so they cam & sawe the Cite that the paynemes assyeged, & gaaf grete sawte / & ouer theire tentes & pavyllons, where were grete numbre of saraxyns. Thenne made Anthony his folk to tary and be styl a while, tyl the ryergarde were nygh to them / and ordeyned archers & crosbowes to be vnder the wynges of hys batayll. and thenne they were appeoeyned, [1]and som of the paynemes, which went & made knowlege therof to theire kyng, sayeng in this manyere: 'Sire, beue the sawte, that in an euyl heure was bygonne, wete it that such a multitude of Cristen peple be comyng hitherward that all the feldes be couered with.' Whan Zelodius vnderstode these tydynges he was wood wroth, & gretly abasshed, and lefte the sawte, and made the trompettes to sowne the retrayte, & that euery man shold assemble togidre vnder hys banere. he thenne ordeyned his batayiles as he coude best. And Anthony commanded hys trompettes to be sowned for to bygynne the batayll, and they approched the paynemes, keping good ordynaunce. Thenne bygan the shotte to be grete & thikk as snowe in the ayer, and syn the men of armes medled togidre, and entred one vpon other, & valyauntly brake speres, & ouerthrew eche other as it happed. The Cristen faught corageously / and the paynemes withstode & susteyned theiro

grete strokes manfully. There was many sarasyn reuersed to therth & slayn. Wel assayed the poyteuyns
them self, & dyde grete faytte of armes vpon theire
4 enemyes. But the king⸱ Zelodyus putte his sheld
tofore his brest, & held his spere alowe, and broched
his hors with the sporys, & rans vpon the Crysten;
and aftir hym folowed xv M⸱ paynemes. Zelodius
8 dide there grete merueylle of armes, and ouerthrew
many a Cristen to therthe, & gretly dommaged them.
For his folke that folowed at back syde of hym faught
meruayllously. Thenne cryed the kyng⸱ Zelodius his
12 baner: 'Lordes, barons, auaunce, the journey is oure,
For they may not vs escape' / And they of poytou
receyued them moch hardyfly, and wete it wel that
there was grete losse of peple of bothe partyes.
16 Thenne came duc Anthony with the swerd [1] in his
fyst / and whan he perceyued his peple recule a lytel,
nygh he deyed for sorowe / and cryed: 'Lusynen!'
with a high voys, and putte hym emong⸱ the sarasyns
20 more hastyfully than thundre falleth fro heuen, and
faught & smote on eche syde vpon his enemyes, and
ouerthrew all them that he recountred. and his peuple
folowed at back syde of hym that were al wondred of
24 his grete fayttes & valyauntnes, For there ne was so
hardy a sarasyn þat durst hym abyde / but fledd &
reculed vnto theire tentes. And this seyng⸱ the king⸱
Zelodius, he cryed: 'auaunt, lordes & barons, and
28 deffend you / how is that for one man alone that ye
flee / it is to you grete shame.' And aftir these wordes
he retourned, & assembled his peple ayen togidre, and
gaaf grete batayl mortal vnto anthony & the poytevyns.
32 Thenne came thadmyral with ten thousand⸱ fighting
men / and thenne enforced the batayll ryght horryble,
For there were many of the sarasyns slayn and sore
hurt.

Marginal notes:

Zelodius with a great host rushes on the Christians,

and greatly hurts them,

and cries 'the day is ours.'

[1] fol. 132 b.

Anthony sees his people retreating; he cries 'Lusignan,' and falls on the Saracens like thunder from heaven.

The Saracens flee.

Zelodius upbraids them,

they rally and fight again.

The admiral arrives with ten thousand men.

Cap. XXXII   How the king of Craco was slayn in bataylle.

† fol. 122.
The vauntgarde, maner the King of Ansony conduytyth and fyghts vygourously.

Anthony and Regnauld gyve marveillous attackes,

and whatever they saw they smote the Sarasyns to ryn.

† fol. 122 b.
Zelodius encourages his folk, and does grete damage.

Regnauld spurs his horse against him.

Zelodius hurts him in the thigh,

but Regnauld hits him back,

Thenne came the ryerward that the kinge of Ansony and the king Ode conduyted þat entred tygourously into the batayll, where was grete occysyon, For the batayll was mortal on bothe parties. And vpon that arryved Anthony & Regnauld, that entered by me smote vpon the sarasyns, making suche occysyon that 8 there ne was sarasyn ne Cristen, but he mervaylled of þe mervayllous strokes that they gaf. And in conclusyon there was none so hardy a sarasyn that durst withstand them, For whatsomever they sawe them 12 they fledd, and so strongly faught the cristen / that the sarasyns tourned theire back, puttyng them self to flight ; but the kyng Zelodyus valyauntly encouraged & retayned them togidre. And wete it wel that he dide 16 grete dommage to the Crysten. But whan Regnauld perceyued the king Zelodius, that rendred so grete a stoure & batayll mortall to hys folke / he sware that he shuld dye or he shuld delyuere the place fro the 20 sarasyns / Thenne tourned he the targe behynde and sporyd his hors by grete yre and came vpon the king of Craco. And whan Zelodyus the kynge sawe hym come he haunced hys swerd and smote hym vpon his 24 helmet / but his swerd glenced doune by the lyfte syde vnto his thye, & hurted hym in such manere that the blood rane vnto his foote / And thenne Regnauld þat was full dolaunt, with bothe handes lyfte vp his 28 swerde and smote the kynge Zelodyus vpon the helmet with so grete yre that he was therwith astonyed, in so moche that the swerd fell out of his hand and bowed vpon his hors neck, and therwith brake the taches of 32 his helmet. And thenne Regnauld retourned & smote hym ayen, and charged hym with so many hydouse strokes that he moste nedes parforce fall to therth.

And fourthwith was the prees grete aboute hym bothe and though Zelodius' people come to defend their king,
of horses & men / but hys peple came & socoured
hym fro the horses feet / but in conclusyon they coude
4 not obteyne nor hym ayde / but he was slayne. And Regnauld slays him.
whan the sarasyns sawe that they went to flight / And The Saracens then flee;
the cristen peple pursiewed þem manfully and slough many are slain,
them bothe in feld & in wodes. And wete it wel
8 that there escaped but few, and thus was the batayll and but few escape.
fynysshed. And this don the Cristen lodged them in
the tentes of the sarasyns. And the two brethern / The Christians take the camp
the kyng of Anssay and the Duc Ode departed with of the Saracens.
12 a C. ¹knyghtes with them toward the Cite, where as ¹ fol. 134.
they were nobly receyued, For the Citezeyns had so The brethren enter the town.
grete Joye of the vyctorye that they had wonne vpon
the sarasyns. And thenne came they & descended at
16 the palays ryall. Thenne came the pucelle Eglantyne
and recountred her vncle the kyng of Anssay and all
his barons.

Cap. XXXIII. How the kynge Zelodius &
20   the other saracyns were brent and bruyled¹.

The pucelle Eglantyne was thenne joyfull & glad The maid Eglantine is glad for
for the dyscomfyture of the paynemes and also of the victory.
the commyng of her uncle. But not withstanding she
24 had sorowe at herte for the kynge, her faders deth,
that she might not forget it. And neuertheles, whan
she cam byfore her vncle she enclyned & honourably
made to hym her obeyssaunce, sayeng: 'My right dere She welcomes her uncle, the
28 vncle, ye be right welcomme / playsed god that ye King of Anssay,
were arryued two ²dayes rather, For thenne ye had ² fol. 134 b.
found my fader on lyue, whiche Zelodius hath slayne
& made to be brent & bruled to the moost vytupere & and tells him how Zelodius has burnt her father's body.
32 shame of the Catholycal feyth.' And whan the kyng
of Anssay vnderstod it he was wroth & dolaunt, and
sware that thus and in suche wyse shuld he do of the He swears

kynge Zelodius and of all the sarasyns, that he coude
fynde ded or alyve.   And thenn were cryece made
thrugh the town, that of every hous one man should goo
in to the feld for to assemble the deed bodyes of the 4
sarasyns togidre vpon a mountayne, and that men
shuld brynge thither wed ynough for to brule & brène
the corps.   And thus it was don.   And was the corps
of Zelodyus sette vpon a stake so that it was seen aboue 8
al other / And so was the fyre grete about them / and
so they were al brent & bruled / and all the deed
bodyes of the cristen men that were found were buryed
there as cristen peple ought to be.   And þenn thinges 12
doon, the kyng of   y made al thing to be redy
for to make thobseq   of the kyng his brother, and
that moche honoure   s it is shewed herafter. /

rofull
her's

In this partye, sayu   hystorye, that wooful & sory 15
was the kynge   nnssay for the deth of his
brother / but syth it pleased god to be so he lefte &
passed his deuel the best wyse that he coude.   Thap-

He has the
cathedral pre-
pared for his
brother's obse-
quies;
¹ fol. 135.

pareyl was thenas made for the obsequye whiche was 20
don in the Chirche Cathedral of the Cite.   And syn
the kyng of Anssay and the duc of bauyere ¹mounted
on horsback and many barons of behayne with them,

and goes toward
the Saracens
camp,

and al clothed in black went toward the sarasyns tentes, 24
where the two bretheren were whiche had do còme

where the breth-
ren were dividing
the spoil.

þer all the Sommage, Cartes, Charyotes, & bagage, And
syn departed among theire peuple all that they had
wonne vpon the paynemes /.   Thenne arryued there 28
the kynge of Anssay, the duc Ode, and all the baronnye
and nobly salued the two brethern, And the duc
Anthony, & Regnauld hys brother receyued them joy-

The King of
Anssay tells how
his brother was
slain and his
body burnt,

fully.   Thenne reccounted the kynge of Anssay to þe 32
two bretheren how the kynge ffederyk was slayn in the
baytayll, and how Zelodyus had made hys body to be

and how he
burned the
Saracens.

brent in despyt of all cristianyte / and therfore he had
doo like wise of Zelodyus body & of all the sarasyns 36

that were founde alyue or deed. And Anthonye þenne
ansuerd, 'On my feyth ye haue don right wel / and
veryly kyng Zelodius mysdede ouermoche grete cruelte, *Anthony thinks Zelodius was cruel.*
4 For syn a man is deed / grete shame is to hys enemy
to touche hym ony more.' 'By my feyth, sire,' said
the duc of Bauyere, 'ye say trouth, but the kinge of *The duke Ode asks the brethren to the obsequies.*
Anssay is come hither to you for to beseche you &
8 your brother to còme to the obsequye of the kyng
Federyke his brother.' And thenne ansuerd the
bretherne, 'we shal thither goo gladly.' Thenne they *They agree to come;*
mounted on hors back & rode toward the Cite, where
12 as the ladyes and damoyselles, knightes & squyres / *and are well received in the city.*
cytyzeyns & commynalte beheld them fayns and mer-
uaylled moche of the Lyons clawe that shewed in
An¹thonyes cheke / and preysed moche his fayre & wel *¹ fol. 135 b.*
16 shappen body, and also of Regnauld hys brother / and
said emong themself, 'these two bretheren ben able for
to subdue al the world.' And thus they came to the
chirch where thobsequye shuld be made and there
20 alyghted.

Cap. XXXIV.   How the two brethern were at buryeng and obsequye of kynge Federyk of behayne.

24 Eglantine that was in the Circh came and re-
countred the two bretheren, whom she made hum- *Eglantine meets the brethren at the church, and thanks them for saving her.*
bly her obeyssaunce, thankyng them mekely of theire
noble socours that they had doo to her, For they had
28 saued her honour, her lyf, and her land. And thenne
anthony ansuerd humbly to her, sayeng, 'Damoyselle,
²We haue nought doo but that we ought to doo, For *² fol. 136.*
euery good cristen is hold & bound aftir the playsire
32 of god toppresse & dystroye thenemyes of God.' The
pucelle was there nobly acompanyed of the ladyes &
damoyselles of the land, thobsequye was honourably &

nobly doon as it apperteyned to suche a noble kyng as he was.   And after the armyes fynysshed the two bretheren mounted on theire horses, and theire meyne

also, and conueyed the pucelle Eglantyne vnto the 4 palays where they descended, & syn mounted in to the hall where the tables were redy couered / and thenne

they wesshe theire handes & satte at dyner / and syn were nobly seruyd & festyed / and after dyner the tables 8 were voyded & take vp & wesshe handes / and syn þey conueyed Eglantyne vnto her chambre, þat was euer sorowful for her faders deth.   And þenne the kinge of

Ansay called to hym al the baronnye of the land, & 12 said to them in this manyere :

'Lordes, barons, ye muste Counseyll emong' you, & take your best aduys how ye myght haue a valyaunt man for to gouerne the royaume, For the land 16 which is in the guydyng & gouernaunce of a woman only is not surely kept.   Now, loke thenne what best is for the prouffyt & honour of my cousyne Eglantine, & for þe common wele of this land.'   Thenne answerd 20 one for them alle & sayd : 'Sire, we knowe none that

oughte to medle hymself therwith tofore you, For yf your Cousyn were passed out of this mortal lyf, that god forbede, al the royalme of Behayne shuld appar- 24

teyne to you.   Wher[1]for we al bes[e]che you that therto ye puruey after your playsire.'   Thenne answerd the king, & thus said : 'Sire, as touching my personne, I may not long abyde with you to be rewler & protectour 28 of this land, For thanked be god I haue land ynoughe

to entreteyne myn estate with / but in conclusyon lete my cousyn take some valiaunt man to her lord, that shal deffende the land ayenst the enemyes of god.' 32 Thenne answered the barons fourthe with, 'Sire, yf it

plaise you þat your Cousyn be maryed, seke for her some noble & worthy man to be her lord & oure, For tofore you none of vs oughte to medle withall.'   Thenne 36

answerd the kyng in this manere, 'We thenne shal
purueye therto to her honour & prouffyt & to yours
also / and that anoone, For I go to speke with her for
4 this cause.' The kynge thenne departed and came in
to the Chambre where his Cousin was, that moche humbly receyued hym. And the kyng said to her in this
manere, 'Fayre cousyne, thankyng to god your affayres
8 be now in good party, For your land is delyuered fro
the paynemes by the puyssaunce of god & of the two
brethern of Lusynen. Now it muste be aduysed &
sene how best your reaume may be guyded in good
12 gouernaunce to your prouffyt & honour, and of your
peuple also.' Thenne answerd the mayden, 'My right
dere vncle, I ne haue noon of Counseyll & comfort but
you / so I requyre you that of good remedye ye pur-
16 ueye therto. And conuenable & lawful it is that I
obey you more than ony other personne in the world,
& so wyl I doo.' Thenne had the kynge pite on ¹her
& said, 'Fayre Cousyn, we haue alredy purueyed
20 therto / ye muste be maryed to suche a man that can
kepe and deffende you & your land ayenst alle enemyes,
the which is fayre, noble, & valyaunt damoyseau, &
not ferre hens.' 'Certaynly,' answerd the pucelle.
24 'Dere vncle, wel I knowe for certayn that ye wold
neuer Counseyll me þat thing but it were to my grete
honour & proffit, and for the commyn wele of all my
land / but ryght dere vncle, I to be maryed so soone
28 after my faders decesse / shuld not shewe semblaunt of
dueyll for his deth. Wherfor me semeth I were
blamed to doo soo / and suche shuld shew to me fayre
semblaunt byfore me,² that wold moke me at a pryvy
32 place /.'

To that answerd the king, & said : 'My right fayre
Cousyn, of two euylles men ought to choose
the lasse, whan nedes muste one be had. But, fayre

² Fr. qui en tendroit mains de compte derrière.

He promises to
find one,
and leaves to
speak to his
cousin on the
subject.

She receives him
humbly.

He tells her that
the way must be
found how best
to govern the
land.

The maid asks
his advice.

¹ fol. 187.

He says she must
get married.

She answers
that she knows
he gives good
counsel,

but she thinks
she should not
marry so soon
after her father's
death.

The King replies
that one must
choose the lesser
evil.

He would like to
wait to be at her
wedding,

but he lives afar
off.

Then the
brethren must
be rewarded,

but half of her
kingdom would
not be sufficient
for this.

I fol. 137 b.
and she is not
worthy to have
Regnauld as
her lord.

Then the maid
was ashamed,

and told her
uncle to do
with her and her
kingdom as he
thought best.

The King bids
her cease weep-
ing.

He goes to the
brethren,

Cousyn, it is wel trouth, that who myght goodly tary
the day of your weddyng⸗ it were your honour / but
what, fayre Cousyn, my dwelling place is ferre hens /
and here I may not make long⸗ soiourne, without my 4
grete dommage, as wel of other mens goodes as of
myn. Also the two brethren most be recompensed &
rewarded of theire noble socours, outher of my goodes
or of yours / and some saith that bettre is to haue 8
more of prouffyt & lasse honour. And to say that ye
coude recompense them as they oughte to be, by raison
of the grete curtoysye by them shewed vnto you ; the
half of your royame shuld not suffise. And ouℝ 12
more, fayre Cousyne, wete it that ye be not to suffysaunt ⸗for to haue suche & so noble a man to your lord
as is Regnauld of Lusynen, For in certayn he is wel
worthy to marye the gretest lady in the worlⅆ. What 16
for his noble lynee, as for his bounte, beaute, & noble
prowesse.' Whan the noble pucelle Eglantyne vnderstode the kyng⸗ her vncle, she was shamfull & hontows /
and on that other part, she consyderyng⸗ the daunger 20
where bothe she & her peple had be & myght be wyst
neuer what to say, and bygane to wepe / but at last
she answerd in this manere : 'right dere vncle, all my
trust, my hoop & comfort is in god & in you, wherfor 24
doo with me & with my reaume what it playse you' /
'Fayre Cousyn,' said the kyng⸗, 'ye say right wel / and
I swere you by my feyth, that nothing I shal say in
this party ne doo, but that it shal be for the best. 28
Now thenne, noble Cousyne, seace your wepyng⸗, &
delyuere you of this affayre, For the more long⸗ that
these baronye with theire peple that be in nombre xv.
M⸗. be soiournyng⸗ in your land the greter dommage 32
shal ye haue.' And she that wel knewe he said trouth,
answerd to hym in this manere : 'Dere vncle, doo therof al your playsyre.' Thenne came the kynge in to
the grete halle where the two brethern were, & the 36

baronye with them, and said to Anthony in this
manyere: 'noble Duc, vouchesaf to understand my
wordes, the barons of this land that be here present,
4 besech your good grace / & as touching my self, I
hertyly praye you that it plese you, that Regnauld your
brother be king of this royalme, and that he take
Eglantyne my Cousyn to his lady / prayeng hym that
8 he this wyl not reffuse, For the barons of the land
desire hym moche to be theire lord.' 'Sire,' ansuerd
anthony, 'this requeste is worthy to be graunted, &
also shal it be. Doo hither come the noble da¹moy-
12 selle.' And fourthwith the kynge & the Duc Ode
yede & fette the pucelle, and despoylled her of her
dueyl & black clothing / and syn was arayed ful
rychely of her noblest raymentes, and acompanyed
16 with her ladyes & damoyselles, she was conueyed by
the forsaid lordes vnto the presence of the noble
bretheren, whiche merueylled moche of her grete
beaute / and she humbly enclyned byfore them, mak-
20 yng her obeyssaunce. Thenne bygan the king of
Anssay to speke, & thus said /

Noble Duc of Lucembourgh, hold ye to vs your
couuenauntes; this is wherof we wyl hold oure
24 promesse.' 'For sooth,' said Anthony, 'it is wel reason.
come hither Regnauld brother, receyue this pucelle to
your lady, For she maketh you kynge of behayne.'
Thenne said Regnauld, in heryng of alle that were
28 there present / 'thankyng be to god, to the kynge, &
to all the baronye of this lande, of the grete honour
that they doo to me. For yf thys noble pucelle had
not one foot of land, yet wold I not reffuse her loue
32 to haue her to my lady, after the lawes of god requyren.
For with thayde of almighty god, I hoop to conquere
ynoughe to hold & entreteyne therwith her noble
estate' / 'Fayre brother,' said þenne anthony / 'ye say
raison / this royaume ye haue wonne alredy / god yeue

and asks Anthony to make his brother marry Eglantine and rule her kingdom.

Anthony agrees.

1 fol. 188.

The maid, richly arrayed,

is brought before the lords and the two brethren.

The King asks Anthony to keep his promise.

Anthony calls on Regnauld to take the maid to wife.

Regnauld accepts her for her merits, not for her lands,

and says he hopes to conquer still more.

you grace to subdue & conquere other reames & landes
vpon her enemyes.' And in conclusyon, the bysshop
was sent for, & assured them togidre. And syn bygane
the¹ feest sumptuous & grete, For soone it was knowen 4
thrugh al the toun, wherof the peple made grete joye /
and were the stretes hanged with ryche clothes, & grete
& noble apparayll was there made, as to suche a feste
apperteyned / and was ordeyned that the weddyng 8
shuld be hold in the feld within the chief pauillon.
Many riche rayments & robes were made what ²for the
spouse / as for the ladyes & damoyselles. That nyght
passed, and on the morne on which day they shuld 12
be espoused / the pucelle nobly was conueyed & ledd
vnto the tentes, whiche were al of cloth of gold / And
that night was good watche made as þe enemyes had
be nygh to them / and there the feste encressed, & 16
were honourably seruyd at souper. And whan tyme
was, euery one went to bed vnto the morow erly, when
Aurora shone clere. /

Cap. XXXV. How Regnauld espoused 20 Eglantyne, daughter to the kynge of Behayne. /

Here sheweth thistorye, & sayth that whan the day
spryng appiered, & the day was ful fayre & clere, 24
the spouse nobly & rychely arayed in her robes of cloth
of gold, & fourred with Ermynes, & purfylled all with
precyous stones, accompanyed with grete nombre of
ladyes & damoy²selles, was right honourably conueyed 28
vnto the place where as the masse shuld be sayd; and
solemply the bysshop espoused them here / and aftir
the masse, she retourned to the pauyllon with al the
noble baronye with her, where they fond al apparaylled 32
& redy to dyner. They were ful wel & nobly seruyd
of al thinges that to suche a feste be requysite & con-

uenable. And after they had dyned, graces were said,
& wesshe theire handes, and syn were the tables after which they danced and made
voyded, thanne bygane they to daunce & to make grete great Joy.
4 joye. /

Cap. XXXVI. How the knightes & esquyers jousted after dyner.

This storye sayth that after the daunce was seaced the
8   ladyes & damoyselles mounted vpon the scafoldes.
Thenne cam the knightes rychely armed, & bygan to The knights be-
gin to joust;
jouste / trompettes sowned, & knightes reuersed eche
other / but none might withstande the noble bretheren, the two brethren
cannot be over-
thrown.
12 but he was ouerthrow, bothe hors & man / so that no
man dide there nought [1] to the regarde of theire prowes. 1 fol. 189 b.
Wherfore, they seyng that the ioustes affeblysshid for
cause of them, they departed fro the lystes & toke of
16 theire armeures / and syn dured the jousting tyl tyme Supper time
arrives.
of souper cams. And thenne the ioustes seaced, and
the knightes & squyers departed, & went & dysarmed
them. Thenne mynestrels with dyuerse Instruments Minstrels play
while it is served.
20 of musique sowned & played melodyously the first
cours of the souper / & syn they were nobly serued of
al maner wynes / and after souper they daunced. But
whan tyme was, the spouse was ledd to bed with grete After some danc-
ing the spouse
is led to bed, and
24 honour & Joye. And anone after came Regnauld is followed by
Regnald.
there, whiche went to bed with the pucelle. Thenne
voyded euery one the chambre / some to theire rest /
some retourned to the daunce / some sang, & other
28 made grete reueyll. Regnauld, thenne that laye nigh
Eglantyne, swetly embraced & kyssed her / and she
to hym moche humbled her self, sayeng in this manere :
'My lord redoubted, ne had be the grace of god / your Eglantine de-
clares that his
prowess has
32 curtoysye & prowes, this poure orphelym had be / no saved her from
exile,
doubt of / exilled, desolat, & lost. Wherfor, my ryght
redoubted lord, I yeld thankyng to god, & to you also

that haue dayned to take to your wyf her that was
vnworthy therto.' 'By my fayth,' said Regnauld,
'dere herte, & my best beloued, ye haue do moche
more for me than euer I dide ne possible is to me to 4
doo for you / sene & consydered the noble yefte youen
by you to me / that is your noble lady / and yet besyde
that of your noble royame ye haue endowed me / and
with me nought ye haue take / sauf only my symple 8
body.' Thenne ansuered Eglantyne, & said / 'Ha /
noble lord, your valyaunt body is derer to me & bettre
worth than ten other suche royames as myn is / &
more it is to be preysed.' Of theire wordes I wyl 12
seace / but that nyght was begoten of them a noble
sone that was named Olyphart / he made in tyme afterward grete faytte of armes, and subdued & gate al the
low marche of holland & Zeland, Vtreyght, & the 16
Royame of Danemarche / and al the partyes of North-
weghe also. On the morne the day was fayre & clere.
Thenne was the noble lady Eglantyne ledd to here the
masse / and al the baronye, ladyes & damoyselles, acom- 20
panyed her thitherward. And after the mass was doo,
they retourned to the ryche pauyllon / and as they were
redy to sette þem at dyner / came there two knightis
fro Lucembourgh, that brought lettres to Duc Anthony 24
from the Duches Crystyne his wyf / the whiche after
theire obeyssaunce honourably made, said to hym in
this wise: 'My lord, ye oughte to take grete joye /
For my lady the Duches is brought to bed of the most 28
fayrest sone that euer was seen in no land.' 'Now,
fayre lordes,' said anthony, 'blessid be god therof / and
ye be right welcome to me' / & syn toke the lettres.
Thistorye sayth that anthony, Duc of Lucem- 32
bourgh, was joyful & glad of these tydynges,
and so was his brother Regnauld. Thenne opened he
the lettres, wherof the tenour was acording to that the
knightes had said. Thenne made anthony moche of 36

them, gyuyng to them grete yeftes of ryches. Thenne
he satte hym at dyner nygh to Eglantyne / and dured
the feest eyght days, sumptuouse & open houshold.
4 And whan the feste was fynysshed, they reentred in to
the Cite with gret honour & joye. And on the morns
next the kyng of Anssay / Anthony & the Duc Ode, &
al theire baronye toke theire leue of [1]Regnauld & of
8 Eglantyne, whiche were dolaunt of theire departyng.
And anthony made couenaunt with Regnauld hys
brother, that yf the paynemes made ony moo werre
with hym, he shuld come & all his baronnye with hym
12 to ayde & helpe hym. And the kyng Regnauld thanked
hym moch. And eche of them thanked & kyssed eche
other at departyng / Soo long marched thoost þat they
came to Mouchyne[2] in Bauyere / & lodged them in a
16 fayre medowe nygh the toun. There the Duc Ode
festyed them right honourably the space of thre dayes /
and on the foureth day they departed & toke theire
leue of the Duc Ode / and rode so long tyl [they][3]
20 came a day journey nygh to Coloyne. And there the
foure knightes that conduyted the Coloyners auaunced
them self byfore Duc Anthony, & to him said in this
manere : 'My lord, it is best that we hast vs byfore
24 you toward the toun, to apparayll & make al thing
redy for your passage.' 'By my feyth,' said the Duc
Anthonye, 'that playseth me wel.' Thenne departed
the foure knightes & theire men with them, & rode
28 tyl they came to the Cite of Coloyne, where they were
receyued with Joye / and the Cytezeyns & gouernours
of the cyte demanded of them how they had exployted
in theire vyage / And they recounted to them all the
32 trouth of the fayte and the valyauntnes & noble prowes
of the two brethern / & how regnauld was made kyng
[of] Behayne. And whan they of Coloyne [4]understode
them they were ryght glad & joyous, sayeng they

them, gyuyng to them grete yeftes of ryches. Thenne

Sidenotes:
Anthony gives the messengers great gifts.
The feast lasts eight days.
Anthony, the King of Anssay, [1] fol. 140 b. and Duke Ode take leave of Regnald.
Anthony promises to help him against the paynims.
They march to Mouchine, where the Duke feasts them, and
on the fourth day they march again.
They arrive near Cologne.
The four knights go in advance to Cologne and
are joyfully received.
They tell the news of the expedition.
[4] fol. 141. The Cologners are glad

[2] Fr. *Muchin.*   [3] MS. has *day.*

R 2

to have the
friendship of
such noble lords.

were wel happy & ewrous[1] to haue acquyred the loue
& good wyll of two lordes of so grete valeur. And
thenne they made grete apparayll for to receyue the
Duc Anthony, and the king of Anssay with theire 4

Anthony and the
king arrive at
Cologne.

baronye. Soo long rode thoost that they came to Coloyne, where the Cytezeyns cam & mete hem honourably / and to the prynces they made grete reuerence,
prayeng them that they wold be lodged that nyght 8

They are nobly
feasted.

within the toun, where they were nobly festyed &
honourably seruyd at souper. And on the morn
Anthony & his oost passed ouer the Ryn, and toke his
leue of them of Coloyne, whiche he thanked moche, 12

and promise the
townspeople
their succour if
it should be
wanted.

sayeng : 'yf they were in ony wyse oppressed by theire
enemyes he woll be euer redy for tayde & socoure them
after hys power.' Wherof they thanked hym moche.
Thenne the Duc Anthony & the king of Anssay dyde 16

Anthony arrives
near Luxem-
bourg.

so moche by theire journeys, that on an euen they
came & lodged them in the medow nygh by Lucembourgh. /

Christine is joy-
ful at her lord's
return.

The duchesse Cristyne was replenysshed with joye, 20
　　whan she knew the commyng of her lord anthony /
and immedyatly she, nobly acompanyed, yssued out of
the toun / and all the noble cyteseyns folowed her to
mete with theire lord, the whiche they recountred a 24
half a myle fro the toun. What shal I say / greter
joye was neuer sene than that was made for the retourne
of Duc Anthony. The Duchesse made humbly her

[2] fol. 141 b.

obeyssaunce vnto hym / and [2] hertyly welcommed hym. 28

His people re-
ceive him with
shouts of wel-
come.
He feasts the
King of Anssay
and frees him
from all his obli-
gations except
the founding of
the priory.

The peuple cryed on hye for Joye, sayeng thus :
'welcomme our lord ryght redoubted.' The joye was
grete thrugh the toun where the Duc festyed the kynge
of Anssay by the space of six dayes contynuelly, & for- 32
gaf & rendred to hym all his obligacions, and held hym
quytte / except the Foundacion of the pryore, where as
sowles shuld be prayed for / for the loue of Regnault

[1] Fr. eureux.

his brother. And the kinge of Anssay thanked hym
moche, & toke his leue of hym / departed, & came in
Anssay, where as he was receyued with joye / And the
4 Duc anthony abode with the Duchesse Cristyne, on
whom he gate a sone that same yere which was clepid
Locher, whiche afterward delyuered the Countrey of
Ardane fro thevys, murdrers, & robbeurs ; and in the
8 wodes there he founded an abbeye, and endowed it
with grete pocessyons / And he also dyde doo make
the bridge of Masyeres vpon the ryuere of Meuze, and
many other fortresses in the basse marche of holland /
12 and dyde many fayre fayttes of armes with the king
Olyphart of behayne, that was his Cousyn, & sone to
kyng Regnauld. It happed not long after the kynge
of Anssay was retourned in to his royame, that warre
16 meuyd betwix hym & the Duc of austeryche & the
[Erle] of Fyerbourgh. wherfor he besought the Duc
Anthony for socour, that gladly obtempered to his
requeste, in so moche that he toke by force of armes
20 the Erle of Fyerbourgh / and syn pas¹sed in Austeryche,
where he dyscomfyted the Duc in batayll, and made
hym to be pacyfyed with the kynge of Anssay, to the
grete prouffyt & honour of the kinge. And bertrand
24 theldest sone of the Duc Anthony, was assured with
Melydee the sayd king of Anssays doughter / the
whiche Bertrand afterward was kynge of anssay, and
hys brother Locher was Duc of Lucembourgh, after
28 the decesse of the Duc Anthony hys fader. But of
this matere I wyl no more speke at this tyme / but shal
retourne to speke of Melusyne & of Raymondyn, and
of theire other children. /
32 Now sayth thystorye, that Raymondyn by hys no-
blenes & grete vasselage conquerd grete countrees / and to hym many barons dyde homage vnto the
land of Brytayne. And Melusyne had two yere after
36 that two sones, the first was named Froymond, that

Marginal notes:

Anssay thanks him, and afterwards returns to his country.

Anthony begets Locher, who frees Ardennes from thieves,

and builds fortresses, and does feats of arms along with his cousin Oliphart of Bohemia.

The King of Anssay asks the help of Anthony against his enemies.

¹ fol. 142.

Anthony assists him.

Bertrand is assured to Melydee, the daughter of the King of Anssay.

Raymondin conquers great countries, and many barons do homage to the land of Brittany.

Melusine bears two sons, Froymond,

entierly louyd holy Chirch, and that was wel shewed in
his ende, For he was professid monke in to thabbeye
of Maillezes, wherof there befell a grete & an horryble
myschief, as ye shal here herafter by thystorye / and
the other child that they had the yere folowyng was
named Theodoryk, the whiche was ryght batayllous.
Here I shal leue to speke of the two children / and I
shal shewe you of Geffray with the grete toth, that
was yrous & hardy / & most enterpryse dide of all hys
bretheren. And wete it wel that the said geffray
doubted neuer man / And thystorye [1]sheweth, & the
true Cronykle that he faught ayenst a knight, that was
gendred with a spyryte in a medowe nygh by Lusynen,
as ye shal here herafter. It is trouth that thesne
Geffray was grete & ouergrowen / and herde tydynges
that there was in Garande peple that wold not obey to
hys fader / thenne sware Geffray by the good lord
that he shuld make them to come as reason requyreth,
and to do that he toke leue of hys fader, that was right
wroth of hys departyng / and had with hym to the
nombre of fyue houndred men of armes, and a houndred
balesters, and so went in to Garande / and anoone enquyred after them that were dysobedyent / and they
that held the party of Raymondyn shewed hym the
Fortresse where they were, & armed them to goo with
hym to helpe to dystroye hys enemyes. 'By my feyth,
fayre lordes,' sayd Geffray with the grete toeth / 'ye
are ryght true & loyal peuple / & I thanke you of
thonour that ye proffre me / but as for this tyme present I shall not nede you, For I haue men of armes
ynough for taccomplyssh myn enterpryse.' 'For soothe,
sire, ye haue more to doo than ye suppose, For your
enemyes ben ryght strong & of meruayllous courage, &
they be frendes & cousyns, and of the grete & moost
noble blood of al the Countree.' 'Fayre sires,' said
Geffray, ' doubte you not, For thrughe thayde of god

Margin notes:

who became a monk,

and Theodorick.

Geffray with the Great Tooth was the most enter-prising of all his brethren.

[1] fol. 142 b.

He hears tidings that the people of Garande will not pay his father their tribute.

He goes to Garande against his father's will.

Raymondin's partizans there offer to help Geffray.

He thanks them,

but declines their aid.

They tell him his enemies are very powerful.

omnipotent I shal the matere [1] wel redresse. And wete
it wel there shal be none so myghty / but I shal make
them to obeye my commandement or to deye of an euyl
4 deth. And also, fayre lordes & true frendes, yf I nede
you I shall send for you' / And they answerd, 'we are
now al redy, and also shal we be at al tymes that it
playse you vs to calle.' 'Fayre lordes,' said Geffray with
8 the grete toth / 'that ought to be thanked for.' Thenne
toke Geffray hys leue of them / and went forth on his
way toward a Fortresse that was called Syon / & within
the same was one of the enemyes of geffray that hight
12 Claude of Syon, & were thre bretheren. Moche were
the thre brethern yrous & proude / and wold haue subdued and putte vnder theire subjection all theire neygh-
bours. Thenne sent geffray with the grete toeth wordes
16 of deffyaunce / outhre to come & make theire obeyssaunce to hym for Raymondin his faders. And they
answerd to the messager, 'that for Raymondyn ner for
no man on his byhalf they shuld nought doo / and that
20 he shuld no more retourne to them for this matere, for
than he were a fole.' 'By my feyth,' said the messager, 'I shal kepe me wel therfro / but that I bryng
with me a maister in medecyne, that shal make suche
24 a lectuary or drynk wherof ye shal be poysonned, &
syn hanged by the neck.' And of these wordes were
the iij bretheren wood wroth. And wete it wel that
yf the messager had not hasted his hors away he had
28 be take & deed without ony remedye, For [2] they were
full yrous & cruell, and doubted not god nor no man
lyuyng. Thenne retourned the messager toward geffray
and recounted hym the grete pryde & auauntyng of the
32 bretheren. 'By my heed,' said Geffray with the grete
toeth, 'a lytel rayne leyeth doun grete wynd / & doubte
you not but I shal pay them wel theire wages.'
Thystorye sayth, that whan geffray vnderstode the
36 grete pryde & the fel ansuere of the thre brethern,

[1] fol. 143.

Geffray says he
will compel his
enemies to obey.

He goes against
Claud of Sion,

one of three
proud brethren.

He sends his de-
fiance, and orders
them to make
obedience to him
on Raymondin's
behalf.

They refuse, and

[2] fol. 143 b.

the messenger
tells Geffray of
their pride and
boasting.
Geffray says that
"a little rain
layeth down a
great wind."

Geffray approaches near the fortress.

He arms, mounts; and takes a squire with him; and orders his men to rest till he sends them word.

without ony moo wordes he came & lodged hym & his peuple half a leghe fro the said Fortresse. Thenne toke he his armures & armed hym of al pieces ; toke with hym a squyer that wel knew the Countrey / 4 mounted on horsback / commanded his men that they shuld not meue them thens vnto tyme they had word of hym, & departed with hys esquyer / but there was a

A knight, who well knew his boldness, follows with x men.

knyght that wel knew hys noble & fyers courage, & 8 that he doubted nothing of the world / which toke x. men of armes with hym and went after Geffray, folowyng hym fro ferre, For he moche loued geffray. Geffray

Geffray arrives at the Fortress of Sion.

He sees its strength on one side,

rode so long that he sawe the Fortresse of Syon vpon 12 a hye roche. ' By my feyth,' said thenne geffray, ' yf the Fortresse be so strong at that other syde as it is at this syde, hit shal gyue me moche peyne or euer it be

and spies all round it.

take, I must see & know yf it be also strong at that 16 other parte.' Thenne he & his esquyer aduyronned the Fortresse about, al along by a lytel wod, that they might not be aspyed ne sene. They came & de-

[1] fol. 144.

scended [1] in a valey / and euer the forsaid knyght that 20 was named Philibert[2] folowed hym a ferre / and so long rode geffray tyl he had ouer sene the said fortres al

He finds that it is weakest by the bridge,

round about / and hym semed wel that it might be take by the brydge syde, For it was the feblest syde of 24 it / Thenne entred geffray & hys esquyer in a lytel

and returns toward his men.

path, & retourned vpon the mountayne toward hys lodgis, where his peple were hym abydyng. Philebert, that sawe Geffray retourne, thought he would lete hym 28

Philebert and his fellowship keep out of Geffray's sight.

passe tofore hym, Wherfor he and his felawship reculed within the wode, to thende thay shuld not be perceyued of hym / but soone after they sawe a companye of men of warre comynge that same way that geffray came 32

He sees xiv armed men in Geffray's way, and is afraid,

toward the Fortresse, and were to the nombre of xiiii personne wel armed. Wherfore the said knight philibert was abasshed & agast, lest they shuld mete with

[2] Fr. Ver. *Philibert de Mommoret.*

geffray, For wel he wyst that geffray wold fyght with
them / as he dide / and that shal ye here herafter./

because he knows Geffray will fight them.

In this partye, sayth thistorye, that vpon the topp of
4   the mountayne geffray recountred the said companye, And who that shuld enquere of me what folke
they were ; I shuld say it was one of Claude of Syon
bretheren that came toward his brother at his mande-
8   ment. And wete it wel, that the way was there so
narow that vnnethe one hors myght passe by other.
And whan Geffray with the grete ¹toeth recountred
them, he sayd to hym that rode first of alle that he
12 shuld tary and make his company to stand asyde tyl
he were passed the mountayne. ' By my feyth,' said
he þat was proude & orgueyllous, ' Sire daw fole,² wel
we muste first knowe what ye be, that say that we
16 retourne vs for you.' ' By god,' said Geffray with the
grete toth / ' that shal you knowe anone, For I shal
make you retourne ayenst your wyll. I am Geffray
of Lusynen / tourne back / or elles I shal make you to
20 retourne by force.' Whan Guyon the brother of Claude
of Syon vnderstode hym & knew that it was geffray
with the grete toeth / he cryed to his folk, ' auaunt,
lordes barons, For yf he escape grete shame shal be to
24 vs / in an euyl heure is he come in to oure land for to
demande seruytude of vs.' Thenne whan geffray vnderstode these wordes he drew out his sword & smote
the nethermost of alle vpon his hed, so grete a stroke
28 that he ouerthrew hym all astonyed doune to the
erthe, and syn passed forth by hys hors, & ouer hym
that laye along the way, in suche wyse that he al to
brusid the body of hym / And thenne geffray atteyned
32 another in the brest foynyng with hys swerd, so that
he fell doune deed to therthe / and syn cryed aftir
the oþer, ' False traytours, ye may not escape, ye shal
retourne to your euyl helthe.' Thenne he passed fourth

Geffray encounters one of Claud's brothers and his men on a narrow road.

¹ fol. 144 b.

Geffray asks them to stand aside till he has passed.

They ask who he is.

He answers, "Geffray of Lusignan," and bids them turn, else he will make them.

Guion cries to his men not to let Geffray escape.

But Geffray draws his sword and smites one of his company so hard that he is overthrown.

He foins at another in the breast, and kills him.

² Fr. *damp musart.*

to the iii^{de}, which was grete & strong, ¹& smote Geffray
vpon the helmet with al his strengthe / but the helmet
was hard and þe swerd glenced asyde & dommaged
hym nought / but Geffray toke his swerd with two 4
handes and smote hym vpon the coyffe of stele vnto
the brayne, & reuersed hym deed to the erth.   And
whan guyon perceyued this myschief he was wode
wroth & full of yre, For he might not come to geffray, 8
wherfore he commanded euery man to retourne, that
they might haue them self at large to deffende eche
other.   Thenne euery man tourned back & fledd, &
yssued out of that narrow way in to a playn feld, And 12
geffray with the grete toth pursiewed them, the swerd
in his hand.   Now shall I speke of the knight philibert, whiche was approched nygh the said way, and
herde the noyse / so he called to hym his felawes. 16
And thenne guyon and his men were in þe playn &
assaylled geffray on al sydes of hym / but as preu &
valyaunt he deffended vygourously his flesshe / and
also hys esquyer bare hym valyauntly / and was ryght 20
strong the batayll.   Now most I speke of hym which
geffray first ouerthrew to therthe in the path forsaid,
For whan he perceyued that guyon was retourned by
the force of geffray / and sawe his two felawes lyeng 24
deed by hym, he was moche dolaunt, and beheld ²all
about hym & fond his hors, wher on he with grete
peyne mounted, for he was al to brusyd in hys body, &
hasted hym as he coude best toward Syon.   And whan 28
he came to the fortresse he fond Claude at yate and
some of his men with hym / the whiche perceyued
that he that was commyng toward hym was al bloody
and knew hym wel / & of hym demanded who so had 32
arayed hym / And he recounted thadventure how they
had recountred geffray, and how he adommaged them
and had made guyon hys brother to retourne fro the
narow lane by force, & that yet lasted theyre bataylle. 36

Thenne whan Claude vnderstode hym he was sorowfull
& angry, and yede and armed hym, and made his men   Claud orders his
men to arm,
to be armed.

4 Moche dolaunt was Claude whan he vnderstod of
the vylonnye & dommage that geffroy had don
to Guyon his brother / and how yet they were fyghtyng
togidre / & armed of al pieces. his men with hym rode   He rides to aid
his brother,
8 thitherward / and were in nombre thre score bassynets.
But for nought he toke hys waye, For philibert with   but is too late;
his ten knyghtes were come to the batayll, & faught in
suche wyse that al guyons meyne were slayne & he   as the men are
slain and his
brother is Gef-
fray's prisoner.
12 take / and soone sware Geffray that he shuld make
hym to be hanged by the neck. Thenne came the said
esquyer, whiche was retourned in to the forsayd land,
to fette a fayre swerd, that he tofore sawe fall fro one
16 of Guyons men / & said to Geffray in this manyere,
'My lord, I haue herd grete bruyt of men armed   A knight tells
Geffray that
more men of
arms are ap-
proaching.
commyng hitherward.' And whan Geffray vnderstode
hym he fourthwith made Guyon to be bound at a tree   ¹ fol. 146.
Guion is bound
20 within the wod ¹nygh by them, & syn retourned with   to a tree.
hys men toward the said path or lane for to abyde   Geffray and his
company return
there his auenture. And philibert rode vnto the top   to the path to
wait the arrival
of the hyll, and perceyued Claude & hys felawship   of Claud.
24 that entred the lane / thanne he retourned to his
felawes & sayd to Geffray, 'Sire, the best that ye can
doo is to kepe wel this pathe, here come your enemyes.' And Geffray with the gret toeth ansuerd /
28 'doubte you not / but it shal be wel kept & deffended.'
Thenne he called to hym the squyer that was come
with hym, & said: 'renne hastily toward thoost, &   Geffray sends a
messenger to his
host.
make my folke to come hither." And he anone de-
32 parted toward thoost, and whan he was there arryued
he said to þem, 'Fayre lordes, now lightly on horsback,
For geffray fyghteth ayenst his enemyes.' And they
armed them & soone mounted on theire horses, and
36 hasted them to folowe the squyer that guyded them   His lords haste

to succour him.

the nerest way there he supposed to fynd Geffray, fighting with his enmyes.

Thystorye sayth that geffray, philibert, & theire knightes were at thentree of the pathe / and 4 thenne came Claude & his men with grete puyssaunce along thrugh the lane, & wel they supposed to haue mounted the montayne. But Geffray was at thentre of the path that vygourously & valyauntly deffended 8 the passage / and wete it wel there was none so hardy but he made hym to recule. For there were two of his knightes that descended fro theire horses, & stode at eyther syde of geffray, & proudly rebuckyd Claudes 12 men with theire speres, & many of them were there slayne. Philibert [1]was thenne descended from his hors, and thre othre of his companye, and recouered the montayne aboue the pathe, where as they gadred 16 stones and threw them vpon them that were in the lane, thrugh suche yre & grete strength, that there was none so strong bassynets nor armure but it was perced; and therwith they were astonyed or elles ouerthrawen / 20 and wete it wel þat there were more than xx[u]. slayn. Thenne câme there the squyer with the batayH that he brought. And whan geffray knew it, he commaunded thre houndred men of armes, that they shuld 24 draw at the other ende of the lane to kepe the passage, that Claude nor hys peple should not retourne to theire fortresse. And anone from thens the squyer with his companye departed, & came hastly to fore the medowe, 28 & passed byfore the Fortresse. And whan Clerevauld, the iii[de] brother of Claude, sawe them, he demed that it was some socours that came to them / For he trowed not that in the land shuld haue be so many enemyes. 32 The whiche esquyer with his companye came with amyable contenaunce, shewyng no semblaunt but as frendes. And thenne Clerevauld, that byleued wel that they were theyre frendes lete faH the bridge, & opened the 36

Geffray blocks the path,

[1] fol. 146 b.

while the Knight Philibert and three men ascend the mountain, and throw stones on Claud and his men.

Geffray's company arrives, and is ordered to prevent Claud returning to his fortress.

Clerevald, third brother of Claud, takes Geffray's company to be friends.

yate where he stode with xx^{ti}. men of armes. And
whan the squyer & his companye perceyued þat the
bridge was doun & the gate open, they drew them
4 hastly in the way to passe the Fortres. And passyng
by the Fortresse, Clervauld demanded what they were /
and they answerd: ¹' We be frendes.' and in approuch-
ing of the said bridge to the nombre xx^{ti} knightes, they
8 enquyred after Claude of Syon: 'For fayn we wold
speke with hym.' And Clereuauld them approuched,
sayeng: 'he shal retourne anoone, For he is departed to
fyght with Geffray with the grete toeth our enemye,
12 that he & Guyon our brother haue enclosed in yonder
mountayne that is there byfore you / and wete it wel
that Geffray may not escape them, though he were
tempred with fyne stele, but that he shal be slayne
16 or take.' 'By my feyth,' sayd the squyer, 'this be
good tydynges.' An thenne he approuched with his
xx^{ti} knightes nerer & nerer, askyng hym where shal
we goo to helpe hym. 'By my feyth,' sayd Clere-
20 uauld, 'gramercys it shal not nede at this tyme.'

Thystorye sheweth that the squyer approched to
Clereuauld so nygh by his fayre wordes, that he
& hys company came vpon the bridge / & thenne he
24 cryed to hys peple / 'auaunt, lordes, the fortresse is
oure.' And whan Clereuauld herd these wordes, he
supposed to haue reculed & to haue lyft vp the bridge /
but the squyer & his peuple came so rudly that it
28 was not in theire powere to haunce the bridge / but
bare it doune by force, and anone alighted & entred in
at the gate / and with two speres vndersette the portecollys / & immedyatly descended more than an houn-
32 dred of the squyers men on foot, & came & entred into
the Fortres. Thenne was clereuauld take, and al hys
peple that were there with hym, & brought vnto a
chambre fast bounden, where they were surely kept
36 with fourty men of armes / ²And after this don, they

He allows them
to come near the
fortress.

Clerevald asks
who they are ;
¹ fol. 147.
"We be friends,"
they answer.

The squire and
his company by
fair words get on
the bridge. He

then cries, "The
fortress is ours."

Clerevald tries
to pull up the
bridge, but is too
late.

He and his men
are taken prison-
ers.

² fol. 147 b.

assembled them, & toke Counseyll how they might
best send word vnto geffray of this faytte, & how they
shuld kepe them within the Fortresse to thentent to
take Claude yf it happed hym to retourne / And thenne 4
said the aquyer that he hym self shuld goo to gyue .

Geffray knowlege of this auenture. And thenne anone
he departed and came to Geffray, to whom he shewed
all the trouth of the faytte / and whan geffray knew 8

thauenture he was joyful, & made hym knight, & gaaf
hym the gouernaunce of a houndred men of armes / &
commanded that he shuld go anoone in to the countrey,
to kepe wal that Claude shuld take none oþer way, but 12
the way to the Fortresse ; For yf he escaped he might
do grete harme tofore he were take, & that bettre it
were to close hym in that lane, & there by force to take
hym. 'Sire,' said the new knight, 'doubte you not he 16
shal not escape you, but yf he cane flee, yf that I may
come by tymes to the lane.' Thenne he departed &
descended the mountayne with hys men of armes. And
geffray taryed at the pathe, that mightily faught with 20
his swerde vpon his enemyes. And wel fourty knyghtes
were alighted on foot vpon þe hylle, & threw stones

vpon Claude & his peple in suche wyse, that by force
he & hys peuple was constrayned to retourne / And 24

Geffray & his peple entred in to the lane & chaced
þem / but vnnethe he might passe to pursiew men
for deed men that were slayn with castyng of stones.
Now shal I shew you of the new knight that was com- 28

myng at the other lanes ende with his company / but
whan he herd the bruyt of the horses / he thought wel

that [1]Claude retourned / and he toke the couert of the

mountayne & suffred Claude to take the way toward 32
the Fortresse.

Thystorye telleth that Claude hasted hym fast to
come out of the lane for to saue hym self &
his peple in the Fortresse of Syon, but that the fole 35

thinketh oftymes commeth to foly.   It is veray trouth
that he spede hym so fast that he was out of the lane
& came to his large / and so he ne taryed neyther for
4 one nor for other / but came walapyng' toward the
Fortresse. And whan he was nygh, he cryed with a
high voyce / 'open the gates' / & so they dide / and
thenne he passed the bridge and entred, & was alyghted
8 afore that he perceyued that he had lost the Fortresse /
and fourthwith he was seasyd & bounde by hys enemyes.
Thenne was he gretly abasshed ; For he sawe not about
hym no man that he knew. 'What dyuel is this!
12 where are my men become?' 'By my feyth,' said a
knight / 'ryght foorth shal ye knowe, For ye shal lodge
with them' / And so immedyatly he was brought to
the chambre where Clereuauld, his brother & his peuple
16 were in pryson. Thenne whan he perceyued them bound
& kept as they were, he was ryght dolaunt. And whan
Clereuauld sawe hym, he said : 'Ha / a, Claude, fayre
brother, we are fall by your pryde into grete captiuite /
20 and doubte it not we shal neuer escape from hens without losse of our lyues, For to cruel is Geffray.' And
Claude ansuerd hym : 'We muste abyde all that therof
shal fall.' Thenne came Geffray [1]ryght foorth to the
24 Fortresse, & had slayn or take all the residu of Claudes
peple / saaf hys brother Guyon which was brought
with hym, & putte prysonner in the said pryson where
as Geffray entred / and emong al oper said to Claude :
28 'How,' said he, 'thou fals traytour, durst thou be so
hardy to hurte or dommage my faders Countre & his
peuple, thou that owest to be his subget / and by the
feyth that I owe to my fader I shal punysshe the, in
32 exemple of all other, For I shal doo the hang' byfore
Valbruyant, the Castel in syght of thy Cousyn Gueryn,
that is a traytour as thou art, vnto my lord my fader.'
And whan Claude herd that gretyng', wete it wel / he
36 was not therwith playsed. But whan the peple of the

Claud and his
people reach the
fortress, and cry,
"Open the
gates."

He is seized and
bound.

He asks about
his men.
He is told that
he will see them,
as he is to be
lodged with
them.

Clerevald sees
his brother, and
upbraids him.

[1] fol. 148 b.

Geffray arrives
and brings his
prisoner Guion.

Geffray tells
Claud that he in-
tends to hang
him before Val-
bruiant, the
castle of his
cousin Guerin,
who is also a
traitor.

The people of the land are glad that Claud and his people are taken or slain;

Countrey knew that Syon the Fortresse, & Claude and his brethern were take & theire peple slayne / thenne came playntes of robberyes & other euyl caas vpon Claude & vpon his peuple, & within that same Fortresse were founde more than a C prysonners of the good peple of the Countrey, as marchants & straungers that were robbed passyng by the way / For tofore that tyme

because they robbed them and despoiled all passers by the fortress.

none passed by the said Fortresse vnspoyled. And whan geffray herd of this tydynges, he made to be

Geffray sets up a pair of gallows and hangs all the people of Claud, but spares his two brothers.

sette vpon the syde of the hille a payre of galowes / & therat dide do be hanged al the peple of Claude / and his two brethern he spared for that tyme / and gaaf the

Geffray leaves the castle in charge of a wise knight,
¹ fol. 168.

Castel in keping vnto a knight of the Countrey that was ryght valyaunt & wyse / & commanded hym ¹vpon his lyf to kepe it wel / and to gouerne lawfully his subgets, & to kepe good justice / And he promysed hym so to doo, For he gouerned the countre wel &

and departs to Valbruiant.

rightfully. And after his commandement he departed on the morowe toward Valbruyant / and toke the thre bretheren with hym, the whiche had grete fere of deth / and that was not without cause / as ye shal here herafter.

Thystory sayth that geffray & his peuple rode ty they cam tofore Valbruyant / wher as tentes were dressed & sett vp, and euery man lodged in ordre Thenne made geffray ryght foorth to sette vp galowe

He erects gallows in front of the castle, hangs Claud and his brothers, and orders them of the castle to yield on pain of hanging.

tofore the Castel gate, and there dide do hang incon tynent Claude & his two bretheren / and sent word to them of the Castel / yf that they yelded not to hym the Fortres, that he wold hang them yf he had it by force. And whan Gueryn of Valbruyant herd these tydynges, he sayd to his wyf: 'It is so for trouth madame, that ageynst this strong dyuell I ne may with

Guerin departs from his castle to Mountfrain to have counsel.

stand ne kepe this Fortresse, wherfor I wyl departe & goo vnto mountfrayn to Guerard my nevew, & to othe my frendes for to haue Counseyll how we may haue

traytye of pais with Geffray.' And thenne the wyf
that was right sage & subtyl said to hym / 'go foorth /
by the grace of god, & kepe you wel that ye be nat
4 take by the waye, and departe not from Mountfrayn
tyl ye haue tydynges fro me, For by thayde of god I
hoop that I shal purchasse a good traytye with geffray
for you; For had ye don after my Counseyll, & byleued
8 me, ye shuld not ¹haue medled with the werkes of
Claude & of his bretheren / not with standing yet haue
ye not falsed your feyth toward your liege lord Raymondyn of Lusynen.' Thenne Gueryn her said : 'My
12 dere sustir & spouse, doo that ye thinke best, For
my fyaunce is in you / and I wyl byleue all that ye
may counseylle.' And thenne departed he by a pryvy
posterne vpon a swyft hors, and passed by the couerts
16 of the wodes, so that he was not aspyed. And whan
he was a lytel passed he sporyd his hors, and the hors
bare hym swyftly, and wete it that he had so grete fere
lest he shuld be aspyed, that he was almost out of his
20 wyt / & thanked god moche whan he fond thentre of
the Forest þat dured wel two leghes / and toke the way
toward Mountfrayn, as moche as he coude ryde.

Thystory testyfyeth, that so long rode Gueryn that
24 he came to mountfrayn, where he found guerard
hys neuew, & recounted to hym al these werkes ; and
how Geffray with the grete toth had take Claude
theire Cousyn & his two brethern, & brought tofore
28 Valbruyaunt, where he dide al thre to be hanged / and
how he was departed thens, doubtyng to be take within the Fortresse. 'By my feyth,' said Guerard, 'Fayre
vncle, ye haue do wysely, For after that men speke of
32 Geffray, he is a valyaunt knight of hye & puyssaunt
enterpryse / and he is moche cruel & moche to be
doubted. Woo is to me that euer we went to Claude !
For wel we knew that he & hys bretheren were of euyl
36 gouernement, & that none passed foreby theire For-

MELUSINE.   S

His wife tells
him not to leave
there till she
sends him tid-
ings ;

she declares she
will make a
treaty with Gef-
fray.
¹ fol. 149 b.

Guerin tells her
to do her best,

and leaves on a
swift horse by a
privy door.

He rides fast, as
he fears to be
seen.

He tells Gerrard
the news, how
Geffray has
hanged Claud
and his two
brethren,

and how he had
fled to escape
capture.

Gerrard says he
has acted wisely,

and is sorry they
had had to do
with Claud,
because Claud
and his brethren
were of evil con-
duct.

¹ fol. 150.

tresse vnrobbed. Now pray ¹We god, that he pre-
serueth bothe our lyues & honour in this affayre. Fayre
vncle, vpon this caas we muste seke remedy / It is good
that we lete haue knowledge to our parents & frendes 4
þerof, þat haue be of this folyssh alyaunce.' And

Guerin and Ger-
rard send to their
friends to come
to Mountfrain to
devise means of
excusing them-
selves to Geffray.

gueryn ansuerd : 'that is trouth.' Thenne they sent
wordes to theyre frendes that they shuld al còme to
mountfrayn, so that they might haue Counseill togidre 8
vpon this faytte, & to seke the meane to escuse them
toward geffray. Now resteth thystory of them / and

The lady of Val-
bruiant

speketh of the lady of Valbruyant that was moche
subtyl & sage / and she euer blamed her lord of that he 12
had consented to Claude & to hys brethern. This lady
had a doughter, whiche was of the age of ix yere / &
fayre & gracyous ; and also a sone that was ten yere of
age, whiche was fayre & wel endoctryned. And thenne 16

mounts her two
children on
horseback

this lady as she had of nothing¹ be abasshed² / mounted
upon a palfray rychely arayed, & dide do be mounted
her two children vpon two horses, and ordeyned two
auncyent gentylmen to conduyte theire horses / and 20

and accompanies
them to the gate
of the castle,

acompanyed with six damoyselles, dide open the gate
where she fond the new knight that brought the
mandement of geffray, which she receyued benyngly,
and he that coude moche of honour made to her the 24

where she tells
the new knight
that she will go
to Geffray her-
self,
² fol. 150 b.

reuerence / and the lady seyd to hym temperatly : ' Sire
knight, my lord is not within / and therfore I wyl go
myself toward my lord your maister to knowe ³what is
his playsyr, For it semeth me that he is come hither 28
to make werre / but I byleue not that it is for my lord
nor for none within this fortresse. For god deffende

as her lord has
done nothing to
displease Geffray
or his father.

that my lord or ony of this place had do that thing
that shuld dysplayse geffray or my lord his fader / and 32
by aduenture yf some of his synester frendes haue informed geffray otherwyse than raison, I wold humbly
beseche & pray hym that he vouche sauf to here my

² Fr. *Adonc la dame ne fut ne folle ne esbahie.*

said lord & husband in his escuses & deffenses' / and
thenne whan the knight herd her speke so sageously /
her ansuerde : 'Madame, this requeste is raisonable,
4 wherfore I shal conduyte you toward my lord / and I
hope that ye shal fynd hym frendly, & that ye shal
haue a good traytye with hym / how be it, he is infourmed of gueryn your lord ryght malycyously / but I
8 byleue that at your requeste he shal graunte a part of
your petycion' / And thenne they departed & came
toward the lodgys of Geffray.

Thystorye sayth that whan geffray saw the com-
12 myng of the lady he yssued out of his tente &
came ayenst her / and she that was wel nourrytured
held her two children tofore geffray, to whom she made
humble reuerence / and thenne geffray enclyned hym
16 to her, & toke her vp right humbly, & said : 'Madame,
ye be right welcome' / and 'my lord,' said she, 'I
see þat I desyre' / and thenne her two children dyde
¹theyre obeyssaunce in the moost humble wyse / and
20 he gaf to them ayen his salut. Thenne toke the lady
the word / and feynyng as though she had knowen
nothing of hys euyl wyll / said vnto hym in this wyse :
'My lord / my lord ! myn husband as for this tyme he
24 is not present in this Countre. Wherfore I am come
toward you to pray you that it may playse you to take
your lodgys in your Fortresse, and take with you as
many of your peple as shal you playse ; For, my lord,
28 thanked be god, there is ynough to plese you with /
and wete it wel that I & my meyne shal receyue you
gladly, as we owe to doo the sone of our souerayn
lord naturall.' Whan geffray vnderstode her requeste
32 he was gretly abasshed how she durst desyre hym /
consyderyng how he was infourmed ageynst Gueryn her
husband. Neuerthele he sayd, 'By my feyth, fayre
lady, I thanke you of your grete curtoysye that ye offre
36 me / but this requeste I ought not to agree, For men

who says that he has been told that her lord does not deserve such recognition,

but that in her lord's absence she and those in the fortress are safe.

¹ fol. 151 b.

The lady answers that neither herself nor her husband have done wrong;

and hopes that Geffray will hear her husband's excuses,

Geffray promises to listen to them,

and gives him a safe conduct for a week.

The lady goes to Mountfrain

and tells her lord of her interview.

² fol. 152.

An ancient knight says that they will have a

haue youen to me knowlege that your husband hatl
not deseruyd it ayenst my lord, my fader, & me / hov
be it, my fayre lady, I wyl wel that ye knowe that I an
not come for to make warre ayenst ladyes & damoy
selles / and be ye of this sure, that neyther to you no
to none of your fortres I wyl nought say nor hurt, y
your husband be not there' / And she thenne said
'gramercy, my ¹lord. But I requyre you, that it playe
you to shew me the cause of your indignacyon that y
haue vnto my lord myn husband, For I am in certai
nother he nor I haue neuer do no thing to our know
leche that shuld be your dysplaysure / and I bylen
that yf it might plese you to here my lord & husban
& his escuse, that ye shal fynd them that thus hau
informed you, be not matere of trouth / and my lord
therupon I make me strong that in conclusyon ye sha
fynde as I say.'

In this partye sheweth thistory, that whan geffra
herd the lady thus speke he thought a lytel, & ay
answerd & said : · By my feyth, lady, yf he goodly ca
excuse hym that he haue not falsed hys feyth, I shalb
glad therof / & I shal receyue hym gladly in his excu:
acyons with his felawes & all theire complyces / an
from this day seuen nyght I gyue hym saaf gooyng
commyng, and fourty personnes with hym.' Thenn
toke the lady her leue & retourned to Valbruyan
where she lefte her children / and acompanyed wit
ten knightes and squyers, & with thre damoyselle
departed, & rode so long tyl she came to Mountfrayn
where she was receyued joyously of her lord & h
frendes, to whom she recounted how gueryn her lor
had safconduyte of geffray for hym, & fourty personne
with hym / & yf he may excuse hym geffray sha
here hym gladly, ²and shal admynystre hym al raysor
'By my feyth,' said an auncyent knight, 'thenne sha
we haue a good traytye with hym / For there nys nor

that may say that euer we mysdyde in eny thing¹ ayenst
our souerayne lord naturel. Yf Claude, that was our
Cousyn, had vs requyred of ayde, yf he neded, & we
4 had promysed hym to helpe hym / not for that we ne
haue yet mysdon / nother geffray nor none other may
not say that euer we had the helmet on heed, nor þat
we yssued euer out of our places for to comforte or
8 ayde hym ayenst geffray by no wyse / goo we thenne
surely toward geffray, & lete me doo there withall, For
I doubte not but that we shal haue good traytye with
hym.' The frendes & cousyns of gueryn confermed
12 this propos, & made theire appareyl for to goo toward
geffray on the iiiᵈᵉ day folowyng. And thenne the
lady departed, & retourned to Valbruyant, where she
sent for breed, wyne, capons, chikkons, conyns, & suche
16 vytayll, with hey & ootys, and presented it to geffray /
but he neuer receyued of it / but suffred that who
wold toke of it for his money / and the said lady lete
geffray haue knowleche how her lord & his frendes
20 shuld come toward hys grace. /

Here sayth thystory, that Gueryn of Valbruyant &
guerard hys neuew, taryed for theire frendes at
mountfrayn / and whan they were come they mounted
24 on theire horses & rode tyl they came to valbruyant /
and on the morne ¹they sent word to Geffray of theire
commyng, and that they were al redy to come toward
hys good grace to theire excuse. And geffray ansuerd:
28 þat he was apparaylled to receyue them. And þenne
they departed fro the Castel & came tofore the tente
of geffray, to whom they made theire obeyssaunce ryght
honourably. And there thauncyent knight of whiche
32 I spak tofore toke the word, & said: " Mighty & puyssaunt lord, we are come hither toward your highnesse
for this, that we vnderstand how ye are infourmed
ayenst vs, that we were consentyng¹ to the ylnesse &
36 dysobedyence of Claude ayenst our souerayne lord

good treaty with
Geffray,

for they did not
help Claud
against Geffray.

The lady returns
to Valbruiant

and sends vic-
tuals to Geffray,

and tells him
how her lord is
about to come
before him.

Guerin and Ger-
rard arrive at
Valbruiant,

¹ fol. 152 b.

and send word
to Geffray,

who announces
his readiness to
receive them.

They present
themselves and
make their obedi-
ence,

The ancient
knight
tells that he has
heard that Gef-
fray thinks they
consented to
Claud's miscon-
duct.

natural, your fader. My lord, it is wel trouth that the
said Claude our Cousyn, tofore hys folysshe enterpryse,
he assembled vs togidre, & thus said to vs : ' Fayre

He relates how
Claud had asked
their help,

lordes, ye be all of my lynage & kynrede / & I of i
yours / wharfore rayson requyreth that we loue eche
other.' Thenne sayd we / ' by my feyth, ye may
trouth / but wherfor say ye soo ?' And thenne he
ansuerd couertly : ' Fayre lordes, I doubte me to haue 8
shortly a strong werre & to haue a doo with a
strong partye ; Wherfor I wyl wete yf ye wold helpe
me ' / & we thenne asked of hym / ayenst whom /

but did not give
the name of the
enemy,

he ansuerd : ' we shuld knowe it al in tyme, & that 12
he was not parfytte frend, who that relenquysshed
hys cousyn at hys nede.' Thenne said we to hym,
' we wyl wel that ye knowe that there nys none so

1 fol. 185.
and how they
promised to as-
sist him.

grete in this countrey, 1ne so myghty, yf he wyl 16
hurt or dommage you, but that we shal helpe you to
kepe & susteyne you in your ryght.' and vpon that

They helped
Claud against
some of his ene-
mies,
but after his dis-
obedience to
Raymondin they
had not aided
him.

he departed / and syn had he many rancoura ayenst
some where we ayded hym / but my lord wete it wel 20
that fro the tyme of hys dysobedyence to my lord your
fader, we ne doubte nor fere neyþer god nor man that
we euer putte piece of harneys on vs / nor that none of
vs all yssued out of his fortres, nother for hym nor for 24
his faytte / and the contrary shal be nother knowen
nor fond, For herof we wyl not haue grace / but we
requyre only right & justice / and yf there be other
cause that our euyl wyllers might haue contryued vpon 28

Therefore he
thinks Geffray
should not be in-
dignant against
him,

vs thrugh enuye or hate / I say by right that ye ne
owe to be therfore indigned ayenst vs, þat are very
subgets & obedyent to my lord, your fader Raymondyn of Lusynen, For yf some were wylling to vexe or 32
moleste vs by ony wyse ye oughte to helpe & kepe vs /
and herof I can no more say, For we can not thinke

because they
cannot think
what they have
done displeasing
to Geffray's
father,

that none of vs dide euer that thing that myght dysplayse my lord your fader. Wherfor we al present 36

beseche & pray you that ye be not infourmed but of
rayson." /

4   Whan geffray had herd thexcuse of the olde knyght
that spake for all, he called his Counseyll to
hym / and syn said to them: 'Fayre lordes, what seme
yow of this fayte ? ¹ me semeth that these folke excuse
them self full wel.' 'By my feyth,' sayd they all in
8   commyn, 'that is trouth / nor ye can not aske of
them, but that ye make them to swere vpon the holy
Euaungylles, that yf the siege had be layed tofore
syon / they had socoured Claude or not ayenst you /
12   and yf they swere ye / they are your enemyes / and to
the contrary, yf they swere that noo / ye owe not to
bere to them euyl wyll.' To this they all accorded /
& therewith concluded theire counseyll.   And thenne
16   were gueryn & hys frendes called tofore geffray / and
after he had recorded to them the sayd conclusyon /
they said that gladly they shuld swere as they dyde.
Wherfore they had peas with geffray, and syn went
20   with hym al about the Countre vysytyng the Fortresses
& places by the space of two monethes.   And after
Geffray toke leue of the Barons there / and lefte gouernours to kepe & rewle the Countrey / and syn departed
24   & retourned to Lusynen, where he was gretly festyed
of hys fader & moder, that were glad of his retourne.
Thenne was there come a knyght of poytou fro
Cypre, whiche had reported tydynges how the Calyphe
28   of Bandas, and the grete Carmen were arryued in
Armenye / and moche they had adommaged the kynge
Guyon.   Also how kynge vryan had tydynges how
they entended to make werre ayenst hym in Cypre.
32   Wherfore he made hys assemble of men of armes & of
shippes, for to recountre & fyght with them in the see.
²For his entencion was not to suffre them to entre in his
lande.   Whan thenne Geffray vnderstode these tydynges
36   he sware by the good lord, that shuld not be without

and beg
to be informed
of their fault.

¹ fol. 153 b.
Geffray tells his
council that he
thinks they have
made a good de-
fence.
The council ad-
vises that Guerin
and his friends
should be made
to swear that
they would not
have helped
Claud had his
castle been be-
sieged.

Guerin is ready
to swear; so he
has peace with
Geffray.

Geffray returns
to Lusignan, and
is greatly feasted.

News comes from
Cyprus that the
Caliph of Bandas
is attacking
Guion, King of
Armenia.

Urian is assem-
bling ships to
fight his bro-
ther's enemies.
² fol. 154.

Geffray resolves
to aid his breth-
ren.

hym, and that to long he had kept his fyre / and said
to Raymondin hys fader, & to Melusyne his moder /
that they wold make hym cheuysaunce of help for to
goo ayde hys bretheren ayenst thenemyes of god / And
they accorded therto / so that he promysed them to
retourne within a yere day toward them.

Geffray asks the
knight from Cy-
pras to accom-
pany him.

Ryght joyous was geffray whan his fader had
graunted hym his wyll. and thenne he prayed
the knight that was come fro Cipre, that he wold
retourne with hym, & that he shuld reward hym wel
therof. 'By my feyth,' sayd the knight / 'men telleth
me as touching your prowes may none compare / and
shal go with you for to see yf ye can doo more than
Vryan & Guyon your bretheren; For thoo two I knowe
ryght wel.' 'By my feyth, sire knight,' said geffray
'it is a lytel thing of my faytte concernyng the puyssaunce of my lordes, my brethern / but I thanke you
of this lyberall offre to goo with me / & I shall meryt
you, therfore, yf it playse god.' Thenne he made hys

He assembles
xiiii C. men of
arms and iii. C.
archers, and
marches them to
Rochelle,
where Raymond-
in had provided
and victualled
many vessels.
¹ fol. 154 b.

mandement & dyde so moch, that he assembled xiiii. C.
men of armes, & wel iij. C. arbalestres, and made them
to drawe toward Rochelle / And raymondyn & melusyne were there, whiche had don arryued man[y]
vesselles, & wel purueyed of¹ vytaylles necessary
And ²thenne Geffray toke leue of his fader & of hys

Geffray sets sail.

moder, & entred into the see with his companye, a[nd]
saylled so þat they lost syght of land, For they made
good way. Here resteth thystorye of them to speke
and begynneth to speke of the Calyphe of Bandas & of
the Sawdan of Barbarye, that was nevew to the sawda[n]
that was slayn in the batayll vpon the heed of Sayn[t]
Andrew aboue the black montayne.

The Saracen
lords resolve

Thystorye sheweth vs that the Caliphe of Bandas a[nd]
the Sawdan of Barbarye / the kyng Anthenor
of Anthioche / and the admyral of querdes² had made

¹ Orig. of of.   ² Fr. Cordes.

togidre theire affyaunce, that neuer they shuld retourne
tyl they had dystroyed the kynge Vryan of Cipre, and
guyon the kyng⸲ of Armanye his brother / and had wel
4 assembled to the nombre of xvi.ᴹᴵ sarasyns, & had
theire shippes all prest to thentent to arryue first in
Armanye / & first of all theire werkes to dystroye
the yle of Rodes, & after the royalme of Armanye / &
8 so passe in to Cypre to dystroye & putte to deth / &
had sworne that they shuld make kyng⸲ Vryan to dey
on the crosse / & hys wyf & his children they shuld
brenne. But as the wyse man saith / 'the fole pro-
12 poseth & god dysposeth' / and at that season were
many espyes emong⸲ them as wel of armenye as of
rodes / and there was one of the maister of Rodes spyes
that was so ¹Lyke a Sarasyn that no man mysdymed
16 hym for other than a Sarasyn, & had the langage as a
man of the same Countrey; the whiche knewe the
secretes of the sarasyns / and syn departed fro them &
came to baruth, where he fonde a barke þat wold sayll
20 to Turckye to fette marchandyse, and entred in it. And
whan they had good wynd they toke vp theire ancres
& saylled so long that they sawe the yle of Rodes,
where they came to refressh them there / and soone
24 after the sayd espye went out of the shipp and toke
hys way toward the Cite of rodes, where he fonde the
maister of rodes, that welcommed hym & demanded
what tydynges. And the spye recounted to hym al
28 that the Sarasyns entended for to doo / the which
tydynges the maister of rodes dyde doo knowe by
wrytyng to the two bretheren kynges of Armenye & of
Cipre / and that they shuld entre in to the see with
32 þeire power / and that he shuld mete with them at the
porte of Japhe / and thenne whan guyon kyng⸲ of
armanye vnderstode this he entred in to the see, & had
with hym to the nombre of six thousand men of armes,
36 & wel iii.ᴹᴵ balesters, & came sayllyng to Rodes, where

to destroy Urian
of Cyprus and
Guion of Ar-
menia.

They intend to
first destroy the
Isle of Rhodes,
afterwards the
kingdom of
Armenia, and
then to capture
Urian of Cyprus,
and make him
die on the cross.

¹ fol. 155.

A spy of the
Master of
Rhodes among
the Saracens

returns to his
master and tells
all that they in-
tend to do.

Word is sent to
the Kings of Ar-
menia and Cy-
prus, and they are
asked to set out
to sea and to
meet the Master
of Rhodes at
Jaffa.

Guion sails to Rhodes, where the prior receives him joyfully.

[1] fol. 155 b.

as he fonde the grete maister at the porte / And whan the grete pryour of Rodes sawe him he had grete joye, & forthwith he entred with hym & al his puyssaunce into the see to the nombre of [1] iii.C bretheren men of armes, & vi.C balesters or crosbowmen. Whan they were assembled togidre fayre was the Flote, [2]For by very estymacion they were fonde to the nombre of ten thousand men of armes / & about xviii.C what balesters as Archers. And wete it wel, it was a fayre syght, For the baners & standarts wayued with the wynd / and the gold & azure vpon the helmets & armures respland-ysshed brigh & clere, that it was grete meruaylt / and syn they rowed toward the porte of Japhe, wher the Sarasyns had made theire nauye to dryue. And here resteth thystorye of them to speke, & sheweth of vryan as ye may here herafter. /

They set sail to Jaffa.

Urian gathers his barons at Lymassou,

Thystory sayth, that the kyng Vryan made & sent his mandement thrugh al his land of Cypre, for to gadre his baronye togidre with theire puyssaunce, & whan they were assembled at the porte of Lymasson he toke leue of the quene Ermyne, his wyf, & entred into the see. And wete it they were in nombre, what men of armes as balesters & archers xiiii.[M], And þenne they departed fro the porte, & saylled by suche force of wynde that quene Ermyne, which was vpon a hye toure, lost soone the syght of them. And wete it wel that geffray with the grete toth, within thre days after arryued vnder Lymasson / but the maister of the porte suffred them not to entre within the porte. how be it he was abasshed to see the armes of Lusynen in theire baners vpon the toppes of theire shippes, & wyst not what to deme or say ; wherfore he went anoone to the Castel & anounced these tydynges to the quene / And she þat was full sage. said to hym / 'go ye to know

takes leave of Ermine,

and soon sails out of sight.

Geffray arrives three days after at Lymasson, but the master of the port will not let him enter.

[2] Fr. *six mille hermins et bien trois mille arbalestriers.* *Hermins* = *Armenians.*

what folke[1] they be, For without treson, they are some
of my lordes lynee / speke thenne with them, hauyng
your men prest & redy vpon the porte to thende, yf
4 they wold arryue by force, that ye may withstand
them' / And he anone fulfylled the quenes commandement & came to the barryers of the clos & demanded
of them what they sought. Thenne ansuerd the knight
8 whiche tofore that tyme had be in Cypre / 'lete us
arryue, For it is geffray, kyng[t] vryans brother, that
commeth to socoure & ayde hym ayenst the Sarasyns.'
And thenne whan the maister of the porte vnderstode
12 þe knight he knew hym anone, & thus sayd : 'Sire,
the kyng[t] is departed from hens thre dayes agoo, &
hath take hys way and hys puyssaunce with hym
toward the porte of Japhe, For he wyl not suffre, yf he
16 may, that paynemes entre in his royame / but pray, my
lord, hys brother, that it playse hym to come & see
the quene that ryght ioyous shal be of hys comyng[t].'
And he al this said to geffray, whiche anoone entred
20 into a lytel galyote, & with hym the said knight and
other of hys felawship, & rowed to the chayne[2] that
anoone was open / & so they entred in to the hauen,
where as they fonde many noble men that honourably
24 receyued geffray & his felawship, whiche meruaylled
them gretly of hys grete courage & of hys fyersnes, &
brought hym toward the queene that abode for hym,
holdyng her sone Henry in her armes.   And as Geffray
28 approched to her she enclyned herself tofore him / and
geffray to her made his obeyssaunce & toke her vp &
kyssed her / & [3]syn said to her, 'Madame, my sustir, god
yeue you ioye of al that your herte desyreth' / And
32 she welcommed hym frendly & honourably.   And
thenne geffray toke vp his neuew Henry, that kneled
tofore hym. What shuld I now make long compte.
Geffray was thenne glad / & the port was open & hys

[2] Fr. chainne.

[1] fol. 156.
The Queen says
thay may be of
her husband's
lineage.

The master of
the port is told
it is Geffray, the
king's brother,
who is in the
ships.

He tells the
knight that the
king sailed for
Jaffa three days
before.

Geffray visits the
queen,

[2] fol. 156 b.

and is welcomed.

His navy enters
the port and is
refreshed.

nauye entred, & whan they were wel refresshed geffray
said to the quene: 'Madame, I wyl departe, lete me

Geffray asks for a
pilot.

haue a maronner that wel knoweth the coutes of this
see, so that I may fynd my brother.'   4

To this ansuerd the quene, 'My right dere brother /
By my feyth, I wold it had cost me a thousand
poundes that ye were now with my lord, your brother,
For wel I knowe he shal haue grete joye of your
commyng.'   and thenne she called to her the maister

The queen orders
the portmaster
to prepare a gal-
ley with the
sagest mariner
that can be
found.

of the porte, & sayd / 'go make a galyot to be shipped
redy with ten oores, & seke for the sagest maronner
& best patron that can be fond, for to conduyte my
lord my brother toward my lord.'   'Madame,' ansuerd

He has a rampin
ready, which
guides Geffray.

the maister of the port, 'I haue wel a rampyn alredy
shipped to rowe, wel armed & vytaylled, & resteth
no more than to meve & departe.'   Thenne was geffray
right glade & toke hys laue of the quene & of his
nevew, & entred in to his shipp / and the said rampyn
or galley gyded hym / & so departed with hys flote, &

who soon sails
out of sight.

rowed & made good way, so that in short space they
of the porte lost the syght of them.   And the quene
Ermyne prayed denoutely to god that they myght retourne with joye   Of hym I shal leue to speke.   But
Vryan his broper rowed so long tyl they perceyued the

1 fol. 157.
Urian comes to
Jaffa,
and sees the
Saracen fleet
there.

porte 1of Japhe, & the bygge & grete vesselles that
were there assembled / and thenne was there comme
the Caliphe / the Saudan of Barbarye, the kyng of
Anthioche, & thadmyral of querdes, with theire puyssaunce.   And was by them concluded the king anthenor
& thadmyrall shuld make vantward, & shuld hold
the way toward rodes / and yf that they neded socour
they shuld wryt to the Caliphe & to the Sawdan,

The Saracens
intend
to sail against
Rhodes.

whiche alwayes be redy to helpe & ayde them / and
the kyng antenor of Anthyoche & thadmyral of Cordes
departed fro the porte of Japhe with fourty thousand
panemes, & toke theire way toward Rodes by suche

wyse that Vryan knew nothing of theire departyng⸱ /
and had rowed but two dayes journey whan they perceyued kyng guyon & the nauye of rodes, and also the
4 Cristens perceyued them / Thenne was there grete
alarme of bothe partes, and soone they borded togidre.
There was grete occysyon & horryble medlee / and at
the first recountryng were six galleyes of the sarasyns
8 sounken & perysshed in the see / And the noble crystens
endeuoyred them self wel & faught valyauntly, But
the force & the quantyte of the Sarasyns was grete /
and the Crysten peuple susteyned grete charge, & had
12 be dyscomfyted yf god of hys grace had not conduyted
geffray that part as it shall be recounted herafter.

They meet Guion, and fight. There is much slaughter,

six Saracen galleys are sunk;

but because of the multitude of Saracens the Christians would have been defeated,

Thystory saith, that geffray & his peple saylled in
the see by force of wynd þat they had at theire
16 wyll so long, that they ¹approuched the place where
the batayll was. And first of all the rampyn that conduyted them approuched so nygh that they sawe them
fyght / and anone retourned & said to geffray, 'Sire,
20 commande al men to be redy, For we haue perceyued
the batayll / & as we suppose they are sarasyns &
crysten fyghting togidre.' Thenne rowed the galyote &
came so nygh the baytayll that they herde crye on hye,
24 'Cordes & Anthioche' / and at the other part 'Lusynen
& saynt John of Rodes' / and immedyatly retourned the
rampyn toward geffray, & said to him, 'Sire, at that one
party they ben sarasyns / and at the other part theire
28 callyng is Lusynen & Saynt Johan of rodes / but certaynly it is not the kyng⸱ vryan / but I byleue, my
lord, that it is the kyng guyon hys brother & the
maister of Rodes that thus fyght with the Sarasyns.'
32 'Ryght foorth,' sayd geffray, 'goo we to them asprely' /
thenne they haunced saylles vp & saylled foorth by
such wyse that it semed as it had be the vyreton of a
Crosbow, & stemed the shippes of the sarasyns in suche
36 manere that they were sparpylled, so that there rested

¹ fol. 157 b. had not Geffray come to their aid.

Geffray is told that it is a fight between Christians and Saracens.

He sails swift as an arrow and breaks up the Saracen fleet.

He cries, 'Lusignan,' which makes the Armenians think Urian has come to help.

The Christians take heart.

¹ fol. 158.

The Saracens rally and attack their enemies.

Geffray damages the Saracens ;

boards the vessel of Anthenor,

and causes many to enter the Admiral of Cordes' ship.

not foure of al the flote, and cryed 'Lusynen' with a high voys. Wherfor the Ermayns & they of Rodes byleued þat it had be the kyng Vryan that were come fro cypre. And thenne toke they good herte to them & courageously. And the kyng of Anthioche [1] & thadmyrall of Cordes gadred ayen theire peple, and rane vpon the crysten with grete force. But geffray & hys peuple, that were fresshe & new, ouerrane them in suche manere that they dommaged gretly the sarasyns / and thenne the vessel where geffray was / borded the vessel of the kynge anthenor & were chayned togidre. And geffray entred into the vessel of the kyng & bygan to make grete occysyon of the sarasyns, & his peuple entred & faught so valyauntly with suche a strength that there was no sarasyn so hardy that durst shew hym or make deffense / and many of them for theyre relyf supposed to haue entred into thadmyral shipp & they were drowned / the whiche admyral, guyon & his peuple assaylled strongly, & drowned foure of the sarasyns shippes.[2] The batayll was fyers & horryble & thoccysyon hydouse / and briefly to say, the sarasyns were putte in suche manere so low that they had noþing them to deffende. /

Moche was the batayll hard & strong, but aboue al other faught geffray manfully, & so dide the poytenyns that were come with hym there, & so dyde guyon the maister of Rodes & theire peple / but they were abasshed for this that they cryed 'Lusynen' / but thenne it was no saison tenquere. And thenne the kyng anthenor & thadmyral perceyued wel þat the dyscomfiture fyll on them, For they þenne [3]had lost more than the two partes of theire peple, wherfore they made the resydu of theire peuple to withdraw them

King Anthenor and the admiral see that they have been discomfited, so set sail to Jaffa.

² fol. 158 b.

² In Fr. *et toutesfois le roi Anthenor se sauua au vaisseau de l'admiral de Cordes et fut tantost son vaisseau pillié de ce qui y estoit de bon, et puys fut effrondé en mer.*

toward the port of Japhe to haue socour / and the said
kyng⸱ & admyral put them self in a shipp of ausauntage
& made grete sayll fro the batayll, and whan the sara-
4 syns perceyued they went after, he that might.   But
the Ermayns & they of Rodes ouertoke the moost part
& putte them to deth & threw þem ouerbord.   But
whan geffray perceyued the departyng⸱ of the kyng⸱
8 anthenor & the admyral, he dyde make sayll & went **Geffray chases them,**
after with al hys nauye, & made so fast way that anoone
he lefte the Ermayns & the maister of Rodes at sterne.
And whan the rampyn ship of ausauntage perceyued
12 geffray, the patron cryed to hys peuple with a hye
voys / 'after / after / fayre sires, For yf geffray leseth his
way & faylleth to mete with hys brother, I shal neuer
dare retourne to my lady.'   And thenne the kynge
16 Guyon, that knew the rampyn, asked of the patron
what was that lord cristen that so had socoured them.
'By my feyth,' said the patron, 'it is geffray with the
grete toth, your brotþer.'   And whan the kyng guyon
20 vnderstod it he cryed with a hye voys, 'make more
sayll, þat we were with our brother, For yf he were **and is followed by the rampin to Jaffa.**
perysshed I shuld neuer haue hertly joye.'   But þe
rampyn went tofore so fast that in short tyme he ouer-
24 toke geffray, that was neer the [1]sarasyns that ap- **[1] fol. 159.**
prouched the porte of Japhe.   Here I shall leue to
speke of them, & shal shew of Vryan that tofore was **Urian had been there, and had set fire to some of the Saracen fleet.**
come to the port and had fyred the sarasyns shippes
28 there / but the paynemes rescued them in theire best
manere / not that withstanding there were more than
ten vesselles brent.

In this partye sheweth thystorye that Geffray with
32 the grete toeth pursiewed so long⸱ the king anthenor
& thadmyral of Cordes, that they approuched nygh to
the port of Japhe, where they entred in / and geffray **Geffray enters the port of Jaffa after the king and the admiral.**
after them; For by no manere he wold leue them /
36 though men shewed to hym the grete multitude of

paynemes that thenne were entred in to the vesselles to
soccoure the kyng⟨ anthenor.   But he anoone bygan the
batayll that was hard & mortall, in so moch that the
kyng and thadmyrall were constrayned to take land, 4
and went to the toune of Japhe, where they fond the
calyphe of Bandas and the Sawdan of Barbarye that
were gretly abasshed that so soone they were retourned,
and demanded of the cause wherfore / and thay re- 6
counted to them al thaduenture, And how the kyng
of armenye & the maister of Rodes were dyscomfyted,
had not a knyght araged or wood that came & socoured them with a few peuple that cryed 'Lusynen' / 12
& there may none witkstand hym, whiche is now
yonder at the porte where he fyghteth ayenst our peuple /
and al that he recountreth is brought to hys ende.
And whan the sawdan vnderstod it he had no wyll to 16
¹ lawghe / but said, 'By machomet, it is tolde me of old
that I, & many other of our sette and lawe, shall
susteyne grete parels vpon the see, by the heyres of
Lusynen / but yf we might haue them on land, and 20
that our peuple were out of þe shippes they shuld be
soone all dyscomfytod.' 'By all our goddes,' said the
Caliphe, 'ye say trouth, / and also yf they were here
dystroyed we shuld subdue lyghtly Rodes, cypre, & 24
armanye / Lete vs thenne make our peuple to come to
land, and suffre the Cristen to take peasybly theire
landing⟨.' But in certayn for nought they spake soo,
For they yssued out without ony commandement, by 28
the vertue & strength of Geffray that therto constrayned
them / and Geffray with his peuple pursiewed them at
land, & chaced them vnto the Cite of Japhe / and all
thoo that were ouertake were put to deth / and they 32
that entred in the toun cryed 'treson, treson!' Thenne
were the gates shette, and euery man went to hys
garde / and geffray retourned to his shippes / and commanded that the horses shuld be had out aland.   For 36

He fights them;

they take to land.

They tell the
caliph and the
sultan their ad-
ventures.

¹ fol. 159 b.
The sultan
repeats an old
prophecy that
says that people
who believe in
Mahomet cannot
withstand the
Lusignans on
the sea.

Geffray mean-
while drives the
Saracens from
their ships.

They fly to Jaffa.

Geffray orders
the horses to be
landed.

he said that neuer he shuld departe but he shuld dey
or he shuld make men to say, that Geffray with the
grete toth hath be here.

4 **T**hystorye telleth vs that whyle Geffray was about
to haue out of the shippes hys horses, the
rampyn perceyued the baners & penons of the kyng‘ Urian is seen by
vryan, that moch strongly scarmysshed the nauye of the men of the
                                                     rampin.
8 the sarasyns that knew nothing‘ that geffray had take
land, For they had take the deep of the porte. And
¹ the kynge and thadmyrall were arryued at the narowest ¹ fol. 160.
syde to be the sooner on land. Thenne departed the
12 rampyn shipp of auauntage, and rowed toward vryan. They row to
And thenne they recountred guyon, whiche asked of him,
the patron tydynges of geffray. ‘Yonder he hath take
land,’ said the patron, ‘& hath chaced the paynemes
16 vnto þe Cite / and yonder is the kyng vryan your
broþer, that scarmyssheth theire nauye, to whom I goo
for to anounce hym your auenture, and the commyng
of geffray, his brother’ / And thenne the rampyn
20 rowed fast, and came to vryan to whom, after his
obeyssaunce don, he recounted al the faytte. Wherof and tell of
Vryan thanked god deuoutely / & cryed to hys peple, Geffray's doings.
‘auaunt, lordes, thinke to doo wel, For our enemyes
24 may not escape vs, but that they be other slayn or
take.’ Thenne the crysten borded theire enemyes, the Urian drives the
which were gretly abasshed of this, that they had Saracens to land.
knowleche that the kyng‘ anthenor & thadmyrall were
28 retourned to Japhe. wherfor they toke land who that
might, & fledd toward the toun. And thenne whan They fly to the
the Calyphe and the saudan sawe theire peple aland, town.
they dyde send ambaxades toward the prynces Cristen The caliph asks a
32 for to haue trews the space of thre dayes, & that they truce for three
shuld suffre theire landing‘, & on the foureth day they days.
shuld gyue them journey of batayll. Kinge Vryan Urian agrees to
accorded therto, and sent word therof to his brethern it.
36 guyon and geffray / and thus they landed peasybly, and

MELUSINE.   T

The brethren
land their hosts,
¹ fol. 160 b.

assembled theire peple togidre. Thenne ¹was the Joye
grete emcng⸱ the thre bretheren, and theire oost was
nombred xxii.ᴹᴵ what men of armes / balestere &
archers.   4

greet each other,
and refresh them-
selves.

Thystorye sayth that the thre bretheren and theire
peuple made moche eche of other, & refresshed
them during⸱ the trews. But þanne the Sawdan of
Damaske that had knowleche of the crystens landing 8
sent word¹ to the Calyphe & to the sawdan of
Barbarye, that they shuld not fyght with the crysten
tyl he were come with them, & that they shuld¹ take

The truce is
lengthened.

othre thre days of trews / & so they dide; wherto the 12
noble prynces crysten accorded. And duryng that
termo the Caliphe &² the sawdan of Barbarye dyde

The Saracens
march inland to
prevent the
Christians escap-
ing after the
battle.

withdraw theyre peuple toward Damaske to thentent
that they might have the Cristen more within the land, 16
so that none might flee to theyre nauye; but he were
ouertake & slayne. For they wend¹ to haue all theire
wyll vpon the Crysten. For they were after the sau-

The hosts are
140,000 Saracens
against 22,000
Christians.

dan of Damaske was assembled with them to the 20
nombre of VII score thousand fyghtyng men / and þe
crysten were but xxii.ᴹᴵ good men / the which, when
they knew of the departyng⸱ of the sarasyns fro Japhe,

The Christians
think the Sara-
cens have fled.

they were full dolaunt; For they supposed they had 24
fledd / but for nought they wend soo / for at ende of
six dayes they came & approuched nygh them, & on
the morne gaf them batayll. Thenne came a trucheman

An interpreter
comes to the
brethren.

mounted vpon a dromadary, whiche alighted tofore the 28
tentes of the thre bretheren, and humbly salued them /

³ fol. 161.

and they rendred hym ³gretyng⸱ / and he beheld them

He wonders at
their fierceness;
especially at Gef-
fray's tooth.

long or he spake. For he wondred moche of theire
noble maynten & fyers contenaunce / and in especial 32
he meruaylled moche of Geffray that was the hyest of
personne, & saw the toeth that passed ouer the lyppe
along hys cheke; wherof he was so abasshed that
almost he coude not speke / but at last he said to 36

² MS. & and.

kynge Vryan in this wyse. 'Noble kyng of Cypre /
my right redoubted lordes the Sawdants of Barbarye &
of Damaske / the Calyphe of Bandas / the kynges of
4 Anthioche & of Danette & thadmyrall of Cordes send
word by me to you that they be prest[1] redy to lyuere
you batayll, & they tary after you in a medowe vnder
Damaske where ye, with al your puyssaunce may
8 come / saf and peasybly there to make and take
there your lodgys tofore them wheresomeuer it playse
you / and by auenture whan ye haue sene theire puyssaunce ye shall fynd some good & amyable traytye
12 with my said lordes. For certaynly it is not to your
power to withstand theire strength.' And whan
geffray herd there wordes, he sayd to hym / 'goo thou
to thy kynges & sawdants, & to thy Caliphe / and say
16 them that yf there were none only but I & my peuple,
yet wold I fyght / & say them þat of theire trews we
haue nought to doo / and whan thou shalt come to
them say that geffray with the grete toth deffyeth them /
20 and anoone after that thou art departed from hens I
shal sawte the Cite of Japhe, & shal fyre it / and al the
sarasyns that I shal fynd, I shal putte them to deth /
and say to them, as thou passe by [2] that they puruey
24 them wel, For I ryght foorth shall departe to asayll
them.' And whan the trucheman or messager herd this
ansuere, he was al abasshed / and without eny more
proces he lept vpon his dromadary, For he had so grete
28 feer of the fyersnes of geffray that alwayes he loked
behynd hym, for fere that he had folowed hym / &
sayd in hym self: 'By mahon, yf al the other were
suche as that with the grete toth, our lordes, nor theire
32 puyssaunce were not able to withstand them.' And
thenne he came to Japhe, & said to them that geffray
with the grete toth wold come anoon tassayll theire
Cyte, and that he had sworne that he shuld putte in

[1] Fr. pretz.

Many fly to
Damascus.

subgeetion of hys swerd al them that he fond. Thenne
were they all abasshed / and wete it wel that the more
parte of the peple there fled for fere toward Damaske,
and toke with them theirs goodes. And anoon geffray 4
dide blow vp hys trompettes, & armed hys peple, & went

Geffray ap-
proaches Jaffa.

incontynent to sawte the toun, and wold neuer cesse
therof, For ony thing that his brethern said / and sware
by god that he shuld shewe them suche tokens that men 8
shuld knowe that he had ben in surya. But here ceeseth
thistorye of hym, & speketh of the forsaid messanger
þat rode so long that he came tofore the lodgys of the
sarasyns at Damaske.   12

The interpreter
returns

In this party, sayth thystory, that the messager rode
so fast vpon his dromadary that he cam / vnto
thoost tofore Damaske / & fond in the tente of the
Calyphe the two sawdans, [1] the king anthenor / thad- 16
myral of Cordes, the kyng golofryn of Damaske, &
many other that asked tydynges of the Cristens. And
the messager them said / 'I haue don your commandement & message / but whan I shewed vnto them, 20
yf that they had seen your puyssaunce it wold haue
be a meane of traytye with you / and thenne one of
them that had oo grete toth, wold not suffre the kyng
of Cypre to haue the wordes, but he hymself said þus, 24

and relates the
result of his em-
bassy.

"Goo thou to thy kynges and sawdants, & say them we
haue not to doo with theire trews, / & that yf there wer
but he & his peple only, yet wold he fyght with you" /
and morouer said to me / that assooue as I shuld come 28
to you that I shuld take you ayen þe patents of your
trews, & that ye shuld beware of hym / and that in
despyte of you all he wold assawte Japhe, & putte the
fyre thrugh al the toun & destroye them for euer / and 32
that thus I shuld say to them whan I passed by the Cite /
and so haue I doo / and wete it wel that the more [2]
part of the Cytezeyns be come after me, & immedy-

[1] fol. 162.
to the Saracen
knights,

[2] MS. has *more* twice.

atly after my departyng⋅ I herd⋅ hys trompettes blowe
thassawte of Japhe / & ye conde neuer thinke thorryble
& fyers contenaunces of the prynces crysten with theire

4 puyssaunce / And wete it wel after the semblaunce that
they shew, ye be not of power tabyde them, & in
especial he with the grete toth hath none other fere
but that ye shal flee or they come to you.'   And whan

8 the saudan of Damaske vnderstod⋅ it, he bygan to lawgh,
& said⋅, ' By machomid⋅, in asmoche as I haue perceyued
now your hardynes, ye shal be the first in batayll ayenst
hym with the grete toth.'   Wherto answerd ¹ the mes-

12 sager / ' vnhappy be that heure or day that I approche
hym / but yf there be a grete ryuere or the toures or
walles of Damaske or some other Fortres betwix hym
& me / and yf I doo other, lete my lord mahomid⋅

16 drowne me,' / & therwith bygans euery personne to
lawhe.   But there were suche that lawhed⋅, that aftirward, yf they might haue had⋅ leyser, they wold⋅ haue
wept.   Now shall I shew how geffray assawted Japhe,

20 and toke it by force, and putte to deth all the sarasyns
there, and toke their hauoir and goodes out of the Cyte /
& bare it vnto the vesselles, and after sette fyre on the
Cite / and this don, retourned the crysten to theire

24 lodgys, where geffray requyred his bretheren that they
shuld take hym, the maister of Rodes, & hys peuple, to
make the vantgarde / & they were agreed⋅ / and that
same nyght they rested them tyl on the morowe.

28 The next day, as the hystory wytnesseth, after the
masse herd⋅, desloged the vanward⋅, and after the
grete batayll, & the sommage & syn the ryergarde /
and it was a noble syght to see thoost & the fayre

32 ordynaunce to departe.   Thenne came a spye to
geffray, & hym said⋅ : ' Sire, about half a leghe hens
ben a thousand sarasyns, whiche drawe them toward
baruth to kepe the hauen of the toune.'   to whom

36 geffray asked / ' canst conduyte me thither ? ' / ' ye, by

He tells the Sa-
racens that he
thinks they are
unable to with-
stand the Chris-
tians.

The Sultan of
Damascus jeers
and says he will
make the inter-
preter the first
to fight Geffray.
¹ fol. 102 b.

The interpreter
declares he will
not fight Geffray.

Geffray assaults
Jaffa, slays the
inhabitants, and
takes their goods
to his vessels.

The battle is
arranged.

The host marches
in good order.

A spy tells Gef-
fray of the march
of a thousand
Saracens to Bey-
routh.

my feyth, sire,' sayd the spye.   Thenne said geffray to
the maister of rodes, that he shuld conduyte the vanwarde, puttyng fyre vpon the way where he went, to
thentent he shuld not fayll to fynd hym by the trasse

of the fumyer / and the maister of ¹Rodes said / ' it shal
be don.'   And thenne departed geffray with the spye,

and went before, where he perceyued the sarasyns
commyng fro a mountayn ; & he shewed to geffray the
sarasyns, which was joyful therof, & hasted hys peuple
and whan he had ouertake them / he sware : ' by god ,
ye gloutons ! ye may not me escape' / & so rane vpon

them, & ouerthrew the first that he recountred to the
erth, & syn drew hys swerd, & dyde mernayllous
fayttes of armes, & his peuple in lyke wyse.   What
nede is to speke more of the sarasyns, they were dys-

comfyte, & fled toward Baruth, & the Crysten in the
chaas.   And whan the sarasyns of baruth sawe the
fleers, they anoone knew them, & lete fall the bridge

& opened the gates & barryers / thenne the fleers entred
within the toune / but alwayes geffray folowed so
hastly, that he entred with them within the town with
wel fyue C men of armes.   And whan Geffray was
entred he commanded to kepe [the] gate² tyl the
resydu of hys peuple were come / And thenne bygan
the batayll to be fyers & stronge / but neuertheles the

Sarasyns might not endure, but fled at another yate out
of the toun.   And he that thenne had a good hors was
wel bestad, For they sporyd fast, som toward the Cite
of tryple, & some toward Damaske.   And geffray &

his peple slew al the sarasyns that they fond in the
toun, and threw them in the see / and he that sawe
the toun strong & the Castel nygh the see, fayre port
garnysshed with toures for the sauegarde of the nauye

sayd / ' that place shuld be kepe for hym self ' / and
there geffray lefte two houndred men of armes & a

² Fr. *à garder.* MS. has *repegate = kepe* [the] *gate.*

C balesters of his peple / and he hymself [1]soiourned
there all that same nyght. And on the morne he toke
leue of his men that he lefte there, & rode after thoost
4 by the trace of the fumyer & smoke / but the maister
of Rodes was aferd lest he shuld haue grete empeschement /. Here seaceth the hystorye of hym / and sheweth
of the fleers out of Japhe toward Damaske, whiche
8 came to thoost at the tente of the Sawdan, where as the
lordes sarasyns were / and pyteously recounted to them
the dystruction of Japhe / how the Cristen had putte
to deth bothe yong & old, & sette fyre on eche part
12 of the toun. Whan the saudants & kynges sarasyns
vnderstod it, they were full dolaunt. 'By al our
goddes,' said the saudan of Damaske, 'Moche hard
ben the crysten, & they doubte nought as it semeth /
16 but full wel they knowe that they are not of power to
withstand our grete puyssaunce ; wherefore they make
semblaunt, that nought they fere vs, & make suche
sawtes while that we are ferre fro them / but yf we
20 marched foorth / no doubte they wold recule & withdrawe them in to theire shippes.' 'By mahon,' said
the sawdan of Barbarye / ' yf they were here alle rosted
or soden, & yf it were custome to ete suche flesshe, they
24 were not to the regarde of our peple suffysaunt for a
brekfast / by my lawe, yf there were but I & my peuple
only, yet shuld none repasse of them homward.' But
whan the trucheman or messager herd hym so speke
28 he coude neuer hold hys tonge, but that he sayd /
' myghty sawdan, yf now ye sawe the kyng Vryan /
the kyng guyon hys brother, & he with the grete toth,
theire horryble & fyers contenaunce, shuld cause [2]you
32 to be in peas & cesse your grete menaces. And wete
it wel, or the werke be ful doo ye shal not haue them
fo[r] so good chep as ye say / but oft he that menaceth
is somtyme in grete fer & drede hym self, & aftirward
36 ouerthrawen' / And thenne whan the saudan vnder-

[1] fol. 163 b.
He leaves three
hundred men to
guard it,

and by the guid-
ance of the
smoke rides to
the Christian
host.

The fugitives
from Jaffa re-
count their mis-
hap to the sultan.

The Sultan of
Damascus says
the Christians
would fall back
if he marched
against them.
The Sultan of
Barbary says
there are not
enough Chris-
tians to make
the Saracen host
a breakfast;

but the inter-
preter says if the
sultan saw the
brethren he
[2] fol. 164.
would cease his
threats and make
peace

stode the messagers wordes, he said to hym: 'By
Mahomid, fayre sire, I see wel by the grete hardynes
that is in you, ye wold fayne be ordeyned at the first
recountre of þe batayll ayenst Geffray with the grete
toeth.' & he answerd: 'By my lawe, sire, yf he be
not recountred of none other but of me / he may wel
cöme surely; For I shal tourne myn heelys towardj
hym / ye / one leghe or two ferre fro his persowne.'
Thenne the lawhing was thare grete / but soone after
they herd other tydynges, wherof they had no wyll
to lawhe, For the fleers fro baruth forsayd came to
thooat, and to them recounted the dommage & pyte of

The fugitives
from Beyrouth

the toune of Baruth, and how geffray with the grete
toth had chased þem by force, & al the resydu of them

relate how they
have been chased
by Geffray,

he had slayn / & 'by mahon,' said they, 'wete it wel
he is not of purpos to flee, For he hath lefte garnyson

and that he is
approaching.

at Baruth, & wel vytaylled it, & commeth hyþorward
in al haste to hym possible / & men see nothing thragh
al the Countre where he passeth but fyre & flame, &
the wayes be all couered with sarasyns that he & hys
peple haue slayn.' Thenne whan the saudan of
Damaske vnderstode it he was moch delaunt & angry.

The Sultan of
Damascus be-
lieves Geffray to
have a devil in
his body

'By mahomid,' said he, 'I byleue fermely that he with
the grete toth hath a dyuel in his body.' Thenne said

[1] fol. 164 b.
He refers to a
saying about the
heirs of Lusignan
destroying him.

the saudan of Barbarye, 'I am in doubte of that is told
me.' 'What is that?' [1] said the saudan of Damaske / ' it
is said that the heyrs of Lusynen shal dystroye me, and
that our lawe shal by theire strengthe be hurt & dommaged.' Thenne was there none so hardy a Sarasyn
but that he shoke for fere. And now cesseth thystorye
of them, & retourneth to geffray.

Geffray over-
takes the Master
of Rhodes,

Thystorye sheweth in this partye, that so long rode
geffray with hys felawship, that he ouertoke the
vanwarde that the maister of Rodes conduyted, whiche
was glade of his retourne, & asked how he had exployted.   And geffray recounted to hym how he & his

peple, with thayde of god, he had wonne the toune, and relates how he captured Bey-routh.
castel, & hauen of baruth, and that by force they had
chased a grete part of them that were within, and the
4 resydu they had putte to deth / & how he had lefte
certayn nombre of his peuple to kepe it. 'By god,'
sayd the maister of Rodes, 'ye haue wel don, & nobly
& valyanntly exployted' / and soone these tydynges The news spreads, and Urian and Guion are joyful.
8 were knowen thrugh thoost / & Vryan & Guyon were
joyfull therof. 'By my feyth,' said Vryan to Guyon:
'Oure brother Geffray is of grete enterpryse & ryght The brothers speak of the prowess of Gef-fray.
valyaunt in armes, and yf god of his grace yeue hym
12 long lyf, he shal do yet many grete actes worthy to be
had in mynde.' 'By my feyth,' said guyon, 'ye say
trouth.' Long tyme went the two bretheren thus spekyng of the prowes of geffray / And so long marched þeir
16 oost, that on an euen they lodged them by a ryuere The host arrives close to Damas-cus.
fyue myle fro Damaske / & there came theire espyes,
that declared to them all the manyere & contenaunce
of the sarasyns. And thenne they toke Counseyl to
20 wete what best was to doo, & they [1]concluded that on 1 fol. 145.
the morne theire oost shuld lodge a leghe nygh to
the Sarasyns as they dide. And thus on the morne
they departed, & was commanded that none shuld
24 sette fyre on his lodgys, nor in none other place; to
thende that the Sarasyns shuld not soone perceyue
theire commyng. And briefly to say, so long they Next day they march still nearer.
went tyl they came to the place where they lodged
28 them togidre, & made þat nyght good watche toward
theire enemyes. & after they souped & lay al nyght in
theire harneys. And anoone aftir middenyght geffray, At midnight Gef-fray ambushes a thousand men near the Saracen host.
accompanyed with a thousand fyghting men, toke a
32 guyde that wel knew the Countre, & went toward
thoost of the Sarasyns al the couert. & nygh therby
was a forest that dured a myle, and there he embusshed
& sent word to thoost that they shuld be redy as to
36 receyue theire enemys.

He takes two
hundred more
men, and tells
those of the am-
bush not to fight
until he and his
company fall
back; and that
then they should
rush upon their
pursuers.

Thystorye testyfyeth that geffray at the day spryn
mounted on horsbake, with ij. C fyghtyng me
& commanded them of thembusshe þat for nothing th
they sawe they shuld not meue them tyl that they saw
hym & hys company recule, and thenne vpon them
the chaas they shuld renne.   Thenne departed geffra
& went vpon a lytel montayne, and sawe the sarasyn
oost all styl, & herd nothing, as nobody had l
there.   Thenne was he dolaunt, that sooner he had n
knowen theire contenaunce, For yf hys bretheren h
be there with theire peple, they shuld haue had goo
chep of sarasyns / but not withstanding, he sware th
ayth he was so nygh, that he shuld make them
knowe his commyng.   Thenne said geffray to hy

Geffray marches
to the Saracen
host.

¹ fol. 165 b.

felawes : 'ryde we fast, & see that ye be not asleps
they are / & make no bruyt tyl I shal command¹ yo
And they said ¹that nomore shuld they doo.   Then
they rode al the couert nygh togidre, & and entre

It is asleep.

When he sees the
great multitude
he says that they
would have to be
dreaded if they
were Christian,
but as they are,
they are only
dogs.

into thoost, & wel perceyued that they were asle
on euery syde / geffray behel & sawe the grete mul
tude of peuple / and syn he said in this wyse : ' By n
feyth, yf þey were crysten, they were to be ferd
dredd / but yet they be not so good as dogges.' and wi

Geffray sees a
rich tent;

his felawship went vnto the myldes of thoost, or th
made eny stryf.   And there geffray perceyued a rycl
tente, and supposyng that it had be other the Caliph
tente or one of the saudants / said vnto hys peupl
'auaunt, lordes & good men, it is now tyme to chere
awake these houndes, for to long they haue slep

he enters and
smites those
inside.

Thenne Geffray, & ten knightes with hym, entred in
the sayd tente, & vpon them that were in smote wi
theire swerdes, makyng heedes, armes, & legges to le
the bodyes.   There was the noyse, & the cry grete
hydous to here / & wete it that it was þe tente of t

They awake;

kyng Gallafryn of Danette ; which anoone rose vp f
hys bed, & wel he supposed to haue fled out at t

backsyde of hys tente, but geffray perceyued, & gaf
hym suche a stroke with his swerd that was pesaunt, &
cuttyng sharp as a raser, that he cleft hys heed vnto
4 the brayne / & the sarasyn kyng fell doun deed / and
none escaped of them that were in the tente; but they
were al slayne. And thenne cryeng 'Lusynen' they
retourned thrugh thoost, puttyng to deth al the sarasyns
8 that they recountred. Thenne was thoost wel awaked
& made grete alarme / And anoone came these tydynges to the tente of the sawdan of Damaske, that
said : 'What noyse is that I here yonder ¹without?'
12 Thenne a sarasyn that came fro that part, which had
a broken heed, in such manere þat hys one eere lay
vpon hys sholder / sayd to hym : 'Sire, that are x
dyuelles, and theire meyne that haue entred into your
16 oost, which slee & ouerthraw al them that they recountre in theire way / and they haue slayn the kyng
of Danette your cousyn, and theire cry is "Lusynen!"'
Whan the saudan vnderstod it he made hys trompettes
20 to blow vp, that euery man shuld be armed. And
thenne the saudan & x. M¹ sarasyns with hym went
after. And geffray went with hys peple thrugh thoost
makyng grete occyson of sarasyns, For they were
24 vnarmed, & might not endure nor withstand. And
wete it that or euer they departed fro thoost, they
slough & hurt more than iii M¹ sarasyns / and whan
they were out of the lodgys, they went al softe &
28 fayre / And the sawdan of Damaske hasted hym after.

Moche dolaunt & angry was the saudan of Damaske,
whan he perceyued the grete occyson that the
crysten had don vpon hys peuple / & sware by hys
32 goddes Appolyn and mahon, that forthwith he shuld
be auenged on them, & that not a crysten shuld be
take to mercy, but shuld al be slayn. thenne he
folowed geffray with x thousand Sarasyns. And
36 thenne geffray that perceyued, & sent word therof to

Geffray cuts
Gallafrin's
heed open.

The Christians
crying 'Lusig-
nan,' return
through the host
and slay many
Saracens,

¹ fol. 166.
The Sultan of
Damascus hears
the tidings,

and with x. M¹
Saracens

hastes after
Geffray.

hys bretheren by his peple feynyng· to flee / and l
entred within the busshe where his peple was, for (
putte them in aray / And the saudan folowed alwa;
& passed byfore thembussh. Wete it wel that tl
maister of Rodes that conduyted the vanward w:

1 fol. 166 *b*.

He is driven back by the vanguard of the Christians.

thenne in fayre [1]batayll. And whan he sawe tl
saudan that folowed the crysten / he renne ayenst tl
sarasyns, the spere in the rest, and there they medle
togidre & faught strongly / and within a lytel space
tyme the Sarasyns were dyscomfyte. For at the fi:
recountre with the speerys, eche cristen overthrew
sarasyn to the erth. And whan the sawdan sav
that he might no lenger withstand he reculed,
assembled his peple in hys best wyse, abydyng tl

Then his host is fallen upon by the ambush,

sarasyns that came after. But geffray & hys cu
panye yssued out of thembusshe and renne vpon the
put went without ordonaunce after the saudan. A:

four thousand Saracens are slain.

within a whyle there were slayn of the sarasyns by tl
way more then foure thousand. And thenne many

Some of them escape to their host

them fledd toward theire oost, and fonde the caliphe
bandas, the saudan of barbarye, the king Anthenor,
thadmyral of Cordes, whiche asked them fro whe

and tell the Saracen leaders of the mishap.

þey came / And they ansuerd : 'we come fro tl
batayll where the sawdan of Damaske hath be dy
comfyted.' And whan they vnderstod it they we
dyscomforted & sorowful, & wyst not what they shu
say or do. Now I wyl retourne to speke of the batay

The Sultan of Damascus fights manfully.

The batayll was horrible & cruel, & the sawdan
Damaske faught manfully þat day, after that
had assembled hys peple. Thenne came geffray, th
renne vpon them at backsyde / and the maister
rodes at the other syde, In so moche that there w
made grete occysyon of sarasyns. What shuld I ma
long compte / the feled them assaylled on bothe syd
wherby [2]they were dyscomfyted, & might no leng
defende. And whan the saudan perceyued the dy

2 fol. 167.

comfyture, he went out of the batayll & tourned the
targe behynd, and sporyd hys hors, & fled fast toward
thoost of the sarasyns / and geffray was at that syde,

4 that wel perceyued hym, & demed wel by hys ryche
armures that it was he, or some grete lord of the
sarasyns.   Thenne he broched hys hors with the sporys
after the saudan, and cryed to hym, 'retourne, or thou

8 shalt dey! For I shuld haue grete vergoyne yf I smote
the behynd / but alwayes, yf thou not retourne, nedes
I most do soo.'   And whan the sawdan vnderstod
hym, he sporyd hys hors, & hasted hym more than he

12 dide tofore / and geffray, that ryght dolaunt was that
he might not ouertake hym, cryed to hym ayen,
sayeng: 'Fy on the! recreaunt coward; that art so
wel horsed, & so nobly & surely armed, and yet darest

16 not abyde a man alone / retourne, or I shal slee the
fleeyng' / how be it, that shal be ayenst my wyll.'
And thenne the saudan, vergoynous of geffrays wordes,
that for fere of a man alone he fledd / retourned at

20 the corner of þe wode, nygh by thoost of the sarasyns,
in that same place where as geffray had that day
embusshed hys peuple / and putte hys shild tofore hys
brest, and the spere in the rest, & thus he cryed to

24 geffray : 'What art thou, þat so hastly folowest me /
by mahon! that shal be to thy grete dommage.' /
'and for thy prouffyt I am not come thus ferre,' said
geffray / 'but syth that myn name thou axest, thou

28 shalt [1]it knowe.   I am Geffray with the grete toeth,
broþer to the kinges Vryan & guyon / and what art
thou?'   'By mahon,' said the saudan, 'that shalt thou
knowe / I am the saudan of Damaske.   And knowe

32 thou, that I were not so joyous who that had gyuen me
a C thousand besans of gold, as I am to haue fond the
so at myn ease, For thou mayst me not escape / I deffy
the, by machomet my god.'   'By my feyth,' said

36 Geffray, 'nother thou nor thy god I preyse not a

When discomfited he flies to the Saracen host.

Geffray recognizes him, and cries to him,

'Return, or thou shalt die!'

He hastes away the faster;

but Geffray again calls on him.

At last the sultan turns round and asks his name.

[1] fol. 167 b.

Geffray replies that he is brother to Urian and Guion, and demands his adversary's name.

The sultan tells him, and defies Geffray.

rotyn dogge ; For soone thou shalt fynd me nerer the,
to thyn euyl helthe / and yf it playeþ to god, my
creatour, thou shalt not escape.' /

Geffray cries that
he will not
escape.

Geffray and the
sultan go apart,
then run upon
each other.

Here sayth thystorye, that Geffray & the saudan, &
that bothe were of grete courage & strength,
reculed eche fro other, and syn ranne vpon eche other /
and the Saudan valyauntly smote geffray, & tronchoned
his spere vpon his shild / but it is wel to byleue that &
the noble & valyaunt geffray, at this first coure, faylled

Geffray bears the
sultan to the
earth

not ; For he smote the Saudan by suche radeur, that he
lefte hym out of hys arsoun, & bare hym vnto therthe.
and so passed foorth, and immedyatly toke in hys hand 1!
hys good swerd / and pretendyng that men shuld speke
of his fayttes & valyaunces, he smote the saudan by

He cleaves his
helmet,

suche vertu that he perced hys helmet, and effoundred
hys heed almost to the brayne, so that the sawdan was l(
sore astonyed and euyl bestad, in suche wyse that he

and is about to
take it from his
head,

nother sawe nor herd / but as geffray wold haue
alyghted to haue take the saudans helmet, to haue

¹ fol. 168.

brought it to hys bretheren, & to see yf he ¹ was deed, 2(

when he sees
sixty Saracens,
who cry, ' Your
end is come.'

he perceyued wel thre score sarasyns, that cryed after
hym, & said : ' By my lawe, false crysten, your ende
is come.' And whan geffray vnderstode it, he sporyd

Geffray smites
the first dead,

hys hors, & brandysshed the swerd ; and the fyrst that 2(
he recountred, he smote doun to therthe al deed. And
who that had be there, he had seen hym execute noble
faytes & armes, as of one man deffendyng hys lyf ; For

and slays many
others.

geffray cutte and smote of heedes & armes, and dyed 2!
the place with grete effusyon of sarasyns blood / and
they casted at hym sperys & dartes, and made grete
peyne for to haue had ouerthrawen hym to therth.

The sultan comes
to his senses,

And thenne the saudan was come at hymself ayen, 3!
and stode vp al astonyed, as he had come fro slepe /
he loke at ryght syde of hym, and mounted on hys
hors, & sawe the batayll, where he perceyued wel
geffray, that made grete occysyon of sarasyns / and was 3(

geffray wounded & hurt in many places of his body.
Thenne cryed the saudan, admonnestyng' his peple,   and incites his
people against
Geffray,
sayeng / 'auaunt ! worthy sarasyns / by mahomid, yf
4 he vs escape, I shal neuer haue joye ; For who might
bryng hym to an euyl ende, the resydu were not to be
doubted.' Thenne was geffray assaylled on all partes /
& he deffended hym hardyly & so valyauntly, that no   who defends him-
self valiantly,
8 sarasyn durste hym abyde / but casted at hym fro ferre
sperys, darts, stones & arowes / vyretons & quarelles,
with theire crosbowes / but it semed not that he ¹made   ¹ fol. 168 b.
ony force therof / but as a hongre wolf renneth vpon   and
as a hungry wolf
12 sheep / so dide he renne vpon the enemyes of god.   runs upon sheep,
so runs Geffray
upon the enemies
of God.
'By my goddes, Appolyn & mahon,' sayd thenne the   The sultan cries
that Geffray is
saudan / 'this is not a man / but it is a grete dyuell,   either a great
devil or the
come out of hell / or the Cristen god, which is come   Christian God.
16 hither to distroye our lawe' / And, For certayn, geffray
was in this auenture wel by the space of two heures.

In this parel was geffray vnto tyme that the new
knight, which had be with hym in garende, which
20 had sene hym departe after the saudan / cam at him
with wel a C men of armes, For he loued hym entierly.
And thenne, whan he approched the wode, he perceyued   Geffray's new
knight sees his
the batayll, and sawe the sawdan, that dyde his best   lord's danger,
24 for to hurt & dommage Geffray, that faught alone
ayenst mahondys peuple ; wherfore he said / 'cursed
be he of god, that shal not helpe hym now' / and the
knightes peple ansuerd, 'to theire euyl helthe they
28 haue recountred geffray.' And forthwith they broched   and rushes at
the head of his
theire horses with theire sporys, & came to the   people to the
rescue.
batayll. but assoone as the saudan perceyued the
socours, he sporyd hys hors, & hastly fled toward   The sultan takes
flight.
32 thoost / & left his peple in that plyght, of the which
neuer one escaped, but were al slayne. Thenne whan
geffray perceyued the new knight, that so wel had
socoured hym, he thanked hym moche, & sayd : 'My   Geffray thanks
the knight,
36 frend, suche rooses ben good, & of swete odour / & the

lorde that hat about hym suche cheualrye, may take
his rest surely.' 'Sire,' said the knyght, ' I haue not
¹ fol. 168.
doo that thing' wherof I owe to be ¹rewarded, For
euery trew seruaunt oweth to take heede to thonour &
prouffyt of hys maister and lord. And thenne, syth it
is soo / no reward ought not to be had therfore / but
departe we hens, For it is tyme that ye take your rest :
ye haue do this day that wel may suffyse. & also we
be lytel nombre of peuple, & nygh our enemyes, that
haue grete puyssaunce / and your woundes and sores
who advises him
to return to the
Christian host ;
must be vysyted and ouerseue / and also, it me semeth
best, that we retourne toward oure oost by our owne
wyll / than yf by force we were constrayned to
retourne ; For no doubte / who that retourneth fleyng,
& is chassed by hys enemyes / that may be to hym but
because it is
often better to
flee than to abide
a foolish enter-
prise.
Geffray follows
the knight's
counsel.
On the way back
they find the field
covered with the
slain Saracens,
who have lost
xxv. Ml men.
blame / how be it, that oftyme it is said / that better
it is to flee, þan to abyde a folysshe enterpryse.' Thenne
said geffray : ' Fayre sire, at this tyme we shal byleue
your counseyll.' And they thenne departed, and went
toward theire oost, & fonde in theire way the feldes
sowen with sarasyns deed. And wete it wel, that
the same day, byfore none, the sarasyns lost wel xxvⁿ
thousand men, that by fayt of armes were al slayne /
and there escaped, fleeyng, XL. Ml. And wete it
also, that the Caliphe and the two saudans, the king
Anthenor and thadmyral of Corles fonde of seuen score
thousand panemes that the euen tofore were in theire
oost, but foure score thousand, wherof they were gretly
abasshed. Now I shal speke of Geffray, that was
retourned to thoost, where he was wel festyed of hys
bretheren, and of theire baronye / and his woundes
² fol. 168 b.
Geffray's wounds
are tended, but
they do not
oblige him to
leave off his
armour.
were vysyted by the Cyrurgyens, that ²said that he
shuld not leue the harneys therfor : and they all
thanked god. And now I shal shew of the sawdan. /

Thystorye sayth, that whan the saudan was departed
fro the batayll, he walaped tyl he came to the

sarasyns oost, where as he fond his peple al abasshed,   The sultan gallops to the Saracen host.
For they wend he had be slayn. And whan they sawe   They thought him to be dead, so receive him with joy.
hym, they made grete joye, & made to hym theire
4 obeyssaunce, and asked how he had exployted. 'By
mahomid,' sayd þe saudan / 'lytel or nought haue I
doo, For my peple is al deed.' And incontynent he
was desarmed, & recounted them al thauenture. And   He relates his adventure.
8 the two oostes rested them that night, without ony
approching or cours don of neyther partye. /

Here sheweth thystorye, that on the morow by   In the morning the Christians arm
    tymes, the Crysten armed them, & rengid &
12 ordeyned them in batayll, and lefte good watche for to
kepe theire lodgys / and them that were wounded &
hurt, that myght bere no harneys / and marched foorth   and march against the enemy.
in fayre ordynaunce toward thenemyes. In the van-
16 warles were geffray, & the maister of rodes, & theire
peple ; & good arblasters were vpon the wynges, wel
rengid. And in the grete batayll was the king Vryan /
and the king Guyon conduyted the ryergard / and so
20 long they marched, that they sawe thoost of the
sarasyns / And anoone was made thenne, on bothe
sydes, a meruayllous cry / with whiche they marched
that one ayenst that other. And bygan the batayll by   The archers begin the battle.
24 the archers and arblasters so aspre that thayer was
obscurid with the quarelles & arowes, that flewh so
thyk. ¹The valyaunt geffray was in the Formest   ¹ fol. 170.
frount of his peuple, and whan the shotte seaced, he
28 toke his sheld & hys spere in escryeng 'Lusynen' by   Geffray shouts, 'Lusignan,' and rushes upon the Saracens.
thre tymes, and smote his hors with his sporys, &
thrested in to myddes of his enemys so swyftly that
the maister of Rodes coude not folowe hym. Ther was
32 thenne horryble bruyt with theire cryes / that one
cryed 'Damaske' / that other / 'barbarye' / some
cryed 'bandas,' & some 'anthioche,' and other were
that cryed 'cordes' / and geffray & his peple cryed
36 'Lusynen & Rodes.' There made the thre bretheren

MELUSINE.   U

so mernayllous faytes of armes / that not only the
sarasyns were abasshed / but also the crystens merneylled
therof. The saudans of Damaske, & of barbarye, perceyued the thre bretheren, that so ouerthrew & slew
theire peple; wherfore they, with xx. M¹ sarasyns,
couched theire sperys & rane vpon them. There
reforced the batayll / and with that ¹cours the cristen
the lengthe of a spere ferre. And whan the thre
bretheren saw the sarasyns, that thus ouerrane theire
peple / bygan to crye ‘Lusynen,’ & said, admounestyng
theire peple / ‘auaunt, lordes barons! these dogges
may not long⁴ withstand our armes.’ And thenne the
Cristen toke herte corageous, & vygourously made an
horryble cours vpon theire enemys; wherby the stour
was strong, & the batayll mortal.² For they ouerthrew
& slough many sarasyns. Thenne was per Geffray,
that effoundred heedes vnto the brayne, & smote doun
to therthe al that he recountred with his swerd;
Whiche perceyued thadmyral of ⁵Cordes, that smote on
the Cristen. Thenne thresed geffray thrugh the prees,
& cam and smote thadmyral by suche vertu, that he
brake bothe helmet & heed vnto the brayne. There
was the prees grete, For ther came the two saudants
and theire puyssaunce, that supposed wel to haue
redressed thadmyrall vpon his hors / but it was for
nought, For he was deed. Thenne came there Vryan,
and sawe the saudan of barbarye, pat moche hated
hym, for cause that he had slayn the saudan his vncle
in Cypre. Thenne came Vryan, & smote hym by
suche strengthe, that he made hys lyft arme to flee fro
the body. And whan the saudan sawe hym thus
arayed, he went out of the batayll, & made ten knightes
to conduyte hym to damaske / and neuertheles faught
euer the sarasyns, For the saudan of damaske, & the
caliphe of bandas, & the king authenor held them in

¹ Fr. se reculèrent le long d'une lance.　　² Fr. greigneur.

vertu. There was grete doleur, & grete pestylence.
And wete it wel, that the Cristens were sore dommaged /
but as the veray cronykle sayth, the sarasyns receyued
4 there ouergrete dommage & losse, For of them were
slayn XL. M¹ & more / and dured the batayll vnto
euen tyme, that they withdrew them eyther other part
to theire lodgyses. And on the morne the Caliphe, &
8 the king anthenor, & the residu of theire peuple, withdrew them in to the Cite of Damaske. And whan the
thre bretheren vnderstod it, they went & lodged, with
theire puyssausce, tofore Damaske. And wete it wel,
12 they were gretly febled, & the more part of them hurt.
And there they rested them by the space of VIII
¹dayes, without sawtyng ne scarmysshing.

T̲hystorye sheweth vnto vs that the kyng Vryan
16   and hys bretheren and the maister of Rodes were
ryght dolaunt & wroth for the grete losse of theire pepla.
For wel they sawe that yf the sarasyns assembled new
men, it myght come therof some euyl to them. For
20 wel they had lost viii^M of theire men. But at that
other part were the saudans al abasshed. For they
knew not the dommage that the Crysten had receyued.
And they had Counseyll that they shuld requyre kyng
24 Vryan journey of traytye vpon fourme of peas / and so
they dide / And the kyng hadd counseyll that he shuld
be greable to it. And the iourney was assygned by
thaccorde of bothe partes on the iii^de day atwix the
28 lodgys & the toun / and were the trews graunted &
were delyuered good pledges & hostages of both partyes.
And thenne came they of the toun to selle theire
marchaundyse in to the Crystens oost. Thenne came
32 to the iourney of traytye that was assigned the saudans
and theire Counseyll. And of the other part came
Vryan & hys bretheren, the maister of Rodes & theire
baronye with them, and spake, & communyked togidre
36 of one thinge & of other, / and dede so moch of eyther

Marginal notes:

Both sides are hurt, but the Saracens the more.

The battle stops at eventide.

Next morning the Saracens, greatly enfeebled, retire to Damascus.

They rest viii. days.

¹ fol. 171.

Urian and his brethren

see that if the Saracens assemble new men they may lose, for they had lost viii. M¹ men.

But the sultans are abashed, and ask for a treaty.

It is granted.

U 2

The Saracens are
to pay the Chris-
tians all the costs
of their voyage,

and a yearly
tribute to Urian
and his heirs of
xxx. Ml besaunts
of gold;

partye that they were accorded, and pacyfyed by co
dycion that the Sarasyns shuld restore to the lord
Cristen all theire expenses & costes made in their vyag
& to payo yerly vnto kyng Vryan & hys heyres f
euermore xxx^{Ml} besauns of gold / and trews were ma
betwenc them for Ȼ & one yere, and therof we
letres patentes sealled. And this couuenaunt a
trayte the sawdan of Barbarye that great doleur felt

1 fol. 171 b.

also they promise
not to wage war
against Urian,
Guion, or the
Master of
Rhodes.

hys sholder for hys arme that ^{1}was of / and the ky
of Anthioche / ratyfyed, / promyttyng that neuer th
shuld bere armes ayenst king Vryan, / ayenst Guyon
Armanye nor ayenst the maister of Rodes, nor the
peple / and that yf other kynges or prynces sarasy
wold attempte ony werre anenst them, they shuld l
them haue knowleche therof assoone as they mig
know it / and yf thrugh that cause they had wei
ayenst ony king or prynce, Vryan promysed them
socoure and gyue them comfort with all hys power, /
in lyke wyse kyng Guyon & the maister of Rod

The brethren re-
turn to Jaffa, ac-
companied by
the Saracen
kings.

The sultan makes
much of Geffray,
but he will re-
ceive no gifts.

promysed to them / And soone after the thre breþe
and theire peple retourued to the port of Japhe. A
the saudan of Damaske, the Calyphe of bandas, & t
kynge Anthenor conueyed hym thither. And t
sawdan made moche of Geffray, and proffred hym gr
yeftes, but he wold nought receyue / but that he moc
thanked hym of his curtoysye.

Urian and Guion
take leave of
Geffray and go to
Jerusalem.

Thystorye sayth that Vryan & Guyon entred in
the see, & vowed themself to Jherusalem. Wh
fore they toke leue of geffray theire broþer, and h
moche thanked of hys noble ayde & socours / and a
they departed fro the porte of Japhe, and rowed towa

Geffray sails to
Rochelle, where
he is honourably
received.

On the morn he
rides to his father
at Merment.

Jherusalem. And Geffray toke hys way by the s
toward Rochelle, & saylled so long that he came the
where as he was honourably receyued & gretly festyed
And on the morn he departed, and rode with hys co
panye tyl he came to Merment, where he fond bot

his fader & and his moder, that knew tofore how he &
his brethern had wrought beyond the grete see &
festyed hym gretly / raymondyn hys fader kept a grete

Raymondin gives
a great feast for
joy of his return.

4 feste & grete Court for joy that he had of his commyng.
But soone aftir [1] came there tydynges that in the
Countre of the Garende was a grete geaunt that by hys
grete pryde & orgueyll, & by his grete strength held all

1 fol. 172.
Tidings come
from Garende of
a great giant who
keeps the coun-
try in subjection.

8 the Countre in subgection. For no man durst gaynsay
his commandement. Of these tydynges was Raymondin
ryght dolaunt ; how be it he made of it no semblaunt,
feryng that geffray shuld knowe & here of it. For he

Raymondin hides
his grief in fear
that Geffray will
see it.

12 knew hym of so grete courage that he wold goo fyght
with the geaunt yf he vnderstod where he was. But
it might not be kept so secret but that geffray vnderstode þe talkyng of hym / and that come to hys

16 knowlege / he sayd in this wyse / 'how dyuel my
bretheren and I haue subdued & made trybutary the
saudan of damask & hys complyces, and that hound
alone shal be suffred to hold my faders ryght enhery-

20 taunce in subgection / by my sowle, in his euyl helthe

Geffray swears
that he will at-
tack the giant.

he thought to vsurpe it, For it shal cost hym hys lyf yf
I may.' Thenne came Geffray to hys fader, & thus
said to hym. 'My lord, I merueyll of you that are a

He tells his father
that he marvels
that he has suf-
fered Guedon to
keep his country
in subjection so
long.

24 knight of so noble enterpryse how ye haue suffred so
long of that hound Guedon the geaunt, that hath putte
your countre of garande in subgection / by god, my
lord, shame is therof to you.' Whan raymondin vnder-

28 stod hym, he said / ' Geffray, fayre sone, wete it is not
long syn we knowe therof / & that we haue suffred
vnto your joyful commyng. For we wold not trouble
the fest / but doubte you not, guedon shal haue hys

Raymondin says
the giant shall
have his pay-
ment.

32 payment after his deserte. He slew my granfader in
the Counte of pouthieu, as it was told me in bretayn,
whan I went thither for to fyght with Olyuer, sone to
Josselyn, that betrayed my fader.' /

fol. 172 b.

Thanne ansuerd Geffray : 'I ne wot nor wyl not enquyre of thinges past, syth that my predecessours
haue therof had thonour & are come to theire aboue /
but at this tyme present that Iniurye shal be soone
mended yf it plese god & I may / and as touching your
personne ye ought not to meue your self for suche a
theef & palyard; For I, with ten knightes of myn

Geffray says he
is ready to go
against him with
ten knights.

houshold only for to hold me companye / not for ayde
that I wyl haue of them ayenst hym, I shal goo fyght
with hym' / And whan Raymondyn hys fader vnder

Raymondin sor-
rowfully con-
sents.

stod hys wordes he was dolaunt & sorowful, and thus
said to hym / 'sethen it may none other wyse be / goo
thou by the grace of god.' And thenne geffray toke
his leue of his fader & of hys moder, and putte hym

Geffray sets out
to find Guedon,

self on the way toward garande accompanyed with
knightes, and there where he passed by he enquyred
after guedon where he might fynd hym / And wel i

and men marvel
why he wants
him,

is trouth that it was told hym where the geaunt was
But men were meruaylled, & asked of geffray why he
speryd after hym. 'By my feyth,' ansuerde geffray

Geffray answers
that he brings
Guedon his pay-
ment for his
outrages.

'I bryng hym the trybut & payment that he by his
foly & outrage thaketh vpon my faders lordship / but
it is neyther gold ne syluer / but it is only the poynt
of my spereheed, For none other payment he shal re
ceyue of me but strokes of my swerd withal.'   And
whan the good peple herd hym thus speke, they said
to hym in this wyse : 'By my feyth, geffray, ye vnder

¹ fol. 173.
They tell Geffray
that a hundred
like him could
not withstand
the giant

take grete foly, ¹For an hondred suche as ye be shuld
not be able to withstand hys cruelte.' 'doubte you
not,' said geffray / 'but lete me haue the feer alone' ,
and they held theire peas, For they durst not make hym
wroth. For moche they fered hys fyersnes & yre, of
whiche he was replenysshed / but þey conduyted hym
vnto a leghe nygh to the sayd geauntis retrette or

Geffray is con-
ducted near the
giant's dwelling

pryue dwellyng / and þene they sayd to geffray : 'Sire,
ye may lightly fynd hym at yonder place within the

forest' / and geffray ansuerd, 'I wold fayne see hym,
For to fynd hym I am come hither' / And here
cesseth thystorye to speke of geffray / and sheweth of
4 Raymondyn & of Melusyne. /

The veray and trew hystorye witnesseth that Raymondin & Melusyne were at merment making
grete joye for the prosperous estate & good Fortune of
8 theire children; but this joye was soone tourned to
grete sorowe, For as ye haue herd how thystorye saith
tofore that Raymondin promysed to Melusyne that
neuer on the satirday he shuld not enquere of her nor
12 desyre to see her that day.   It is trouth that on a
Satirday a lytel byfore dyner tyme, Raymondyn vnderstode that hys brother the Erle of Forests was come
to Merment for to see hym & hys Noble Court.
16 wherof Raymondin was ryght Joyous, but aith grete
myschief came to hym therfore as herafter shal be
shewed.   Thenne made Raymondin grete apparayll &
ryght noble for to receyue his brother / And shortly to
20 shewe, he came & recountred hys brother [1] with noble
company & welcommed hym honourably, & dide moche
that one of that other, & went to chircheward togidre /
And after the deuyne seruice was don they came
24 agayn to the palleys where al thinges were redy to
dyner / they wesshe theire handes and syn sett them
at dyner and þey were worshipfully scrued / ha / las !
thenne bygan a part of the doleur & heuynes. For hys
28 brother coude not kepe hym, but he asked after Melusyne, suyeng in this manere : 'My brother, where is
my sustir Melusyne ? lete her come, for moche I desyre
to see her.' And Raymondyn, whiche thought none
32 euyl, ansuerd, 'she is not here at this tyme / but to
morne ye shal see her & shal make you good chere.'
But for that ansuere the Erle of Forests held not hys
peas / but thus said ayen to his brother : 'Ye are my
36 brother / I owe not to hyde to you your dyshonour.

One set of folk says your wife goes to another man every Saturday,

and others that she is a spirit of the fairies, and goes on Saturdays to do penance.
I know not which to believe.'

¹ fol. 174.
Raymondin rises from the table full of jealousy; he girds on his sword and goes to the place where Melusine retires on Saturdays.
He finds a strong door,

and pierces a hole in it with his sword.

Now, fayre brother, wete it that the commyn talking the peple is, that Melusyne your wyf every satirday the yere is with another man in auoultyre / & so blyr ye are by her sayeng' that ye dare not enquere n knoweth wher she becommeth or gooth / and also oth sayen, & make them strong' that she is a spyryte of tl fayry, that on every satirday maketh hir penaunce. wot not to whiche of bothe I shal byleue / and f none other cause I am come hither but to aduerty you therof.' Whan Raymondin thenne vnderstod the wordes that his brother hym said he roos ¹fro the tab and entred in to his chambre, and anoone all esprys with yre & Jalousy, withall toke hys swerd & gird it about hym, & syn went toward the place where Melusyne went every satirday in the yer / and wh he cam there he fond a doore of yron thikk & strong and wete it wel he had neuer be tofore that tyme ferre thitherward / and whan he perceyued the doo of yron he toke hys swerd, that was hard & tempere with fyn stele, and with the poynte of it dyde so moc that he perced the doore, and made a holl in it, a loked in at that holl, and sawe thenne Melusyne th was within a grete bathe of marbel stone, where we steppis to mounte in it, and was wel xv foot of lengtl and therin she bathed herself, makyng there her pen tence as ye shal here herafter. /

Cap. XXXVII. Here aftir foloweth ho
     Raymondin by the admounesting of h;
     brother beheld Melusyne hys wyf with
     the bathe, wherfor he toke hys broth
     the Erle of Forest in grete indignacio

fol. 174 b.

Thystorye sayth in this partye that Raymond
     stode so long at the yron doore that he perced
with the poynte of his swerd, wherby he might wel

all that was within the Chambre / and sawe melusyne   Raymondin sees
within the bathe vnto her nauell, in fourme of a woman   Melusine in the bath,
kymbyng her heere, and fro the nauel dounward in   half woman, half serpent.
4 lyknes of a grete serpent, the tayll as grete & thykk as
a barell, and so long it was that she made it to touche
oftymes, while that raymondyn beheld her, the rouf of
the chambre that was ryght hye.   And whan Ray-
8 mondyn perceyued it, wete it wel that he was ryght   He becomes sorrowful, and
dolaunt and sorowful & not without cause, and coude   laments that he has betrayed
neuer hold hys tonge, but he said, 'My swete loue, now   her.
haue I betrayed [1]you, & haue falsed my couenaunt by   [1] fol. 175.
12 the ryght fals admounestyng of my brother, and haue
forsworne myself toward you.'   Raymondin thenne was
smyten to the herte with suche sorow & dystresse that
vnnethe he coude speke / and pensefull with a heuy
16 contenaunce retourned hastly toward hys chambre, and   He returns hastily to his cham-
toke some wax wherwith he went & stopped the holl   ber, to procure wax to stop the
that he had made at the doore of yron, and syn came   hole in the door.
agayn to the hall where he found hys brother.   And   This done he re-
20 thenne whan therle of Forest perceyued hym and sawe   turns to the hall,
hys heuy contenaunce / wel supposed he that he had
fond Melusyne in some shamful fayt, and said to him
in this wyse : 'My brother, I wyst it wel / haue ye not
24 fond as I said ?'   Thenne cryed Raymondin to hys
brother of Forest in this manyere : [2]'Voyde this place,   and orders his brother out of
fals traytour, For thrugh your fals reporte I haue falsed   the place,
my feyth ayenst the moost feythfullest & truest lady
28 that euer was borne.   ye are cause of the losse of al my
worldly joye & of my totall destruction / by god, yf I
byleued my courage, I shuld make you to dey now of   and tells him that were he not
an euyl deth / but rayson naturel kepeth & deffendeth   his brother he should die.
32 me therfro, bycause that ye are my brother / goo your
way & voyde my syght, that al the grete maisters of

[2] Fr.: *Fuiez d'icy, faulx triste, car vous m'avez fait, par
votre tresmauvais rapport, ma foy parjurer contre la plus
loyalle et la meilleure des dames qui oncques naquit, après celle
qui porta notre seigneur Ihesucrist.*

hell may conduyte you thither' / And whan
Erle of Forest apperceyued Raymondyn his brotl

that was in so grete yre, he went out of the halle &
his peple, & mounted on horsbak and rode as fast
they might toward Forests ryght pensefull & he

repentyng hym of hys folysah enterpryse ; for he kn
wel that Raymondin his brother wold neuer loue h
nor see hym. Here I leue to speke ¹of hym, & s
shewe you of Raymondin that entred in to his cham

wooful & angre. /

'Halas, Melusyne,' sayd Raymondin, 'of whom
the world spake wele, now haue I lost you
euer. Now haue I fonde the ende of my Joye / s
the begynnyng is to me now present of myn euerl
yng heuynes / Farwel beaute, bounte, swetenes, ar
ablete / Farwel wyt, curtoysye, & humilite / Farwel
my joye, al my comfort & myn hoop / Farwel m
herte, my prowes, my valyaunce, For that lytel
honour whiche god had lent me, it came thrugh yo
noblesse, my swete & entierly belouyd lady. Ha /

falsed & blynd Fortune, aigre, sharp, & byttir / wel h
thou ouerthrawen me fro the hyest place of thy wh
vnto the lowest part of thy mansyon or dwellyng pla
there as Jupyter festyeth with sorow & heuynes, t
caytyf & vnhappy creatures / be þou now cursed

god. by the I slough ayenst my wyll my lord, m
vncle, the whiche deth thou sellest me to dere. hels
thou had putte and sette me in high auctoryte thru
the wyt and valeur of the wysest, the fayrest, & mo
noble lady of al other / and now by the / fals blyn

traytour and enuyous, I must lese the sight of her
whom myn eyen toke theire fedyng¹ thou now hates
thou now louest, thou now makest / thou now vndos
in the, nys no more surety ne rest than is in a fa
that tourneth at al windes. Halas / helas ! my ryg
swete & tendre loue / by my venymous treson I ha

maculate your excellent fygure / helas! myn herte & al
my wele ye had heeled me clene of my first soore / yt
I haue now rewarded you therfore.   Certaynly yf I

<table>
<tr><td>4 now lese you / none other choys is to me / ¹but to take</td></tr>
</table>

4 now lese you / none other choys is to me / ¹but to take
myn vtermost exill there as neuer after no man lyuyng
shall see me.'

He cries that he
will
¹ fol. 176.
go into exile if
he loses her,

  Here sayeth thistorye, that in suche doleur & be-
8   wayllinges abode raymondin al that nyght tyl it
was day light.   And as sone as aurora might be perceyued, Melusyne came & entred in to the chambre /
and whan Raymondyn herd her come he made sem-
12 blaunt of slepe.   She toke of her clothes, and than al
naked layed herself by hym.   And thenne bygan Raymondyn to sighe as he that felt grete doleur at herte /
and Melusyne embraced hym, & asked what hym eyled,
16 sayeng in this wyse: 'My lord, what eyleth you, be ye
syke?'   And whan Raymondin sawe that she of none
other þing⁴ spake, he supposed that she nothing had
knowen of this faytte / but for nought he byleued soo,
20 For she wyst wel that he had not entamed nor shewed
the matere to no man / Wherfor she suffred at that
tyme & made no semblaunt therof / wherfore he was
right Joyous, and ansuerd to her: 'Madame, I haue be
24 somewhat euyl at ease & haue had an axez² in maner
of a contynue.'   'My lord,' said Melusyne, 'abasshe you
not, For yf it plese god ye shal soone be hole.'   And
thenne he that was right joyous said to her, 'By my
28 feyth, swete loue, I fele me wel at ease for your
commyng' / and she said, 'I am þerof glad' / and
whan tyme requyred they roos and went to here masse /
and soone after was the dyner redy / and thus abode
32 Melusyne with Raymondyn al that day / and on the
morne she toke leue of hym & went to Nyort, where
she bylded a fortresse.   ³And here seaceth thistorye of
her / and retourneth to speke of geffray.

and bewaills all
the night long.

In the morning
Melusine re-
turns.
Raymondin
feigns sleep.

Melusine lies by
him.   He sighs.

Melusine in-
quires what is
wrong.

Raymondin
thinks she does
not know of his
deed.

She does, but
makes no show
of her know-
ledge.

He replies he has
a fever.
Melusine says he
will soon be well.

He says he is
better since her
return.

Melusine goes to
Niort and builds
a fortress.

³ fol. 176 b.

² Fr. *ung peu de fièvre en manière de continue.*

Geffray is received with joy in Garande.

He asks after Guedon, and is taken to his tower of Mermount.

Here sayth thystory, that Geffray cams in garande, where as he was receyued with gret joye / and he asked where the geant guedon held hym self / and, as before is said, they conduyted hym, and shewed to 4 hym the strong tour of Mermount, where the geaunt was, & said: 'Sire, wete it / that yf ye byleue vs, it shal suffyse you to haue sene the toure, & shal retourne

His guides leave.

with vs; For as touching our personnes, we shal goo 8 no neer þat horryble geaunt, algaf you to eyther of vs your pesaunt or weyght of fyn gold.' 'By my feyth, sires,' said geffray, 'I thanke you moche, that thus ferre ye haue brought me.'   13

Geffray dismounts and arms himself.

Geffray thenne, as thystory saith, descendid from his hors, & armed hym, and syn girded hys swerd[1] about hym, & remounted on horsback; and after toke hys sheld, & heng it tofore hys brest: & 16 toke a clubbe of stele, & faste it at tharsons of his sadell; and syn toke a trompe of yuory, and heng it at hys neck behynd; and syn asked hys spere / and thenne said to his tene knightes, in this manere: 20

He tells his knights to wait for him in the valley, and bids them come to him when they hear his horn.

'Fayre lordes, abyde me in this valey / and yf god graunte me the vyctory of the geaunt, I shal thenne blowe this horne / and whan ye shal here it, ye shal lyghtly come to me.' And they were dolaunt that he 24 wold not suffre them to go with hym, and bade hym farwell, prayeng god for hys good spede. Thenne

Geffray mounts to the tower.

departed the valyaunt & hardy geffray, and mounted the montayne; and anoone cam to the first gate of the 28 toure, & found it open / thenne entred he in to the bassecourt, & went toward the dongeon, that strong was to meruayll. And whan he was nygh, he beheld

[2] fol. 177.

it, & moche [2]playsed hym the facion and byldyng of 32 hit; but he sawe the brydge, that was drawen vp. For

He calls to the sleeping giant.

the geante slepte. Thenne he cryed with a hye voys, sayeng in this manere: 'hourys sone & fals geaunt,

[1] hys swerd twice in MS.

cŏme speke with me! For I bryng to the / the syluer
that the peuple of my lord, my fader, owen to the.'
And, for certayn, geffray cryed so long that the geaunt
4 awacked, & came at a wyndowe, and beheld geffray,
armed of al pyeces, mounted vpon a courser, that held
hys spere couched / and thus bygan to crye, with a
lowde voyce, 'knyght! what wold thou haue?' 'By
8 my sowle,' said geffray, 'I seke for the, & for none
other / and I come hither to chalange the, and bring·
with me the trybut that thou hast ouersette vpon the
peuple of my lord, Raymondyn of Lusynen, my fader.'
12 Thenne whan the geant vnderstode geffray, he was
nygh aragid & mad, that of one knight alone was so
bold to make hym warre, & had sette hym so nygh hys
place. but, notwithstanding, when he had wel aduysed
16 hym, he consydered in hym self that he was a man of
grete valyaunce. Thenne the geaunt armed hymself,
and laced the taches of hys helmet; & toke a grete
barre of yron, and a grete sythe of stele, & came to
20 the brydge, and lete it fall; & came in the bassecourt,
& demanded of geffray : 'What art thou, knight, that
art so bold to come hither?' And geffray ansuerd, in
this manere : 'I am geffray with the grete toeth, sone
24 to Raymondyn of Lusynen, that commeth hither to
chalenge the patiz or trybut, that thou takest thrugh
thy grete pryde, of my lord my faders peple.' Thenne
whan Guedon vnderstod it, he bygan to lawhe, and to
28 hym thus said : 'By my feyth, poure fole, for thy grete
hardynes & the grete enterprise ¹of thyn herte, I haue
pyte of the. Now wyl I shew to the curtoysye / that
is, that thou retourne lyghtly to make thy warre in
32 other place ; For wete thou wel, yf now with the were
V. C suche foles as thyself art, yet coudest thou not
endure and withstand my puyssaunce. but for pyte
that I haue to putte to deth so hardy a knight, as I
36 suppose thou art, I gyue the lycence & congie to

who comes to his
window and asks
what he wants.

Geffray answers
he bears him his
tribute for his
misduings.

The giant is
enraged;

he arms

and descends to
the bassecourt,
and again asks
who Geffray is.

He answers that
he is the son of
Raymondin, and
has come to chal-
lenge the tribute
he has heretofore
exacted.

Guedon laughs
at him,

¹ fol. 177 b.

and tells him to
go back, because
V. C like Geffray
could not over-
come him.

retourne to Raymondyn thy fader / goo thou lyghtly hens / and for loue of the I shal forgyue to thy faders peple the payement of a holl yere of the trybut that they owe me.' Thenne whan geffray with the grete toth herd that the geaunt made so lytel of hym, & that as nought he preysed hym, he was of it ryght dolaunt, and said to hym in this wyse: 'Meschaunt creature, thou alredy ferest me moch / I wyl wel thou wete that of thy curtoysy I sett nought by, For thus spakest thou for the grete feer that thou hast of my toeth. but wete þou, for certayn, that I shal neuer departe fro this place vnto that tyme I haue separed the lyf fro thy body / and therfor, haue pyte of thyself, & not of me, For I hold the for deed where as thou art / & ryght foorth I deffye ye.' And whan the geaunt herd hym, he made semblaunt of lawghing, sayeng al this : 'Geffray, fool, thou commest in to batayll, & thou mayst not endure one stroke of me only, without I falle the to þe erthe.' And thenne geffray, without ony more sayeng, smote hys hors with hys sporys, and charged hys spere, & dressed hym toward the geaunt, asmoche as the hors might ranne ; and strak hym thrugh the brest by suche strength that he bare hym to the ground, the bely vpward. [1] but the geaunt stert vp lyghtly, in grete yre, & as geffray passed by, he smote hys hors behynd with hys sythe of fyn stele / and whan geffray wyst it, he descended lyghtly from hys hors, & came toward the geaunt, the swerd drawen. and thenne came the geaunt toward hym, holding his sythe in his hand : where as was grete batayll.

Cap. XXXVIII.   How geffray slough Guedon, the geaunt, in garande.

Al thus, as ye haue herde, geffray was on foot tofore the geaunt, that held his syþe in his fyst, & supposed to haue smyte geffray / but he bare

it vp / & with that, he smote with hys swerd vpon the
hafte[1] of the geantis sythe, that it fell in two pyeces.
And thenne the geaunt toke hys flayel of yron, & gaf
4 geffray a grete buffet vpon his bassynet, wherwith he
was almost astonyed. Thenne came [2]Geffray toward
hys hors, that laye on the erthe, & toke hys clubbe of
yron, that hyng at tharsons of hys sadell, & lightly
8 tourned toward the geaunt, that haunced hys flayel,
supposyng[t] to dyscharge it vpon geffray / but geffray,
that was pert in armes, smote with hys clubbe suche a
stroke vpon the flayel, that he made it to flee out of the
12 geantis handes. And thenne the geaunt, full of yre,
put hys hand in hys bosom, where were thre hamers of
yron; of the whiche he toke one, & casted it by suche
radeur, that yf geffray had not receyued that strok vpon
16 his clubbe, he might haue be myschieuyd therwith / by
the force wherof hys cluble flough out of hys handes:
and the geaunt toke it vp / but geffray drew lightly his
swerd, & cams to the geaunt, that supposed to haue
20 smyte geffray with the cluble of stele on the heed / but
geffray, that was light & strong, fled the stroke, & the
geaunt faylled; & the stroke fell to therth, by the force
wherof the heed of the clubbe entred in to the grounde
24 a large foot deep. And thenne geffray smote the geaunt
vpon the ryght arme with hys swerd, in suche vyolence,
& hys swerde was so sharp & trenchaunt, that he made
it to flygh fro hys body to the erthe. Thenne was þe
28 geant gretly abasshed, whan he sawe thus his arme
lost / notwithstanding, he haunced his swerd with hys
other hand, and trowed to haue smyte geffray at herte /
but geffray kept hym wel therfro, & smote the geaunt
32 vpon the legge, vnder the knee, by suche strength that
he smote it in two. Thenne the geaunt fell, & gaf
suche an horryble crye, that al the valey sowned þerof,
so that they that bode for geffray, herd it / but they

who cuts it in
halves.

The giant takes
his flail and
smites Geffray.

[2] fol. 173 b.

Geffray takes his
iron club

and knocks the
flail out of the
giant's hands.

The giant throws
a hammer at
Geffray

and drives his
club out of his
hands.

The giant thinks
to hit Geffray,

but he flees the
stroke.

Then Geffray
smites off the
giant's right arm.

The giant tries to
strike at Geffray
with the other
hand, but he cuts
the giant's leg in
two.

The giant falls,
and utters a
horrible cry.

---

[1] Fr. *manche*, a haft or handle. Written 'haste' in MS.

fol. 179.

Geffray cuts off the giant's head. He blows his horn, and the people land God when they know the giant is dead.

Geffray tells them that the giant will never trouble them again.

knew not the certayn what it was / but ¹alwayes they had grete meruayll of that horryble sowne. Thenne geffray cutte the taches of the geant helmet, and after cutte of his heed / and syn toke hys horne, & blew it; Wherby his peple, that were in the valey, might here it / and so dide other that were of the countre / and by þat they knew the geaunt was deed; wherof they gaaf lawdyng· to our lord god denoutely. and imme- diatly they mounted the mountayns, & came to the place, where they fonde geffray, that said to them of the Countre / 'this fals traytour geaunt shal neuer more patyse you, For he as now this tyme present, hath neyther lust nor talent to aske ony tribut of you.' And whan they perceyued the body & the heed of the geaunt, lyeng in two partes, they were al abasshed of hys gretnes, For he was XV foot of lengthe / sayeng to geffray, that he had enterprysed a grete faytte, to haue putte hym self in so grete parel tassayll suche a dyuell / 'By my feyth,' said geffray, 'the parel is past. For, fayre lordes, I wyl that ye knowe / thing· neuer bygonne / hath neuer ende / In euery thing most be bygynnyng, tofore the ende commeth.'

fol. 179 b.

²Cap. XXXIX. How Froymond, brother to Geffray, was professed monke at Mayl-lezes, by consentement of hys fader & moder.

The tidings of Geffray's deed are spread in the country

Geffray sends the giant's head to his father

Moche were thenne the knightes abasshed, as the storye reherceth, of this that geffray had slayn the geaunt, that was so grete & mighty. And the tydinges therof were spred in the Countre, & in the marches about. And also geffray sent, by two of hys knightes, to hys fader, the heed of the geaunt. And in the meane season he went & dysported hym in the Countre, where as he was gretly fested, & receyued

with grete joye, & presented with gret ryches.   Here I
shal leue to speke of hym / & shal shew you of Froymond, hys brother, who that prayed so moche hys fader
4 and his moder, that they were greable that he shuld be
professed monke at Maylleses / & so he was shorne, by
the consentement of hys fader, & of [1]his moder;
Wherof thabbot & all conuent was ryght joyous.
8 And wete it wel, there were within the place to the
nombre of an hondred monkes.   And yf they had
thenne grete joye of ·Froymonds professyon / it was
afterward reuersed in to grete doleur / as ye shal here
12 herafter / but wete it wel, that it was not thrughe the
faytte of Froymond, For he was right deuoute, & ledd
a relygious lyf / but by the rayson of hym came to
the place a merueyllous auenture.   It is trouth that the
16 two forsaid knightes that geffray sent vnto hys fader
with the heed of the geant, rode tyl they came to
merment, wher they fond Raymondin, & presented
hym with the heed of the geaunt, wherof he was joyful.
20 And the heed was moche loked on / & euery man
merueaylled how geffray durst assayll hym.   And thenne
Raymondin sent a lettre to geffray, how Froymond, his
brother, was professed monke at thabbey of maylleses.
24 helas! that message was the cause of the trystefull
doleur of the departyng of his wyf, wherof neuer
after he nor she had hertly joye, as ye shal here herafter.   Trouth it was that Raymondyn gaaf thenne
28 grete yeftes to the two knightes, and delyuered them
the lettre; and sayd that they shuld grete wel geffray,
& that they shuld bere the hed of the geaunt to
Melusyne, that was at Nyort: For it was not ferre out
32 of theire way.   Thenne so departed the two knightes,
& held on theire way tyl they came to nyort, where
they fonde their lady; the whiche they salued, &
presented her with the heed of the geaunt.   Wherof
36 she was ryght joyous, [2]and sent it to Rochelle, and was

MELUSINE.

Froimond prays
his father and
mother to
allow him to
become a monk
at Mailleses.

[1] fol. 180.

They consent;
he is shorn.

The abbot is
glad,

but Froimond's
profession causes
them much pain
afterward.

The knights
bring Raymondin
the giant's head,

He sends back
word to Geffray
how Froimond
was professed
monk.

He gives the
knightes gifts,

and bids them
take the head to
Melusine.

[2] fol. 180 b.

X

sette vpon a spere at the gate toward guyenne. *A*
Melusyne gaf the two knight*es* ryche yeft*es* ; and a
that toke theire leue, and went toward the toure
mou*n*tyouet,[1] where geffray was for hys dysport & so
And here cesseth thystory, & sheweth other matere.

Thystory sayth that the tydyng was ancone sp
thrughe the Countre, how geffray with the g
tooth slough the geau*n*t guedon in batay*H*, and a*H* t
that her*d* therof were gretly abasshed.   And for t
tyme regned in northomberlan*d* a geau*n*t that hy
Grymault, & was the moost cruel that eue*r* man so
For he was xvii foot of heyght / and that same g
dyue*H* held hym nygh a mountayne called Brombel
and wete it wel for trouth he had dystroyed a*H* t
Countre about in so moche that there ne durst no
sonne inhabyte nygh hym by eyght or nene leghes
so a*H* the Countre was desert & wyldernes.   It be
that in Northomberlan*d* came tydynge*s* how gef
wit*h* the grete tooth had slayn the geau*n*t gued
Wherfore they of the same Countrey made a g
counsey*H*, that they shuld sende to geffray, & pr
hym so he wold delyuero them of the cruel mur*d*
grymaul*d*, eue*r*y yere duryng hys lyf he shuld h
x. M[1] besans of gold ; & yf he hath yssue male of
body they to possesse the said annuel rente of x.
besans / and yf he hath a doughter to hys heyre, w
be quytte after his decesse of *ou*r sayd trybute.   W]
upon they choose eyght of þe moost noble person
of theire Countre, & sent he*m* in ambaxade tow
geffray / the whiche depa*r*te*d* & came to Mou*n*tyo
where they fonde geffray, to [2]whom they proposed
cause of theire comm*y*ng.   And thenne whan gef
v*n*derstode it / he a*n*suer*d* nobly : ' Fayre lord*es*, I
not reffuse your demande, how be it I shul*d* haue g
thither to fyght wit*h* þat geau*n*t, For I her*d* tydy]

[1] Fr. *Monjouet.*

of hym tofore your commyng', for the pyte that I haue
of the destruction of the peple, & also for to seke
honour. Wete it that now foorthwith I wyl departe
4 with you without ony lenger delay / and by the help
of god I suppose texille the geaunt.' And þey thenne
gaaf hym grete thankinges.

Cap. XL. How the two messangers of Ray-
8 mondin cam in garande toward geffray.

Thenne came the two knyghtes that he had sent
toward hys fader, and salued hym honourably,
and recounted hym the noble chere that they had
12 hadd of hys fader & of his moder, whiche ¹greted hym
wel : ' By my feyth,' said Geffray, ' that playseth me
wel.' and after they delyuered to hym the lettre from
hys fader, which geffray toke & opend it / the tenour
16 of whiche made mencon how Froymond his brother
was shorne monke at Mayllezes. And whan geffray
vnderstod it he was wroth, & shewed thenne so fel &
cruel semblaunt that there ne was so hardy that durst
20 abyde the syght of hym ; but they all voyded the
place except the two knightes and the ambaxatours of
northomberland. /

In this party sheweth thistory, that whan geffray
24 knew the tydynges of Froymonds professyon he
was so dolaunt that almost he went fro his wyt. And
wete it wel that thenne he semed bettre to be araged
& madd than man with rayson. And he said in this
28 wyse : ' how deuell ! had not my fader & my moder
ynough for to entreteyn & kepe thestate of Froymond
my brother, & hym to haue maryed som noble lady of
the land / and not to haue made hym a monke / by
32 god omnipotent these flatterers monkes shal repente
them þerof, For they haue enchaunted my lord my
fader, & haue drawen Froymond with them for to fare

The knights salute Geffray, and tell him of the noble cheer they had at his father's.

¹ fol. 181 b.

They deliver the letter which tells how Froimond had professed himself monk.

Geffray waxes wroth at the news.

He seems to be mad,

and declares that the monks shall repent of their guile and their greed.

X 2

þe bettre by hym / but by the feyth that I owe to g
I shal pay them so, therfore, that they shal neuer ha
neyther lust ne talent to withdraw no noble man to
shorne monke with them.' And thenne he said to t

Geffray tells the embassy that they will have to wait.

bassade of Northomberland: 'Sires, ye muste soiour
a while & abyde my retourn hither / For I must g
to an affayre of myn that toucheth me moche.' A
they that knewe hys wrathe & anger ansuerd: 'I
lord, so shaH we doo with a good wyH.' Thenne ma
geffray his ten knightes to mounte on horsback / a

With his ten knights he goes to Mailleses,
1 fol. 182.

also he armed hym and lept on hys hors / & syn
parted [1]fro Mountyoued, esprysed with grete yre aye
the abbot & Conuent of Maylleses / and at that ty
the said abbot & hys monkes were in Chapitre. A

and finds the monks in chapter.

geffray thanne come to the place, entred, the swe
gird about hym, in to the Chapitre. And whan
perceyued thabbot & hys monkes, he said al on hye

He upbraids them for having shorn his brother monk.

them: 'Ye false monkes / how haue ye had the har
nes to haue enchaunted my brother, in so moche t
thrughe your false & subtyl langage haue shorne h
monke / by the toeth of god yl ye thought it, For
shal drynk therfore of an euyl drynk.' 'helas!
lord,' said thabbot, 'for the loue of god haue mercy
vs / and suffre you to be enfourmed of the truth

The abbot denies having so counselled him.

rayson, For on my Creatour, I nor none of vs aH co
seylled hym neuer therto.' Thenne came Froym

Froimond comes forward and says he became monk of his free will.

foorth, that trowed wel to haue peased the yre
geffray hys brother / and þus said: 'My[2] dere, d
brother / by the body & sowle which I haue gyuen
god, here is no personne, nor within this place that
spake ony word to me touching my professyon, Fo
haue it doon of myn owne free wylle & thrugh de

Geffray says he will pay him with the rest.

cíon.' 'By my sowle,' said geffray, 'so shalt thou
therfore payed with the other, For it shal not
wytted[3] me to haue a brother of myn a monke' /

[2] *By* in MS. (Fr. *Mon.*)   [3] Fr. *reprouché*.

with these wordes he went out of the Chapter, &
shetted the doores fast after hym, & closed thabbot &
the monkes therynne / and incontynent he made al
4 the meyne of the place to bryng there wode & strawe
ynoughe al about the Chapter, and fyred it / & sware
he shuld brenne them all therynne, & that none shuld
escape.   Thenne came the ten knightes foorth tofore
8 geffray, whiche blamed hym of þat horryble faytte /
sayeng : 'that Froymond, his broþer, was in good.
purpos, & that happly thrughe hys [1]prayers & good
dedes the sowles of his frendes & other myght be
12 asswaged & holpen.' 'By the toeth of god,' sayd
thenne geffray, 'nother he nor none monke in this
place shal neuer syng masse nor say prayer, but they
shal all be bruled & brent.' Thenne departed the x
16 knightes from hys presence / sayeng that they wold not
be coulpable of that meruellous werke.

Cap. XLI. How Geffray with the grete
toeth fyred thabbey of Mayllezes, & brent
20   bothe thabbot & al the monkes there.

In this partye, sayth thystorye, that Geffray anoon
after that the ten knightes were departed fro hym,
he toke fyre at a lampe within the chirche, & sette the
24 fyre in the strawe all about the Chapter, where as were
in thabbot, & al the monkes of the place, & hys brother
Froymond with them. It was a pyteous syght, For
as soone as [2]the monkes sawe the fyre they bygan to
28 crye piteously, & to make bytter & doulorous bewayl-
lynges, but al that preuaylled them nought. What
shuld I make long compte ? Wel it is trouth, that all
the monkes were brent / and wel the half of the said
32 Abbey or euer geffray departed thens. That don he
came to hys hors & lepte vp / but whan he cam in to
the feldes he retourned hys hors, & beheld toward

He goes out of the chapter, closes all the monks inside, and has wood and straw brought, and swears he will burn them.

His knights remonstrate with him,

[1] fol. 182 b.

without avail,

and leave him because they will not be culpable of such a deed.

Geffray takes fire from a church lamp and lights the straw.

[2] fol. 183.

The monks cry bitterly when they see the fire.

They are all burnt, and half of the abbey.

Geffray feels re-
morse, and be-
gins to sigh
bitterly.
He upbraids
himself,

thabbaye / & perceyuyng that grete myschief & the
dommage that he had don there, & his vnkynd & abhomynable deelyng, remors of conscience smote the
herte of hym, and bygan to syghe and bewayll byttirly /
sayeng vnto him self in this wyse : ' helas ! fals, wycked,
& vntrue prodytour[1] & enemy of god / woldest thou
that men dide to the that / whiche thou hast doo to
the true seruauntes of god ! / nay certayn.'   And than
blamed & wytted hym self, so that no man myght

and is full of de-
spair, and like
to slay himself.

thinke the dyscomfort & grete dyspaire that he thenne
toke / & wel I byleue that he had slayn hym self with
hys owne swerde yf it thenne had not fortuned that

His knights ap-
proach, and one
says that it is too
late to repent.

hys ten knightes cam to hym there / one of the whiche
bygan to hym says / ' ha / a, my lord, ouer late is this
repented.'   And whan geffray vnderstode hym / he
thenne had greter despyte than tofore / but he dayned
not ansuere to the knyght, but rode so fast toward the

Geffray rides
swiftly to Mount-
jouet,

toure of Mountyouet, that with grete peyne myght his
men folow hym / & so long rode he tyl he came

and gets ready
to go with the
ambassadors.

thither / And thenne made his apparayll for to goo
with the ambaxatours there as they shold conduyte
hym / & toke with hym but his x knightes.   And
here seaceth thystorye of hym, & speketh of Raymondin his fader /

A messenger
from Mailleses
recounts to Ray-
mondin the pite-
ous tidings

[2] fol. 182 b.

H ere sayth thistory, that a messager came toward
 Raymondin at merment that came fro mailleses, [2]and after hys obeyssaunce recounted to Raymondyn ryght pyteous tydynges, sayeng to hym in this
manere : ' My lord, wel it is trouth, that geffray with
the great toth your son hath take so grete malencolye
& suche dueyl of the professyon of your son Froymond
that he is com to maylleses, & there he hath fyred the

of the burning of
the abbey and
the monks.

Abbay / & within the chapter brent & bruled all the
monkes, pryour, & Abbot.'   ' What sayst thou ?' sayd

Raymondin says
he cannot beleve
the story.

than Raymondyn / ' that may not be / I can not beleue

[1] Fr. proditour.

it.' 'By my feyth, my lord,' said the messager, 'it is
trouth that I telle you; &, morouer, your son Froymond is brent & deed with them / and yf ye byleue
4 me not make me to be putte in to pryson, & yf ye
fynde otherwyse than I says, lete me be hanged therfore.' Thenne Raymondyn sorowfull & heuy mounted
foorthwith on horsbak, & toke hys way toward mayl-
8 lezes as fast as hys hors myght bere hym / and hys
men, who þat myght folowed hym / and he neuer
seaced tyl he cam thither / where he fonde, as the messager said, & sawe the grete doleur & myschief that
12 gaffray had don. Wherof he toke suche yre & anger
at herte, that almost he was out of hys wyt. 'ha / s,'
sayd he, 'Geffray, thou haddest the fayrest begynnyng
of hys prowes & cheualrye to haue coms to the degree
16 of high honour more than ony prynce son lyuyng at
this day / and now thrugh thy grete cruelte thou shalt
be reputed & holden vnworthy of al noble fayttes, &
abhomyned for cause of thys vnkyndnes & horryble
20 dede of al creatures. By the feyth that I owe to god,
I byleue it is but fantosme or spyryt werke of this
woman / and as I trowe she neuer bare no child that
shal at thende haue perfection, For yet hath she
24 brought none but that it hath some strange token / see
I not the ¹horryblenes of her son called Horryble, that
passed not vii yere of age whan he slew two squyers of
myn / and or euer he was thre yere old he made dye
28 two gentyl women his nourryces, thrugh hys byttyng of
theire pappes? / sawe I not also theyre moder of that
satirday, whan my brother of Forestz to me brought
euyl tydynges of her / in fourme of a serpent fro the
32 nauel dounward? / by god, ye / and wel I wote certayn /
it is som spyryt, som fantosme or Illusyon that thus
hath abused me / For the first tyme that I sawe her /
she knew & coude reherce all my fortune & auenture.'

But the messen-
ger says it is the
truth, and that
Froimond was
burnt with them.

Raymondin rides
to Maillezes,

and when he sees
the mischief

he complains of
Geffray,

and how he will
be hated for his
cruelty.

He cries that he
believes it is
spirit work.

He complains
that Melusine
never bore a
perfect child,
and of the
horribleness of
her son Horrible.

¹ fol. 184.

He speaks of
seeing Melusine
half woman, half
serpent, on a
Saturday,

and says he
believes her to
be a spirit.

Raymondin goes
to Marment.
He retires to his
chamber

and makes pite-
ous lamentation.

The barons are
sad,

and send word
to Melusine at
Niort,

but this aug-
ments the grief
of Raymondin
and Melusine.

¹ fol. 164 b.
When Melusine
reads the letter
she is sorrowful,
more for the
wrath of Ray-
mondin than
anything else.

She comes to
Lusignan,
where she looks
so sad,

and sighs so
much, that it is
pitiful to see her.

In this partye, sayth thystorye, that Raymondyn,
pensafull and wroth ouer meruayllously, departed
fro Mayllezes, & rode agayn toward Marment. And
whan he was come thither, he alyghted, & went in to
hys chambre, where as he layed hym vpon a bed / and
there he made suche lamentacion, & so pyteous bowayl-
lynges, that there nys in the world herte so harde / but
that it had wepte to here hym. Thenne were al the
barons ryght dolaunt / and whan they sawe that they
myght not gyue none allegeance to hys dolour, they
toke Counseyll that they shuld lete it wete to theire
lady Melusyne, whiche was at Nyort that tyme / and
thither they sent a messanger, to recounte to her al the
matere of the fayt. Halas! full euyl dide they, For
they augmented thereby bothe Raymondyn & Melusyne
in theyre doulour & myserye. Now bygynneth theire
hard & bytter departyng, eche fro other, whiche dured
to Raymondyn his lyf natural / & to Melusyne shal
laste her penitence vnto domysday. The messanger
thenne rode tyl he came to Nyort, & made his
obeyssaunce, & syn delyuered the lettres to his lady:
¹the whiche she toke, & opened it. And whan she
vnderstode the tenour of the lettres, she was ryght heuy
& dolaunt, & more for the yre & wrath of Raymondin
than for ony other thing; For she sawe wel that the
meschief that geffray had doon might none otherwyse
be as for that tyme present. She thenne made come
all her peuple & aray, and sent for many ladyes &
damoyselles, for to hold her companye / and so departed fro Nyort, & came to Lusynen / and there she
sojourned by the space of thre dayes / and euer she
was of symple & heuy contenaunce / and went al about
in the place, vp & doun, here & there / gyuyng ofte
syghes so grete that it was meruaylle & pyteous to
here / And the hystory & cronykle, whiche I byleue
be trew, sheweth to vs that wel she knew the doleur &

sorow that was nygh her to come / and as to me, I
byleue it fermely / but her peple thoughte nothing of
that / but they trowed that it had be for cause of the
4 grete myschief that was befell thrugh the fayttes of
geffray, to thabbay of maylleses / and also for the
wrathe & anger that Raymondyn toke therof. Melusyne thenne, on the III⁴ᵉ day, departed fro Lusynen, &
8 came to merment wel acompanyed of ladyes & damoyselles, as tofore I haue sayd. And thenne the barons
of the land, that were there assembled for to haue
recomforted Raymondin, that they loued entierly / came
12 ayenst her, & honourably receyued her / & sayd how
they by no wyse coude make Raymondyn to leue hys
dolour. 'Wel,' sayd she / 'doubte you no; For, by
the grace of god, he shalbe soons recomforted.'

16 Melusyne, the good lady, that thenne was wel
acompanyed of many ladyes & noble damoyselles, & of the barons of the land, entred in to þe
Chambre where as Raymondin was in / the which
20 chambre had regarde towand the gardyns, that ¹were
commodyous & delectables, and also to the feldes
toward Lusynen. Thenne whan she sawe Raymondin,
humbly & ryght honourably salued hym / but thenne
24 he was so dolaunt & replenysshed with yre, that he to
her ansuerd neuer a word / and thenne she toke the
word, & sayd : 'My lord, grete symplenes & foly it is
to you that men repute & hold so sage & so wyse a
28 prynce / you thus to maynten & make suche sorowe of
that thinge that may none other wyse be, & whiche
may not be amended nor remedyed / ye argue ayenst
the playsire & wyll of the Creatour, whiche all thinges
32 created, & shal vndoo at al tymes whan it playse hym,
by suche manere wyse aftir his playsire. Wete it that
there nys so grete a synnar in the world / but that
is more piteable & mysericordyous whan the synnar
36 repenteth hym, with herte contryte, of his mysdede &

She knows of the sorrow that is coming,

but her people think she is sad on account of Geffray's mischief.

She comes to Merment,

where they receive her honourably, and tell her of Raymondin's grief.

Melusine enters his chamber

¹ fol. 185.

and salutes him.

But he answers not a word.

Melusine chides him for his grief,

and says what is done cannot be undone,

and that God had allowed Geffray so to do because of the sins of the monks.

synne / yf geffray, your sone & myn, hath doon that oultrageous folye thrugh his mervaylloes courage, Wete it certaynly that suffred god for cause of the monkes mysdedes & synnes, whiche were of euyl, inordinate, & vnrelygious lyuyng / and wold our lord god haue them to be punysshed in that manere wyse / how be it, that it is vnknowen to creature humayns, For the jugements of god be ryght secret & mervayllous. And, moreouer,

She says they have enough to rebuild the abbey, and to endow it richer than it was before,

my lord, thankyng to god, we haue ynough wherof to do make ayen thabbey of Maylleses as fayre & bettre than euer it was tofore, & to ampossesse & endowe it bettre & rychelyer, and therin to ordeyne greter nombre of monkes than euer were there ordeyned. Also, yf it

and she hopes that Geffray will amend his life.

playse god, geffray shal mende hys lyf, bothe toward our lord god & the world. Wherfore, my lord, leue your sorowe, I pray you.' Whan thenne Raymondyn

¹ fol. 165 b.

Though Raymondin knows she speaks wisely, he is so full of anger that in a cruel voice he cries,

vn¹derstode Melusyne, he knew wel that she sayd trouth of that she had sayd to hym / and that it was best, after rayson, so to doo / but he was replenysshed & perced with yre, that al rayson natural was fled & goon from hym. And thenne, with a right cruel voyce, he said in this manyere:

Cap. XLII. How Melusyne felle in a swoune, for this that Raymondyn, her lord, wyted her.

'Go hence, false serpent! Thou and thy children are but phantoms.

How can the dead have life again?

Froimond, your only perfect child, by devilish art has suffered death.

'Goo thou hens, fals serpente / by god! nother thou nor thy birthe shalbe at thende but fantosme / nor none child that thou hast brought shal come at last to perfection / how shal they that are brent & bruled haue theire lynes agayn / goode fruyte yssued neuer of the, saaf only Froymonde, that was youen to god & shorne monke; the whiche, thrugh arte demonyncle, hath myserably suffred deth: For all

they that are foursenyd[1] with yre obeye [2]the comande-
ments of the prynces of helle. And þerfor, thorryble
& cruel geffray commanded of his masters, alle the
4 deuelles of helle, hath doon that abhomynable &
hydouse forfaytte, as to brenne hys owne propre brother
& the monkes, that had not deserued deth.' Thenne
whan melusyne vnderstode these wordes, she toke suche
8 douleur at herte, that foorthwith she fell in a swoune
doun to therthe, & was half an ooure long that nother
aspyracion nor breth was felt nor perceyued in her, but
as she had be deed. And thenne was Raymondyn
12 sorowfuller & more wroth than euer he was tofore, For
thenne he was cooled of his yre, & bygan to make
grete dueyll, & moche repented hym of that he had
sayd / but it was for nought, For þat was to late / And
16 thenne the baronnye of the land, & the ladyes & damoyselles were ryght sory & dolaunt, and toke vp the lady,
& layed her on a bed / and so moche they dide, that
she came ayen to her self. And whan she myght
20 speke, she loked on Raymondyn pyteously, and said /

Geffray burnt his brothers by command of his masters, the devils of hell.'

Melusine is overcome by his cruel words, and swoons.

He repents, but it avails nought.

When Melusine comes to herself she looks piteously at Raymondin and says,

[2]fol. 186.

Cap. XLIII. It is shewed herafter, how Melusyne came to her self ayen, and spake to Raymondyn.

24 'Ha / a Raymondyn / the day that first tyme I
sawe the was for me ryght doulourous and
vnhappy / in an euyl heure sawe I euer thy coynted
body, thy facion, & thy fayre fygure / euyl I dyde to
28 desire & coueyte thy beaute, whan thou so falsly hast
betrayed me / how wel thou art forsworn toward me,
whan thou puttest thy self in peyne to see me / but for
this, that thou haddest not yet dyscouered nor shewed
32 to no man nor woman, myn herte forgafe [2]the / and no
mencion I neuer shuld haue had made therof to the /

'It was an evil hour when I first saw your figure.

When you falsely betrayed me I forgave you because you kept my secret.

[2] fol. 186 b.

[1]. Fr. *enforcenez.*

and god shuld haue pardoned the. Halas, my frende /
now is our loue tourned in hate, doleur & hardnes /
oure solace, playsire & joye ben reuersed in byttir
teerys & contynual wepynges, and our good happ is
conuerted in ryght hard & vnfortunate pestilence /
Halas, my frend ! yf thou haddest not falsed thy
feythe & thyn othe, I was putte & exempted from all
peyne & tourment, & shuld haue had al my ryghtes, &
hadd lyued the cours natural as another woman ; &
shuld haue be buryed, aftir my lyf natural expired,
within the chirche of our lady of Lusynen, where myn
obsequye & afterward my annyuersary shuld haue be
honourably & deuoutely don / but now I am, thrughe
thyn owne dede, ouerthrowen & ayen reuersed in the
greuouse and obscure penytence, where long tyme I haue
be in, by myn auenture : & thus I muste suffre & bere
it, vnto the day of domme / & al through thy falsed /
but I beseche god to pardonne the.' Melusyne began
thenne to make suche doleur, that none was there that
sawe her but he wept for pyte. And whan Raymondyn sawe her douleur & heuynes, almost hys herte
brake for sorowe, in so moche that he nother herd, nor
sawe, nor coude hold contenaunce. /

Thystorye sayth that Raymondyn was right dolaunt ;
and, for trouth, the true cronykle testyfyeth that
neuer no man suffred so grete dolour, without of his
lyf expired. but whan he was a lytel come to hys
mynde, & sawe Melusyne tofore hym, he kneeled doun
on hys knees, & joyntly¹ handes, thus bygan he to
saye : 'My dere lady & my frend, my wele, my hoop,
& myn honour, I beseche & pray you that it playse you
to pardonne me, & that ye wyl abyde with me.' 'My
swete frend,' sayd Melusyne, that saw the grete habundaunce of teerys fallyng fro hys eyen / 'he that is the
very forgyuer, creatour & omnipotent, forgyue you your

¹ Fr. *joingnist.*

Our loue is now turned to hate.

If you had kept your oath, I was to be exempt from torment.

I should have been buried at Lusignan,

and my anniver-sary would have been devoutly kept.

But now my fate is altered.

I must suffer grievous peni-tence till dooms-day.'

Melusine shows such grief that all pity her.

The heart of Ray-mondin is nearly broken by her grief.

He kneels to Melusine and beseeches her pardon

Melusine calls on God to forgive him.

forfaytte ; For as touching myself, I forgyue & pardonne
you with al my very herte / but as to myn abydyng
with you ony more / it is Impossible / for the veray
4 jugge & almighty god wold neuer suffre me ¹to doo
soo.'

as she does;
but declares that
God will not let
her abide with
him.

¹ fol. 187.

Cap. XLIV.   How Raymondyn & Melusyne
felle bothe in a swoune.

8   A nd with thoo wordes Melusyne toke vp Raymondyn, her lord / and thenne, as they wold haue
embraced & kyssed eche other, they fell both at ones in
a swoune, so that almost theire hertes brake for grete
12 douleur : Certayn there was a pyteous syght. There
wept & bewaylled barons / ladyes & damoyselles, sayeng
in þis manere : 'Ha, fals Fortune! We shal lese this
day þe best lady that euer gouerned ony land / the
16 moost sage / most humble / moost charytable & curteys
of all other lyuyng in erthe.' And they al lamented &
bewaylled so pyteously, & rendred teerys in habund-
ance, in so moche that it was a pyteous syght. Thenne
20 retourned Melusyne to her self out of swounyng, and
herd the heuynes & dolour that the baronnye made for
her departyng / and cam to Raymondyn, that yet laye
on the grounde, & toke hym vp / and thenne to hym,
24 in heryng of thassistaunce, she said in this manere /

Melusine raises
Raymondin.

They kiss,
and immediately
swoon on ac-
count of their
grief.

The barons and
ladies weep at
the thought of
losing their lady.

Melusine re-
covers,

and comes to
Raymondin and
says—

Cap. XLV.   How Melusyne made her testa-
ment. /

'M y lord & swete frend Raymondyn, Impossible
28   is my lenger taryeng with you ; Wherfore
lyst, & herke, & putte in mynde that I shal saye.
Wete it, Raymondyn, that certayn after your lyf naturel
expired, no man shal not empocesse nor hold your land
32 so free in peas as ye now hold it, & your heyres &
successours shal haue moche to doo / and wete it shal

'My sweet
friend, it is im-
possible to stay
with you, there-
fore listen and
keep in mind
what I say.
After your life no
man shall hold
your land in
peace.

Your heirs
through their
folly shall lose
their inheritance.

1 fol. 137 b.
Keep Geffray
with you, he will
prove a vaillant
man. I will
take care of
Raymond and
Theoderic,
though after I go
you will never
see me again in
woman's form.
I bequeath Par-
tenay to Theo-
deric;

Raymond shall
be Earl of Forest;
Geffray will pro-
vide for himself.

I charge you to
put Horrible to
death.'

Raymondyn asks
Melusine to stay
with him.

but she says that
it cannot be done.

She then kisses
him tenderly and
bids him adieu.

be ouerthrawen & subdued, thrugh theire foly, from
theire honour & from theire ryght enherytaunce / but
doubte you not, For I shal help you duryng the cours
of your lyf natural / and putte not geffray, oure sone, &
fro your Court / he is your sone, 1& he shal preue a
noble & valyaunt man. Also we haue two yong children male, Raymond & theoderyk / of them I shal take
good heede / how be it, aftir my departyng / that ryght &
soone shal be / ye shal neuer see me in no womans
fourme. And I wyl & bequethe to theodoryk, yongest
of all our children, the lordshipes with al thappurten-
aunces of Partenay / Vernon / Rochelle, & the port
there / And Raymond shal be Erle of Forest / and as
touching geffray, he shal wel purueye for hym self'
Thenne drew she Raymondyn & hys Counseyll apart,
& sayd to them in this wyse : 'As touching our sone,
that men calle Horryble, that hath thre eyen / wete it
for certayn, yf he be lafte alyue / neuer man dide, nor
neuer shal doo, so grete dommage as he shall. Wherfore I pray & also charge you that, anoone aftir my
departyng, he be put to deth ; For yf ye doo not soo /
his lyf shall full dere be bought, & neuer ye dide so
grete folye.' 'My swete loue,' sayd Raymondyn, 'there
shal be no fawte of it / but, for goddis loue, haue pyte
on yourself, & wyl abyde with me.' And she said to
hym : 'My swete frend, yf it were possyble / soo wuld
I fayne doo / but it may not be. And wete it wel, that
my departyng fro you is more greuous & doubtous a
thousand tymes to me than to you / but it is the wyll
& playsire of hym that can do & vndoo al thinges.'
and, with these wordes, she embraced & kyssed hym
full tenderly / sayeng : 'Farwel, myn owne lord &
husbond, Adieu, myn herte, & al my joye ; Farwel, my
loue, & al myn wele / and yet as long as thou lyuest, I
shal feel myn eyen with the syght of the / but pyte I
haue on the of this, that thou mayst neuer see me but

in horryble figure' / and therwith she lept vpon the
windowe that was toward the feldes & gardyns ayanst
Lusynen. /

4 Cap. XLVI.   How Melusyne in fourme of a
Serpent flough out at a wyndowe.

[1] In this partye, saith thistorye, that whan Melusyne
was vpon the wyndowe as before is said, she
8 toke leue sore wepyng, and her commanded to all the
barons, ladyes, & damoyselles that were present / and
after said to Raymondyn : 'here be two rynges of gold
that be bothe of one vertue, and wete it for trouth that
12 as long as ye haue them, or one of them / you / nor
your heyres that shal haue them after you, shal neuer
be dyscomfyted in plee nor in batayll, yf they haue
good cause / nor they that haue them shal not dey by
16 no dede of armes,' and Immediatly he toke the rynges.
And after bygan the lady to make pyteous regrets and
greuouse syghynges, beholdyng Raymondyn right pyteously / And they that were there wept alway [2]so ten-
20 derly that eueryche of them had grete pyte, they
syghyng full pyteously.   Thenne Melusyne in her lamentable place, where she was vpon the wyndowe
hauyng respection toward Lusynen, said in this wyse,
24 'Ha, thou swete Countre / in the haue I had so grete
solas & recreacion, in the was al my felicite / yf god
had not consented that I had be so betrayed I had be
full happy / alas! I was wonnt to be called lady / &
28 men were redy to fulfylle my commandements / &
now not able to be alowed a symple seruaunt / but
assygned to horryble peynes & tourments vnto the day
of fynal judgement.   And al they that myght come
32 to my presence had grete Joye to behold me / and fro
this tyme foorth they shal dysdayne me & be ferefull
of myn abhomynable figure / and the lustes & playsirs
that I was wonnt to haue shal be reuertid in tribulacions

She leaps to the window.

[1] fol. 188.

and again takes leave, weeping sorely.

She gives Ray-
mondin two
magic rings.

[2] fol. 188 b.
Those present
weep, so full of
pity are they.

She looks from
the window to-
wards Lusignan,

and speaks of her
sad future,

and how all will
disdain her be-
cause of her
abominable
figure.

& grieuous penitences.' And thenne she bygan to say
with a hye voyce : 'Adieu, my lustis & playsirs / Far
wel, my lord / barons / ladyes, & damoyselles, and I
beseche you in the moost humble wyse that ye vouchesauf to pray to the good lord deuoutely for me / that
it playse hym to mynnsshe my dolorous peyns / not-

She telle that her father was

withstanding I wyl lete you knowe what I am & who
was my fader, to thentent that ye reproche not my
children, that they be not borne but of a mortal woman,
and not of a serpent, nor as a creature of the fayry /
and that they are the children of the doughter of kynge

Elinas, King of Albany, and her mother Queen Pressine , and that she is one of three sisters.

Elynas of Albanye and of þe queene Pressyne, and that
we be thre sustirs þat by predestinacion are predes-
tynate to suffre & bere grieuous penaunces, and of this
matere I may no more shew, nor wyl.' And therwith
she said : ' farwel, my lord Raymondyn, and forgete not
to doo with your sons called Horryble this that I have
you said / but thinke of your two sones Raymond &

She gives a sore sigh, and be- comes like a great serpent ; ¹ fol. 189.

Theodoryk.' Thenne she bygan to gyue a sore syghe,
& therwith flawgh in to thayer out of the wyndowe,
trans¹figured lyke a serpent grete & long in xv foote of
length. And wete it wel that on the basse stone of

and to this day her serpent's footprint is on the base-stone of the window.

the wyndowe apereth at this day thetmprynts of her
foote serpentous. Thenne encreaced the lamentable

The grief of Ray- mondin and his people increases.

sorowes of Raymondyn, and of the barons, ladyes, &
damoyselles / and moost in especial Raymondyns heuynes aboue al other / And foorthwith they loked out of
the wyndowe to behold what way she toke / And
the noble Melusyne so transffygured, as it is aforsaid,

They see Melu- sine fly thre times about the place, uttering horrible cries ;

flyeng thre tymes about the place, passed foreby the
wyndow, gyuyng at euerche tyme an horrible cry &
pyteous, that caused them that beheld her to wepe for
pyte. For they perceyued wel that loth she was to
departe fro the place, & that it was by constraynte.
And thenne she toke her way toward Lusynen, makyng

then she makes her way to Lusig- nan, moaning so

in thayer by her furyousnes suche horryble crye &

noyse that it semed al thayer to be replete with thundre & tempeste. /

loud that it sounded like thunder.

Thus, as I haue shewed, went Melusyne, lyke a serpent, flyeng in thayer toward Lusynen / & not so hygh / but that the men of the Countre might see her / and she was herd a myle in thayer, For she made suche noyse that al the peple was abasshed. And so she flawgh to Lusynen thre times about the Fortres, cryeng so pyteously & lamentably, lyke the voyce of a Mermayde. Wherof they of the Fortresse & of the toun were gretly abasshed, & wyst not what they shuld thinke, For they sawe the fygure of a serpent, and the voyce of a woman þat cam fro the serpent. And whan she had floughe about the Fortresse thre tymes she lyghted so sodaynly & horrybly vpon the toure called poterne, bryngyng with her such thundre & tempeste, that it semed that bothe the Fortres & the toun shuld haue sonk and fall / & therwith they lost the syght of her, and wyst not where she was becoms. But anoone after that cam messagers fro Raymondyn, [1]that he sent thither to haue tydynges of her / to whom was shewed how she fyl vpon the fortresse / & of theire fere that they had had of her / and the messagers retourned toward Raymondyn, & shewed hym al the caas. And thenne bygan Raymondyn to entre into hys sorowe. And the tydynges were knowen in the Countre, the poueere peuple made grete lamentacion & sorowe, & wysshed her ayen with pyteous syghes, For she had doo them grete good. And thenne bygan thobsequyes of her to be obseruyd in al abbeyes & chirches that she had founded / and Raymondin, her lord, dede to be doon for her almesses & prayers thrugh al his land.

She flies through the air to Lusignan, making a great noise, and then flies three times round the fortress,

lamenting piteously like the voice of a mermaid.

She alights on Postern Tower in such wise that it seemed the fortress would fall.

She disappears.

[1] fol. 189 b.
Messengers are sent by Raymoudin to get tidings of her.

Raymondin and all the people lament.

Her obsequies are observed in all the churches she had built.

Cap. XLVII. How Raymondyn dide do brenne his sone called Horryble.

MELUSINE.　　　　　　　　　Y

The barons remind Raymondin of Melusine's command about Horrible.

Thenne came tofore the presence of Raymondyn the barons of the land, and said : 'My lord, it behouyth that we doo of your sone horryble this that his moder hath charged you & vs to doo.' And Raymondyn to them ansuard, 'doo you in this that ye are commanded to doo.'

He bids them fulfil her order.

And then they went and take by fayre wordes this Horryble / & led hym in to a caue.

Horrible is led to a cave

For yf he had had warnyng of theire purpos they shuld not haue had take hym without grete payne.

and suffocated.

And thenne they closed hym in smoke of wet hay. And whan he was deed they buryed hym honnourably in the Abbey called the Neufmoustier.

He is buried at Neufmoustier.

Cap. XLVIII. How Melusyne came euery nyght to vysyte her two children.

Raymondin goes to Lusignan, and brings his children Raymondin and Theoderic.
[fol. 100.]

Thenne departed Raymondyn from thens & came to Lusynen, & brought with hym his two children, Raymond & theodoryke / and said that he shuld neuer entre ayen in to the place wher ¹he had lost his wyf.

Melusine visits them every day.

And wete it wel that Melusyne came euery day to vysyte her children, & held them tofore the fyre and eased them as she coude / and wel sawe the nourryces

They grow faster than other children

that, who durst no word speke. And more encreced the two children in nature in a weke than dide other children in a moneth; wherof the peuple had grete meruayll.

Raymondin when he hears of her coming,

but whan Raymondyn knew it by the nourryces that melusyne came there euery nyght to vysyte her children / released his sorowe / trustyng to haue her

hopes to have her back, but in vain.

ayen / but that thoughte was for nought, For neuer after sawe he her in fourme of a woman / how be it dyuers haue sith sen her in femenyn figure. And wete it that how wel Raymondyn hooped to haue her ayen /

Raymondin is so woful that he never laughs.

neuertheles he had alway suche hertly sorowe that there is none that can tell it / And there was neuer man syth that sawe hym lawgh nor make joye / and

hated gretly geffray with the grete toth / and yf he   He hates Geffray.
myght haue had hym in his yre, he wold haue dystroyed
hym. But here seaceth the hystorye of him And speketh
4 of geffray. /

Thystorye sayth, that geffray rode so long· that he   Geffray comes to Northomberland.
came in Northomberland with the ambaxatours
and hys ten knyghtes with hym / And whan the barons
8 of the Countre vnderstod his commyng· they cam ayenst
hym honourably, & receyued hym solemply, sayeng :
'ha, sire, of your joyful comyng we owe wel to lawde   The barons tell him they are joyful at his arrival,
& preyse our lord god, For without it be by you &
12 thrugh your prowes we may not be delyuered of the   because they will be delivered of Grymauld.
horryble geaunt and meruayllous murdrer, Grymauld,
by whom all this countre is dystroyed.' Thenne an-
suerde geffray to them : 'And how may ye knowe that   Geffray asks how they know.
16 by me ye may be quytte & delyuered of hym ? ' to
whom they answered, 'My lord, the sage astronomyens
haue said to vs that the geaunt grymauld ¹may not dey   ¹ fol. 190 b. They answer that wise astrono-mers have said that he alone can slay Grymauld, and the giant knows this too, so Geffray must not tell him his name.
but by your dede of armes / and also we knowe for
20 certayn that he knoweth it wel. Wherfore yf ye go to
hym, and that yf ye telle hym your name ye shall not
kepe hym, but he shall you escape.' Thenne sayd
geffray to the barons, 'Sire, lede me toward the place
24 where I may find· hym, For grete desyre I haue to see
hym.' And Immedyatly they toke hym two knyghtes
of the land that conduyted hym toward the place / but
that one of them said to that other þat they shuld not
28 approche al to nygh grymauld / and that they myght
not beleue that geffray shuld haue the vyctory of hym.
And thenne geffray toke leue of the barons and de-   Geffray is taken to the mountain of Brombelyo,
parted, the two knyghtes with hym, and so long they
32 rode tyl they saw the montayne of Brombelyo. Thenne
sayd the two knyghtes to geffray, 'My lord, yonder ye
· may see the mountayns where he holdeth hym / & this
way shal lede you thither without ony fayll, For cer-   where the knights show
36 taynly he is euer at yonder trees vpon that mountayne

where Grymold
is to be found.
Here they leave
him for fear of
hurt.

for to espye them that passe by the way. Now may
ye goo thither, yf it playse you, For as touchhing our
personnes we wyl goo no ferþer that way.' And geffray
answerd to them in this manere, 'Yf I had come vpon
thaffyaunce of your ayde I had fayled therof at this
tyme.' 'By my feyth,' sayd one of them, 'ye say
trouth.' Thenne came they to the foot of the hyll /
and there geffray descended & armed hym, and syn
remounted on his hors, and layed the sheld tofore hys
brest, and toke his spere, and thenne he said to the
two knyghtes that they shuld abyde hym vnder the
mountayne, and that they shuld soone see what therof
shuld befall. And they sayd that so shuld they doo.

Cap. XLIX. How geffray with the grete toeth rane ayenst the geaunt & ouerthrew hym with hys spere.

In this partye sayth thistorye that Geffray take leue
of the two knyghtes, & mounted the mountayne,
so that he approched nygh the trees where as he
apperceyued the geaunt þat satte vndernethe them. but

He sees the
giant,
who is astonished
at Geffray's bold-
ness in coming
against him
alone

assoone as he sawe geffray he meruaylled gretly how
one knyght alone had the hardynes to haue dare
come toward hym, and thenne he thought in hym self
that he cam to treate with hym for som patyse or for
som peas. but he sware hys lawe that lytel or nought
he shuld entrete hym. Thenne rose vp the geaunt and

toke an horryble grete Clubbe in hys handes, which
ony man had ynough to doo to lyft it vp fro the

ground. ¹And so he came ayenst Geffray, and cryed

He demands
Geffray's name,
and threatens
him with death.

with a hye voys, 'What art thou that darest come so
boldly toward me in armes / by my lawe wel shal thou
be payed therfor. For who that sendeth the hyther
wold haue the deed.' And geffray cryed to hym, 'I

deffye the / deffend thou thy self yf thou canst.' And

with these wordes geffray couched hys spere & sporyd
hys hors and ranne & smote the geannt in the brest so
myghtily that he ouerthrew hym, the legges vpward to

4 the ground / and anoon geffray descendid fro his hors,
fesryng that the geannt shuld slee hym vndre hym,
and fasted it by þe brydel at a tree / & pusshed his
sheld behynd, and toke his good trenchaunt swerd;

8 For wel he sawe that it were grete foly to hym to
abyde the stroke of the geauntis Clubbe. And thenne
cam the geannt toward geffray, but almost he conde not
perceyue hym for cause he was so lytel of personne to

12 the regarde of hym. And whan he was nygh hym he
said to hym, 'Say me thou lytel body, who art thou
that so valyauntly hast ouerthrawen me? / by mahomid
I shall neuer haue honour but I auenge me.' And

16 thenne geffray ansuerde to hym, 'I am Geffray with
the grete toeth, sone to Raymondyn of Lusynen.' And
whan the geannt vnderstod hym, he was ryght dolaunt,
For wel he wyst that he myght not be slayne but with

20 geffrayes handes. not that withstanding he ansuerd to
hym, 'I knowe the wel ynough. thou slough that
other day my Cousin Guedon in Garande, al the
deuelles of helle haue brought the now hither.' And

24 geffray hym ansuerd, 'no doubte / but I shal slee the
yf I may.' And whan the geant vnderstod it, he
haunced his Clubbe & wold haue dyscharged it vpon
geffrayes heed, but he faylled, And thenne Geffray

28 smote hym with his swerd vpon the sholder. ¹For he
myght not reche to his heed, & cutte the haulte piece
of his harneys, and made his swerd to entre in his
flesshe wel a palme deep, and thenne the blood fell

32 doon along his body vnto the heelys of hym. And
whan he felt that stroke he cryed & said to geffray /
'cursed be that arme that by suche strengthe can
smyte, & hanged be the smyth that forged that swerd.

36 For neuer blood was drawen out of my body of no

Side notes:

and rushes forward and overthrows him.

Geffray dismounts,

fastens his horse to a tree, and takes his sword and shield.

The giant approaches Geffray, but can hardly see him.

He asks Geffray who he is.

Geffray answers that he is the son of Raymondin of Lusignan. The giant is sad at this news, because he knows that Geffray alone can slay him.

The giant says he knows him as the slayer of Guedon.

Geffray tells the giant that he will kill him too.

The giant raises his club, but misses Geffray.

¹ fol. 192.

Geffray wounds the giant,

who curses Geffray's arm,

and stykes back.

manere wepen al were it neuer so good.' And thenne with his clubbe he wend to haue smyte geffray / but geffray fled the stroke. For wete it for trouth that yf he had atteyned hym he had slayn hym / but god, on ī whom hys trust was, wold not suffre it. And ye owe to wete for certayn that with that same stroke the Clubbe entred into the grounde wel a foot deep / but or euer the geaunt myght haue haunsed his Clubbe, Š geffray smote on it with his swerd by suche strengthe that he made it fligh out of the geauntes handes, and therewith he cutte a grete piece of it.

Geffray avoids the blow.

The force of the giant's stroke drove his club a foot into the ground.

Before it is raised Geffray strikes it from his hands.

Cap. L. How the geaunt fled & Geffray 1 folowed hym.

Thenne was the geaunt ryght dolaunt & abasshed whan he sawe his Clubbe jus cutte lyeng on the grounde, For he durst not bowe hym self to take it vp. 1 Thenne he lept on geffray & strake hym with his fyst vpon the helmet with so grete myght & yre that almost geffray was astonyed therwith all. but geffray, cora-geous & hardy, smote the geant vpon the þye, so that Š he cutte a grete part of it. And thenne whan the geaunt sawe hym thus hurt he withdrew hym a lytel backward, and syn bygan to flee / but geffray, holdyng his swerd, folowed hym / and the geaunt entred into Š a holl within the mountayne, Wherof geffray was abasshed /. Thenne came geffray ¹ to the holl and loked in, but it was so obscure & derk & so deep that he sawe nor wyst where the geaunt was become. And he Š retourned and toke & mounted ayen vpon his hors, and descended into þe valey, & came to hys meyne that abode for hym there, whiche had grete meruayll whan they sawe hym retourne hole & sauf / and in especial Š the two knightes wondred moche & were abasshed of it / and they asked hym yf he had sene the geaunt / and he said to them, ' I haue faught with hym / and

The giant fears to bend to lift his club, so he strikes Geffray with his fist.

Geffray smites the giant on the thigh.

He flies to a hole in the mountain. Geffray follows

¹ fol. 192 b. and looks in, but it is so dark that he cannot see the giant.

Geffray rises to his meyn, who marvel at his safe return.

The two knights ask if he has seen the giant.

he is fled & entred in to an holl, where as I may not see hym.' And they demanded of geffray yf he had told hym hys name / and he ansuerd, 'ye' / and thenne

4 they said that it was for nought to seke hym, For wel he wyst that he shuld dey by the handes of geffray. 'Doubte you not,' said geffray, 'For wel I knowe where he is entred in / and to morne, with goddes

8 halp, I shal fynd hym wel.' And whan they vnderstode Geffray to speke they had grete joye, and said that geffray was the moost valyaunt knight of the world.

Geffray tells how he fought him, and how he entered a hole in the mountain.

They say that there is no use of looking for the giant, because Geffray has told his name.

Geffray says that with God's help he will find him next day.

12 Cap. LI. How Geffray went & entred into the holl for to fyght with the geaunt./

And thenne on the morowe by tymes Geffray armed hym & mounted vpon his hors & rode tyl he

16 came to the said holl vpon the mountayne. 'By my feyth,' said geffray thenne / 'this geaunt is twyes as grete as I, & sith he is entred here in, wel I shal goo thrugh it / and so shal I do whatsomeuer it befell

20 therof.' And thenne he toke hys swerd in his hand, & fayre & softly lete hym self fall into the holl / and as he was in to the botome of it, he perceyued some light, & sawe a lytel path. And thenne he made the

24 signe of the cros & foorth [1]went that way./

Geffray rides in the morning to the hole where Grimold disappeared.

He jumps in sword in hand, and sees a light and a path.

He makes the sign of the cross and follows it.
[1] fol. 193.

Cap. LII. How Geffray fonde the sepulture of the king of Albany, his granfader Helynas, within the mountayn.

28 Geffray thenne went not ferre whan he fond a ryche Chambre, where as were grete ryches and grete Candstykes of fyn gold, and vpon them grete tapers white wax, brennyng so clere that it was

32 meruayll. And in the myddes of the Chambre he fonde a noble & ryche tombe of fyn gold, al sette with

Geffray comes to a chamber

that contains a noble tomb,

and an alabaster
statue of a
queen,

with this inscrip-
tion, 'Here lieth
my husband,
King Elynas of
Albany,'
and other writing
regarding his
burial, and his
daughters Melu-
sine, Mellor and
Palestine;

and how the
giant was put on
guard until
the arrival of an
heir of one of the
daughters.

1 fol. 101 b.
Geffray looks
a long while at
the inscriptions,
but knows not
that he is of the
lineage of Elynas.

Geffray leaves
the chamber, and
makes his way to
a field where
he sees a great
tower.

He finds the gate,
and enters the
hall, where there
are over a hun-
dred prisoners.

perlys & precyous stones, & vpon it was figured the
fourme of a knyght, that had on hys head a ryche
croune of gold with many precyous stones / and nygh
by that tombe, a grete ymage of Albaster, kerued & /
made aftir the fourme of a quene, crouned with a ryche
crowne of gold / the whiche ymage held a table of
gold / where-as were wryton the wordes that folowen.
' Here lyeth my lord myn husband the noble kyng &
Elynas of Albanye' / and also shewed al the manyere
how he was buryed there, and for what cause.   And
also spake of theire thre doughtirs, that is to wete,
Melusyne, Melyor, and Palestyne / and how they were so
punysshed bycause that they had closed theire fader /
as in thystory tofore is rehersed.   Also it shewed by
wrytyng how the geaunt had be there ordeyned for the
kepyng & sauegarde of the place, vnto tyme he were
putte therfro by the prowesse of one of the hayres of
the said thre doughtirs / and how there myght none
neuer entre within yf he were not of that lynage / and
in these tables of gold was wel dyuysed along as it is
wreton in the Chapytre of king Elynas / and thus geffray
beholding & seeyng, [pondered] by grete space[1] vpon
[2]the tables as vpon the beaute of the place / but he
knewe not yet that the tables shewed that he was of the
lynee of kyng Elynas & Presyne his wyf.   And whan
he had wel beholde a long tyme he departed, & went by
a waye obscure tyl he fond a feld, thenne loked he
tofore hym, & sawe a grete toure, square, wel batel-
mented, & went toward and went about the toure tyl
he fonde the gate the whiche was open, & the bridge
let faH doun, & entred in, & came to the haH, where
he fonde a grete yron trayH,[2] wherin were closed a
hondred men & more of the Countre that the geaunt

1 Fr. Et à ce veoir et regarder advisa Geuffroy par grant
temps.
2 Fr. traillis.

held for hys prysonners./   And whan they sawe
geffray they mervaylled moche, & hym sayd, ' Sire, for
the loue of god flee you, or ye shal be deed ; For the
4 geaunt shall come ryght foorth that shal dystroye you
al, were ye an C suche as ye are' /   And geffray
answerd them al thus : ' Fayre lordes, I am not here
come but only the geaunt to fynde / & I shuld haue
8 don to grete foly to be come fro so ferre hither to
retourne so hastly.'   And after these wordes cam the
geaunt fro slepe.   But whan he sawe geffray he knew
hym, and sawe wel that his deth was nygh, and had
12 grete feer / and thenne he fledd vnto a chambre, the
whiche he sawe open, & speryd the doore to hym.
And whan geffray that perceyued, he was ryght sorowful
that he had not mete with hym at the entryng of the
16 Chambre./

Thystorye sayth that geffray was right dolaunt whan
he sawe the geaunt was entred into the chambre,
and that he had speryd the doore to hym.   Thenne
20 cam geffray toward the doore, rennyng with a grete
radeur, & smote with his foot so mightyly that he
made the doore to flye vnto the myddes of the chambre.
[1]And thenne the Geaunt swyftly went out at the doore
24 bycause he might none other way passe, and held in
his hand a gret mayllet wherof he gaaf to geffray suche
a stroke vpon the bassynet that he made hym al
amased.   And whan geffray felt the stroke, that was
28 harde & heuy, he foyned with his swerd at his brest,
with suche yre that it entred in the geaunt thrughe to
the cros of the swerd.   And thenne the geant made vp
[2]an horryble cry, sayeng, ' I am deed, I am deed.'   And
32 whan they that were in the traylles of yron herd it /
they cryed with an hye voys, ' Ha, noble man, blessid
be the ooure that thou were borne of a woman.   We
pray the for the loue of god, that thou haue vs hens,

² MS. has ' &.'

Side notes:

They are astonished to see Geffray, and advise him to fly from the giant.

Geffray replies that he has come to find him;

and just as he finished speaking the giant appeared. When he saw Geffray he knew his death was at hand. He fled to a chamber, and barred the door.

Geffray bursts it open.

¹ fol. 194.

The giant rushes on Geffray, and strikes him with a mallet;

then Geffray thrusts his sword into the giant right up to the hilt.

The giant cries out, 'I am dead, I am dead!'

The prisoners on hearing the cry bless the hour of Geffray's birth, and beg their deliverance.

For thou hast at this day delyuered this londe out of
the gretest myserye that euer peuple was in.'/

Cap. LIII.   How geffray delyuered the prysonners that the geaunt kept in pryson.

And thenne geffray cerched the keyes so longe tyl
he fonde them, & lete the prysonners out; and
this doon, they all kneeled tofore hym / & asked hym
by what way he was come. And he said to them the
trouth. 'By my feyth,' said they, 'it is not in
remembraunce that this foure hondred yere was no
man so hardy to passe by the Cane, but onely the geaunt
and his antecessours, that fro heyre to heyre haue
dystroyed all this Countre / but wel we shal bryng you
another way.' And thenne geffray gaf to them al the
hauoir of the toure./

Cap. LIV.   How the prysonners led the geaunt deed vpon a Charyott.

The prysonners thann toke the Geaunt deed, & putte
hys body in a Charyot, and sette hym ryght vp,
& bounde hym so that he shuld not fall, & putte fyre
all about hym. And this don, they led geffray to the
place where he had left his hors, vpon the whiche he
mounted, & descended toward the valey with al the
goodes that they had. Wherof euery man had his
part / and toke the heed hool of the geaunt with them /
and came foorth tyl they sawe geffrayis knightes and
the more part of the nobles & peple of the Countre,
the which fested & dide to geffray grete honour / and
to hym wold they haue youen grete yeftes, but he wold
none take / but toke his lene, & departed fro them.
And the prysonners bare the heed of the geaunt thrugh
al good tounes for euery man to see, of the whiche

sight euery man had grete merueyll that one man alone
durst be so hardy to assaylle such a deuell.   And here
seaceth thistory of that more to speke / and retourneth
4 to speke of geffray.

country, and the
people marvel
that one man
should have been
brave enough to
have fought such
a devil.

In this partye sayth thistorye that geffray rode so
long that he came to mountyoued[1] in garande,
where they of the countrey receyued hym nobly.   And
8 for thenne was come his brother Raymond to enfourme
hym of the yre that theire fader had, & of his wordes
that he had said of hym, And hym recounted fro the
bygynnyng vnto the fyn.   And how theire moder was
12 departed and al the manere / And how the first
bygynnyng of her departyng was thrugh theire vncle
of Forestz.   And how she had said at her departyng
that she was doughter of kyng Elynas of Albanye.

Geffray is well
received at
Mountjouet.

His brother Ray-
mond tells of
their father's
rage, and how
their mother had
departed owing
to the behaviour
of the Earl of
Forest; and that
she was a daugh-
ter of King
Elynas.

16 And whan geffray herd this word he bethought hym
of [2]the table that he fond vpon the tombe of kynge
Elynas.   And by this he knew that he and his brethern
were come of the same lynage; wherof he thought
20 hym self the bettre, but this not with standing he was
ryght sorowfull of the departyng of hys moder, & of
the heuynes of hys fader / and knew thenne wel that
this misaduenture was cõme & grew by therle of

[2] fol. 195.
Geffray recollects
the inscription
on the tomb of
Elynas, and
understands that
he is of the king's
lineage.
He is sorry for
his mother,

24 Forestz his vncle.   Wherfor he sware by the holy
trynyte that he shuld quyte hym.   And thenne he
made to go to horsback hys brother and his x. knightes,
and rode toward the Countee of Forestz / and had
28 tydynges that the Erle his vncle was in a Fortresse
that was edyfyed vpon a roche ryght hye / and was
the self Fortres named at that tyme Jalensy, and now
it is called the Castel Marcelly.

and swears re-
venge on the
Earl of Forest.

Geffray takes his
brother and ten
knights, and
rides to his
uncle's castle.

32 Cap. LV. How Geffray was the deth of
the Erle of Forestz hys vncle.

[1] Fr. *Monjouet*.

He enters his uncle's hall, and finds him among his barons, and calls out 'To death traitor, for through thee we have lost our mother.'

Geffray approaches the Earl, with sword drawn.

The Earl runs out of a door followed by Geffray, who chases him to the top of the tower.

1 fol. 196 b.

The Earl gets out of a window to pass to another tower, but loses his hold and falls dead at the foot. Geffray looks out of the window and upbraids him for the loss of his mother.

Geffray descends to the hall, where none dare to speak against him.

He orders his uncle to be buried, and explains to the barons his uncle's misdeed.

Geffray makes his uncle's barons do homage to his brother Raymond.

So long rode geffray that he came to the Castel and anoone he alighted & went into the hal where he fond the Erle emong᷒ his barons / and thenne he cryed with an hye voyce / ' to deth traytour For thrughe the we haue lost our moder ' / and forthwith drew his swerd & yede toward the Erle / And the Erle whiche knew wel hys fyersnes and anoon fled toward a doore open / and that part geffray folowed hym / and so long chassed hym fro chambre to chambre to the hyest part of the toure where he sawe he myght no ferder flee / he toke a wyndowe / and supposed to haue passed vnto a tour ¹nygh but so to saue hym from the yre of geffray / but footyng fayled hym, & fell doun deed to the grounde. And thenne geffray loked out of the wyndowe, & sawe hym al to rent & brused lyeng᷒ deed on the erthe / but therof he toke no pyte / but sayd ' False traytour by thyn euyl report I haue lost my lady my moder / now haue I quyted the therfore.' And thenne he cam doun ayen to þe halle / but none so hardy was there that durst say one work ayenst hym. And he thenne commanded that his vncle sholde be buryed / and so he was and his obsequye don. And after þat geffray recounted & shewed to the barons of the land why he wold haue slayne his vncle / and bycause of the Erles mysdede and false reporte they were somewhat peased. And thenne Geffray dide make them to doo hommage to Raymond his brother, that was aftirward Erle of Forestz. And now seaceth thistory of hym to speke / and retourneth to shewe of Raymondyn his fader /

Cap. LVI. How Geffray went to Lusynen toward hys fader and prayed hym of mercy.

Thystorye sayth that soone aftir this delyt was
shewed to Raymondyn, wherof he was ryght
dolaunt & sorowful / but he forgate it lyghtly, bycause
4 that his brother had announced hym the tydynges
whereby he lost his wyf / and said to hym self / ' this
that is doo may be none otherwyse / I most pease
geffray or he doo ony more dommage.' And [1]therefore
8 he sent word to hym by hys brother Theodoryke that
he shuld come toward hym at Lusynen. And geffray
came to his fader at his mandement / and as ferre as
he sawe hym he putte hym self on his knees / and
12 prayed hym of pardon & mercy, sayeng in this wyse,
' My ryght redoubted lord, my dere fader, I beseche
you of forgyfnes & pardon / and I sware you that I
shal doo make ayen thabbay of Maylleses fayrer than
16 euer it was afore / and there I shal found ten monkes
ouer the nombre of them that were there byfore.'
' By god,' said Raymondyn, ' al that may be doo with
the helpe of god / but to the deed ye may not restore
20 theire lyf. But geffray it is trouth that I muste go to
a pelgrymage that I haue promysed god to do. And
therfor I shal leue you the gouernaunce of my land /
and yf by auenture god dide hys wylle of me, al the
24 land is yours / but I wyl & charge you this that
your moder hath ordeyned by her last wylle to be doo
be fulfylled. She hath bequethed to Theodoryke
Partenay, Merment, Vouant & al theire appurtenaunces
28 vnto Rochell, with the Castel Eglon with al that
therof dependeth / and fro this tyme fourthon I
enpocesse hym therof for hym and for his heyres.'
Thenne said Geffray to him, ' Dere fader, wel it is
32 raison that it be so don.' This doon Raymondyn made
his apparayll, & with hym mounted on horsback
many lordes & knightes, and toke with hym grete
fynaunce & hauoir and so departed and foorth rode
36 on his way. And Geffray & [2]Theodoryke conueyed

Sidenotes:

Geffray's father is told the story.

He determines to appease Geffray. [1] fol. 196.

He sends Theodoric to ask Geffray to come to Lusignan.

Geffray obeys, and on seeing his father falls on his knees and asks pardon, and promises to rebuild the abbey of Mailleses better than it was before.

Raymondin answers that with God's help he may fulfil his promise, but that will not bring the dead to life. He tells Geffray that he is going on a pilgrimage, and that he leaves his land in his care, and makes him his heir.

Raymondin declares that Theodoric has been left Parthenay and other lands and castles by his mother.

Raymondin then starts on his pilgrimage, accompanied by many knights, and well provided with money and goods.

[2] fol. 196 b.

hym tyl he bade them to retourne.   And as they rode
geffray recounted hym how he fonde the tombs of
Helynas his granfader within the mountayns of
Brombelyo, vpon foure Coulonnes of fyn gold and of
the ryches of þe place / and of the fygure of the quene
Pressyne that stod vp ryght, and held a table of gold,
and of this that was there writon / and how theire
thre doughters were predestyned / 'of the whiche,'
said geffray, 'our moder was one of them' / and shewed
hym al the begynnyng of the matere vnto themf of
hit.   And wete it wel that Raymondyn harkned hym
gladly, & was wel pleased of that he said that hys wyf
Melusyne was doughter of king Elynas & of Pressyne
hys wyf.   And thenne he gaf lycens to his children
to retourne.   And so þey departed & retourned toward
Lusynen / and Raymondyn held on his way toward
Romme.   And to theodoryke he gaf the ryng whiche
Melusyne gaf hym at her departyng fro hym.

Cap. LVII.   How Raymondyn came toward the pope of Romme and confessed hys synnes to hym.

Here sayth thystorye that Raymondyn rode so
long that he came to Romme and his companye
with hym, where he fonde the Pope named Benedictus /
& drew hym toward hym to whome humbly he made
reuerence, & syn kneeled tofore hym & confessed his
mysdedes & synnes in his best wyse / and as touching
this that he was forsworne ayenst god and Melusyne
hys wyf, the pope gaf hym therfor such penaunce as it
playsed hym.   and that same day Raymondyn dyned
with the pope Benedicte / and on the morne he yede
& vysyted the holy places there.   And whan he had
doon there al that he muste doo, he toke leue to the
Pope & said to hym in this wyse, 'Ryght reuerend
holy fader, I may not goodly considere in me how euer

I may haue joye.   Wherfore I purpose to yeld myself
into some hermytage.'   And thenne the Pope hym
demanded thus, 'Raymondyn, where is your deuocyon
4 & wylle to goo?'   'By my feyth, holy fader,' said
Raymondyn, 'I haue herd say that there is to Mountferrat[1] in Aragon a deuoute & holy place / & there wold
I fayn be.'   'My fayre sone,' said the pope, 'soo it is
8 said.'   And to hym said Raymondyn, 'holy fader, my
intencion is thither to goo and to yeld my self there
hermyte, for to pray god that it playse hym to gyue
allegeaunce to my lady my wyf.'   'Now fayre sone,'
12 said the Pope, 'with the holy gost may ye goo / & al
that ye shal doo with good wyll I remysse it to your
penaunce.'   And thenne Raymondyn kneeled & kyssed
the popes feet.   And the pope gaf hym hys benedic-
16 tion. / And thenne departed Raymondyn & came to
hys lodgys / & dide doo [2] trusse & make all redy for
to departe / and as touchyng his meyne nor of hys way
I wyl not make long mencyon / but he rode so long
20 that he came to Thoulouse / and there he gaf lycence
& leue to all hys meyne to departe & retourne / except
only a Chappellayn & a Clerc that he toke with him /
and wel & truly he prayed [3] euery one so that they
24 were content / but sory they were all of theire maister
that so departed fro them / and he sent letres to geffray
& to the barons of hys land that they shuld doo theire
hommage to his sone geffray, & receyue hym for theire
28 lord.   And his meyne toke the letres / and soo they
departed fro theire lord with grete sorow & heuynesse,
For he neuer told them what way he shuld take / but
wete it he had with hym goodes ynough / and dyde so
32 moche that he came to Nerbonne where he rested hym
a lytel space of tyme.

Thystorye sheweth in this partye that whan
Raymondyn was come to Nerbonne he dide

---

[1] Montserrat, the correct reading.   [2] Fr. *trosser les sommiers.*

Side notes:

and telle him that he wishes to be a hermit.

The Pope asks where he would like to go.

Raymondin answers Mountserrat in Aragon.

The Pope bestows his blessing, after Raymondin had kissed his feet.

Raymondin gets on his way, and when he arrives at Toulouse he pays off his men,

[3] fol. 198.

and sends them home with letters to Geffray, which order the barons of his land to do homage to Geffray.

His men return sadly, without knowledge of where their master is going. Raymondin goes to Narbonne, where he makes a halt;

and has hermits' habits made for himself, his chaplain and his clerk.

He continues his journey

till he arrives at Mountserrat.

He attends divine service.

He is asked if he will stay the night, and answers 'yes.'

[2] fol. 196 b.

Raymondin visits the hermitages, and finds the third cell empty, the hermit having died lately.

doo make many hermyte habytes, and also for his Chappellayn & Clerk suche as they owe to haue / and syn departed & went tyl he came to [1] Parpynen where he soiourned one day / and on the morne [2] he passed the destraytte & mounted the mountaynes of Aragon / and so foorth he came to Barselone the Cite where he toke hys lodgys and soiourned there thre dayes, and on the fourth toke hys waye toward Mountserrat where he came & yede & vysyted wel the Chirche & the place there, whiche semed hym ryght deuoute / and there he herd the deuyne seruyse deuoutly / but yet had he on hys worldly gownes / And thenne came to hym they that were ordeyned for to lodge & herberowe the pelgrymes, and demanded of hym yf it playsed hym to abyde there for þat nyght / and he answerd 'ya.' Thenne were his [3] horses stabled / and they gaf hym a fayre Chambre for hym & for his men. And in the meane while Raymondyn yede & vysyted the hermytages / but he went no ferther than to the v^m celle, for that place was of so grete heyght that he myght not goodly goo thither / and fonde the III^de celle exempt. For the hermyte there was deed but late tofore that. And there was stablysshed of old a Custome that yf within a terme prefix none came there to be hermyte, he of the nerest Celle gooyng vpward muste entre into that other Celle so exempted / and so al the hermytes benethe hym to chaunge theire places vpward. And so by that maner wyse was the nedermost Celle of al exempt & without hermyt. And the cause of this permutacion was that alwayes the nedermost hermyte most serue hys brother hermyte next aboue hym of meet & drynk after theire pytaunce & manere of etyng, and so foorth dide that one to that other vpward / and

[1] Fr. *Perpignen.*
[2] Fr. *passa le vellon et le pertuys, et vint à diener à Funères, et au giste à Gnemie.* Omitted above.

thus one serued other. And so ferre enquyred &
knew Raymondyn of theire maner of lyuyng that he
toke grete deuocion to it more than tofore / that is to
4 wete to be hermyte there. And thenne he toke leue
of the vth hermyte & so dide as he descended of the
other.   And he demanded after the pryour of
thabbey / and it was told hym that he was in the
8 vyllage nygh by thabbay that was hys, whiche vyllage
was called Culbaston / and thenne he desyred them
that they wold conduyte hym there as he was. And
so Ray¹mondyn left there his Chappellayn & his
12 Clerc, and with a seruaunt of the place went there as þe
pryour was, whiche receyued Raymondyn with joyful
chere. And there shewed Raymondyn al hys wyll and
deuocyon and how the place playsed hym. And thenne
16 the pryour that sawe Raymondyn of fayre coutenaunce
& man of grete worship graunted hym the exempted
place, wherof Raymondyn had grete joye at herte. /
Thenne was Raymondyn ryght joyous whan the
20   pryour had graunted hym the place of the
nethermost hermytage and moche þanked god therof.
and so he bode there with the pryour al that nyght /
and on the morow they mounted and came ayen to
24 thabbay where as Raymondyn toke his habytes and
was there made hermyte. And thenne was the deuyne
seruyce doon, where Raymondyn offred ryche jewels
as gold and precyous stones. And after the seruyce
28 they went to dyner / and raymondyn dyde doo send
to hys bretheren hermytes besyde theire pytaunce other
meetes for recreacion, letyng them knowe hys professyon & commyng. Wherof al they lawded god,
32 deuoutely prayeng hym that he wold hold & encres
Raymondyn in good deuocyon. And so dwelled
Raymondyn in thabbay, and on the morne he entred
in to his Celle wher he bygan to led a holy & strayt
36 lyf.   And anoone after was the tydynges spredd

MELUSINE.   Z

Side notes:

Raymondin, after his enquiries, takes a greater liking to the place than ever.

He takes leave of the hermit in the fifth cell and descends.

Raymondin asks to be taken to the prior of the abbey.
¹ fol. 199.

The prior entertains Raymondin,

and at his request grants the empty cell.

The next day Raymondin is made a hermit,

and after divine service makes a rich offering.

Raymondin tells his brother hermits of his profession, and supplies them with extra meats. The hermits praise God, and pray for Raymondin.

He enters his cell, and begins to lead a holy life.

thrugh all Aragon & Langgedok how that a g
prynce was made hermyte at Mounferrat / but t
knew not of what Countre he was.   And ¹also
wold neuer vttre it / And many noble men went
see hym / and in especial the king⸱ of aragon was tl
hym self, which asked hym of his estate & Count
but of hym he coude neuer wate it.   And hare res̄
thystorye of them / and retourneth to shewe
Raymondyns men that departed fro Thoulouse. /

Thystory recounteth that so long rode the ¹
of Raymondyn after they were departed
Thoulouse that they came in Poytou & so foertl
Lusynen, Where they fonde geffray and many of
barons of the land / and after theire obeyssunce d
they delyuered theire letres to geffray & to the ba
as they were commanded by Raymondyn theire l
Whan the baronye vnderstod the tenour of th
letres they said to geffray in this manere / 'My
syth it playseth not your fader vs more to gouer
and that he wyl that we doo our hommage to you,
are al redy thereto.'   'By god,' said geffray, 'grame
Fayre lordes, and I am redy to receyue you to y
lygeauns.'   And þenne they dyde to hym homm
And anoone after was knowen thrugh al the Cou
how Raymondyn had exilled hymself for the g
sorow that he had for his wyf Melusyne that he
lost.   Who thenne had sene the doleur & lament
heuynes that men dide thrugh all the Cou
wysshyng theire lord & theire lady, he shuld haue
hertely pyte.   For many one fered geffray for caus
his yre & fyersnes.   But for nought they doubted,
he gouerned hym rightously & wel.   Here I sh
leue of þem ²to speke / and shal shewe of geffray
was ryght dolaunt & sorowful of that he had lost l
hys fader & his moder thrugh his owne mysdede
synne.   For they that were retourned fro hym co

not say where he was come. Thenne remorse of
conscience toke geffray at herte & remembred how he
fyred thabbaye of Maylleses, & brent hys brother
4 Froymond and al the monkes *þer* *without* hauyng ony
lawfull cause so to doo / and that thrughe hys synne
he angred bothe hys fader & moder, and by that cause
he had lost his moder. Wherfore he toke suche sorowe
8 that it was *meruaylt* / and also he remembred the deth
of the Erle of Forest hys vncle, which thrugh his faytte
fell doun fro the hyest toure of the Castel Marcelly to
the erthe. And thus remembred geffray all hys
12 my[s]dedes and synnes, and sore wepyng bygan to say /
that but yf god had pyte on hym he was lyke to be
lost & dampned for *euer*. And thenne he hymself
alone entred into a chambre / and there he bygan to
16 make grete sorowe & lamentable wepynges prayeng god
with herte contrite that he wold haue *mercy* on hym /
and as god wold he toke there *deuocion* to goo to
Romme for to confesse his synnes to *our* holy fader the
20 pope. And thenne he sent for his broder theodoryke
that he shuld come to speke *with* hym, For he loued
hym aboue al *oþer*. And assoone as Theodoryke
vnderstod the mandement of hys brother geffray, he
24 foorth*with* mounted on horsback & rode tyl he came
to Lusynen where geffray was, that receyued hym
with joye, & said to hym that he wold leue al hys
land in his gou*ernaunce*, For he ¹wold go to Romme to
28 confesse his synnes tofore the pope / & that he wold
neuer come ayen tyl he had found hys fader. Thenne
Theoderyk prayed hym that he wold suffre hym to goo
with hym. And geffray shewed to hym that it were
32 not good for them bothe so to doo / And thenne
geffray with noble companye departed and toke *with*
hym grete goodes, and toke *with* hym one of hys
faders seruaunts that was retourned fro Thoulouse for
36 to conduyte hym all that way that hys fader yede /

(margin notes:)
Geffray is full of remorse when he thinks of the loss of his father and mother, and how it was caused by his misdeeds.

Geffray enters a chamber alone, and prays with a contrite heart for mercy.

He resolves to go to Rome to confess to the Pope. Geffray sends for Theodoric

¹ fol. 200 *b*.
to tell him that he is going to Rome to confess to the Pope, and that he leaves his lands in Theodoric's charge. Theodoric wants to go with him, but Geffray says it would not do. Geffray takes plenty of goods, and sets out on his journey with one of his father's servants.

and he shuld euer take hys lodgys there as hys fader
was lodged by the way. And the seruaunt hym
ansuerd that gladly he shuld so doo.

Cap. LVIII. How Geffray went to Romme & confessed hys synnes tofore the Pope.

Thystorye sayth that whan geffray was departed
fro Lusynen he rode so long by hys journeyes
that he came to romme, and drew hym toward our 8
holy fader the Pope, to whome he made humble
reuerence and syn deuoutely confessed hym of hys
synnes. And the Pope charged hym to make thabbay
of Maylleses to be edyfyed agayn & therto ordeyne six 12
score monkes, & many other penitences the pope
charged hym doo, the whiche as now present I shal not
shewe. And thenne geffray said to our holy fader the
Pope how he wold goo to seke hys fader, and the pope 16
told hym that he ¹shuld fynd hym at Mountferrat in
Aragon. And thenne he toke leue of the pope &
kyssed his feet / and the pope gaf hym hys benediction. And so geffray departed fro Romme & toke 20
hys way toward toulouse where he cam & hys meyne
with hym and was lodged where as his fader dede
lodge tofore. And there the seruaunt asked of theire
hoste yf he coude not telle which way hys lord 24
Raymondyn toke / And thoste said to hym that hys
lord had hold the way toward Nerbonne & that no
farther he knew of hys way. And the seruaunt told
it to geffray. 'By my feyth,' said geffray, 'that is 28
not the next way for to goo to Mountferrat / but syth
my fader went that way so shal we doo.' And thus
on the morne geffray & hys meyne departed & hasted
them toward Nerbonne, where they cam & were lodged 32
there as Raymondyn had tofore lodged. For so moche
enquered the servaunt that he knewe þat hys lord dide

Geffray confesses
to the Pope.

He is charged to
rebuild the abbey
of Maillezes.

Geffray learns
that his father
¹ fol. 201.
is at Mount-
serrat.

He kisses the
Pope's feet,
and receives the
benediction.
Geffray goes to
Toulouse, and

finds that his
father went from
there to Nar-
bonne.

He follows the
same route,
though it is not
the direct way to
Mountserrat.

lodge there, & how he dide do make there many
habytes for an hermyte. And on the morne geffray
toke hys way toward Parpynen, where he cam, & fro
4 þens he rode with hys meyne to Barselone, & þenne to At last Geffray reaches Mount-serrat.
thabbey of mountferrat where he alyghted & sent hys
horses to Culbaston / and syn he yede & entred in to
the Chirch.   And anoon the seruaunt beforsaid sawe
8 the Chappellayn of Raymondyn his lord within a His servant re-ports that he has seen his father's chaplain.
Chapell And immedyatly he told of it to geffray. ¹ fol. 201 b.
Wherof ¹he had grete joye and yede toward the
Chappellayne, the whiche whan he sawe geffray he
12 kneeled tofore hym and said, 'My lord ye be ryght The chaplain wel-comes Geffray, and tells him of the good life his father leads;
welcome' / and syn he recounted to geffray the good
lyf that hys fader led / and how euery day he confessed how he confesses and communi-cates daily, and that he eats no-thing that has had life.
hym & receyued his creatour / and that he ete nothing
16 that receyueth deth.   And thenne geffray asked hym
where he was.   And the Chappellayn to hym said, The chaplain says Geffray can-not see his father till next day.
'he is in yonder hermytage / but my lord as for this
day ye may not speke with hym, but to morne ye shall
20 see hym.'   'By my fayth,' said geffray, 'fayn I wold
see hym today / but sith it is soo I must take it in
patience ty[l] tomorowe.'   'My lord,' said thenne the
Chappellayn, 'yf it playse you ye may here the hye
24 masse, and therwhiles I shal ordeyne and shew your
meyne where your Chambre shal be dressed, and also I
shal doo make your dyner redy at your retourne fro
the masse.'
28 Thenne departed the Chappellayn fro geffray, that Geffray hears mass;
went to here masse acompanyed with x knyghtes
and wel xx squyers.   And thenne came the monkes and when he is out of sight the monks ask the chaplain, 'Who
of the place to Raymondins Chappellayn and demanded is that great devil with that great tooth?'
32 of hym in this wyse.   'What is that grete deuell with
that grete toth? he semeth wel to be a cruel man /
wherof knowe you hym / is he of your Countre?'
'By my feyth,' said the Chappellayn, 'ye / It is He tells them,
36 geffray with the grete toeth of Lusynen, one of the best

¹ fol. 202.

and they ask if
it is not the same
one who killed
the Northumber-
land giant, and
burnt the Abbey
of Mallesea and
all the monks
therein.

The chaplain an-
swers that he is.

The monks are
much afraid.

The chaplain
tells them to be
at ease, because
the hermitage
contains the per-
son Geffray loves
most of all in the
world.

The monks clean
and decorate the
church,

and send word
to the prior of
the arrival of
Geffray.

The prior finds
Geffray in the
church, and does
him reverence.

Geffray thanks
him, and pro-
mises that the
place will be
none the worse
for his visit.

² fol. 202 b.

& moost valyaunt knightes of the world & wete it he
¹holdeth grete possessions & grete landes.' And the
monkes answerd, 'Wel we haue herd speke of hym /
is it not he that sloughe the geaunt in garand and that 4
other geaunt also of Northomberland / he is also he
that brent thabbay of Maylleses with all the monkes
perinne bycause that hys brother was there shorne
monke without hys leue.' 'By my fayth,' said the 8
Chappellayn, 'certainly it is that same.' And þenne
the monkes al abasshed and aferd sayd / he is come
hither for to doo vs some myschief and dommage.
Thenne said one of them, 'wete it wel that I shal hyd 12
myself in suche place that he shal not fynd me.'
'Noo,' said the Chappellayn, 'Forsooths I warraunt
you he shal doo you no hurt nor dommage, but al ye
shal soone be glad of hys commyng, For suche one is 16
within this place that he loueth aboue al creatures of
the world.' And whan they vnderstod the Chappellayn
they were somwhat assured and went & hanged the
chirche, and made al the place fayre & clene to theire 20
power as god hymself had descended there / and sent
word to the Pryour that was at Culbaston that he
shuld come there, and that geffray with the grete toth
was come in pelgrymage in to theire abbaye, and noble 24
companye with hym. Thenne came there fourthwith
the pryour that fond geffray in the Chirche, and
honourably made hym reuerence and sayd that he
hymself / the monkes & al the place was at his 28
commandement. 'Sire,' said geffray, 'gramercy and
wete it wel I loue this place / and yf god gyf me
helthe it shal ²not be the wers for my commyng.'
'My lord,' said the pryour, 'god yeld you.' Thenne 32
cam the Chapellayn to geffray and hym said, 'My
lord, your dyner is redy.' And therwith geffray toke
the pryour by the hand and togidre went into the hall,
where they wesshed theire handes & syn sette them at 36

dyner; geffray and the pryour deuysed long space
togidre of one thing & of oþer. And thus passed
foorth that day. /

4 In this partye sayth thystorye that on þe morne
geffray roos vp and fonde the priour and his faders
Chapellayn waytyng after hym whiche led hym to
here masse / and after the masse they led hym toward
8 the hermytages. And thenne the pryour toke his leue
of geffray & retourned to Chirchward supposyng none
other but that geffray went for to see thestate of the
hermytes and for none other cause. For he had neuer
12 trowed that his fader had be þer. And thenne mounted
geffray toward the first hermitage that was wel lxxx
stepes highe vpon the mountayns. And wete it that
the Clerc was at Raymondyns Celle doore waytyng for
16 the Chappelayn that shuld say masse tofore Raymondin.
And as the Clerk loked dounward, he perceyued geffray
that came vpward & wel knew hym, and forthwith
entred in the celle & said to Raymondin, 'My
20 lord, here commeth your sone geffray.' And whan
Raymondin vnderstod it he was ryght joyous and said,
'blessed be god / he is welcomme.' Thenne entred
first the Chappellain in to the Celle & salued
24 Raymondyn / but he bade the Chappellayn to say
geffray that he myght not speke with hym tyl þat hys
masse were doon. And foorthwith the cha¹pellayn
dyde as Raymondyn hym commanded. And geffray
28 answerd, 'his playsire be doo.' This doon Raymondyn
was confessed and herd his masse & receyued the holy
sacrament. And in the meane sayson geffray beheld
vpward the great mountaynes whiche were high &
32 ryght vp and sawe thermytages that were aboue hym /
and sawe the Capell of Saynt Mychel whiche was the
vᵗʰ hermytage, and after loked dounward / and in hym
self had grete meruayll how man durst there take
36 habytacyon / and to hym appered the Chirche and

housyng of thabbey but as lytel Chapelles. Thenne
cam the Chapellayn & called geffray and he entred
within the Celle of his fader / and anoone kneeled on
his knees & dyde to hys fader reuerent salutacion / 4
And Raymondyn toke hym vp in his armes and kyssed
hym / and thenne made hym to sette vpon a stoole
with hym tofore the awter. And there bygan geffray
to shewe to hys fader how he was at Romme, and how 8
he was confessed of the pope / and the pope hym said
that he shuld fynd hym at Mountferrat. And in this
communycacion had they many materes togidre /
geffray alwayes prayeng hys fader that he wold 12
retourne to his countre. 'Fayre sone,' said Raymondyn,
'that may I not doo. For here I wyl spend my lyf,
always prayeng god for thy moder & me, & for the,
that god wyl amende the, my sone geffray.' And soo 16
geffray was there al that day with his fader. And the
next day in the morowe herd Raymondyn his masse,
& receyued our lord, as hys custome was to doo / and
after, said to geffray, 'Fayre sone, it behoueth the to 20
parte from hens, & to retourne in to thy Countre;
and grete wel al ¹my children & my barons.' And
thenne geffray toke leue of hys fader al wepyng; and
loth he was to departe from his fader. And after 24
came doun fro the mountayn vnto thabbaye, where
he was honourably receyued / and the monkes had
grete meruayll wherfore he was so long aboue.

Thystorye sheweth that geffray gaf grete ryches & 28
fayre jewelles to the Chirche, & after toke leue of
the pryour & his monkes, but the pryour hym conueyed
vnto Culbaston, wher geffray dyned with the pryour /
and told hym in secret wyse that Raymondyn was 32
hys fader, whom geffray besoughte to take hede to
hys fader, and that the Chirche shuld not lese nothing
therby, For euery yere ones duryng hys lyf he wold
come & vysyte hys fader. Thenne ansuerd the pryour, 36

Geffray enters
his father's cell,
and salutes him.

Raymondin
takes him in his
arms and kisses
him.
Geffray tells his
father how he
had been at
Rome, and how
he confessed,
and was told by
the Pope that
his father was at
Mountserrat.

Geffray asks his
father to return
to his country,
but he answers
that he cannot,
as he intends
to stay at Mount-
serrat, and pray
for Geffray's
mother, for him-
self, and for
Geffray.

¹ fol. 203 b.
Geffray takes his
leave.
His father sends
a greeting to his
children and his
barons.

Geffray gives
presents to the
Church;

and at dinner
tells the prior
that Raymondin
is his father, and
asks him to take
care of him, and
the Church will
lose nothing
by it.

'doubte you not, my lord, there shal be no deffawte but
I shal vysyte & remembre your fader.' And thenne
toke geffray leue & went to Barselone to hys bed.

4 And on the morne he departed toward Lusynen wher
as Theodoryk hys brother & the barons receyued hym
with ryght grete joye, and were glad of his commyng.
And whan they were at leyser, geffray shewed to hys
8 brother theodoryk the very effect of euery thing
touchyng theyre fader. Foorthwith Theodoryk that
moche loued his fader bygan to wepe ful tenderly.
And geffray seeyng his broþer make suche sorowe to
12 hym said thus, 'My ryght dere brother, yet must ye
abyde here, For wete it wel that I wyl goo see our
two bretheren in almayne, that is to vnderstand
Regnauld king of behayne and the Duc Anthony of
16 Lucembourgh / but I wyl not departe with̃out aray
of men of armes, For þer be in thoo marches ryght
euyl peple the which ¹gladly wold robbe them that passe
by the way.' 'By my sowle, my brother, I hold wel
20 with̃al that ye doo as ye say / but I beseche you ryght
entierly brother that we leue our countre in the
gouernaunce of our barons & take *with* vs v.C. men of
armes, and that it may playse you I to go wit̃ you ;
24 For I haue herd say that there is grete werre betwix
them of Ansay & them of Austeryche.' 'By my
feyth,' said geffray, 'Ye say wel, For perauenture our
brother Anthony is in hand *with* them.' And whan
28 they had made theire ordonnaunce, Odon the Erle of
Marche came and spake with geffray, and brought in
hys company thre score men of armes, For at that
tyme he had warre ayenst the Earle of Vandosme /
32 and also Raymond their brother Earle of Forestz cam
there the same day. And there the foure bretheren
made there moche one of other / and were joyfull for
the tydynges that they herd of theire fader / and said /
36 ones they hoped to see hym togidre.

Geffray returns
to Lusignen,
where he is joy-
fully received.

He tells Theo-
doric about their
father.

Theodoric weeps
at the story.

Geffray proposes
to visit Reginald
and Anthony.

¹ fol. 204.

Theodoric wishes
to go with him,

because he has
heard there is
war between
Ansay and
Austria.

They are joined
by Odo, Earl of
March.

The brothers
make much of
each other, and
are glad of the
news of their
father.

Cap. LIX. How Geffray reedyffyed the monastery of Maylleses.

Geffray arrange for the rebuilding of the abbey of Maylleses.

Geffray afore his departyng charged & ordeyned peuple for the reedyfyeng of the Abbaye of 4 Maylleses, as hym was youen in Charge by the pope by way of penaunce / and to them assygned where they shuld take bothe gold & syluer therwith to paye the werkmen. And so lefte he a good gouernour in 8

He and Theodoric appoint good governors for their countries.

hys countre / And in lyke wyse dyde his broper theodoryk in his Countre. And whan Odon &

1 fol. 204 b.

Raymond sawe that they wold departe to go ¹to see

Odo and Raymond propose to go with them to Allmain.

theire bretheren in Allemayne, they sayd in lyke wyse 12 wold they doo. And commanded anoone theire peple to mete with them at Boneuall. And at that tyme were the bretheren acompanyed with two thousand men of armes & a thousand Crosbowes. And whan 16 the Erle of Vandosme herd tydynges therof he supposed certaynly that they came to exille hym, and that Odon had complayned hym to hys bretheren of hym, and so

The Earl of Vendôme makes his peace with Odo.

moche he doubted geffray that he came to Boneuall 20 and yelded hym to the grace of Odon erle of Marche. And he pardonned hym of al the mysdedes that he had doo to hym. And the erle of Vandosme made hym homage of the land that was in debat atwix 24 them. /

The four brethren ride with their company to Castle Duras, near which they lodge.

Here sheweth thystorye that the foure bretheren departed fro Boneual & were in theires companye many grete lordes, and rode in fayre aray tyl they cam 28 vpon an euen and lodged them nygh a ryuere called Meuze, by a Fortresse named the Castel Duras. But as now I shal cease of them to speke / and shal

The King of Anssay was at war with the Dukes of Freibourg and Austria. He was besieged by them at Pourrencru.

begynne to speke of the kyng of anssay, that had grete 32 warre ayenst the Erle of Frebourgh & with the Duc of Austeryche, the which had besieged hym within a Castel of hys that was called Pourrencru. Wherfor he sent worde to Regnault kyng of Behayne that was

He had sent for help to Anthony and Regnald.

maryed with his Cousyn / and lyke wyse to the Duc
Anthony of Lucembourgh prayeng them of ayde &
4 socour ayenst his enemyes, at the whiche instaunce &
prayer / the two bretheren Regnald & Anthony made
theire apparayll. ¹And Regnaulde departed out of his

¹ fol. 205.

Royalme of Behayne and came to Lucembourgh with

Regnald with four hundred men goes to Anthony, to accompany him to the siege of Pourrencru.

8 IIII. C men of armes for to haue hys brother Anthony
with hym toward the siege of Porrencru, wher the
kyng of ansamy was besieged within. And þat meane
mayson came two knightes to Lucembourgh from geffray
12 and his thre bretheren þat were with hym, the which

Geffray sends word that he and his three brothers are on their way to Luxembourg.

. two knightes brought worde bothe to regnauld &
anthony of theire bretheren commyng, and that they
were nygh the toun and cam for to see them. And
16 whan kyng regnauld and the Duc Anthony knew that
theire bretheren were commyng toward them, they
were full glad & immedyatly commanded that al the
stretes shuld be rychely hanged, and syn mounted on
20 horsbak, and with noble companye they went to mete
them ; and rode tyl they mete with the vanwarde of
theire armee & asked where theire bretheren were /
and it was shewed to them where they were commyng

Regnald and Anthony meet their brethren outside the town.

24 vnder the standart. Geffray thenne, that wel vnderstod that anthony & regnauld his bretheren came to
mete hem, he made euery man to stande apart / and
soone after the six bretheren mete togidre and embraced
28 & made moche one of other / and after rode foorth
toward the toun / and aftir theire age they rode two
& two togidre. Odon and Anthony were the formest,
and after them rode Regnauld & Geffray / and them
32 folowed theodoryk & Raymonnet / and al theire
oost came after in fayre ordynaunce / and in this
manere they entred in to the toune, where as the
Cytezeyns were in theire best rayments al in a rowe
36 on bothe ²sydes of the stretes, that were rychely

² fol. 205 b.

hanged / and the ladyes & damoyselles loked out of t
wyndowes / and so grete & noble apparayll was the
made for theire commyng that it was a fayre syght.

Trouth it is that whan the bretheren entred with
Lucembourgh, Anthony & Geffray rode ther
the formest of al theire bretheren. And wete it th

The citizens
marvel at their
appearance.

the notable Citeseyns, ladyes, & damoiselles mervayll
moche of the fyeranes and grete height of theire lor
bretheren, sayeng that they six togidre wer able
wel shapen to destroye a grete oost / And thus th
rode thrugh the toun into the Castel and there th
alighted. There were the six bretheren recountred

The brethren
are received at
the castle by
the Queen of
Behaim and
the Duchess of
Luxembourg.

two noble ladyes, that is to vnderstand the que
of Behayn and the Duches of Lucembourgh, th
honourably receyued theire lordes and brethern. A
aftir they went into the hall that was al hanged w
ryche cloth of gold / and þer were the tables ryche
couered & redy to dyner. And thenne after ma
playsaunt deuyses and joyfull wordes, they wessh
theire handes and sette them at dyner and were no
serued. And after dyner geffray shewed & recount

Geffray tells of
his adventures.
How he had
found the tomb
of King Elinas
and Queen
Pressine, from
whom they had
all sprung, and
how their father
had become a
hermit at
Montserrat.
Anthony and
Regnold tell
their brethren
that they are to
help the King
of Ansay.
1 fol. 205.

Geffray answers
that he and his
brethren are
ready to do so
as well.

all hys auentures & fayttes / and how he fonde
tombe of Elynas / & of the quene Pressyne of whic
lynee they were yssued, wherof they were al joyfull
glad to mervayll / and how theire fader was depart
and where he was. For of all other thinges th
knew ynough. And thenne Anthony & regnau
told to theire brethern how the kyng of Ansay v
besieged & that they wold help hym. Then
answerd Geffray, 'My lordes, my brethern, wete
wel we are not come hither to take our rest / but
al are redy to goo with you whersomeuer ye wyl /
therfor lete vs not make long soiourne / but go v
vpon our enemyes to helpe & socoure our frende
And soothwold Geffray and hys brethern that w

1 'we' repeated in MS.

come there with hym toke theire leue of bothe the
queene & duchesse theire sustirs & retourned to theire
oost / and thenne Regnauld & Anthony wold haue
4 conueyed them / but geffray said, 'Fayre lordes &
bretheren, ye shal come no forther / but make al your
apparayll & take leue of your wyues, and to morne, god
before, we wyl departe toward the said Castel wherin
8 the king of Anssay our frend is besieged.' And soo
Anthony and regnauld retourned sayeng eche one to
other, 'Certaynly this man may not long endure / but
he be other take or slayn. For he fereth of nothing
12 in the world / & also to counseylle hym, it were but
for nought, For he suffreth nothing, but as his wyt &
mynde gyueth hym. For yf he had with hym but
X. Ml men, & that he sawe his enemyes tofore hym to
16 the nombre of IIC. Ml yet wold he fyght & medle
with them, wherfore we must take heede to hym that
he vaunce not hym self so moche with the enemyes,
but that we be nygh hym to socoure hym with our
20 peuple / but for this haste that he maketh we owe
not to wete hym euyl gree For cause that assoone as
oon may, he muste aduyse the wayes to hurt &
dommage his enemys.' And thenne they lefte of
24 geffray theire brother more to speke / but bothe they
said that he was ryght hardy & valyaunt. And on the
morne they [1] toke leue of theire wyues and left in the
land a good gouernour. And also geffray on that
28 other part ordeyned & purueyed of al thinges that were
necessary to hys oost. /

In the next day Geffray made blowe vp hys trompettes,
that euer[y] man shuld be armed, and after herd
32 his masse and syn marched forth with hys oost / And
immedyatly Anthony & regnald came out of the toun
with theire peuple in fayre aray. And so they departed
and rode togidre tyl they came into the land of
36 Anssay / and on an euen lodged them thre leghes nygh

he then returns to his hoost.

Geffray refuses Anthony and Regnald's company, and asks them to prepare to start to succour the King of Anssay in the morning.

They speak of Geffray's bravery.

[1] fol. 206 b.

In the morning they take leave of their wives and appoint a governor.

Geffray orders every man to arm, and after mass is said his hoost marches.

Anthony and Regnald join him with their people.

They arrive home again from Fribourg.

the toune of Frebourgh. Thenne called geffray al his bretheren and shewed to them that it behoued not them for theire honour to ronne vpon no man but that they had defyed hym tofore / And they answerd that 4 he said trouth. Wherfor they lete make a letre of deffyaunce of whiche the tenour foloweth. 'Regnauld

A letter of defiation is written to the Duke of Austria and the Earl of Fribourg.

by the grace of god kyng of Behayne, Anthony Duc of Lucembourgh, Odon Erle of Marche, Geffray lord of 8 Lusynen, Raymond Erle of Forestz, and Theodoryk lord of Partenay. To the duc of Austerychs and to the Erle of Frebourgh, and to al theirs alyaunces gretyng. And whore we haue vnderstand that with- 12 out ony lawfull quarell or raysonnable cause ye haue gretly hurt & dommaged bothe the land & pouple of our ryght welbeloued vncle the kyng of Anssay, the whiche as now ye haue besieged within his Castel of 16 Pourrencru, And for as moch that we be therfor meued, & entende & purpose to entre in your land to dystroye you & al your pouple / consyderyng the

(&c. &c.

noble ordre of knyghthode that it shal not be by vs 20 myunsshed. We perfor by our messenger send you oure letres of deffyaunce, &c.' Thenne was delyuered the letre to a herault, which rode tyl he came to the

and sent by a herault to the Duke of Austria at Pourrenenu. It is read in hearing of all the nobles there. They say that the devil has sent the brethren against them, and that only the name of the Lusignans is now spoken of. The herault returns to the brethren's camp.

siege of Pourrencru wher he presented the said letre 24 to the Duc of Austrych, the whiche letres were redd in heryng of al þe lordes there. Thenne said they of Allemayne the Deuell hath brought hem hyther, none other renowme is now thrugh al the world but of them 28 of Lusynen. Thenne retourned the herault toward the six bretheren, and to them shewed the manere how they of theire enemyes oost were meruaylled. 'By my feyth they haue herd speke of vs from ferre ; but now 32 they shal see vs nere to them.' It is trouth that

Geffray takes two hundred men, and ambushes them in a wood near Fribourg.

thenne geffray departed with four hundred men of armes from his oost & went and embusshed his pouple in a lytel wood nygh the toun of Frebourgh. This 36

doon he & ten knyghtes with hym, & a squyer of
Lucembourgh that ryght wel coude speke Almayn
tonge & knew al the Countre, went vpon a lytel
4 mountayne to behold & see how he myght entre in
the toun / but or he departed he said to them of his
embusshe in this manere : ' Sires, I entende & purpose
with the help of god to haue the toun of Frebourgh or
8 to morne pryme at our playsire. Wherfor this nyght
I shall departe with this X knyghtes and this esquyer,
& at the spryng of the day I shal bygynne myn
enterpryse / and but loke wel when ye perceyue vs
12 within the gate that fourthwith ye marche toward vs.'
And thenne about thre of the clokk after mydnyght
Geffray / his ten knyghtes and his guyde toke ¹eche
of them a sack full of hey and bare it before them
16 vpon tharsons of theire sadels. In this manere they
went & came tofore the gate of Frebourgh, where as
the said esquyer called the watche þat they myght
entre, sayeng that they were frendes and that they had
20 be all that nyght in fourrage. Thenne asked hym the
porter what they had in thoo sackes, the squyer ansuerd
there ben in gownes & suche thinges and suche ware /
that we haue take vpon our enemyes and we bryng
24 them . hyther to selle them. The porter thenne
supposyng they had be of Allemayne & theire frendes
opend the gate & lete fall the bridge. Thenne entred
geffray first of alle, and foorthwith drew his swerd and
28 slew the porter / and in conclusyon they slough al
them of the watche. Thenne was there the cry of
them of the toun ' treson / treson ' / And immedyatly
marched thembusshe & came & entred in the toun.
32 There was grete occisyon of them of the toun / but
many of them escaped and fledd. And whan this was
doon geffray lefte there foure hondred men of armes &
retourned with the residue toward hys oost that he
36 mete by the way toward the siege. Of this noble

enterpryse & valyaunt fayt the brethern of geffray and
al theire peple were meruaylled / saymng that guffray
was the moost valyaunt knyght & subtyl in the faytte
of armes that lyued at that day. And joyous & glad 4
they marched courageously ¹toward theire enemyes.

Anoon after came tydynges to the siege how Frebourgh
was lost, wherof the Duc of Austeryche and in especial

the Erle of Frebourgh were sorowful & wroth. 'By 8
my fayth,' said thenne the Duc of Austeryche, 'they
be subtyl men of warre & moch to be doubted. Yf we
loke not wel about vs they myght wel gyue vs a grete
shak.' Wherfor they called theire Counseyll.　　　12

In this partye sayth thystorye that on the next day
by the morowe the six bretheren hard masse, and
after ordeyned peire batayltes / geffray & his thre
bretheren that were come with hym conduyted the first 16
batayll, Anthony had the second, And regnauld the
III^de. And so marched forth in fayr ordynaunce, and
so wel renged that it was a fayre sight to behold.
And whan the sonne bygan to shewe bryght & clere 20
they came vpon a lytel mountayn into the valey.

Thenne were they percyued, and they of the siege
bygan to cry alarme. Thenne armed hym euery man,
And in theire best wyse came & renged them before 24
the batayltes of the brethern. Thenne bygan the
batayltes of bothe sydes to approche eche other / and

with grete cryes of one part & of other medled & ranne
with theire sperys vpon eche other. The grounde was 28
there soone dyed rede with grete effusyon of blood.
For Geffray with hys swerd smote at the lyfte syde
& at the ryght syde vpon his enemyes & ouerthrew or

sloughe all them that he recountred. And ²the six 32
baners of the bretheren rengid them togidre in fayre
army. There were the armes of Lusynen wel shewed
and knowen in pycture, and also by pesaunt and
horryble strokes, For the six bretheren perced the 36

prees & smote, cuttyng heede*s*, armes, & leghes of
theire enemyes here & there, and made suche occysyon
that it was meruaylle / Geffray recountred by aduenture

4 the Duc of Austrych, on whom he descharged hys
swerd by such myght that he made hym to staker al
astonyed, And the*n*ne theodoryk that was nygh by,
strak hym fourthwi*th* and ou*er*threw hym, and so

8 incontynent he was take. And the noble and valyaunt
Anthony dyde ryght valyauntly, For he toke the Erle
Freburgh and made hym to delyu*er*e his swerd to hym,
and after betoke hym to foure knigh*tes*. What shuld

12 I make long compte . they of Allemayne were dyscomfyted and bygan to flee. The*n*ne came the kyng
of Anssay out of the Fortres glad & joyou*s* of the
dyscomfyture of hys enemyes, and cam*e* to the brethern

16 tent*es* where he thanked them moche of theire noble
socour and gretly festyed them. And were brought
there tofore hym the Duc of Austeryche & the Erle of
Frebourgh wi*th* syx noble barons / and to hym said

20 the bretheren, 'Sire, here ben your enemyes as
prysonners, doo of them your playsyr.' And the kyng
thanked them gretly & humbly. And this doon geffray
and hys bretheren that were cōme [1]wi*th* hym toke

24 leue of the kyng of Anssay, of theire brethern Anthony
& Regnauld, and retourned in theire Countre. But
thystory sayth that aftirward all the bretheren fonde
eche other togidre at Mountferrat, where they held a

28 noble feste for loue of Raymondyn theire fader, whiche
was ryght glad and joyou*s* to see there his children,
but soone he toke leue of them and retourned in to hys
hermytage. And thenne the six bretheren gaaf grette

32 ryches & jewels to the chirche there, and after departed
and toke leue eche one of other & retourned to theire
Countrees, some by the see & other by land.

H ere testyfyeth thistorye that as long as Raymondyn
36 lyued, Geffray & theodoryk cam*e* there eu*ery*

Side notes:

The brethren slay many of their enemies.

Geffray encounters the Duke of Austria, and strikes him with his sword.

Theodoric, who was at hand, gives him another stroke, and overthrows him. The Duke is taken. Anthony captures the Earl of Freibourg.

The Germans begin to flee. The King of Anssay comes out of his fortress, and thanks the brethren,

and feasts them. The Duke of Austria and the Earl of Freibourg are brought before him, and the brethren tell him to do what he pleases with them.

[1] fol. 209.

The brethren return home.

They afterwards meet at Mountserrat on a visit to their father, who is joyful at seeing them.

They give rich gifts to the church.

Geffray and Theodoric go to Raymondin every year;

but one day when they were about to journey to Mountserrat, a great serpent is seen on the battlements of Lusignan castle. It has a woman's voice. The people are abashed, and know it to be Melusine ; the brothers weep. When the serpent sees them she inclines her head, and utters a dolorous cry.

yere ones to see hym / but it befell on a day, as they were bothe at Lusynen redy for to go to Mountferrat, a mernayllous auenture, For there was seen vpon the batelments of the Castel a grete & horryble serpent the 4 which cryed with a femenyne voys, wherof all the peuple was abasshed / but wel they wyst that it was Melusyne / whan the two bretheren beheld it, teerys in habundaunce bygan to fall fro their eyen ; For they 8 knew wel that it was their moder. And whan the serpent sawe them wepe, she enclyned the heed toward them, casting suche an horryble cry & so doulorous that it semed them that herd it that the Fortres shuld 12 haue fall. And anoone aftir the two brethern geffray & theodoryk departed toward Mountferrat where they came and fond their fader deed, wherof they lamented & made grete sorow [1]and anoone clothed 16 themself and al theire meyne in blak, and ordeyned for thobsequye of their fader. There came the kyng of aragon with many grete lordes that offred at the masse. And whan the scruyse was doon & the corps 20 buryed honourably / geffray went & thanked the kyng and his barons of thonour that þey had doon to hys fader and to his brother & hym. /

Geffray and Theodoric go to Mountserrat and find their father dead.
[1] fol. 209 b.
They mourn, and dress themselves and their men in black, and arrange their father's obsequies.
The King of Aragon, and many lords, attend and hear mass.
After the burial Geffray thanks them.

Thus as thystorye sheweth was thobsequye of 24 Raymondyn deuoutly & nobly doon, and a ryche sepulture was made & sette vpon his graue, & trouth it is that Bernardon the neuew of Geffray was there that ryght wel coude behaue hym among the ladyes, 28 in so moche that the quene of Aragon, that was there, desyred her lord to demande of Geffray what that yong gentylman was / and that / the kyng dide gladly. And thenne geffray ansuerd, 'Sire, he is my neuew, 32 sone to the Erle of Marche my brother.' 'Certaynly, Geffray,' said the kyng, 'Wel I byleue that, For he is wel nourrytured and semeth wel to be of noble

A tomb is placed over Raymondin.

extraction / and wete it wel that his contenaunce
playseth vs ryght wel· and so dooth lyke wyse to the
quene / and veryly yf it playsed you to suffre hym
4 abyde with vs in our Court we wold doo for hym that
he & you bothe shuld be playsed therwith.' 'Sire,'
said geffray, 'his fader hath another sone and two
doughtirs, & syth it is your playsir to haue hym he is
8 come hither with vs in a good heure & that playseth
me wel.' And thenne the kyng thanked hym moche,
and so dyde the quene.   And wete it that Bernardon
[1] Wedded aftirward, at thinstaunce & prayer of the
12 kyng of Aragon, the doughtir of the lord Cabyeres that
had none to hys heyre but her.   And thenne the
kyng· and the quene, lordes & ladyes, toke theire leue
of the two bretherne, the whiche after grete yeftes of
.16 ryches by them youen to the chirch toke leue of the
pryour and hys monkes, and after departed and
retourned to Lusynen, where as they called to them all
the baronnye and there was thobsequye of Raymondyn
20 honourably doon.   And aftir Geffray shewed to his
brother Odon, Erle of Marche, how & wherfore hys
sone Bernardon was lefte with the kyng of Aragon,
wherof he was glad.   And thenne the bretheren and
24 the barons toke leue of Geffray and retourned to theire
countrees.   And Geffray abode at Lusynen and dyde
aftirward moche good ; For he reedyfyed the noble
Abay of Maylleses and dyde grete almesse to the poure
28 peuple.

Thystorye sayth that all the heyres of Raymondyn
and Melusyne regned nobly, that is to wete
Vryan in Cipre, Guyon in Armenye, Regnault in
32 Behayne, Anthony in Lucembourgh, Odon in Marche,
Raymonet in Forestz, Geffray in Lusynen, and
Theodoryk in Partenay.   And of theyre lynee are
yssued them of Castel Regnault, They of Penbrough

The Queen of
Aragon takes
Geffray's nephew
to her court.

1 fol. 210.
He afterwards
marries the only
child of the Lord
of Cabyeres.

Geffray and
Theodoric give
great gifts to
the church,

and return to
Lusignan, where
the obsequies of
Raymondin are
honourably done.

Geffray tells
Odo that Bernar-
don had been
left with the
King of Aragon.

Geffray rebuilds
the Abbey of
Mailleses.

The nine heirs
of Raymondin
and Melusine
reign nobly,

and from them
are issued the
lords of Castle
Regnault, of
Pembroke,

A A 2

of Cabyeres, and
of Cardillac,

in England / they of Cabyeres in Aragon,[1] and they
[2]Cardillak in Quercyn. /

Geffray governs
his land well,
and administers
good justice.
For ten years he
asks no ac-
counts from his
receivers, who

* fol. 110 b.

are told when
they wish him
to examine the
accounts, that
when justice is
done, and his
towns and
castles are well
provided for, and
he has plenty
of money, he
is content.

But his stewards
ask, for their
own safety, that
he should give
them quittance.

Here after saith thistory that geffray ten yere af
the deces of Raymondin· his fader governa
ryght wel & kept good justice in his land / but dury
that long space of tym he asked of his receyuours no
acomptes, but whan the [2]receyuours wold haue shew
theire acomptes he to them answerd in this maner
'What acomptes wold ye shew to me? For as touchi
myself I wyl none other acompte, but that justice
wel and truly kept throgh al my land, and my town
& Castels wel entreteyned, and gold & syluer to he
& kepe myn estate / trow ye that I wyl make a pala
of gold / the stone that my lady my moder me g
suffyseth me ryght wel.' And thenne hys stywardes
gouernours answerd, 'certaynly, my lord, it behoue
wel to a prynce to here and see what he spendeth,
lest ones in a yere / al were it but for the saluacy
of hys receyuours in tyme to come and for to gy
them quytaunce.'

Geffray looks at
his accounts,
and sees an item
of ten sous that
was paid yearly
for the pommel
of the highest
tower of Lusig-
nan Castle.

He is told that
it is an annual
rent.

Geffray declares
he holds the
castle direct
from God,
his Creator.
His stewards
tell Geffray that
they do not know
to whom they
pay the ten sous.

Here sayth thistory that geffray consentid to he
thacomptes of his receyuours. And it came
an article where he vnderstod that [4]X. ß were pay
euery yere only for the pommel of the hyest toure
hys Fortresse of Lusynen / he anone rested there a
asked why it was not made so strong that it myg
laste many wynter. 'My lord,' answerd the receyuour
'it is rente annuell.' 'What say ye?' said geffray /
hold not the fortresse but only of god my Creatour
wel happy I were yf he held me quyte therfor of a
my synnes / but telle me to whom ye paye.' 'Certaynly
said they / 'we wot not' / 'How thenne,' said Geffray
'ye desyre of me quytaunce therof / so wyl I hav

---

[1] Fr. version gives in addition 'ceulx du Chaurenage e
Dauphine: ceulx de la Roche.'
[2] Fr. Candillat.　　　　　[4] Fr. dix soubz.

quytaunce of hym that receyueth it of you / as rayson
is / but by god ye shal not begyll me soo, for yf I may
knowe who that taketh that annuel rente of me, he

Geffray says that
he who takes the
money must
show letters
patent proving
his right,

4 shal shew me good letres therof made / or he or ye
shall yeld me ayen the said annuel rente fro the tyme
that ye first alowed it in your acomptes ¹vnto now.'

or he will have
to return it.

¹ fol. 211.

Thenne said the receyuours to Geffray in this manere :

The receivers
tell how six years

8 'My lord, trouth it is / that six yere agoo after the
doulorous departyng of my lady your moder from your
fader / euery yere vpon the last day of August was
sene a grete hand that toke the pommel of the said

after the depar-
ture of Melusine,
and the last day
of August every
year,

a great hand
pulled down the
pommel of the
tower, which
cost twenty to
thirty livres to
repair.

12 toure & pullyd it fro the toure by so grete strength
that the rouf of the tour brak therwithal, and so it
costed euery yere to make ayen xx¹¹ or xxx²li. thanne
came a man to my lord your fader which he nor no man

Then an un-
known man came
and advised Ray-
mondin to put
thirty pieces of
silver on the
pommel the last
of August each
year,

16 knew what he was, and counseylled hym that euery
yere vpon the last day of August he shuld doo take
a purse of hertis leeder and to be put in it xxx pieces
of syluer, eche piece worth ³foure penys, that made in

20 summa ten sheling, And that this purse shuld be putte
vpon the pommel of the said toure / and by that shuld
the pommel abyde styl and not hurt nor dommaged /
and euer syth tyl now it hath thus be doon.' And

and the tower
would be un-
injured.

24 whan geffray vnderstod this meruayll he bygan to
thinke, and long he was or he ansuerd or said ony
word. /

Geffray marvels
much at the
story:

Thystorye witnesseth that long thought Geffray
28 vpon this faytte, and after he said in this manere :
'Sires, how wel that I byleue that it is as ye say,
Neuertheles I charge you vpon peyne of deth that ye
no more paye the said annuel, but at the last day of

at length he for-
bids his steward
to pay the rent
again on pain
of death ;

32 August bryng to me the purse and the money, For I
wyl make the payement myself.' Thenne sent geffray
for hys brother theodoryk in Partenay, and also for
hys brother Raymond in Forestz, that they shuld be

but says on the
day the money
is to be given to
him, and he will
pay it himself.
Geffray sends for
Raymondin and
Theodoric,

² Fr. livres.   ³ Fr. quatre deniers.

with hym at Lusynen the xxvi[th] day of August.   And
when they were come he shewed [1]to them al the
maters of the said second rente, and said that he neuer
should suffre it to be payed; but that he first knew to 4
whom and why the fortres of Lusynen was bound thus
for to doo.   And when the last day of August came,
Geffray herd hys masse and receyued ryght deuoutely
the holy sacrement and immedyately armed hym, and 8
had the preste putte the stolle about his nek / and
aftir toke the purse with the money therin.   And
penne he had his bretheren farwel, sayeng in this

manere: 'I wyl departe and serche for hym that thus 12
yerly taketh trybute of my fortresse / but I assure you
yf he be no more of strength than I am I shall hastly

hyreue hym of hys trybute.'   And so he yede vp to
the vpermost stage of the donjon / and his bretheren 16
and the barons taryed benethe in grete doubte and fere
that geffray shuld be peryshed / but geffray was therof
not agast / but loked long yf he coude see any thing.

AH thus as thystory sheweth geffray rested there 20
fro none to thre of the clok, that he ne herd nor
sawe nothing.   but anoone after he herd a grete noyse
wherwith all the donjon shook / and as he loked
tofore hym he perceyued a grete knyght armed of al 24
poynts, that said to hym with a hye voys, 'Thou
geffray, wilt thou denye my trybute that of ryght I
ought to haue vpon the pommel of this toure of the
which I was seasyd & enpocessid by thy fader!' 28

'Thenne,' said Geffray, 'where are the letres? yf thou
hast them, shew it how my fader was bound, and yf I
see thou hast good ryght   here is the money redy to
paye the.'   and thenne the knyght answerd in this 32
manere: 'I had neuer letres therof / but wel & truly
haue I be payed and neuer denyed tyl now.'   'By my
feyth,' said geffray, 'al were it good debte and thy
ryght to haue it   yet shuldest thou haue grete peyne 36

to recouere it of me. And on the other part thou
holdest me for thy subget & ¹woldest holde me in
seruitude and thou hast therof nothing to shew. but

4 what art thou that thus by the space of ²XVI. yere
hast thevely take this trybute? / I now deffye the by
the myght of my sauyour and the I chalenge for myn
herytage.' 'By my feyth,' said the knyght, 'doubte

8 not therof but that I am a creature of god, and myn
name shalt thou knowe tyme ynough.' And without
eny more questyon eche of them recountred other with
myghty & gret strokes. And what with that and with

12 the stampyng of theire feet, the noyse was so grete
that al þey that were benethe were abasshed, and
supposed that the donjon shuld haue fall. Wherfor
they wyst wel that geffray had somwhat to doo. And

16 his bretheren shuld haue assysted hym, but geffray had
them deffended so to do. And wete it wel whan the
knyght of the tour fond Geffray so fyers & so strong,
he putte his swerd vp in the shede and thrugh his

20 paueys behind hym. And whan Geffray sawe hym
that doo / he dyde lyke wyse with his sheld / but he
with bothe his handes smote the knyght vpon the
helmet with his swerd so myghtyly that he stakerd

24 þerwith. And thenne the knight toke geffray in his
armes / and with that geffray lete fall his swerd and
wrestled with hym / and wete it wel ther was lytel
fauour shewed on neyther part. And whan the

28 knyght perceyued the purse about geffrays neck he
supposed to haue had it from hym / but geffray kept
hym therfro / sayeng / 'or thou haue purse or money
it shal cost the the best blood in thy body / but for

32 trouth I meruayll how thou mayst so long withstand
me.' 'By my feyth,' said the knight, 'I haue more
meruaylle how thou mayst withstand my strengthe /
but to morowe shalt thou haue a new day with me,

² Fr. *quatorze ou de xr. ans.*

¹ fol. 212.

but as he has nothing to show that it is due, he demands his name, and defies him.

The knight replies that he is a creature of God, and that Geffray will learn his name soon enough.

They fight, and make so great a noise that those below think the donjon will fall.

His brethren would have come to his help, but Geffray had forbidden them to do so. The knight sheathes his sword, and puts his shield behind him.

Geffray strikes him on the helmet so that he staggers.

He wrestles with Geffray,

and tries to take the purse from him.

¹ fol. 212 b.
The knight appoints another struggle in a meadow by the river next morning on condition that Geffray comes alone. Geffray agrees, and the knight disappears.

For now the sonne is to his rest, ¹and thou shalt fynd
me yonder vpon that medowe beyond the ryuere al
redy armed to chalenge the end my ryght. But thou
shalt assure me þat no persoone shal passe the ryuere
but thou.' 'By my feyth,' said geffray, 'I the assure
no more ther shal not,' and with that he departed that
geffray wyst not where he became. 'By my feyth,'
sayd thenne geffray, 'here is a pert messager, I haue
grete mernaylle what this may be,' and so came he
doun and brought with hym the knightes sheld that
he had wonne.

Geffray comes down and brings the shield he had won in his right hand, and the purse in his left.

Thystorye witnesseth whan Geffray was come doun,
hys sheld about his neck and the knyghtes
paueys in his ryght hand that he had wonne / and in
his other hand the purse with the money, hys bretheren
and the barونnye þere were abasshed therwith, and
asked hym whom he had fond. And thenne he said

His brethren are abashed, and ask whom he had found.

he had fond the moost valyaunt knyght that euer he
dyde dedes of armes withal. And to them shewed al
the maner of batayll & of theire couenaunt / and how
he wold haue had the purse, and how he departed so
sodaynly. and they bygan to lawhe, sayeng þat neuer
tofore they herd of suche a thing. But whan they
sawe geffrays helmet & al hys harneys so peryssshed
with strokes, they had no courage to lawhe, For they
knew wel there was sore batayll. And on the next
day erly geffray roos, and he & hys brethern herd
masse & drank ones. And thenne armed hym at al

He answers, the most valiant knight he had ever seen, and tells of his covenant, and of the sudden departure of the knight.
They laugh at the story, but when they look at Geffray's helmet they see there has been a great fight.

pieces & mounted on horsbak / And his bretheren and
þe barons yede to conueye hym to the ryuere, where he
toke leue of them and passed ouer on the other syde

In the morning Geffray goes to the meadow.

of the ryuere. /

Thystorye telleth that anoone Geffray fond þe
knyght and to hym said with a hye voys, 'Sire
²knyght, be ye he that wyl take the trybute vpon my
Fortresse?' And he answerd, 'ye by my feith.' And

He calls to the knight.
'Be ye he that will take tribute upon my fortress?'
² fol. 213.
The knight says he is.

12

16

20

24

28

32

36

ryght forth said geffray, 'I chalenge the, wherfor
deffende the.' And whan the knight vnderstod this,
he sette the spere in the rest and geffray lyke wyse /
4 and so eche of them recountred other / by force wherof
they brak thaire speris to the hard fyst in many pieces.
And whan they had thus manfully broken theire speris
they drew out theire swerdes and smote eche other
8 with grete & myghty strokes that the fyre sprang out of
theire harneys, wherof the peple vpon the ryuere syde
had grete meruayH & were al abasshed how that euer
they might endure the grete strokes, For they left not
12 one piece of harneys hool. And they faught fro the
morow vnto thré of the Clok at aftirnone and neuer
seaced. And so grete was the batayH that none
¹[wist] which of them had the bettre. And thenne
16 the knight bygan to say to geffray / 'here me now, I
haue the wel assayd / and as touching the trybute I
the quyte. And wete it wel that / that I haue doo,
it hath be for the prouffyt of thy fader & of his sowle,
20 For it is trouth that the pope enjoyned hym by way
of penaunce for the forsweryng that he had don to
thy moder to founde a monastery, the whiche penaunce
was not by hym obserued. but it is so yf thou
24 wylt edyfye an hospital, and founde therin a preste to
syng dayly for thy faders sowle ; thy fortres fro this
day fourthon shalbe quyte of ony trybute / how be
it there shal be sene about the tour more meruaylles
28 than in eny other place of þe world.' And geffray
ansuerd, 'yf I knew for certayn that thou were of god
I wold gladly ²fullfuH thy wyH in this byhalf.' /
And he said he was. And thenne geffray said / 'be
32 thou sure this shal be doon yf it playse god. but I
pray the say me what thou art.' And the knyght
ansuerd, 'Geffray, enquere no ferther, For as for this
tyme thou mayst knowe no more / but only that I am

¹ which *in MS.*

Marginal notes:

Geffray chalenges him.

They break their spears,

and draw their swords, and give each other mighty strokes.

They fight till three o'clock, and no one can tell who has the better of the fight.

The knight tells Geffray that he forgives him the tribute.

What he had done was for the good of Geffray's father's soul, who was to have founded a monastery as penance, but had not done so.

If Geffray will build an hospital and endow a priest, he will quit him of his tribute altogether.

Geffray answers, that if he knew the knight were of God he would do his will.

² fol. 213 b.

He declares he is, and Geffray promises that his will shall be done.

¹a Creature of god.' And therwith he vanysshed that geffray wyst not where he became / wherof mervaylled moche they that were by þe ryuere. And thenne came geffray ouer the ryuer to his bretheren, whiche asked 4 hym how he had doo and where hys party aduerse was become. And geffray to them sayd that they were acorded togidre, but where he was become he coude not tell. And thenne they retourned to Lusynen 8 where geffray dide doo hang the paueys, that he had wonne vpon the knyght of the toure, in the myddes of his hall. Where as it hong tyl geffray had edyfyed the said hospytal, For thenn it vanysshed away that 12 no man wyst where it became. And here fynyssheth the hystory of the heyres of Lusynes. but bycause that the kynges of Armanye ben yssued of that lynee, I wyl shewe herafter an auenture that befell to a kyng 16 of Armanye.

Thystorye sayth that long after the deces of kyng guyon of Armanye, Ther was a kinge of that land yong and fayre, lecherous and folowyng his wyll. 20 The kyng vnderstod by the report of som knightes vyageours, that there was in the grete Armanye a Castel whereas was in the most fayre lady that men wyst at that tyme in al the world / the whiche lady 24 had a ²sperhauk / and to al knightes of noble extraction that thither went & coude watche the said sperhauk duryng the space of thre ³dayes and thre nyghtes without slepe / the lady shuld appiere tofore them and 28 gyue them suche worldly yeftes as they wold wysshe and were desyryng to haue, except only her self. This kyng thenne that was lusty and in his best age, and that vnderstod the renommee of thexcellent beaulte of 32 the said lady / said he wold go thither / and that of the lady he shuld nothing take but herself. But wete it that in the said Castel might none entre but ones in

¹ Fr. de par Dieu.   ² Fr. esprevier.

a yere / and that was the day tofore the vygille of
saynt Johan / and the next day after saynt Joh*a*ns
day e*ue*ry man must departe thens.   Whan the said
4 kyng was redy he departed & rode wit*h* noble company
so long that he cam to the forsaid Castel at the day
assygned, tofore the which he dide dresse vp a ryche
pauyllon and there he souped, and aftir went to rest.
8 And on the morne he roos and her*t* masse / and after
that the masse was do, he drank ones, and syn armed
hym and toke leue of them that were come wit*h* hym,
which were sorowful for his departing, For they
12 trowed that neu*er* he shuld haue come ayen. And
this doon the kyng yed toward the sperhauk in the
Castel. /

Here saith thistory that whan the king was at
16 thentree of the Castel, an old man al clothed in
whyte cam ayenst hym, & asked hy*m* who that had
brought hym thither / and he answerd in this manere :
'I am come hither to seke thauenture and to haue the
20 Custome of this Castel.' And the good old man said to
hym / 'ye be ryght welcome, folow ye me, and I shal
shew you the auenture that ye seke for.' Thenne
yede the king aftir the old man / and gretly was he
24 meruaylled of the grete & inestimable riches ¹ that he
sawe, wit*h*in the place. And thene entred the old
man into a noble hall rychely hanged, And aftir hym
entred the kyng that perceyued in the mydde*s* of the
28 hall a long horne of a vnycorne that was fayre &
whyte / and therupon was spred a grete cloth of gold
wheron stod the sperhauk and a gloue of whyt sylk
vnder his feet. Thenne said the old man to the kynge
32 in this wyse : 'Sire, here ye may see thauenture of
this Castel / and wit*h* it sethen ye are so ferfoorth
c*o*me ye must watche this sperhauk thre days and thre
nyghte*s* wit*h*out slep. And yf Fortune suffre you so
36 to doo, wete it wel *þ*at the noble lady of this ryall

the lady of the
castle will ap-
pear on the
fourth day, and
grant what he
desires most to
have, except
herself; if he
asks to have her
evil will befall
him.

Castel shall appiere tofore you on the fourth day, to
whom ye shal aske that thing of the world whiche ye
desyre moost to haue / except har body / and, no
doubte of but ye shal haue it / but wate it certaynly
yf ye desire and aske to haue herself, euyl auanture
shal fall to you therof.'

Cap. LX.   How the king of Armanye watched the sperhauk.

8

1 fol. 215.

The old man laft
the King alone
in the hall.

There was a
table covered
with all manner
of dainties,

but the King
eat sparingly,
so that he might
be able to keep
awake.

2 fol. 215 b.
He spent his
time looking at
the pictures,

and among
others, sees
figured the
history of King
Elinas and Queen
Pressine, and
their three
daughters, and
how they were
punished for
shutting their
father in Mount
Brombelyo.

The King
watches until
the third day,

1The forsaid old man aftir that he had declared
and shewed to the kyng the manere of watching
of the sperhauk, he departed fro the halle / and the
kyng abode alone and had grete meruayll, what of the 12
grete ryches þat he sawe there, as of a ryche table that
was in the hall couered nobly with al maner deyntes of
meetes.   And þat part he drew hym self & ate a lytel
and drank of that lyked best & kept good dyete and 16
made none exces, For wel he knewe that to moch
meet & drynk causeth the body to be pesaunt & slepy.
And to dryue fourth the tyme walked vp & doun the
hall, taking grete playayr of the grete noblesse that 20
he sawe, 2For there were ryche pictures where as were
fygured many a noble hystory, and the wrytyng
vndernethe that shewed the vnderstandyng of it.
And emong other hystoryes was there fygured the 24
noble hystory of kyng Elynas & queen Pressyne his
wyf, and of their thre doughtirs, and how they
closed their fader in the mountayne of Brombelyo in
Northomberland / and how Pressyne theire moder 28
punysshed them therfor / and al the circonstaunces of
þeir faytes were there shewed in letres of gold fro þe
bygynnyng vnto the ende.

Grete playsir toke the king to rede & see the said 32
hystoryes.   And thus he watched lokyng here
and there vnto the thirde day.   And thene he per-

ceyued a right noble chambre, and sawe the doore al
wyd open / and that part he went and entred in the
chambre, and beheld þer many knyghtes armed fygured
4 and rychely paynted on the walles, and vnder their
feet were their names writon in letres of gold and of
what lynee & countre they were / and aboue their
heedes was writon in this manere : 'Vpon suche a
8 tyme watched this knight in this Castel the noble
sperhauk, but he slept / and theifore he most hold
company with the lady of this place as long as he may
lyue, and nothing worldly shal he wante of that his
12 herto can desiie saf only the departyng fro the place.'
And there nygh were paynted thre sheldes in a rowe,
and on them were fygured the armes of thre knyghtes
and their names / their lynee & their Contre that they
16 were of were writon vnderneth / and aboue the sheldes
was shewed by wrytyng this that foloweth : 'In suche
a yere watched our sperhauk this noble knight ¹wel
and duely and departed with joye and had his yeft of
·20 vs with hym.' And so long beheld the king that he
almost slept / but he anoon came out of the Chambre
and sawe the sonne almost doun and passed fourth
that nyght without slepe.

24 Thenne was he glad whan he perceyued þe day.
And foorthwith at the rysyng of the sonne cam
the lady of the Castel in so noble and so ryche aray
that the kyng had grete meruayH therof / and what of
28 her ryches as of her excellent beaute, he was gretly
abasshed. And thenne the lady dide her obeyssaunce,
sayeng in this manere : 'Noble kyng of Armanye, ye
be ryght welcome. For certaynly ye haue wel &
32 valyauntly endeuoired you. now aske of me what
yefte that so euer playse you worldly and raysounable,
and ye shal haue it without ony taryeng.' Thenne
answerd the king that right sore was esprysed of the
36 loue of her, 'By my fey.h, gracyous & noble lady, I

Side notes:

when he sees
an open door.
He enters the
chamber,
and sees the wall
figured with
many knights,
and reads their
names and the
writing :

'This knight
watched the
sparrowhawk,
but slept,
and so must
remain in the
castle all his
life.'

He also sees
three shields
painted with the
arms of three
knights,

and a writing :
'This knight
watched our

¹ fol. 216.

sparrowhawk,
and departed
joyfully with
his gift.'
The King nearly
fell asleep look-
ing at the figures,
but left the
chamber, and
kept awake all
the night.

At sunrise the
lady of the castle
comes to the
King,

and welcomes
him, and asks
him to name
what gift he
would have.

The King
answers,

aske neyther gold nor syluer, Cyte, toun, nor Castel,
For thanked be god I haue of al worldly rychas ynough /
but yf it playse you, my ryht dere & right entierly
beloued lady, I wyl haue you to my wyf.' And whan 4
the lady vnderstod this she was wroth, and by grete
yre she said to hym in this wyse: 'Ha, thou grete foole,
For nought hast thou asked my body, For thou mayst
not by no wyse haue it.' Thenne said the king to 8
the lady, 'Wel I haue, to myn aduys, endeuoired me.
Wherfor, noble lady, be you fauourable to me and haue
regard to the custome of this castel.' 'By my feyth,'
answerd the lady, 'as touching thaduenture & custome 12
of this Castel, I wyl that it be obserued & kept / but
aske of me yaft raysounable / and no doubte ¹of but
thou shalt haue it.' 'By my feyth, noble lady, I desyre
none other thing erthly nor none other I shal not aske 16
nor take of yon, but only your gracyous body.' 'Ha,
fole, fole,' said thenne the lady, 'suyl myschauance
shal fall on the, yf thou soone chaungest not thy
purpos, and so it shal to al thin heyres & successours 20
aftir þe / though they be not culpable therof.' And
tho kyng her answerd, 'It is for nought, For my
herte is rauysshed of your beaute, and only fedde with
your syght. And therfore your body wyl I haue and 24
none other thing erthly.' /

Cap. LXI. How the kyng wold haue
rauysshed by force the lady, but she
vanysshed away. 28

Whan thenne the lady sawe that the kyng
chaunged not his purpos, she was ryght wroth,
and to hym said in this manyere: 'Thou folyssh kyng,
now shalt thou lese the syght of me, & shalt fayll of 32
thy reste, & hast putte thyself in auenture to abyde
within for euer in grete payne & tourment, bycause that

thou art yssued of the lynee of kyng guyon that was sone to Melusyne my sustir, and I am his ante / and thou art so nygh of my blood and kynred that though 4 I wold be consentyng to thy wyll holy Chirch wold neuer suffre it.' And aftir she reherced & shewed to hym al that is tofore said in the ¹Chapter of Elynas and Pressyne, and also fro hed to heed all the heyres 8 of Lusynen and their fayttes. And after she said to hym / 'grete myschief shal happe to the & vpon thyn heyres successours ²after the, and that shal endure vnto the ix lynee, For they shal fall in decaye, & exilled fro 12 their contrees & fro their honour, wherfor departe lightly hens, For here mayst thou no lenger abyde.' The kyng thenne vnderstod wel the lady. but neyþer for her wordes, nor for fere that ought shuld hym 16 mysfall, he neuer chaunged his folysh wyll & vnhappy purpos, but wold haue take the lady by manere of vyolens and by force. but soone Melyor vanysshed away that he wyst neuer where she was become.

because she is the aunt of King Guion his ancestor, and that they are too near of kin to marry, and even if she consented, Holy Church would forbid their union. Then she tells the history of Elinas and Pressine, and of the heirs of Lusignan, and foretells of the decay of his ² fol. 217. line, and of their exile from their lands. She advises him to leave the castle.

The King persists and tries to take her by force, but Melior vanishes he knows not where.

20 Cap. LXII. How the king was bete & ouerthrawen and knew not of whom.

And immediatly after the departyng of Melyor there fell vpon the kyng gret & pesaunt strokes, 24 as thykk as rayn falleth fro the skye. Wherof he was al to brusid in euery part of his body, and was drawen by the feet fro the halle vnto the barrers without the Castel. And wete it that he neuer saw none of them 28 that so cruelly seruyd hym. And as soone as he myght he stode vpon his feet, cursyng a thousand tymes hym that first brought hym tydynges of this auenture, and the heure also that euer he cam thither. 32 And thenne he went toward his meyne that saw his harneys al to broken and perysshed, and demanded of

The King is thrashed so hard that he is bruised in every part of his body, and is pulled by the feet out of the castle.

He cannot see who it is that serves him so.

He rises and curses the man that brought him the news of the adventure,

and returns to his men,

¹ Cap. I. page 6, *et seq.*

who ask if he has been fighting? He tells them he is hurt, but that he has had no fight because he would not pray who struck him.

3 fol. 217 b.

hym in this manere: 'My lord, vs semeth that ye be sore hurt, haue ye had batayll there as ye haue be?' And he asnsrerd, 'I am somwhat hurt / but no batayll I haue not had / but so ferre I knowe that shrewdly 4 I haue be festyed[1] [2]how wel I perceyued no body / but I assure you I felt wel the strokes, and wete it wel I reuenged me not / and thus haue I had no batayll / For he that gyueth the first strokes dooth not the batnyll. 8 but he that reuengeth hym bryngeth it to effect.' /

The King returns home,

Anoone aftir the king & his peuple departed and entred in the see and sailled toward his countre, euer thinking vpon this that Melyor had said to hym, 12 and doubted moche to haue lost his good fortune as he

but he had no joy after this adventure, though he reigned a long time. His heirs were unlucky.

had. For wete it wel that neuer aftir this faytte he had no hertly joye and regned long tyme, but fro day to day fell in decaye by dyuerse manere. And wete it 16 wel that his heyres after his decesse were not fortunat, but vnhappe in al their actes. Here shal I leue to speke of the king of Armanye. For ynough it is knowon that they came of the noble lynee of the 20

This volume was ended on Thursday, Aug. 7th, 1394.

king Elynas of Albanye & of Lusynen. vnto this thursday vii day of August vpon the whiche was ended this present volume. The yere of our lord a thousand [ccc] [3]lxxx & foureteen./   24

I have told the story of Lusignan Castle, and of its builders, and of their issue, from the true chronicles.

Now have I shewed to you after the very Cronykles and true history how the noble Fortresse of Lusynen in Poytou was edyfyed & made / and of the noble yssue & lynee of the foundatours therof, on whos 28 sowles god haue mercy / the whiche fortresse of

It has lately been conquered by the Duke of Berry,

Lusynen is a now come but of late, by manere of Conqueste, into the handes of the ryght noble & myghty

---

[1] Fr. batu.

[3] Note to C. Brunet's Fr. Ed., page 420. *Le texte porte: mil iiij cinqz et xiiij. C'est évidemment une erreur puisque Jean d'Arras dit, dès les premières pages, qu'il a commencé cette histoire en 1387.* In the Harl. MS. of Melusine the date is given as 'le VIIe jour d'avust l'an de grace Mil iiiC iiiXX et XIII.'

prynce my right redoubted lord Johan sone to the kyng
of Fraunce, Duc of Berry, Auuergne, &c., by whos commandement I haue endeuoired me after my rude and
4 symple entendement to collige & gadre emong⸱ many
gestes & true Cronykles the trouth of thystory ¹byfore
specyfyed.   And wete it for trouth that oftentymes I
haue herd¹ my said lord say that a knyght called
8 Sersuell that held the said Fortres as lieuftenaunt &
Captayne there for the kyng of England / at that tyme
that my said lord had besieged / said to hym after the
reducyon of the Fortres / that thre dayes tofore, tofore
12 that he gaf it vp / he lyeng in hys bed with a woman
hys concubine named Alexaundryne / perceyued a
grete & horryble serpent in the myddes of the Chambre,
wherof he was gretly abasshed & sore agast / and wold
16 haue take the swerd to haue descharged it vpon the
serpent / but Alexandryne said thenne to hym in
this manyere : 'Ha, valyaunt Sersuel, how ofte haue
I sene your mortal enemyes tofore your presence that
20 neuer ye were aferd, and now for a serpent of femenyne
nature ye shake for fere.   Wete it for trouth that this
serpent is the lady of this place & she that edyfyed it /
she shal by no manere wyse hurt nor dommage you /
24 but so ferre I vnderstand by her apparysshing that
nedes ye shal hastly delyuere & gyue vp this Fortres
to the Duc of Berry' /   And morouer said the said
Sersuell to my said lord that hys Concubyne fered
28 nothing⸱ the serpent / but that he was neuer in his
dayes so aferd.   And that he sawe thenne the said
serpent tourned in to a fourme of a woman clothed in
a gowne of Cours cloth & gyrded with a grete corde
32 vndernethe the pappes of her / and soone after tourned
herself in the figure of a serpent and so vanysshed
away.

36   Also there was a man named godart dwellyng at
that tyme within the said Fortresse, whiche

MELUSINE.   B B

Godart sware to my lord on the gospels that he had often sene

1 fol. 218 b.

the serpent on the walles of the fortrese, and that he had passed her without harm.

Ivon of Wales sware that three dayes before the surrender of the castle by Berswell, he saw a great serpent on the donjon of the castle, and that many others saw her.

affermed for a trouth / and sware to my foresaid lord vpon the holy euaungilles that many tyme he had sene vpon the walles of the fortres [1]the said serpent, and that he had passed oftymes nygh her without receynyng 4 of ony harme.   Then another also called Yvon of Walles sware his feyth vnto my said lord that thre dayes tofore the reducyon of the said Fortresse made by the said Seruell into the handes of my said lord, 8 þat he sawe an horryble grete serpent vpon the batelments of the donjon of the said Castel of Lusynen. And many other also had the vision and syght of her./[2]

And where it is soo that at thinstaunce requeste 12 and prayer of my said lord haue be examyned many prynces[3] and dyuerse oþer for the makyng & compilacion of this present hystorye vpon the said maters.   And also I haue putte my self to myn 16 vtermost power to rede & loke ouer the Cronykles & many bokes of auncyent hystoryes, to thende that I might knowe the trouth of tho foresaid maters.   Therfore yf I haue wryton or shewed ony thing that to som 20 semeth neyther possible to be nor credible, I beseche them to pardonne me.   For as I fele & vnderstand by the Auctours of gramaire & phylosophye they repute and hold this present hystorye for a true Cronykle & 24 thinges of the fayry.   And who that saith the contrary / I say the secret jugements of god and his punyssh-

I have done my utmost to know the truth of the matter,

and if I have written what appears to some incredible, I beg for pardon.

Some authors hold this to be a true chronicle of fairies.

To those who object, I say the judgments and

---

[2] Fr. adds: Et encore plus avant y a ung chevalier poiterin, nommé messire Percheval de Coulongne, qui fut chambellain du bon roy de Chippre, avec le roy, la serpente s'estoit apparue à icelluy roy, comme celluy roy luy avoit dit en ceste manière parlant a luy : Percheval, je me doubte trop ! Pour quoy, monseigneur? dist le chevalier.   Par ma foy, dist le roy, pour ce que j'ay veu la serpente de Lusignen qui c'est apparue à moy : si me doubte qui ne me adviengne aulcune perte dedens brief temps, ou à Perrin mon filz : car ainsi apparut-elle quant aulcuns des hoirs de Lusignen doibvent morir.   Et jura messire Percheval que dedens le tiers jour aprez, la dure adventure que chascun scet bien advint.

[3] Harl. MS. reads prouues = proofs.

ments are inuysible & impossible to be vnderstand or
knowe by the humanyte of man./ For the vnderstanding of humayne Creature is to rude to vnderstande the
4 spyce espirytuel, & may not wel comprehende what it
is / but as ferre as the wylle ¹of god wyl suffre hym.
For there is found in many hystoryes Fayries that
haue be maryed & had many children / but how this
8 may be the humayn creature may not conceyue. For
these poynts and suche other god hath reteyned þem
in his secrets. And the more that the personne is of
rude entendement the ferther is he fro knowlege of it.
12 And he that is replet of scyence naturel, the rather
shaH haue affection to byleue it. Notwithstandyng no
creature humayn may not obteyne the secrets of god./
how be it saint paule saith in hys epystles to the
16 Rommayns, 'that al thinges ben knowen by humayn
Creature' / but the glose reserueth & excepteth the
secrets of god. For the kynde of man is to vnderstand
the ferther that he trauaylleth in reaumes and Countrees/
20 the greter knowleche hatH he of euery thinge / than he
that resteth in his owne Countre and neuer remevyth.
And semblable wyse this historye is more credible for
as moche as it is not auctorised by one man only / but
24 also by many noble Clerkes. Now of this proces I wyl
make no ferther mencion / but humbly I beseche you
and alle them þat shaH here or rede this hystorye /
that yf there be ony thing that be nuyouse or desplay-
28 saunt to you / wyl pardonne me & hold me escusid.
For yf a man dooth as wel as he can / he ought to be
accepted. For in som cas the good wylle of a man
is accepted for the dede./ And here I, Johan of Aras,
32 ende the hystorye of Lusynen / ²besechyng god of his
hygh mercy to gyue to þem that be passed fro this
mortaH world hys eternaH glorye / and to them that be
lyuyng, prosperous and blessidfuH endyng./
36 [Here fynyssheth the noble hystorye of Melusyne.]

punishments of
God are not to
be understood
by man.

¹ fol. 219.

There are many
histories of
Fairies that have
married, and had
children. No
man can under-
stand how this
can be.
God has kept
these things
secret.
Ignorant people
cannot believe
such things.
Those who are
learned can more
readily do so,
but no man can
fathom the
secrets of God.

The more men
travel the more
they learn.

This story is
made more
credible by the
number of clerks
who vouch for it.

I ask forgiveness
of my readers for
anything tire-
some or displeas-
ing I may have
written.
If a man does as
well as he can
he ought to be
accepted.

I, John of Arras,
end the history
of Lusignan,
² fol. 219 b,
asking God to
give those who
have left this
world His
eternal glory,
and to the living
a blessed ending.

NOTES AND ILLUSTRATIONS.

PAGE 1, line 19. In the Catalogue of the Duke of Berry's Library, published in Le Labourer's *Histoire de Charles VI.*, there is a volume relating to the subject of this romance, 'Vn liure de l'Histoire de Lezignem, escrit en Latin, de lettre de fourme, bien historié & au commencement du second fueillet apres la premiere Histoire, a escrit, *sola sed tantum*, couuert de drap de damas rouge, formant à deux fermoirs de laiton, & tixus de soye.' Jean d'Arras declares in several places that the romance is founded on old Chronicles; see end of Cap. I.

p. 2, l. 11. Text should read: 'the Wednesday before St. Clement's Day.' The 'before' has been accidentally omitted by the translator or the transcriber. The French version reads: 'le mercredi devant la Saint Clement en yver.'

p. 2, l. 18. This heading seems out of place.

p. 3, l. 9. Is the reference to Romans, Cap. I, verse 20?:—'For the invisible things of him from the creation of the world, are clearly seen, being understood by the things that are made: his eternal power also and divinity: so that they are inexcusable.'

p. 3, l. 33. He appears to refer to local traditions, of which he makes some use; see, for example, the description of Melusine's appearances in his own time, on pages 369 and 370.

p. 4, l. 17. Probably Gervaise of Tilbury (fl. 13th century), a nephew of King Henry II. of England; he was appointed Marshal of Arles by the Emperor Otto IV. He was a voluminous writer. Warton says, in the *History of English Poetry*, § XXIV, that his *Otia Imperialia* was translated into French by Jean de Guerre between 1412 and 1427. His treatise is full of the most extraordinary marvels. In the British Museum MS., leaf 85, he tells of men being born without heads, having their eyes and mouths in their breasts. He is very full on lamia and dragons, and all kinds of monstrosities. He says that there have been cases in Italy of men being turned into beasts by eating cheese given them in taverns by enchantresses. Gervaise dedicated his *Description of the World* to Otto IV.

p. 4, l. 32. French text reads: 'les ungz qu'ilz ne verroient jamais l'ung l'aultre; que le samedi ilz ne les enquerroient que elles seroient devenues en aulcunes manieres; les autres que se elles avoient enfans, que leurs maris ne les verroient jamais en leurs gessines.'

p. 5, l. 21. He may be referring to the tales of Marco Polo, a copy of whose travels Jean d'Arras had access to in the Duke of Berry's collection.

p. 5, l. 24. The following appears to be the passage in *Gervaise of Tilbury* referred to: 'Scio equidem jampridem relatum veridica narratione, quod in Aquensi provincia paucis ab Aquis milliaribus est castrum

Rameturn, quod vallem Trezenaem sub se missam respicit. Hujus castri
Dominus, Raimundus nomine, cum uno aliquo die solus in aquo vectaretur
juxta decursum interlucentis Laris fluvii, ex improviso occurrit domina
nulli decore secunda, in palafredo phalerato, vestibus et apparatu pretiosis,
cumque salutata a milite ipsum ex nomine resalutasset, ille ab ignota se
nominatum audiens, miratur et nihilominus illam, ut moris est, coepit
verbis lasciviis interpellare, ut ei consentiat. Cui illa opponit, hoc praeter
conjugalem copulam nulli licere verum si in ejus nuptias consentiat, ipsius
possit optatis frui complexibus. Quid ultra? acquiescet conditionibus miles
in nuptiis: at illa replicat, illum summa temporalium felicitate ex ejus
commansione fruiturum, dum ipsam nudam non viderit; verum ut ipsam
nudam conspexerit, omni felicitate spoliandum asserit et vix ei vitam
miseram servandam esse praeponit. Pendet dubius ne timeret optaretne
mori? tandem in nuptias consentit et conditionem admittit. Inflam-
matus et aestuans omnem conditionem facilem arbitratur, qua cupitam
thorum possit obtinere. Consentiunt in matrimonium et contrahunt, et
crescente militis felicitate, in brevi favore et hominum gratia, temporalium
copia et corporis strenuitate in tantum excrevit, quod pares excessit et
paucis proceribus et illustribus secundus invenitur. Hominibus amabilis,
apud omnes gratiosus, liberalitatem discreta largitate atque urbanitate
condiebat, filiis et filiabus summae pulchritudinis procreatis. Cum post
longa tempora una die domina, ut assolent, in thalamo balnearet, Raimundus miles, a venatu rediens et aucupatu, perdicibus aliisque carnibus
ferinis dominam exeniat, et dum parantur eibaria, nescio quo motu vel
spiritu militi venit in mentem, quod nudam videat dominam balneantem,
constituens in animo siquidem, quod ex inhibita nuditatis conspectione
potuit ex fatis esse periculum, temporis diuturnitate tamque diuturnae
commansionis longinquitate evanuisse. Affectum maritus exposuit uxori,
quae diuturnam felicitatem ex conditione servata objicit et infelicitatem
minatur secuturam, si contemnatur. Tandem praeceps in praecipitium
miles, non temperatur interminatione poenae neque precibus flectitur, ut
a stulto proposito desisteret suae consulat utilitati:

> "tangunt animum motusque metusque
> et timet eventus indignaturque timere,"

Quid moror? erepto linteo, quo balneum operitur, miles ut uxorem nudam
videat, accedit, statimque domina in serpentem conversa, misso sub aqua
balnei capite, disparuit, nunquam visa imposterum nec audita, nisi quando-
que de nocte, cum ad infantulos suos visitandos veniebat, nutricibus
audientibus, sed ab ejus aspectu semper arctatis. Sane miles pro maxima
parte felicitate ac gratia minoratus, filiam illius dominae cuidam nostro
affini ex nobilibus Provinciae oriundo postea dedit in uxorem, quae inter
coaetaneas et confines suas plurimum extitit gratiosa et cujus jam suc-
cessio ad nos usque pervenit.' Prima Decisio XV Otia Imperialia.

The theories of Paracelsus people rivers, &c., with Melusinae. They
have no spiritual principle, but can obtain one by entering into a union
with man: 'Melusinae & meliorae filiae regiae quondam propter peccata
desperabundae, fuerunt a Sathana raptae, & in spectra transmutatae, spiritus
malignos, lemures horribiles, & in immania monstra. Vivere putantur
absque anima rationali & in brutali solum corpore phantastico, nutriri
elementis, atque una cum istis, in extremo die judicii transiturae, nisi cum
aliquo homine forte fortuna matrimonium contrahant, tum demum, ut
ipse, naturali morte interire posse, ut matrimonio naturaliter vivere virtute
hujus unionis. Ejusdem status atque generis plura spectra haberi creditur

in desertis, in sylvis, ruinis, monumentis, arcibus vacu:s, & in extremis littoribus maris. Vulgo maledicti vacantur homines, sed proprio nomine spectra vocantur, atque diabolorum sancti, cum quibus versantur cacodæmones, suas illusiones & portenta perficiunt.'—W. Johnson's *Lexicon Chymicum* [to the writings of Paracelsus], London 1652.

p. 5, l. 24. The name of Regnald does not occur in the list of the kings of Bohemia.

p. 5, l. 25. The Lusignans do not appear to have had any connection with Luxembourg.

p. 5, l. 28. The name Theodoric does not occur on the roll of the lords of Partenay-l'archevêque. The house was founded, according to French genealogists, by William, the son of Gilles Lusignan (fl. 1100—1130). Valence, daughter of Geoffray with the Great Tooth, married Hugh III. of Partenay-l'archevêque.

p. 7, l. 15. couered, Fr. *couvertement.*

p. 11, l. 3. Fr. 'je ne pense en nul cas deshoneste.'

p. 12, l. 26. There is a romance entitled 'L'Histoire du noble & vaillant Roy, Florimont fils du noble Mataquas duc d'Albanie.' Florimont is the son of Mataquas, sire of Duras and Duke of Albany. His mother was Edozie or Flory, daughter of Fragus, King of Persia. It is bound up with a Rouen edition of Melusine. Warton notices a romance of 'Florimont et Passeroze,' *History of English Poetry*, § XII, note.

p. 12, l. 32. In Coudrette's version of Melusine, Aualon is called fairy land.

p. 13, l. 7. In some editions of the French version Ybernie is substituted for Albany, others have Albany as here.

p. 14, l. 8. Fr. ver. adds 'filles' after 'lawfull.'

p. 15, l. 11. They should be allowed to leave Aualon.

p. 15, l. 32. One of Melior's adventures is described at page 362.

p. 16, l. 4. The eve of St. John's Day comes on June 23. Many curious customs used to be observed on the vigil of St. John. In London the Watch was paraded through the city. In Paris a number of cats and a fox were burnt in the Place de Grève. In Ireland the people used to light fires on the hill tops, and according to Rev. Donald McQueen, they danced round them, and then made their children and cattle walk through the fires. McQueen thinks the custom a relic of sun-worship.—Brand's *Antiquities.*

p. 16, l. 13. There is a mountain named Guygo in Lesser Armenia. No account of Palatine is given in this romance. In Coudrette's versification of the romance there is briefly narrated her story, l. 5704, *et seq.* Palatine's place of abode is there given as Arragon.

p. 17, l. 3. Geoffray with the Great Tooth discovers the tomb, see page 327.

p. 17, l. 24. The Castle of Lusignan was founded in the tenth century by Hugues II., known as the *Bien Aimé.* It had many masters, and was a formidable stronghold. It was razed in 1569, after its capture from the Hugenôts. Little trace of it now remains.

p. 17, l. 27. 'fell at debate'; translates *eut riot.*

p. 17, l. 32. Fountains are usually made the scenes of the fairy love-making. Elinas meets Pressine at 'a moche fayre fontayne'; Henry of

Leon, father of Raymondin, meets the 'fayr lady to whom he told all his Fortune,' 'nighe by a fontain,' &c.

p. 18, l. 7. Jean d'Arras was fond of etymology; this appears a reasonable guess.

p. 19, l. 14. The 1478 edition makes the third chapter begin here. The edition published at Rouen by Pierre Mulot begins Cap. III at the same place as our text.

p. 21, l. 7. 'h. . . . s.'], in Fr. *sur le col.*

p. 31, l. 35. Melusine protests throughout that 'she is of god.' See pages 316 and 320.

p. 32, l. 32. Compare the promise exacted by Pressine, Melusine's mother, page 11.

p. 33, l. 12. 'hys doughtir,' i. e. Earl Emery's daughter.

p. 33, l. 25. Melusine has a store of magic rings:

1. Makes the holder proof against death from wounds.
2. Gives victory in war, in law, &c., to the holder.
3. Gives victory, and protects against enchantments and poison, p. 110, l. 20.
4. Gives victory so long as the wearer fights in a good cause, p. 191, l. 11; p. 319, l. 10.

Magic rings appear to have come from the East. They figure in many Arabian tales. In classical literature we have several Magic ring stories, which probably have been taken from Semitic sources. Plato's story of the ring of Gyges, that made the bearer invisible, is well known. Solomon had a ring that gave him command over the genii. It was made of copper and iron, and had the sacred name of the deity engraved on it. Solomon sealed his orders to the refractory genii with the iron part, those to the good genii were sealed with the copper portion. Once when Solomon was bathing, and had taken the ring from his finger, it was stolen by a wicked genie. Solomon was so concerned about the loss that he was unable to attend to affairs of state. It was afterwards recovered from the stomach of a fish that was caught for the king's table.

Petrarch relates that Charlemagne became infatuated with a woman of low degree to such an extent that he neglected the affairs of state, and even the care of his person. She fell ill and died, but her death did not break the charm : Charlemagne would not allow her corpse to be buried. One day Archbishop Turpin examined the body, and found a ring in her mouth, which he took possession of; Charlemagne then came under the influence of the Archbishop. The prelate, tired of the king's special attentions, and afraid that the ring might fall into the hands of some unworthy person, so he threw it into a lake near the town. From that time Charlemagne refused to quit Aix-la-Chapelle. He built a palace and a monastery there, and in his will directed his successors to be crowned at Aix.—*Epistolæ familiares*, Lib. I, Cap. 3.

p. 35, l. 33. Jean d'Arras was evidently of the opinion of Rabelais, that　　　　　'Mieulx est de ris que de larmes escrire,
　　　　　Pour ce que rire est le propre de l'homme.'

p. 42, l. 4. Note that the Earl is unable to give land without the consent of his barons.

p. 42, l. 19. Brunet reads 'Montiers'; the Rouen edition has 'l'abbaye demonstiers.'

p. 45, l. 13. There is an 'onde limpide' near the Forest of Coulombyers, known as the 'Fontaine-des-Fees.'—*Annales de la Société Royal Académique de Nantes*, 1831, p. 405.

p. 48, l. 26. The power of love is a favourite theme of John of Arras. See 122, 135, 164, &c. The book was written for the amusement of the Duchess of Bar. This may account for the elaborate treatment of love affairs, dress, &c., in the book.

p. 54, l. 14. Coudrette makes the wine-list an extensive affair. See *The Romans of Partenay*, E. E. T. S. ed., p. 39 :

> 'With wine of Angoy, and als of Rochel tho,
> Which would eschawfe the braines appetite,
> Wine of Tourain, And of Bewme also,
> Which iawne [yellow] colour applied noght vnto ;
> Clarre Romain, with doucet Ypocras
> Thorught al the hal rynnynge hye and bas.
> Wine of Tourisnz, and also of Digon,
> Wine of Aucerre, of seint Jougon also :
> Wyne of Seint Johan of Angely good won,
> Of it ful many ther spake and tolde tho ;
> Wine of Estables, of Uiart also ;
> After thaim cam the wyne,
> Wine of Seint Pursain, and of Ris hys brood.
> Ouer all thes wines ther had the prise,
> The nouel osey of Dingenon.'

p. 55, l. 3. The magic ring that Melusine gave Raymondin has made him invincible. See p. 33.

p. 59, l. 9. The custom of the newly-wedded couple making presents to the wedding guests, instead of receiving them, resembles what takes place in India in our time, where the parents of the bride make gifts to those who attend the marriage ceremony.

p. 63, l. 3. Fr. reads : 'Et avec tout ce il y a forte braies entaillées de mesmes la roche.'

p. 64, l. 13. There are a number of suggested etymologies of the name Melusine, none of them satisfactory.

Jean Bouchet says it is a combination of Melle and Lusignan. She was lady of Melle, and her husband was lord of Lusignan. Bouchet says that this was the accepted etymology in his time (16th century). Baron Dupin adopts this etymology. It appears, however, that women did not add to their name the name of their husband's seignory, nor was it usual for women to bear the name of their own manors.

Bouchet thought the tail signified that Melusine was an adultress. N. Chorier imagined that it symbolized her prudence !

Salverte says that the name is a combination of Mere and Lusignan. He makes its signification to be 'Mother of the Lusignans.' The name is spelt Merlusine by Brantôme, and the popular pronunciation is Merlusine.

Grimm derives it from Meri menni, a syren, or scylla.

Littré derives it from Melus, a Celtic word meaning agreeable.

Bullet says it is made up of Me = half, llysowen (pronounced lusen) = serpent : the name thus signifies half serpent.

A writer in the *Nourelle Biographie Générale*, thinks that Melusigne is an Anagram of Leusignem. I have not observed any case in which the family name is spelt in this manner, and I am not aware that the fashion of Anagram-making was much practised in the 14th century

M. de Freminville, in *Antiq. de la Bretagne, Côtes du-Nord*, p. 23, derives Melusine from morlusein = vapour or sea fog.

In Quaritch's catalogue, 1887 (vol. I, p. 90) it is stated that the name comes from a Breton word signifying 'the woman with a tail,' mer' hlostek, which the writer believes was at one time pronounced something like Merlusec.

Mascurat surmises that Melusine was a lady who used a seal engraved with a syren, and from that was at last imagined to be a mermaid herself.

p. 65, l. 3. The following list of Melusine's children shows the blemishes that each of them bore:

1. Urian: A broad face, ears like the handles of a vannus, and one eye red and the other blue.
2. Odon: One ear greater, without comparison, than the other.
3. Guion: One eye higher than the other.
4. Anthony: Had on the cheek a lion's foot (grif de lyon).
5. Reguald: Had only one eye.
6. Geoffray: Had a great tooth, which protruded more than an inch out of his mouth.
7. Froimond: Had a mole (tache velue) or tuft of hair on his nose.
8. Horrible: Had three eyes—one in his forehead.
9. Raymond: Blemish not recorded.
10. Theodoryk: Blemish not recorded.

p. 65, l. 5. 'handlyng of a fan' translates 'manilles d'ung van.'

p. 65, l. 11. Fr. reads: 'Guerande et Penicense.'

p. 66, l. 17. Fr.: 'mal enformé.'

p. 65, l. 12. Hugues IV. of Lusignan had a dispute with Joscelin, lord of Parthenay, about some lands that the latter had usurped. The dispute descended to the heirs of Joscelin. Hugues appealed to his suzerain William, Count of Poitiers. The count sided with the lord of Parthenay, and Hugues' stronghold, the Castle of Lusignan, was burnt down. *B. Ledain* in *La Gatine.*

The Lusignans possessed the domain of Porhoët, in Brittany, from the 18th century. Phillipe le Bel took it from Guy, Count of Marche and Angoulème, in the 14th century.

Perhaps these historical events may have suggested the story in the romance.

p. 79, l. 24. 'the cranes flighing' translates 'les grues en vollant.' The cranes are said to be the earliest birds to migrate.

> 'E come i gru van cantando lor lai,
> Facendo in aere di se lunga riga.'
> > Dante, *Inferno*, Canto V.

p. 84, l. 15. The Rouen Fr. ed.: 'Raimondin le frappa de la lance au coste.'

p. 91, l. 30. There is an omission here in the translation. The French text reads: 'Il avoit entendu par aulcuns des varlés d'icelluy chastelain que ilz actendoient gens à qui ilz ne vouloient point de bien.'—Brunet's ed., p. 104.

p. 92, l. 15. Fr reads: 'que ilz ne nous trouvent à descouvert.'

p. 94, l. 24. 'high' seems to be a mistake for 'his.' 'traist l'espee' is the French reading.

p. 97, l. 28. There is a legend current that the convent of the Trinita'res of Sarzeau was founded by Melusine. John III., Duke of Brittany, founded it in 1341, forty-six years before John of Arras wrote this account of its origin. Jehan de la Haye, in *Memoires et recherches* (1581), says that Melusine and Raymondin were buried in this convent.

p. 104, l. 10. Such excrescences apparently do appear, as can be seen from the following statement, made by a man of recognized accuracy of observation:—

'On the 29th [of Feb. 1839], being requested by some friends of the town, I visited a wonderful man there. It appears that nature, deviating from the usual course, gave this man a small trunk, like an elephant, on the right side of his face, beginning from the forehead to his chin. With his left eye only could he see, the other being covered with this superfluous part of the body. He was a young man of about twenty, sound in mind, as he gave rational answers to the several questions I put to him in the Sindhi language.'—*Autobiography of Lutfullah*, p. 311, edited by E. B. Eastwick, 1858.

p. 112, l. 35. This advice to kings reads as if it had been specially written for the Duke of Berry's edification.

p. 116, l. 23. The Knights Hospitallers of St. John captured Rhodes after a siege of three years, in 1309, and made the island their headquarters.

p. 117, l. 32. In the Apocryphal Book, known as the Gospel of Nicodemus, the names of the two thieves are given as Dimas and Gestas. In the 'Narration of Joseph of Arimathæa' it is related that Demas was born in Galilee. He was an innkeeper, and was kind to the poor. He followed the example of Tobias in secretly burying those who died in poverty. He robbed Jews, even in Jerusalem. He plundered the daughter of Caiaphas. It was for this crime that he suffered death.

p. 120, l. 2. Fr. reads: 'Urian n'avoit mie encores, à compter les gens du maistre de Rodes, plus de quatre mille combatans.'

p. 128, l. 25. Alexander is said to have had 30,000 foot soldiers and 4,500 horsemen when he crossed the Hellespont. (Plutarch.)

p. 136, l. 26. 'he cast at hym the dart [with great] yre.' The Fr. 'par grant' is omitted by mistake.

p. 141, l. 21. Fr. text reads: 'Adonques le maistre de Rhodes et les capitaines de Lymasson se mirent tous ensamble.'

p. 142, l. 9. The 'paueys,' according to Viollet-le-Duc, were large oval or square shields, chiefly carried by the crossbowmen. They did not come into use until the fourteenth century.

p. 155, l. 20. For the true version of the story of how Cyprus passed into the hands of Guy of Lusignan (not Urian, as the Romance says), see the Introduction. The *Itinerary of Richard Cœur de Lion*, by Vinsauf, is the authority relied on.

p. 159, l. 24. The 'for to wete & know, for to here & know,' is a double translation of the French phrase, 'pour aller sçavoir.'

p. 159, l. 22. 'fortres' is plural here and on p. 160, l. 6.

p. 169, l. 13. 'they . . . . . ancres' translates 'ilz desancrèrent.'

p. 169, l. 32. 'them,' *i. e.* their ships.

p. 171, l. 1. See page 129, *et seq.*

p. 176, foot of page. In John Stow's *Survey of London* (W. J. Thom's ed., 1842, p. 119), the cost of writing out the works of D. Nicholas de

Lira in two volumes is given at 100 marks = £66 13s. 4d. W. Stevenson, in his *Life of William Caxton* (p. 12), says that this sum most likely included the cost of the illuminations. The volumes may have been sumptuously bound, in which case comparatively little would be left for the copyist's work.

It is quite probable that the 17/8, written on the margin of the Melusine MS., may be a memorandum having no relation to the copyist's pay.

p. 178, l. 10. Modern economists would not approve of this summary way of treating forestallers. Adam Smith believed that the dread of witches and of forestallers were on a par.

p. 179, l. 28. The Fr. ver. has the following sentences after 'armanye':—'Et se il vous samble qu'elle n'en soit digne, si luy aidas à assener à quelque noble homme qui bien sache le pays gouverner et deffendre des ennemis de Jhesucrist. Or y vueillez pourvoir de remède convenable car à tout dire, se il vous plait, en la fin je vous fais mon heritier du royaulme d'Armanie; mais pour l'amour de Dieu prenes en garde et ayes pitié de mon povre enfant, qui est orpheline desolée de tout conseil et de tout confort, se vous lui faillez.' The nine succeeding lines of the English version, 28 to 36, are not represented in the French version published by Brunet.

p. 180, l. 8. After Guyon's address the Armenian lords reply in the French version: 'nostre seigneur le vous vueille meriter, qui vous doinct bonne vie et longue.'

p. 180, l. 31. The following paragraph is omitted in the English version:

'En ceste partie nous dist l'histoire que ceux de Calis furent moult joyeulx quant ilz virent approucher la navire, car jà spavoient les nouvelles que leur seigneur venoit, pour ce que les barons qui estoient allez en Chippre pour porter les lettres dont je vous ay fait mention par avant, leur avoient mandé toute la verité, affin de ordonner et pourveoir de le recepvoir honnourablement; et y estoient tous les haultz barons du pays et les dames et damoiselles venues pour le festoier et honnourer. A celle heure la pucelle Florie estoit à la maistresse tour, qui regretoit moult la mort de son père, et si avoit moult grant paour que le roy Urian ne le voulsist pas accorder à son frère, et estoit une cause qui moult luy angoissoit sa douleur. Mais adoncques une damoiselle luy vint dire en ceste manière: Madamoiselle, on dist que ceulx qui estoient allez en Chippre arriveront bien brief au port. De ces nouvelles fut Florie moult joyeuse, et vint à la fenestre, et regarda en la mer, et vit navires, gallées, et aultres grans vaisseaulx qui arrivoient au port, et oyt trompettes sonner, et pluiseurs aultres instruments de divers sons. Adonc fut la pucelle moult lie, et vindrent les barons du pays au port, et recepvoient moult honnourablement Guion et sa compaignie, et le menèrent à mont vers la pucelle, laquelle luy vint à l'encontre de luy. Et Guion la salua moult honnourablement en ceste manière: Ma damoiselle, comment a-il esté à vostre personne depuis que me partis d'icy? Et elle luy respondist moult amoureusement et dist: Sire, il ne peut estre gaires bien, car monseigneur mon père est nouvellement trespassé de ce mortel monde, dont je prie à nostre Seigneur Jhesucrist, par sa saincte grace et misericorde, qui luy face vray pardon à l'ame, et à tous aultres; mais, sire, comme povre orpheline je vous remercie et gracie tant humblement comme je puys des vaisseaulx que vous m'envoiastes, et aussi de la grant richesse et avoir qui estoit dedans.'

p. 183, l. 25. Afterwards (p. 217) called Metydee.

p. 190, l. 11. This passage should be compared with that beginning on page 110, where Melusine gives parting advice to her two elder children, Urian and Guion.

p. 190, l. 34. Passages like this (see also p. 112) show that John of Arras pleaded for a more humane treatment of conquered provinces. He shows that even from selfish considerations a ruler should treat his people well (p. 112). It is true he does not directly condemn the marauding expeditions, which were the curse of the Middle Ages; but it should be noted that the sons of his heroine were always called to assist the oppressed. They never started out as mere plunderers. John of Arras was a forerunner of Rabelais in his condemnation of the barbarities of feudal warfare. He resembled Rabelais in character. It required considerable boldness for an officer of the Duke of Berry—one of the most rapacious plunderers of France—to make a stand against injustice.

p. 192, l. 20. Did the author of *Melusine* intend Anthony and Regnald's system of warfare to be an example to be followed by the Duke of Berry?

p. 202, l. 33. Fr. reads: 'le jeta si roidement encontre la terre que peu faillist que il ne lui crevast son cœur ou son ventre.'

p. 211, l. 2. It is interesting to note that all the kings in the Romance are constitutional kings. They are obliged to consult their barons before they enter into treaties or alienate land. (See pages 42, 211, 263.)

p. 214, l. 18. 'pryuy meyne,'—a private or select company or following.

p. 222, l. 29. Fr. reads: 'paiez pour huyt moys.'

p. 228, l. 13. 'Catell & goodes' translates 'biens.'

p. 229, l. 14, there is an omission after 'city.' The Fr. text reads: 'mais le roy Zelodus avoit fait armer ses gens et faisoit fort assaillir la cité, car grand desir avoit de la prendre, et ceulx de dedens se deffendoient lachement, et bien le appercevoient les Sarrazins; et pour ce ilz assuilloient tant plus vigoureusement. Et fut la besoigne mal allée quant l'ancien chevalier vint qui bien apperceut la besoinge et la faible deffense de ceulx de dedens' (Brunet's ed., p. 254). The Fr. text then continues: 'A doncques acheoa l'assault,' &c., as in the English version.

p. 233, l. 31. 'the moost vytupere' translates 'pour plus vituperer.'

p. 246, l. 6. Fr. 'Thierry.'

p. 246, l. 12. Fr. 'ung chevalier faye au maulvais esperit.'

p. 246, l. 13. The belief in Incubi and Succubi (demons who consort with men and women and engender children) was current in the time of John of Arras, and for long after. The fathers of the Church taught the doctrine, as can be seen from Augustine: 'It is so general a report, & so many auerre it either from their owne tryall or from others, that are of indubitable honesty & credit, that the Syluans and Fawnes, commonly called Incubi, haue often iniured women, desiring & acting carnally with them: and that certaine diuells whom the Frenchmen [Gauls] call Dusies, do continually practise this vncleannesse, & tempt others to it; which is affirmed by such persons & with such confidence that it were impudence to deny it.'—*City of God*, Bk. XV, Cap. XXIII, ed. 1620, translated by J. H.

Lodovico Vives, in commenting upon this passage, says: 'There are a people at this day that glory that their descent is from the devils, who visited women in the guise of men, and men in the guise of women. This in my conceit is viler than to draw a man's pedigree from pirates, thieves, or famous bullies, as many do. The Egyptians say that the devils can only accompany carnally with women and not with men.'

The following quotation from Michæl Psellus, a Byzantine savant of the eleventh century, explains the mediæval ideas on this subject. The text is from a translation by Pierre Morean Touranio, published in 1576: 'Or me suis-ie trouué quelque-fois auec vn moine, en la Cherronese de Mesopotamie, lequel apres auoir esté spectateur & chirurgeur des phätosmes diaboliques, mutant ou plus expert en cela, que nul autre, depuis il les a mesprisez & abiurez, comme vains & friuoles, & en ayant fait amende honorable, s'est retiré au gyron de l'Eglise, & a fait profession de nostre foy seule vraye, & Catholique: laquelle il a soigneusemêt appris de moy. Ce moine donc me dit alors & declara plusieurs choses absurdes & diaboliques. Et de fait, m'estant quelque-fois enquis de luy, s'il y a quelques diables patibles: ouy vrayement, dit-il, comme on dit aussi, qu'aucuns d'iceux iettent semence, & engendrent d'icelle des vers. Si est-ce chose incroyable, luy dis-ie lors, que les diables ayent aucuns excremês, ny membres spermatiques, ny vitaulx. Vray est, respondit-il, qu'ils n'ont tels, membres, si est-ce toutefois qu'ils iettent hors ie ne scay quel excrement & superfluité, croyez hardiment ce que ie vous en dis. Dea, luy dis-ie lors, il y auroit danger qu'ils fussent alimentez & nourris de mesme nous. Ils sont nourriz, respondit frere Marc, les vns d'inspiration, comme l'esprit qui est aux arteres & nerfs, les autres d'humidité: mais non par la bouche, comme nous, ains comme esponges & huistres attirent à soy l'humidité adiacente exterieurrement. Puis iettent hors ceste latente & secrete semence. A quoy ils ne sont tous subiects, ains seulement les diables qui sont enclins à quelque matiere, sçauoir est, ou celuy qui hait la lumiere, le tenebreux, l'aquatique, & tous soubsterrains.'—Psellus, *De l'energie or operation des diables* (leaf 19 b, et seq.), ed. 1576.

In Ambroise Paré's collection (died 1590), livre xix, ch. 30, we read : 'Or quant à moy ie croy que ceste pretendue cohabitation est imaginaire procedante d'une impression illusoire de Satan .... car à l'execution de cet acte, la chair et le sang sont requis, ce que les esprits n'ont pas.'

Fuller accounts of the ancient opinions on Incubi and Succubi will be found in Iohn Wierus, *De Prestigiis dæmonum*, 1569 and 1579, and in Jean Bodin's *Refutation of Wierus*, 1593.

Modern thought ascribes the belief in Incubi & Succubi to Dreams, see E. B. Tylor: 'From dreams are avowedly formed the notions of incubi and succubi, those nocturnal demons who consort with women and men in their sleep. From the apparent distinctness of their evidence these beings are of course well known in savage demonology, and in connection with them there already arises among uncultured races the idea that children may be engendered between spirits and human mothers. (See Martin, *Mariner's Tonga Islands*.) For an ancient example of the general belief in this class of demons, no better could be chosen than that of the early Assyrians, whose name for a succubus, "lilit," evidently gave rise to the Rabbinical tale of Adam's demon wife Lilith. (See Lenormant, *La magie chez les Chaldéens*.) The literature of mediæval sorcery abounds in mentions of this belief, of which the absurd pseudo-philosophical side comes well into view in the chapter of Delrio (Lib. II, quæsto 15): "An sint unquam dæmones incubi et succubæ, et an ex tali congressu proles nasci queat ?" But its serious side is shown by the accusation of consorting with such demons being one of the main charges in the infamous bull of Innocent VIII., which brought judicial torture and death upon so many thousands of wretched so-called witches. (See Roskoff, *Geschichte des Teufels.*) It further throws light on demonology, that the frightful spectres seen in such affections as delirium tremens have of course been interpreted as real demons.'

p. 253, l. 19. 'hym,' *i. e.* Claude of Syon.

p. 264, l. 16. 'concernyng' here means 'compared with.' Fr. phrase is 'envers la puissance.'

p. 273, l. 31. Jaffa changed hands several times in the 4th Crusade, 1196.

p. 279, l. 34. 'ye shal not haue them for so good chep,' *i. e.* 'You will not overcome them as easily as you think.' Fr. reads : 'Vous n'aurez pas si bon marché.'

p. 281, l. 33. Fr. 'tout le couert.'

p. 282, l. 18. Fr. 'tout couertement.'

p. 287, l. 11 : 'Si cum li cerfs s'en vait devant les chiens,
Devant Rollant si s'en fuient Païen.'
La Chanson de Roland, ll. 1874-5.

p. 290, l. 7. 'cours' translates 'se reculèrent.' 'There reforced the batayll [*et souffrirent cristiens moult grant affaire*], and with that cours [retires] the cristen,' &c.

p. 291, l. 3. 'sarasyns' in Fr. text is 'Turcs.'

p. 295, l. 9, page 32.

p. 296, l. 6. 'esperit fae.'

p. 297, l. 5. 'quaque à harenc' = a herring barrel.

p. 303, l. 3. 'ung flayal de plomp à trois chainnes.' The flail was rarely used in France. The MSS. of the 12th and 14th centuries show it very seldom (*Viollet-le-Duc*).

p. 309, l. 19. The date of the ravaging of the Abbey of Mailleres by Geoffray with the Great Tooth was 1232.

p. 312, l. 8. Coudrette makes the Castle of Vouvant the scene of the catastrophe. *The Romans of Partenay*, E. E. T. S. ed., line 3453.

p. 314, l. 26. 'Si quelqu'un aussi se fondoit sur la non vérisimilitude de tant d'aventures, enchantements, de la flûte d'un roi Oberon, tant de somptueux palais soudainement se perdant et évanouissant, et du cheval de Pacolet, qui est encore plus en çà, d'une Mélusine, de Merlin ; je lui répondrai que le christianisme étant pour lors bien peu avancé aux contrées de par deçà, le diable avoit beau jeu à faire ses besognes, essayant, en tant qu'est en lui, nous empêcher et divertir du vrai service de Dieu, par ses moqueries et illusions ; et, gagnant toujours pays, allant de pied en pied, a si bien fait cet esprit calomniateur, que d'eteindre, en ce qu'il a pu, le nom de notre Seigneur Jésus-Christ, et icelui obscurcir et cacher aux hommes.'—*Contes d'Eutrapel*, by Noel du Fail, 1548.

p. 315, l. 2. The theory that anger is the work of demons is hinted at by the Byzantine Psellus. This writer declares that there are six varieties of demons: Leliurium, or fiery, haunting the upper atmosphere, Aërial the lower atmosphere, Earthy, Aqueous, Subterranean, and Lucifugus, the lowest class of all. The aërial and earthy enter into the soul of man, and urge him to all kinds of lawless thoughts and deeds. If a Lucifugus obtain an entrance into man it makes him ungovernable. The

Lucifugus is devoid of intellect, is ruled by whim, and is regardless of reproof. The possessed person can only be saved by divine assistance.

There is an old saying : 'via furor brevis est.'

p. 318, l. 12. 'Vernon'; Fr. 'Warnont.'

p. 318, l. 23. French text adds: 'car certainement il destruiroit tout ce que j'ay edifie, ne jamais guerres ne fauldroient au pays de Poictou ou Guienne.'

p. 319, l. 27:   'nessun maggior dolore,
        Che ricordarsi del tempo felice
        Nella miseria.'—Dante, *Inferno*, Canto V.

p. 321, l. 19. There is a legend that Melusine flew to the caves of Sassenage in Dauphiny, natural hollows in the mountain which lie at the back of Grenoble, and made her abode there. N. Chorier, in his *Histoire Générale de Dauphiné*, describes these caverns: 'Les grotte de Sassenage ne font pas moins digne d'estre contemplée. L'vne est d'vne grandeur incroyable, & elle gette de l'horreur dans les ames les plus ferme. En l'autre ces cuves si célèbres, & dans la troisième est vne table de pierre, que l'on appelle communement la table de Melusine. C'est l'opinion d'vn grand personnage que les nymphes y estoient reverées autrefois d'vn culte particulier.' 'Estienne Barlet fait passer pour vne verité ce qu'il raconte d'vne autre. Il dit qu'apres que l'on y est entré par vn long & difficile chemin, on y voit distinctement des choses estranges. Vn roy y paroist assis dans vn thrône, la couronne à la teste & des thresors infinis à ses pieds. Il adjoûte que l'on croit que les fées, ou ces nymphes que les Grecs nomment les Oreades, y ont habité, & qu'ayant eu longtemps de la peine à le croire, il en a esté à fin persuadé. Cette caverne n'est pas fort éloignée de Montcluz, mais ce que l'on en dit l'est beaucoup de la vérité.'—Lib. I, Cap X.

p. 335, l. 8. Montserrat (mons serratus) rises abruptly from the plain of Catalonia. The ridge of peaks makes it look from a distance like an enormous saw. There are a number of natural caverns in the rock. A monastery was founded at Montserrat in the tenth century. The legend tells that one evening the shepherds of Olea heard celestial music as they tended their sheep. While they listened they saw a bright light among the rocks. The Bishop of Manresa hearing of their vision, resolved to ascend the mountain. He found there an image of the Virgin, made of black wood. It was recognized as the statue that had been sculptured by St. Luke, and brought to Spain by St. Peter. He erected a chapel near where he found the image. A few years afterwards the Count of Barcelona built a convent on the spot, and appointed his daughter Abbess. Later the building passed into the hands of the Benedictines. The Virgin's image worked miracles, and an immense number of pilgrims were drawn to the shrine. The ascent to the chapel was very difficult, and it was regarded as a very meritorious task. The kings of Aragon, Castile, and Navarre enriched the foundation. New buildings were added from time to time. At the wars at the end of last century the Spaniards turned the monastery into a fortress. The French captured it, and when they blew up the fortifications much damage was done to ancient portions of the buildings.

The hermitages are now in ruins, and the ascent to them is very difficult. They were all built on the same plan. Each had an antechamber, a cell with a recess, a study, a kitchen, and a plot of garden with a chapel. The hermits took a vow to die on the mountain. They followed an austere rule, and lived on vegetables and a little salt fish.

Their only amusement was carving little wooden crosses for the pilgrims who visited their cells.

It was at Montserrat, in the Church of the Virgin, that Ignatius Loyola vowed constant obedience to God and the Church, on the Vigil of the Annunciation, 1522.—*Visite au Montserrat*, by G. de Lavigne.

p. 337, l. 9. Fr. 'Culbaton.' The village of Collbató is the starting-point now-a-days for Montserrat.

p. 340, l. 8. Geoffray visited Pope Gregory IX. in 1233. Before he left France he made restitution to some of those he had wronged, as the letter dated 1232, still extant, proves: 'To all who shall see these letters. Geoffroi de Leziniem, Vicomte of Châttellerault, lord of Voluent and Mayreuent, salut éternel.

'You know that I am about to journey to the court of Rome, to put an end to my differences with the church of Maillezais. I wished to satisfy to the best of my ability, before my departure, all who have claims against me, especially such as are in holy orders.

'Geoffroi, Abbot of Absie, having heard of my will, has demanded restitution for damages done, and losses and injuries that I and my father have caused to the Abbey of Absie.

'I have learnt, from the testimony of men worthy of belief, that these claims are just; and for the salvation of my soul, and of my father's soul, I have satisfied the said abbot, 1232.'—From Thibaudeau's *Histoire de Poitou.*

p. 368, l. 18. Coudrette's versification of the Romance carries the fortunes of the Armenian kings to Leo VI., the last of the line, who died at Paris in 1393. This king was driven from his throne by the successful arms of the Egyptians. He was taken prisoner, and obtained his release through the good offices of John of Castile. Leo VI. visited Spain, where he was received as a champion of the Christian faith, and the King of Castile allowed him a pension of 150,000 maravedis. He afterwards travelled to France, where he was kindly received by Charles VI. A pension of 6,000 francs was granted to him there. Leo came over to England, where his reception was as warm as in Spain and Portugal. He obtained an English pension in addition to those from Spain and France. Leo VI. was a far-sighted man. He wanted to bring about a permanent peace between France and England, and he told the rulers of both countries that the only way that the Mahomedan arms could be checked in the East was by the aid of a united West. Unfortunately, his wise policy was rejected, and the rivalries of the kings of Christendom lost some of the fairest lands of Europe to the followers of Mahomet. Leo VI. told the King of France that Amurath aimed at being crowned at Rome, and that he had sent an expedition out with that purpose, which was annihilated by a stratagem of the King of Hungary.

> 'Thay lost ther lande and all ther honour,
> Inclinyng and comyng vnto mischaunce.
> On of thes kynges cam to Fraunce þat houre,
> So fro hermeny chaced into Fraunce.
> Full long the kyng ther gaf hym sustinance.
> At Parys died as happned the cas,
> At the Celestines entered he was.'—l. 5685.

After the death (29th Nov. 1393) of Leo VI. the title of King of Armenia was assumed by James I. of Cyprus. Neither James I. nor any of his successors ever reconquered the country.

p. 570, l. 5.   Yuon, Yvain, Owen, or Evan of Wales claimed to be the rightful heir of the kingdom of Wales, and the French king treated him as such.   Yuon was a favourite of John the Good, King of France, and took a part along with the French in the battle of Poitiers.   When peace was made between England and France, Yuon went to Lombardy, where he remained until the war was renewed.   In the reign of Charles V. he held a number of commands.   He led an expedition of Welsh knights against Guernsey.   His hope was that he would be able to reconquer Wales.   Charles V. assisted him with money and supplies, but he was unable to land in Wales.   He took part in the expedition of Bertrand du Guesclin in Spain.   On his return to France he won some victories over the English.   Froissart says that he was greatly hated in England on account of his claims to the Welsh crown, and for his treatment of his English prisoners, some of whom he would not allow to be ransomed. Yuon fell a victim to treason.   He took into his service a James Lambe, a knight who represented himself to be a Welsh exile.   He appointed this man his chamberlain.   When Yuon was before Mortagne (1378), directing the siege against the English garrison, he was assassinated by James Lambe, who fled to the English camp, where he received protection. Yuon was buried at the church of St. Leger with great pomp.

LIST OF PROVERBS IN THE ROMANCE OF
MELUSINE.

The loue of ladyes causeth peyne & traueyll to the amerous louers, and deth to horses, 56.

Old synne reneweth shame, 79.

Such weneth to auenge his shame that encreassith it, 93.

It is euyl companye of a traytour, 97.

Good it is to shette the stable before the hors be lost, 97 and 184.

Wel fole is he that fighteth ayenst the wynd wenyng to make hym be styll, 107.

Long taryeng quenchith moch the vertu of the yefte, 111.

Yf the peple is pouere, the lord shall be vnhappy, 112.

A flyes of a yere is more prouffytable than a flyes that is shorne twyes or thryes a yere, 112.

In long treatee lyeth sometyme grete falshed, 113.

Wyse men goo abacke for to lepe the ferther, 113.

One grayne of peper alone smertith more on mans tonge, than doth a sacke full of whete, 128.

Victorye also lyeth not in grette multitude of peuple, but in good rule & ordynaunce, 128.

Goodnes & bounte is betre than fayrenes & beaulte, 138.

All is not yet lost that lyeth in parell, 147.

Who lerneth not his crafte in his yougthe, with grete peyne & hard it shal be for him to be a good werkeman in his old age, 193.

That God doth, he done anone, 203.

Whan the yron is hoot it moste be wrought & forged, 211.

Of two euylles men ought to choose the lasse, whan nedes muste one be had, 237.

Bettre is to haue more of prouffyt & lasse honour, 238.

A lytel rayne leyeth doun grete wynd, 247.

That the fole thinketh oftymes cometh to foly, 255.

The fole proposeth & god dysposeth, 265.

He that menaceth is sometyme in grete fer & dredo hymself, & aftirward ouerthrawen, 279.

Bettre it is to flee, than to abyde a folyssh enterpryse, 288.

Thing neuer bygonne hath neuer ende, 304.

In euery thing most be bygynnyng tofore the ende cometh, 304.

He that gyueth the first strokes dooth not the batayll, but he that reuengeth hym bryngeth it to effect, 368.

GLOSSARY.

Words in Italics are the corresponding words of the French version, Ch. Brunet's Edition 1854. Cot. = Cotgrave's French Dictionary.

Abhomyned, page 311, abominated.
aborde, 71, waited.
absteyn, 16, abstain.
abused, 7, beguiled.
abysmes, 5, abysses.
accorded, 213, agreed.
acompte, 356, account.
acoyntaunce, 71, acquaintance.
acoynte, 190, become familiar; acoynted, 205.
adiouste, 16, adjust.
admounested, 228, warned; admounestyng, 287.
adommage, 32, harm; adommaged, 182.
adrecyd, 226, directed.
aduyronned, 123, surrounded.
aduys, 71 (*avis*), opinion.
affeblysshid, 241, became depressed, lost spirit.
affectuelly, 148 (*humblement*), earnestly.
affettuously, 159, affectionately.
affyaunce, 324 (*fiance*), assurance, trust.
affyns, 89 (*proesmes*), near relatives.
affrayenge, 10, fearing.
afrayed, 28, frightened.
agree, 259, accept.
aigre, 298, harsh.
albaster, 328, alabaster.
alez, 218, allies; alyed, 92.
algaf, 300, although (lit. al if).
allegeaunce, 335, relief.
aluese, 106; almesses, 321, charity.
alowed, 200, lowered.
altogidre, 41, altogether.
ambaxade, 183, embassy.

amerous, 56, amorous.
amongis, 27, amongst.
amyable, 275, friendly.
an, 90, one.
ancres, 114, anchors.
anenst, 21, against.
ansuerde, 10, answered.
ante, 367, aunt.
antecessours, 330 (*antecesseurs*), predecessors.
aourned, 51, 53 (*aourne*), attired.
aparteyned, 20, belonged.
apas, 27, apace.
apayed, 111, 192, pleased.
appareylled, 118, made ready.
apparysshing, 369, appearing.
apperceyued, 230, 324, observed.
appert, 125, expert.
appertly, 131, promptly (Cot.).
appertyse, 83, deeds.
appiere, 15; appyeren, 4, appear.
arblaster, 289, men who worked the arblastes, machines for throwing missiles.
archegaye, 226 (*archegaie*), dart.
ardaunt, 142, burning.
argued, 150 (*argue*), perplexed.
arregarde, 132, rearguard.
arsouns, 286, saddle-bows.
aspre, 145, fierce.
asprely, 132, fiercely.
aspye, 117, spy.
aspyracion, 315, respiration.
assayed, 171, attested.
assoted, 12, infatuated.
assurest, 171, boldest.
astonyed, 202, astonished.
astromy, 20, astronomy.

astronomyens, 325, astronomers.
asuryd, 155 (*fiancé*), betrothed.
auantgarde, 174, vanguard.
auauntynge, 11, boasting.
auctoures, 3, authors.
auncyent, 4, ancient.
auoultyre, 296, adultery.
awondred, 50, wondered.
awter, 344, alter.
axe, 41, ask.
axes, 299, attack of fever.
ayen, 180, again.

Bake, 9, back.
bare, 351, bore.
barers, 124; barreres, 65 (*braies*), defences.
bassade, 309, embassy.
bassecourt, 300, inner court of a castle.
bazyn, 8, mug.
basyneta, 125, helmetted man.
batayll, 289, battalion.
batayllous, 246 (*batailleroux*), given to fighting.
beaulte, 7, beauty.
beed, 149, bed.
begonne, 12, begun.
behauf, 17, use.
behel, 282, beheld.
behighte, 111, 190, promise, promised
heryng, 8, hearing.
besily, 3, busily.
betoke, 110, committed.
bewte, 7, beauty.
bigge, 86, build.
bigynne, 17, begin.
bikled, 17; bykled, 6, builded.
bode, 18, bid.
bourgeys, 200; burgeys, 151, burghers.
braunche, 23, branch.
braundysshed, 145, brandished.
brede, 41, breadth.
brennen 17; brenne, 4; brennyng, 184, to burn.
bright, 266, bright.
broche, 24, pierce.
broched, 130, spurred.
browded, 83; browded, 81, embroidered.
bruled, 234, burnt
bruyt, 254, noise.

brygandyners, 128, men wearing brigandines, canvas coats covered with iron plates or iron rings.
buffet, 303, blow.
busshe, 264, ambush.
butyn, 146, booty.
bycomme, 4, gone to.
bye, 39, boy.
bygoten, 6, begotten.
bynethe, 22, beneath.

Caas, 128, cause.
candelstykes, 17, candlesticks.
carrykes, 104, cargo ships.
caruell, 117, a light ship.
cas, 11, case.
castel, 15, castle.
castellayne, 92, castellan.
catholicatt, 215, catholic.
causer, 89, originator.
cepter, 179, scepter.
cerched, 330, searched.
certyfyen, 3, to certify.
cesse, 155, cease.
chaffed, 22, excited, vexed.
champaynes, 100, open fields.
chanoyne, 40, canon.
chappen, 193, shapen.
charyte, 12, charity.
chasse, 20, chace.
chaunfreyn, 84 (*gauffrain d'acier*), the headpiece of a barbed horse (Halliwell).
chayere, 82, chair.
cheryed, 98, treated.
chevaunce, 155 (*chevance*), achievement.
cheuysaunce, 264, promise.
cheyned, 177, chained.
childed, 104, gave birth to.
chirch, chirche, 36, church.
cleme, 142, climb.
clemme, 25, climb.
clepen, 187, called; clepid, 245, named
cleue, 26, cleave.
clos, 118 (*clos*), enclosure, 267.
cluble, 303, club.
cohortacion, 97, company.
cohorte, 97, company.
coler, 53, collar.
collige, 369, collect.
commevyd, 123; commouyd, 154, excited.

communyked, 291, talked.
commynalte, 184 (*communes*), commons.
comparacion, 17, comparison.
compleyned, 12, complained.
complices, 96, accomplices.
condampned, 68, condemned.
condycion, 14, condition.
congie, 301, leave.
conne, 12, to be able.
connyng, 2, cunning, knowledge.
conspiracion, 75, conspiracy.
constreyned, 7, constrained.
contrefaytte, 135, deformed.
contynue, 299 (*continue*), prolonged attack.
conuenable, 40, convenient.
convers, 100, menials.
convyne, 133, 142, 172 (*commune*)? assembly, militia, soldiery.
conyns, 261, rabbits.
corset, 84, a cloth coat worn over the cuirass.
coste, 134, disbursement.
costes, 268, coasts, shores.
cotidiane, 100, daily.
cotte, 129, coat.
coude, 7, could, was able; 20, knew.
couenaunce, 5, covenant.
couert, 254, 257, 281, 282, covert, concealed way.
couertly, 262, obscurely, secretly.
couetyse, 87, covetous.
coule, 168, cool.
couloure, 4, colour.
courcer, 9, courser.
cours, 15, course; cours, 290, rush.
courteyns, 57, curtains.
coyffe, 250 (*coeffe*), head-dress.
coynted, 315, comely.
cradelles, 4, cradles.
cramesyn, 205, crimson.
cronykle, 6, chronicle.
cryded, 82, cried, shouted.
curee, 99, entrails, quarry.
curtoysye, curtoisye, 9, courtesy.
cyrurgyens, 288, surgeons.

Dalt, 177, divided.
damoyseau, 163; damoyseaulx (pl.), 125, youth.
dampned, 339, damned.
daw fole (*damp musart*). French text means Sir Fool or Sir Thoughtless, "damp" being equivalent to the O.E. Dan, as: "Dan" Chaucer. *daw fole* may mean "melancholy" fool; see Bradley's Stratmann's M. E. Dictionary, under "dan."
debonnaire, 190, gentle.
deceneryd, 169, ? unfurled their sails.
decez, 356, decease.
dede, 321, caused; dede, 323, deed; dede, 12, did.
deele, 190, divide.
deeling, 111, bearing.
def, 29, deaf.
deffawte, 345, default.
delyt, 333, misdemeanour.
demanded, 20, related.
demened, 80, 125, 136, depressed; demeneth, 147, conducted.
demesurably, 132, greatly, immeasurably.
demysed, 87 (*s'en est deffait*), got rid of.
denounced, 188, declared.
departed, 116, divided.
departement, 98, departure.
despyt, 234, contempt.
desray, 123, disorder.
destraytte, 336 (*le vellon et le pertuys*), ? district, or territory.
destrier, 81; destrer, 82, horse.
detrenched, 146, hacked.
deuel, 234 (*doeul*); dueyll, 237, mourning.
deuoyre, 82, duty.
deuysed, 67, told.
deuyses, 348, talks.
dey, 15, die.
diches, 88, ditches.
distourned, 55, turned aside.
do, 321; doo, 239; doon, 13, 26, cause to.
dogge, 21, dog.
dolaunt, 312, doleful.
doleur, 305, dolor.
dombe, 29, dumb.
dome, 13, doom.
dommage, 145 (*dommaige*), harm.
don, 118 (*donne*), given.
dongeon, 300, main tower of a castle, donjon.
doubtid, 1, feared.
doubtous, 193, fearful.

doughtir, 11, daughter.
doun, 13, down.
dowbed, 18, dubbed.
dresse, 30; dressed, 21, direct,
    turned.
dressyng, 155 (*adressant*), address-
    ing.
duc, 6, duke.
duchery, 214, duchy.
dueil, 138; dueyl, 216, mourning.
dysempare, 215, dethrone.
dyspens, 148, outlay.
dysployed, 119, 230, unfurled, dis-
    played.
dysporte, 77, 98, sport; dysported,
    304, enjoyed.
dyspoylle, 136, pillage.
dyspreyse, 115, contemn.
dyspytous, 29 (*despiteux*), angry,
    spiteful.
dysymyle, 113, dissimulate.
dystourne, 25 (*destourneray*), turn
    away; distourned, 88.

Eche, 17, each.
effoundred, 266, ran into.
egaly, 148, equally.
emonge, 116, among.
empeche, 89, prevent.
empechement, 279, hindrance.
empossesse, 99; empocesse, 333, put
    in possession.
empryced, 81, undertaken.
ench, 83, inch.
encheson, 65, motive.
encres, 337; encresse, 32, increase.
eneysed, 62, cut.
endenoyre, 152, endeavour; en-
    denoyred, 157.
endoctryne, 55, instruct.
enfourmed, 308, informed.
enharnashed, 9, accoutred.
enjurous, 66, injurious.
enlyberte, 99, liberate.
ensiew, 184, follow.
ensured, 68 (*asseurout*), assured.
entamed, 211, 295, broached.
entaylled, 50, carved.
entende, 1, to give heed.
enterdement, 369, understanding.
entent, 91, intent, purpose.
ententyfly, 70, attentively.
enterprenaunt, 122, enterprising.
enterprysed, 12, undertaken.

entremete, 83 (*se mesler*), inter-
    meddle.
entreteyne, 239, keep up.
enuahisshing, 188 (*enuoye*): enua-
    hysshed, 147; enuahys, 201, as-
    sault.
envertued, 200 (*se envertued*),
    strengthened.
eny, 16, any.
erable, 99, arable.
erle, 6, earl.
eschiewed, 145, avoided; 270,
    rescued.
escryed, 77, 115, p.p. of escrien, to
    call to.
escuse, 258, excuse; 10, excused.
eslongyd, 133 (*se eslongérent*), separ-
    ated.
espirytuel, 371, spiritual.
esprised, 11, 34 (*surpris*), overtaken.
esprouued, 224 (*esprouoions*), tried.
esprysed, 77 (*espris*), smitten.
espyes, 193, spies.
esquyer, 248, squire.
essoye, 192, try.
estimed, 117, estimated.
estraungers, 178, strangers.
estymacion, 366, estimate.
euerche, 320; eueryche, 154, every.
euerychon, 38, every one.
ewrous, 244 (*eureux*), lucky, happy.
excusacion, 107, excuse
exercyted, 221, exercised.
exployted, 123 (*exploita*), worked;
    81, fought; 289, acted.
eyled, 299, ailed.

Facion, 225, build, make.
fader, 7, father.
faicte, 13; faict, 71; faytte, 119;
    fayt, 312, deed.
falshed, 13; falsed, 315, falsehood;
    fals, 12.
fan, 65 (Latin *vannus*), a corn win-
    nowing fan or sieve.
fantosme, 311, phantom.
fasted, 44, fastened.
fauntesye, 4, 31, fantasy.
fawte, 57 (verb), fail; 196, wrong;
    58 (noun), failure.
feith, 24, faith.
fel, 134, 200, fierce, cruel.
felawship, 8, fellowship.
fer, 60, far; ferre, 327.

ferder, 332, further.
ferfourth, 106, widely.
fest, 19, feast ; festyed, 98, feasted ; feste, 8, rejoicing.
festyed, 368 (*batu*), thrashed.
fette, 251 ; fete, 213, fetch.
feynted, 66, faint.
feynyngly, 28, pretending.
flayel, 303 (*flayel*), a baton carrying a lump of iron attached by a chain.
flawgh, 321, flew ; floughe, 321.
flemed, 112, fled.
florysshed, 13 (*florie*), flowered.
flote, 268, fleet.
flyes, 112, fleece.
fole, 24, fool.
fore, 184, early.
foreby, 251, past.
forfaytte, 315 (*fourfait*), crime.
forgate, 7, forgot.
forwayed, 101, wandered, lost.
foundatours, 368, founders.
foundement, 62 (*fondament*), foundation.
founs, 172 (*font*), bed.
fourne, 17, form.
foursenyd, 315 (*enforcenez*), furious, enraged.
fourueyeth, 76, wanders.
fowel, 206, foul.
fownd, 103, founded.
foynyng, 67, thrusting.
foyson, 21 (*foison*), abundance.
fro, 3, from.
fuldoo, 1, accomplish.
fullyssh, 149, 208, fully.
fumyer, 278, smoke.
fust, 85, fist.
fuste, 116, a rowing and sailing ship.
fyaunce, 257, trust.
fyers, 17, fierce.
fyerste, 118, boldness.
fyl, 321, fell.
fyn, 331, end.
fynaunce, 17 (*finance*), ready money.
fyreyron, 23, flint and steel.

Gadre. 266, gather.
gaf, 19, gave.
galyote, 167, little galley ; galyotte, 118.
gan, 22, began.
garnysons, 135, garrisons.

garnysshed, 184, 230, furnished, adorned.
gate, 203, got, obtained.
gaynstode, 137, withstood.
geaunt, 17, giant.
gendred, 246, begotten.
gent, 8, gentle.
gerdell, 53, girdle.
gerland, 59, garland, wreath.
gestes, 369, histories.
glanched, 77, glanced.
gobelyns, 4, goblins.
gonnes, 115, guns.
good chep, 279, 282 (*bon marché*), easy mastery.
gorgeret, 175, a piece of armour to protect the throat.
gramaire, 370, grammar.
gramercy, 9, great thanks.
grauntfader, 19, grandfather.
gree, 109, 121, favour, will, pleasure.
gree, take in, 2, agree to.
greef, 13, grief.
gret, grett, 7, great.
greve, 130, injure.
guerdon, 204, reward.
gyfte, 15, gift.

Haake, 20, hawk.
haboundonne, 99, give up.
habundauntly, 228, abundantly.
halid, 161, hauled.
halowed, 158, blessed.
handlyng, 65 (*manilles*), handles.
hap, 15 ; happ, 5, 12 (noun), luck, chance.
happe, 4 ; happed, 5 ; haped, 118 (verb), to happen.
hardyly, 10 ; hardyfly, 231, boldly.
harneys, 115, armour.
hauen, 118 (*clos*), haven.
haunce, 112 ; enhance, 325, raised.
haunted, 113, practised.
hauoyr, 67, goods.
haused, 166 (*getter*), lowered overboard.
hawtepyece, 145 ; haulte piece, 325, helmet.
heest, 21,
hehge, 21, hang.
helmets, 199, 251 (*bassines*), fighting men.
henne, 211, hen.
hens fourthon, 17, henceforth.

herberowed, 70, harboured.
herde, 7, heard.
here, 2, hear.
herke, 317, harken.
herte, 9, hart; hert, 39.
heued vp, 24, raised.
heure, 146, hour.
heuyer, 35, heavier.
heyer, 66, heir.
hit, 7, it.
hold, 190, keep.
holt, 302, whole.
holped, 46, helped.
honestly, 73, worthily.
hontous, 238, ashamed.
hool, 361, whole.
hoop, 36, hope.
hores, 177, oars.
hors, 10, horse.
hourys son, 300, whore's son.
hurted, 25, p.p. of hurten, to rush
    against.
hurtelyd, 95 (*hurta*), pushed.
hydouse, 315, hideous.
hye, 76 (*hault*), aloud; 94, high.
hyerid, 134, hired.
hyndre, 24, hynder.

Impetred, 14, procured (Cot.).
importable, 153, unbearable.
incontynent, 276, immediately.
indigned, 262, made indignant.
infortunate, 16, unfortunate.
iugge, 15, judge.
iuggement, 3; jugement, 15, judg-
    ment.
Iung, 16, June.

Jacke, 205 (*Jaques*), coat.
jape, 79, jest.
journey, iourney, 291, a fixed date.
jugge, 317, judge.
justiser, 97, justiciary.

Kennyng, 104 (*Veues*), far sight,
    extent of vision. Cotgrave trans-
    lates "kenne": *veoir de loin*.
    Motteux (*Rabelais*, Bk. 1V, cap.
    22) translates "ne sommes pas
    loing de port" by "within a ken-
    ning."
kepe, 112, guard.
kerle, 28, churl.
kerued, 17, carved.

keruyng, 43, carving, cutting;
    kerued, 50.
knowleche, 2, knowledge; know-
    leched, 96.
konne, 108, show.
kychons, 50, kitchens.
kymbyng, 297, combing.
kynge, 6, king.
kynne, 90, kin.
kynrede, 24, kindred.
kyst, 78 (*jetta*), cast.

Langing, 136, longing.
large, 111, liberal.
largenes, 111, liberality.
launche, 123, hurl; launchid, 94,
    rushed.
lawghe, 272; lawhe, 101, laugh.
lawmentyng, 147, lamenting.
lectuary, 247 (*electuaire*), electuary.
leder, 39; leeder, 357, leather.
lefte, 286, lifted.
legge, 99; leghe, 129; leghis (pl.),
    194, league.
leghe, 294 (*lieue*), place.
leghes, 358, legs.
lepe, 10, leap.
les, 22, lest.
leser, 144 (*loisir*), leisure.
lette, 10, delay; late (imp.) let, 20;
    letted, 196.
leued, 23, left; leve, 33, leave.
leuyed, 135, levied.
leyd, 34, laid.
leyser, 277, leisure.
locucion, 20, circumlocution.
lodgis, 119, lodgings.
lost, 147, faith.
lustis, 320, pleasures.
lyf, 7, life.
lyflod, 108; lyuelod, 31 (*terrien*),
    landholding.
lygeauns, 338, allegiance.
lyghtly, 300, quickly.
lykwyse, 15, likewise.
lynee, 6, line.
lyuere, 275, give.

Machecolyd, 63, 103, parapetted,
    holes are left in the parapets to
    pour out molten lead, &c.
machined, 96; machyned, 68, ma-
    chinated.
maculate, 299, blemished.

mageste, 1, majesty.
magre, 142, maugre.
maister, 1, master.
manded, 73 (*manda*), sent for.
mandement, 153, 183, mandate, commandment.
manoyr, 100, mansion.
marches, 183, districts.
maronner, 268, mariner.
maryage, 16, marriage.
mate, 147, dull (*mat*), dejected; mated, 216.
mayllet, 329, mallet.
maynten, 126, bearing.
medled, 132, mingled.
medowe, 5, meadow.
meney, 9, retinue.
mercy, 71, thank; mercyed, 90.
meruaylle, 11, marvel.
meryte, 15, merit.
meschaunt, 302, wicked.
mesprysed, 79, calumniated.
messagery, 69, corps of messengers, embassy.
messe, 54, dish.
metes, 38, meats.
meued, 122; mevyd, 8; menyd, 21 (*mue*), stirred up.
meure, 160, mature.
meyne, 23, men; meney, 9, 280, company.
moche, 6, much.
moder, 14, mother.
mone shyn, 22, moonshine.
moneth, 208, month.
morow, 361, morning.
most, 29, must.
moustre, 165, muster.
mowe, 23, be able.
musarde, 29 (*musart* from *muser*, to loiter), dawdler.
myddes, 54, midst.
mynnsshed, 350, lessened; mynusshe, 320.
myscheaunce, 366, ill luck, mischance.
mysdon, 261, done amiss.
mysdymed, 265, mistook.
mysericordous, 313, forgiving.
myserye, 13, misery.
mysknewe, 102, mistook.
myster, 219, need; mystier, 222.

Nat, 2, not.

naturell, 15, natural.
nauye, 109, navy.
nauyll, 15, navel.
nayle, 81, hoof.
ne, 1, nor.
nedermost, 336, nethermost.
ner, 212, nor.
nevew, 17, nephew.
none, 358, noon.
nones, 63, nonce.
nothre, 39, neither.
nourrytured, 354, nurtured.
nouryces, 103, nurses.
nuyouse, 371, tiresome.
nyghte, 179, niece; nyghtis (pl.), 162.
nys, 8, is not.

Obscurte, 22, obscurity.
obsequye, 235, funeral ceremony.
obtempering, 9, submitting.
occysyon, 132, slaughter.
on, 131, 233, in.
ones, 360, once.
oo, 79; oon, 4, one.
oost, 193, host.
ootys, 91, oats.
ordonne, 14, order; ordonned, 79.
orgueyll, 293, haughtiness.
orgueyllous, 249, haughty.
orphanite, 147, state of orphanage.
orphelym, 241; orphenyme, 213; orphenyns (pl.), 187, orphan.
ouch, 126; owche, 59, jewel.
ouergrowen, 65, full grown.
ouerredde, 1, read over.
ouertredde, 112, overstep.
ought, 134, owes.
oultrage, 196, outrage.
oultrageous, 89, outrageous.
outhre, 95, either.

Paas, 21, pace.
pais, 257, peace.
palfrener, 52 (*varlet*), page.
palfroy, 9, palfrey.
palleys, 147, palace.
palyard, 294 (*ribault*), rascal.
pannes, 4, pans.
panser, 84, a steel plate covering that part of the body between the breast and the waist. *Viollet-le-Duc*, the front part of the cuirass.
pappes, 311, breasts.

parels, 31, perils.
parement, 57, ornament.
parfounde, 167, deepest.
parfytt, 3, perfect.
partrych, 175, partridge.
pas, 136, pass, passage.
patron, 115, master.
patyse, 304, 324, tribute ; patiz, 301 ; patise (verb), 304, tax, exact tribute.
paueys, 142, 359, shield.
paueysed, 167, shielded.
paynemys, 106, pagans.
pees, 12, peace ; peased, 100, pacified.
pensefull, 28 (pensif), thoughtful.
perfightly, 22 ; perfyttly, 5, perfectly.
peris, 39 ; peers.
perpetred, 76, perpetrated.
perske, 126 (pers.), blue, sky coloured (Cot.).
pert, 105, expert.
pesaunnt, 142, weight.
pesaunt, 145, heavy.
peupled, 118, peopled.
peyne, 12, 322, pain, painstaking.
plaisir, 10, pleasure.
playntes, 12, plaints.
playsaunce, 14, pleasure.
playsaunt, 7, pleasant.
plee, 53 (plait), story.
plee, 319 (plet). play.
pletyng, 33, pr. part. of plete, to plead.
portable, 209, bearable.
portecollys, 253, portcullis.
potence, 117, cross, gibbet.
pouere, 6, poor.
pouldre, 115, powder.
poursiewe, 155, seek.
poyuted, 149, appointed.
prately, 9 (doulcement), prettily.
prechement, 196 preaching
prees, 137 (presse), throng.
prest, 265, 275, ready, now.
preste, 358, priest.
preu, 21 (preus), valiant.
preyse, 23, praise.
preysed, 302, approved.
prodytour, 310 (proditeur), traitor.
proesse, 15, prowess.
promyssion, 16, promise.
promytte, 15, promise.

promyttyng, 292, promising.
propice, 188 ; propyce, 108, propitious.
propos, 261, proposal.
propre, 196, own.
propriete, 133, property.
proufytte, 3, profit.
proy, 132, prey.
prymat, 40, primate.
pryme, 148, six A.M.
pryuy, 214, select, intimate.
publyed, 64, published.
pucelle, 179, maid.
punysshe, 13, punish.
purchasse, 257, procure.
purfeld, 53 ; purfylled, 240, trimmed.
puruey, 19, purvey.
purveyaunce, 109, provender.
purueyed, 109, purveyed, provided.
pytaunce, 336, allowance.
pyte, 14, pity.

Quarell, 287, a kind of arrow.

Radeur, 329 (radeur), swiftness ; 386, violence.
raisonably, 18, reasonably ; raisson, 260, justice.
rampyn, 117 (rampin), a light ship.
rannyng, 8, running.
raser, 283, razor.
rauysshed, 7, ravished.
realyed, 145, rallied.
renume, 238 ; renme, 240, realm.
rebuckyd, 252, struck, attacked.
rechaced, 126, chased back.
reche, 325, reach.
reconforte, 107, comfort again.
recorded, 263, related.
recountred, 168, encountered.
recule, 124, 231, fall back, retreat.
rede, 2, read.
redeuaunce, 4 (redevance), rent, service
redressid, 193, rearranged.
reforced, 176 (se renforcha). 290 (reforcha), increased, reinforced.
regarde, 200, desert.
regenered, 140, regenerated.
regue, 6, reign.
regracy, 23, regracye, 124, thank.
rejoye, 157, gladden.
relacion, 42, reference.
released, 322, relaxed, diminished.

releuyd, 95 (*se remit*), 103, 131, rose.
relygyon, 181, order.
remenant, 44, remnant.
remevyth, 371, removeth.
remyse, 207, 210, restore ; remysed, 137.
renommee, 108 ; renoumee, 74 (*renommée*), renown.
resoyngne, 140 (*ressongner*), to fear (Cot.).
respection, 319, outlook.
restablysshe, 196, establish again.
retche, 14 (*challoir*), reck, regard.
reuertid, 319, turned.
reueste, 97, endow.
reuested, 40, clothed.
reueyll, 241, revelry.
rewled, 68, ruled.
rightwyse, 69, righteous.
roche, 248, rock.
roos, 22, rose.
roste, 4, roast.
rote, 60, root.
rotyn, 286, rotten.
rought, 67, recked.
route, 136, squadron (Cot.).
royalme, 118 ; royame, 245, realm.
rudesse, 28, rudeness.
ryall, 363, royal.
ryalte, 214, royalty.
ryuage, 2, 114 (*ripve*), shore, landing.

Saaf, 3, except.
sac, 39, sack.
salades, 130, helmets.
saluacyon, 356, safety.
salue, 126, salute ; salued, 8 ; salewed, 10.
Satirday, 15, Saturday.
saudant, 291, sultan.
sauegarde, 17, safeguard.
sauf, 177, except.
sawdees, 148, soldiers' pay.
sawdoyers, 208 ; sawdyours, 149, soldiers.
sawdan, 105, sultan.
sawte, 229 ; sawtyng, 291, assault, assaulting.
saynct, 3, saint.
scafoldes, 241 (*eschafauds*), grandstands.
scaped, 34, escaped.
scarmusshing, 131, skirmishing.
schall, 2, shall.

scourers, 224 (*coureus*), runners.
seaced, 311, ceased.
seale, 39, seal.
seased, 75, seasyd, 358 (*saisir*, connected with *seisin*), seized from.
sechyng, 10, seeking.
see, 7, sea.
semblable, 210, similar.
semblaunt, 33, 150, show.
semynge, 7, seeming.
sene, 153 (cf. syn) since.
senester, 84 ; senyster, 137, left.
separed, 302, separated.
sepulture, 354, tomb.
serche, 1, search.
seruytude, 249, feudal dues.
sethen, 163, since.
sette, 17, set, placed ; 272 (noun), sect.
seuene nyght, 91, week.
shadd, 22, shed.
shede, 359, sheath.
shelynges, 43, shillings.
shett, 14, shut.
shul, 16, shall.
siege, 133, seat, camp.
siew, 123, follow ; siewed, 219 ; siewyng, 73.
sith, 10, since.
sitte, 23, set.
slee, 24, slay.
slough, 306, slew.
sodan, 128, sultan.
soden, 279, boiled.
solas, 306, amusement.
solemply, 323, solemnly.
sommage, 143, baggage.
sommed, 65, summoned.
songe, 7, sang.
sonne, 174, sun.
sorow, 13, sorrow.
sonne, 360, sun.
sort, 110, spell, sorcery.
souped, 363, supped.
sourdred, 46 (*est sours*), 50 (*sourdit*), sprung forth.
sowle, 41, soul.
sowne, 101, sound.
sparpylled, 165 (*esgarez*), scattered.
spek, 6, 19, speak.
sperhaak, 16 ; sperohak, sparrow hawk.
speryd, 294, asked.
spoused, 11, espoused.

spyce, 371 (*espèce*), element.
stablyshed, 17, stablished.
stalage, 54, stands.
start vp, 302 (*saillist*), jumped up.
straunged of, 48, estranged from.
stake, 254, a pile of wood.
stakered, 82; staker, 353, staggered.
staung, 98, pool.
stere, 185, stir, move.
sterop, 27; sterope, 85, stirrup.
stode, 7, stood.
stoure, 132, 146, tumult, battle.
straunge, 183, foreign.
straunger, 10, stranger.
strengest, 33, strongest.
streyte, 118, street.
styed, 94, mounted.
styl, 7, still.
subgect, 24, subject.
subgection, 17, subjection.
suposen, 8, suppose.
supposed, 30, intendest.
surprysed, 10, overcome by.
surquydous, 96, arrogant.
suscited, 151 (*ressuciter*), raised from.
suster, 118, sister.
swette, 7, sweet.
syke, 147, sick.
sylenceth, 48, becomes silent.
symplenes, 194, ignorance.
syn, 17, 71, 116, since, then.
synester, 258, evil.
synowen, 138 (*veines*), veins.
synner, 313, sinner.
synne, 339, sin.
syth, 26, since.
sythe, 301, scyth.

Tache, 22 (*tache*), spot; tache, 232, buckle, clasp.
tambours, 110, drums, a kind of tambourine.
targe, 175, shield.
termyned, 149, terminated.
terryen, 60, landholder.
thaketh, 294 (*pris*), taketh.
the, 284, they.
thenne, 7, then.
thevely, 359, thieflike.
thikk, 18, thick.
thoo, 16, those.
thrested, 77, thrusted.
thrugh, 359, threw.
thurst, 7, thirst.

thye, 232, thigh.
tierce, 157, In summer eight of the clock, in winter ten (Cot.).
toard, 96, towards.
to fore, 20; to forne, 178, before.
togidre, 11, together.
toke, 4, took.
top, 105, tuft.
tourment, 15, torment.
tourned, 9, turned.
tranchis, 43 (*tranchée*); trenchis, 50, carvings, hewings.
trasse, 278, trace.
trauerse, 126, across.
trayll, 320 (*treillis*); traylles (pl.), 329, cage.
trayttee, 182, treaty.
trenchaunt, 145, sharp.
trew, 1, true.
trewu, 276, truce.
tronchoned, 286, truncheoned.
troussage, 132 (*troussages*), goods, bundles.
troussed, 141, prepared to leave.
trouth, 17, truth.
trucheman, 274, interpreter.
trusse, 335, pack.
trychery, 110, treachery.
trystefull, 305, sad.
tyres, 53, attire.

Valew, valewe, 41, value.
valiauntie, 122, valiantness.
vasselage, 145 (*vasselage*), fealty; 200 (*vasselages*), feats of arms (Cot.).
vergoyne, 285 (*vergoingne*), shame.
vergoynouse, 21, ashamed.
vertu, 291; vertue, 200, strength.
very, 1, 25, veracious.
vitupere, 89 (*blasme*), reproach.
vmbrel, 85 (*maisselle*), the shade for the eyes placed immediately over the sight of a helmet, and sometimes attached to the vizor (Halliwell).
vnfortune, 209, misfortune.
vnnethe, 202, 249, scarcely, nearly.
vnpurveyed, 121 (*despourveu*), unprovided
vnyed, 131, united.
volente, 207, will.
voyded, 209 (*ostées*), removed.
vpso-dounne, 25, upside down.

vyageours, 362, travellers.
vylayne, 28, bondman.
vylonnye, 251, disgrace.
vynaigre, 114, vinegar.
vyreton, 269, arrow or bolt.
vysyted, 288, examined.
vytupere, 233 (*vituperer*), shame.

Wakked, 7, was awake.
waloped, 130; waloping, 21, galloped.
warauntyse, 200; waraunt, 136, protect.
warde, 62, wall of defence.
wardes, 170, guards.
wareyne, 99, preserve, enclosure.
wast, 18, waste.
waymentyng, 13, lamenting.
wedryng, 206, weather.
wele, 11, weal.
wend, 72; weneth, 2; wenyng, 29, weened, thought.
wende, 137, turned.
wepen, 25, weapon.
wered, 21, fought, warred, worried.
were, 129, wear.
werre, 65, war.
wers, 216, worse.
wery, 145, weary.

wete, 115; wot, 12; wote, 120, know.
whom, 52, home.
wodd, 272, mad.
wode, 285, wood.
woo, 85, woful.
wood wroth, 247, madly angry.
worship, 111, respect.
worshipfully, 10, honorably.
wounderly, 5, wonderfully.
wraunt, 158, guarantee.
writon, 17, written.
wrorthy, 68, worthy.
wysshyng, 177, wish.
wytted, 310, blamed.

Yaf, 181, gave.
yede, 7, 21, went.
yeft, 16, gift.
yl wyller, 211, ill-wisher.
ymage, 17, image.
ynough, 13, enough.
yonde, 70, yonder.
yonge, 4, young.
ypocras, 54, a spiced and sweetened wine.
yrous, 246 (*fier*), angry, fierce.
ytaken, 9, taken.

INDEX OF PROPER NAMES.

PART I.—PERSONS.

Adam, page 3.

Alayn of Quyngant, 68, Raymondin's uncle.

Alexaundryne, 369, concubine of Sersuell.

Anthenor, King of Antioch, 264; helps to form a league to fight Urian of Cyprus; is defeated, makes a treaty with Urian, and agrees to pay tribute, 292.

Anthony, 6, fourth son of Raymondin and Melusine; birth, 104; leaves home to succour Christine of Luxembourg, 190; conquers the King of Anssay, 308; marries Christine, 214; goes to the siege of Pourrencru, 347; captures the Duke of Freiburg, 353.

Appolyn, 283.

Aragon, King of, visits Raymondin at Montserrat, 338; is present at Raymondin's burial, 355.

Argemount, Lord of, 218, a baron of Poitou, appointed by the Duke Anthony as captain of Luxembourg in his absence at the siege of Prague.

Aristote, 3; Aristotles, 20, quoted.

Asselyn, 183, Earl of Luxembourg, father of Christine.

Austeryche, Duke of, fights against the King of Anssay, is defeated, 245.

Bandas, Caliph of, goes against Cyprus with the King of Brandimount, 164; attacks Lymasson, 167; he retreats on hearing of the damage to the fleet by the storm, 168; his fleet captured, 170; fights Urian, 175; makes his escape, 176; defeated at sea by the Master of Rhodes, 177; escapes in a small boat, 177; forms a league against the kings of Cyprus and Armenia, 264; defeated by the Christian forces, and is compelled to make a treaty, 292.

Bar, Duchesse of, Marie, 1, daughter of John le Bon, King of France; born Sept. 12, 1344; married 1364 to Robert, Duke of Bar; died 1404.

Barbary, Sultan of, nephew of King Brandimount, one of the league against Urian, King of Cyprus, 264; believes the league will be successful against the Lusignans on land, 272; loses his arm in a fight with Urian, 290; makes a treaty, 292.

Benedictus, Pope, 334; Benedicte; visited by Raymondin.

Bernadon, 354, son of Odon, Earl of Marche, marries the heiress of the lord of Cabyeres.

Berry, Duke of, John, 1, son of John le Bon, King of France; born Nov. 30, 1340; died June 15, 1416; commands John of Arras to compile the history of Melusine, 2; captures Lusignan Castle, 369.

Bertrand, 18, 102, son of Emery, Earl of Poitiers; succeeds to the

PART II.—PLACES.

R. CLAY & SONS, LIMITED, LONDON & BUNGAY.